GM
9.2
WAT

Information Systems For Management

A Book of Readings

Edited by

Hugh J. Watson
Professor of Management and
Director of MIS Programs
University of Georgia

Archie B. Carroll
Professor of Management
University of Georgia

Pcp

Robert I. Mann
Associate Professor of Information Systems
Virginia Commonwealth University

3046137500.

1991
Fourth Edition

Richard D. Irwin, Inc.
Homewood, Illinois

Senior sponsoring editor:	Larry Alexander
Developmental editor:	Lena Buonanno
Project editor:	Rebecca Dodson
Production manager:	Ann Cassady
Designer:	Larry J. Cope
Compositer:	TCSystems, Inc.
Typeface:	10/12 Times Roman
Printer:	R. R. Donnelley & Sons Company

ISBN   0-256-09390-3

Library of Congress Cataloging-in-Publication Data

Information systems for management: a book of readings/edited by
 Hugh J. Watson, Archie B. Carroll, Robert I. Mann.—4th ed.
    p.   cm.
  Includes bibliographical references.
  ISBN 0-256-09390-3
  1. Business—Data processing.   2. Management information systems.
 I. Watson, Hugh J.   II. Carroll, Archie B.   III. Mann, Robert I.
 HF5548.2.I42433   1991
 658'.054—dc20   90–28255

Printed in the United States of America
1 2 3 4 5 6 7 8 9 0 DOC 8 7 6 5 4 3 2 1

Contents

PART I   **Introduction**   **1**

    1   Information Technology 3

PART II   **Computer Hardware and Software**   **33**

    2   Computing Is the Medium for the Message
Michael Antonoff, 35

    3   At Last, Software CEOs Can Use
Jeremy Main, 44

    4   Software Catches the Team Spirit
Louis S. Richman, 50

    5   Telecommunications in the 1990s
Randall L. Tobias, 56

    6   Corporate Videotex: A Strategic Business Information
System
Gene Kusekoski, 66

PART III **Information Systems and Their Applications**   **81**

    v   **7** A Framework for Management Information Systems
G. Anthony Gorry and Michael S. Scott Morton, 83
CLASSIC

    V   **8** A Framework for the Development of Decision Support
Systems
Ralph H. Sprague, Jr., 103
CLASSIC

    9   The Management Information and Decision Support (MIDS)
System at Lockheed-Georgia
George Houdeshel and Hugh J. Watson, 133

10 Expert Systems: The Next Challenge for Managers
*Fred Luconi, Thomas W. Malone, and Michael Scott
Morton,* 151

11 Prototyping: The New Paradigm for Systems Development
Justus D. Nauman and A. Milton Jenkins, 168

12 Computers of the World, Unite!
Jeremy Main, 189

13 Wired for Speed
William R. Ruffin, 195

14 The Compleat Angler
B. G. Yovovich, 200

15 Let the Customer Do It
Jerry Kanter, Stephen Schiffman, and J. Faye Horn, 208

PART IV   Management of Information Systems   215

16 Strategic Planning for Management Information Systems
William R. King, 217
CLASSIC

17 The Line Takes the Leadership—IS Management in a Wired
Society
John F. Rockart, 233

18 End User Computing: Are You a Leader or a Laggard?
Thomas P. Gerrity and John F. Rockart, 246

19 Creating Competitive Weapons from Information Systems
Charles Wiseman and Ian C. MacMillan, 261

20 Rattling SABRE—New Ways to Compete on Information
Max D. Hopper, 276

21 Managing the Introduction of Information Systems
Technology in Strategically Dependent Companies
James I. Cash, Jr. and Poppy L. McLeod, 289

22 The Shape of I/S to Come
Robert F. Morison, 307

Information
Systems
For Management
A Book of Readings

23   Measuring Information Systems Performance: Experience
with the Management by Results System at Security Pacific
Bank
*John P. Singleton, Ephraim R. McLean, and Edward N.
Altman*, 319

**PART V   Computer Impact on Personnel, Organizations, and
Society   337**

24   The Coming of the New Organization
Peter F. Drucker, 341

25   Computers and Managerial Choice
Peter G. W. Keen, 351

26   IT in the 1990s: Managing Organizational Interdependence
John F. Rockart and James E. Short, 368

27   Four Ethical Issues of the Information Age
Richard O. Mason, 387

28   Ethics in the Information Age
Bruce E. Spiro, 399

29   Jesse James at the Terminal
William Atkins, 406

30   Deterring Computer Crime
Kenneth Rosenblatt, 413

31   The Growth of the Home Office
Roberta Furger, 421

32   The Terrors of Technostress
John P. McPartlin, 430

Preface

Computers are found in organizations of every kind and size. In fact, it is becoming increasingly difficult to find an organization that does not have several. Recognizing this trend, most colleges of business administration now require one or more courses in computers and information systems in their common body of knowledge. Without this training, graduates would be poorly equipped in the skills required to function effectively in the contemporary business world. With this training, graduates are ready to use and to help manage this important organizational resource.

What do business school graduates need to know about computers and information systems? From the editors' perspective, the answer to this question is "A little about a lot of things." From our point of view, a student entering the business world needs to know about:

1. Computer hardware and software.
2. Computer-based information systems and their applications.
3. Management of information systems.
4. Computer impact on personnel, organizations, and society.

A knowledge of *computer hardware and software* is necessary in order to actively use the computer and communicate with data processing specialists. In a previous course or the course that you are currently taking, you probably learned about bits, bytes, and other hardware and software concepts; how to use computer software for word processing, spreadsheet, and database applications; and perhaps how to write your own computer programs. In this book of readings we assume an elementary knowledge of computer hardware and software and build from there.

Information systems and their applications are why computers exist. They continue to evolve in response to organizational needs, hardware and software advances, better understandings of how to develop them, the efforts of information systems personnel and end users, and so on. In this book, we discuss various types of applications, describe how they are developed, and give many examples.

Computers and information systems are an important organizational resource. Companies have committed enormous sums of money to their purchase, development, operation, and maintenance. Many firms could not function or compete without them. Consequently, the *management of information systems* is an important organizational concern not only for information systems managers but general management as well. Given such recent developments as computer hardware and software advances, end users developing their own applications, and information systems being used for competitive advantage, managing computers and information systems is a challenging task.

Computers and information systems are responsible for a number of *impacts on personnel, organizations,* and *society.* They eliminate, modify, and create positions within the organization. They affect how managerial and nonmanagerial work is done. They create fear and resistance among those unfamiliar with the technology. They pose a challenge for both computer specialists and users as they strive to understand each other. Computers affect the organization's structure, with departments not only being created, modified, or eliminated but the organizational placement of departments being changed. Finally, computers are affecting society in such areas as privacy, employment, and computer-related crime.

There is much that needs to be learned about computers and information systems in order to be an effective information systems specialist, user, or manager. The objective of this book is to provide you with some of the knowledge that is required. It should assist you when entering a computerized environment—to function effectively both personally and as a contributing organizational member.

This book of readings was prepared for use in courses with a significant information systems focus. Articles were selected on the basis of their readability, level of interest, contributions to understanding, and coverage of current and future topics of importance. Consequently, articles were selected from leading sources, such as *Harvard Business Review, Computerworld, MIS Quarterly, Journal of MIS, Sloan Management Review, Fortune,* and others.

Because the information systems field changes so rapidly, most of the readings are recent. There are some selections, however, that are classics in the sense that they are as relevant today as when they were first published. They remain as the definitive writing on a topic. Three of these CLASSICS are included and are identified as such in the book.

The topics covered include:

- An introduction to the wide-range of developments that are occuring in the information systems field.
- How computers are affecting how people communicate.
- Computer software targeted at executive users.
- Computer software to support groups of people working together.
- Future developments in telecommunications.
- How videotext can be effectively used in organizations.
- Management information systems—concepts and applications.
- Decision support systems—concepts and applications.

- Executive information systems—concepts and applications.
- Expert systems—concepts and applications.
- Applications in various functional areas and industries.
- The design of information systems and their applications.
- Information systems planning.
- The information systems responsibilities of line management.
- End-user computing and its management.
- Information systems as a competitive weapon.
- Creating an information technology platform for application development.
- How to structure information systems resources.
- Measuring information systems performance.
- How information systems are affecting organizations.
- How information technology can be used to support organizational interdependence.
- How information systems affect decision making.
- Ethical issues.
- Computer-related crime.
- Telecommuting.
- Computer-related stress.

We want to acknowledge that the major contributions to this book come from the authors of the articles. While we have written introductions to each of the parts, the articles have made the substantive contributions. We would like to express our appreciation to the authors and the publishers of the journals in which the articles appeared for allowing us to reprint them. Also, we would like to thank Linda Volonino of Canisius College and Tyona Lyons and Robert Bennett, our graduate assistants, for helping in the development of this book.

Hugh J. Watson
Archie B. Carroll
Robert I. Mann

I Introduction

The purpose of this introduction is to provide the reader with a broad overview of information technology evolution, uses, applications, and impact. This "big picture" perspective gives the reader a glimpse of the breadth of information technology before looking in detail at more specialized topics and issues. It becomes apparent in our initial reading that computers and information technology are no longer just tools of business. Instead they comprise the environment of business because of their ubiquitousness. With estimates that, by 1995, 90 percent of American workers will have desktop computer screens, it becomes evident that computers are transforming business, though often in ways not foreseen by those using them.

Reading 1, "Information Technology," presents a comprehensive survey of information technology published by *The Economist*. This article is appropriate for an initial orientation to the computing environment of business and other organizations because it quickly gets into current applications and specific uses. Beyond this, the survey interviews and quotes leading experts on information systems and provides various concepts appropriate for understanding the evolving role of information technology in business. For example, the article provides initial answers to broad questions, such as "What can the machines do?" and, more appropriately, "What do we want them to do?" Three general answers to these questions provide us with helpful initial understandings of computers and technology: enhancing productivity, gaining competitive advantage, and increasing the effectiveness and timeliness of organizational responsiveness. The article contains many of these useful conceptualizations of the role and function of information technology, which should provide a firm basis for later articles directly addressing hardware and software, information systems and their applications, the management of information systems, and computer impacts on personnel, organizations, and society.

1 *Information Technology**

THE UBIQUITOUS MACHINE

It has been a momentous change. Information technology is no longer a business resource; it is the business environment. Most white-collar workers now have computers on their desks. By 1995, predicts the Institute for the Future, a California think tank, 90 percent of American white-collar workers will have a screen. In a generation or two, electronic mail, electronic databases, and, no doubt, one or two computer tricks as yet unimagined, will be as ubiquitous, and as taken for granted, as the telephone, the mailbox, and the book today. But getting from here to there promises to be a wild and wonderful ride.

Perhaps the hardest problem posed by information technology is that it is so flexible. Computers can be programmed to do all sorts of things. Already they are adding up payrolls, storing data on crop pests, helping design electronic circuits, and advising motor mechanics on how to fix the latest model. As individual computers are increasingly linked together over communications lines, the machines both send messages and act as a sort of collective memory to record and analyse who said what to whom, when. Increasingly, the right question to ask about computers is not "What can the machines do?" but "What do we want them to do?"

So far, a generation of automation has evolved three broad answers to that question. Each presents its own opportunities and creates its own problems. They are:

---

* Source: "Information Technology," *The Economist,* June 16, 1990, pp. 5-20.

• *Productivity.*   By replacing people in routine jobs with machines doing the same work, companies can cut their wage bills. Unfortunately, planned-for productivity improvements have a nasty habit of failing to materialise.

• *Competitive advantage.*   By building information technology into their products, companies can influence their customers. So American Airlines automated travel agents, and by so doing made it easiest for the agents to buy seats on its flights, rather than its competitors'. American Hospital Supply put terminals on the desks of hospital administrators to help them purchase its potions. But companies are quickly learning how to blunt the competitive impact of rivals' information systems—often simply by joining with others in the industry to copy them.

• *Responsiveness.*   Information technology enables many companies to deliver a more customised product faster than the old-fashioned way of doing things. McGraw Hill will this autumn offer professors the chance to create textbooks tailor-made to their courses by choosing individual chapters from a database of texts on topics like computer science and accounting. Information technology also enables firms to build up a companywide encyclopedia of their customers' likes and dislikes. And that raises a vision of a sort of corporate utopia—the "learning organisation," which uses technology ceaselessly to refresh its knowledge of its customers' wants and to devise new ways of satisfying them. But while many have been inspired by this vision, none has yet worked out in detail how such perpetual-learning machines will overcome human inertia, sloth, and bureaucracy.

Setting broad goals for the use of information technology has always been easier than reaching them. Part of the problem is that the technology itself keeps moving the goal posts. Some of the biggest recent goal-post movements have been brought about by huge declines in the price of technology.

Never mind how many supersonic Volkswagens could fit on the head of a pin if the price, size, and performance of cars had changed as quickly as those of computers. The real consequence of cheaper computing is simply that the machines are no longer so expensive that humans must dance attendance on them. Machines are instead going to work alongside humans—typically in one of three roles. As assistants, computers do boring, routine work, like adding numbers, editing documents, or preparing dossiers of information from databases. As advisers, the machines store and search huge quantities of information to provide facts and advice on everything from maintaining aircraft engines to plant diseases. And as communicators, they spread information across companies and countries.

It is as communicators that the effect of computers is likely to be felt most strongly over the next decade. Now that it is economic to put a terminal on every worker's desk, wiring those terminals together creates new communities of knowledge. If they want to, everybody can see everybody else's work as it is done. Though few will carry things to this extreme, easier access to information can have a revolutionary effect on organisations. Mr. Paul Strassman, former head of data processing at Xerox and now a business academic, reckons that many organisations spend most of their time and energy on internal communications. Why should they continue to work so hard passing around buckets when they can now all dip straight into the same well?

Take two small examples of the sorts of things which the newly ubiquitous computers can do. A company marketing brand-name consumer goods now uses computers to help local managers react quickly to local market opportunities. If that manager wants to organise, say, a promotion, the computer shows him what inventories are available (from the warehouse computer) and helps him to coordinate delivery of product and promotional material (with the shipping computer). A container-shipping company, by contrast, uses its new system to put its salesmen a step ahead of the competition. Before a salesman calls on a prospective client he summons up on his laptop computer a briefing on the client's past shipments. The briefing also provides any news garnered from the grapevine about what discounts or other temptations competitors might be offering the client, plus advice from regional headquarters on how to fight back.

The Carnegie Group, a firm of consultants in Pittsburgh which is involved in state-of-the-art applications of information technology, uses the word *disintermediation* to describe the impact of many of its systems. Instead of Joe asking Sally to ask Fred to get a certain piece of information from George, Joe gets it straight from the computer, where George left it. At some companies cutting Sally and Fred out of the line of command also puts them out of a job. But at most firms something far more interesting and complex is happening.

When the agricultural revolution in the 19th century enabled a few men to produce what had previously required a nation, the Western world was not converted *en masse* to lives of leisure. Instead, it invented disposable income and new "necessities" to buy with it—like factory-made clothes, cars, and television. So some information workers who find machines providing the answers will simply find new questions to ask. As one manufacturing executive complains, only half-jokingly: "We've automated our payroll clerks out of a job four times already—and now they are 'compensation consultants' earning 50 percent more than we paid them as clerks."

One of the side effects of installing information technology is that it gives information workers an unprecedented view of how their organisation works—and thus suggests new ways of working within it. As Miss Shoshana Zuboff of the Harvard Business School pointed out in her book, *In the Age of the Smart Machine,* mechanisation makes it harder for employees to understand their work. Instead of a roomful of people, the industrial revolution put workers alongside machines with levers that clunked up and down. They could not ask the machines questions or look inside—and even if they could work out what the machine was doing there was little they could do to change it. Information technology, Miss Zuboff argues, has the opposite effect. Once a person gets over the initial shock of things happening intangibly behind the screen, it is easy to deduce the logic of a computerised process, and to use the technology as a window on the organisation as a whole.

One British insurance giant had this lesson brought home to it in an unexpected way. It installed a computer system to speed the processing of claims. Unfortunately, the system came to a near halt, deluged by a flood of claims. The problem, it turned out, was that clerks had quickly discovered that the system had rules built into it to weed out dubious claims—so asking it to decide on a dubious claim was much easier than asking a supervisor or fumbling through obscure rulebooks. This extra volume flooded the system. A relatively easy technical fix unclogged the computer. But managerial conundrums remain: If the computer can administer rules for checking claims, part of the existing staff is doing useless work. But which part—those writing the rulebook or those using it? And how should their jobs be reorganised?

Such surprises can give managers an unprecedented opportunity to create a new breed of "self-aware" corporations in which all work together to assess weaknesses and to create and teach the new skills needed to overcome them. They also wreak havoc with the best-laid plans of managers installing information technology. But from the confusion springs a wealth of opportunities.

Often the key to success is to sit back and ask the simplest of questions. "What would make our customers happiest?" "What would make our employees happiest?" Too few organisations do this. Instead, they typically reason something like: "Computers are good; computers typically do such and such; therefore, we will be better if we use computers to do such and such"—which is a recipe for expensive disaster. The encouraging realisation for many of those independent-minded enough to ask simple questions is that information technology can make many of their wishes come true. The snag, however, is that all involved must first agree on what they want, and how they are willing to change in order to get it. That is the challenge of the information revolution. To see how companies are coping, read on.

NOW FOR SOMETHING COMPLETELY DIFFERENT

Productivity, competitive advantage, and responsiveness—all three visions of automation have created both successes and failures. But they are increasingly united by a common theme. To reap the benefits of new technology, companies must create new organisations, doing new things in new ways. That means questioning the day-to-day traditions of centuries of business.

Mr. Michael Treacy, an information technology consultant, tells an instructive tale about Ford's efforts to reduce the number of paper-shufflers. What seemed at first to be a mundane efficiency campaign became a challenge to Ford's long-established ways of doing business. Ford employed about 500 people to order components, receive the parts, and pay suppliers. Mazda, a Japanese carmaker with which Ford has formed an alliance cemented by a 25 percent shareholding, did the same job with less than 100. An elaborate automated system cut Ford's order-shufflers only to about 400. So Ford's folk took a harder look at Mazda. Mazda, Ford discovered, had fewer computers than Ford. Its secret was that it did not wait for invoices from its suppliers. When goods arrive at the loading dock, a warehouseman waves a bar-code reader over each box. That single action enters the parts into inventory, updates production schedules (if necessary), and sends electronic payment to the supplier.

This seemed a bit like magic to some of Ford's managers. They had viewed invoices as a capitalist essential, like double-entry bookkeeping. Once shown the trick, the possibilities for boosting efficiency by eliminating the complications of matching parts and invoices seem obvious. But tapping these efficiencies requires changes in the way people work: close relations with suppliers, a warehouse that can talk directly to the finance department, and workers who adapt happily to new ways of doing things. Ford is working on all those, and it hopes within a few years to institute payment on receipt worldwide.

Creating such change is hard; creating it with information technology is harder still. Though computers have become catalysts of change for Western companies, it is not a role to which they are completely suited. Information technology is expensive and complicated. It introduces new ways of getting things wrong. British banks, for example, first organised their automated systems by account number, because that is how transactions are recorded. Now, however, they want to reorganise their systems to work by customer name to provide more sophisticated services and marketing. One bank, which prefers to remain nameless, calculates that reorganising all of its systems will require about five years and cost nearly £1 billion ($1.7 billion).

More daunting than the technical obstacles to successful automation, however, are the organisational ones. Information technology throws a searchlight on the most uncomfortable question any organisation can ask itself: What should be each worker's responsibilities? Worse, each successful application of the technology changes the answer.

Mr. N. Venkatraman, who studied the impact of information technology on business as part of the "Management in the 1990s" project for the Sloan School of Management at the Massachusetts Institute of Technology, reckons that there are five stages to the exploitation of information technology. Each creates different opportunities.

- *Automating existing jobs.*   Jobs within a company are automated, typically to boost productivity—for example, by installing a computerised accounting system. Little changes but the number of people and the capital costs of doing business.
- *Electronic infrastructure.*   Islands of functional automation are linked together. Nothing has to change in order to create ways of sharing information between all of a firm's computers. But without change there is usually little economic incentive to overcome the inevitable technical incompatibilities and to battles over who does what. That incentive typically comes bundled up in one of three other sorts of change:
- *Business-process redesign.*   Just as Ford found it could do away with invoices, computers enable things to be done in new and more efficient ways.
- *Business-network redesign.*   Creating links with suppliers and customers not only creates new opportunities for changing business processes it also changes the balance of competition.
- *Business-scope redesign.*   As part of the process of self-improvement, information technology enables some companies to move into new businesses. Merrill Lynch's cash-management account, for example, put the firm into competition with banks by each day sweeping the cash balances of brokerage accounts into interest-bearing securities.

Each step changes jobs. Putting a design engineer on to a computer-aided design system (CAD) changes the way he works. His work changes again when that CAD system is linked to manufacturing. And yet again when the newly integrated computer system is linked with similar systems at its suppliers. Part of the change is personal. The engineer may miss the feel of drafting paper, or rejoice at an end to ink smudges. But many of the most confusing changes concern the engineer's relationships with his fellow workers—both inside his company and out.

As Mr. Richard Walton of the Harvard Business School notes in a shrewd book, *Up and Running,* the same basic technology can promote either centralisation or the opposite, decentralisation. Automating a process captures a pool of information—such as a record of sales or a history of inventory levels. Viewed from the top of the organisation, this information gives bosses an unprecedented ability to look over the shoulders of their subordinates, and to centralise decision-making. But giving the same information, packaged slightly differently, to front-line workers can act just as powerfully for decentralisation by giving them a bird's-eye view of their work previously available only to their superiors.

Fitting the style of automation to a particular company and task is one of the hardest challenges facing today's managers. For some companies the basic choice is straightforward, though challenges remain in the implementation. Fast-food restaurants—who employ inexperienced, uneducated workers to do routine jobs—have long traditions of centralised control. At McDonald's just about everything an employee does, from how he greets a customer to the order in which he puts the food into the bag, is laid down by company policy. Automated systems simply reinforce that central control. Investment banks, on the other hand, employ educated, responsible adults (well, mostly) and thus require a decentralising approach to automation.

Most companies fall somewhere in between. They often end up using automation to centralise control over some parts of an employee's job and decentralising others. Though often neither decided nor presented as such, each new computer system is in effect a statement of priorities. In apportioning work between man and machine, a company tells its workers which skills it values in its people. Identifying those core skills is hard. It is also sometimes painful for employees who suddenly discover that they are not loved for the reasons they thought they were. But setting priorities is only half the challenge of successful automation. Companies must also learn to build computer systems that can enable workers to do their redesigned jobs more comfortably.

Both challenges are hard. Take the example of Mrs. Fields Cookies, which in 1989 sold $130m-worth of chocolate-chip cookies from shops around the world.

Mrs. Debbi Fields, who founded the first cookie store in 1978, oversees the over 400 stores now in her empire from Park City, a ski resort in Utah, together with her husband, Mr. Randy Fields. Over the past few years they have installed an elaborate automated system to manage the stores. The idea is that the system should take over many of the administrative, number- and policy-geared tasks, leaving store managers free to concentrate on people-oriented jobs like selling and creating a pleasant environment in the store. So the system monitors hourly sales and plans hourly production. It handles accounting and stocks, and it administers personnel tests for hiring. Through voice mail and electronic mail, store managers are also encouraged to talk direct to Mrs. Fields and she to them.

Whether this system is controlling or enabling depends on each store manager's personality. Those that had enjoyed the administrative part of their work presumably felt crushed; those who preferred the people side, liberated. But even for those in tune with the basic thrust of the system, questions remain over whether or not the detailed division of labour between man and machine is viable. Is the presence of the system's supervising eye reassuring or intrusive? How about all those little messages from Mrs. Fields? Can store managers really create the "right" environment with the system's strong, centralised influence on hiring? The jury is still out. Mrs. Fields Cookies has not made much money recently, and a recent reorganisation, in which Mr. and Mrs. Fields stepped back from day-to-day operations, adds to the uncertainties.

In meeting the challenges of automation, each company must rely on three sets of skills: engineering the technology (getting the machines to work), managing the technology (getting machines to work with people) and managing the organisation (getting our people and machines to work more efficiently than their people and machines). Twenty years ago just getting computers to work was a challenge, and companies rightly stressed engineering over management. But the priorities are shifting. Look at each skill in turn.

HELP WANTED

A sign said to hang in IBM's Tokyo office sums up the capabilities of computer technology. It reads:

IBM: FAST, ACCURATE, STUPID
MAN: SLOW, SLOVENLY, SMART

One of the most common mistakes about computers is the impression that a machine which can calculate pi to several thousand decimal points in the twinkling of an eye must somehow be cleverer than the average toaster. And the most common manifestations of that false impression are attempts to put computers in charge of people. Changes in technology and economics now allow men to put computers in their place.

Around 1970, when a computer cost several times the combined annual salaries of a typical accounting department in a medium-sized company, there was little choice but to organise work to make the most of this expensive asset. Now that similar computing power can be purchased for less than a clerk's holiday pay, there is no excuse for doing so. Computers make bad taskmasters, and researchers are creating technologies which enable them to be better assistants. That means building systems which are both flexible and easy to understand.

The history of attempts to automate computer programming shows the challenges and progress. In the late 1960s, researchers were confident that computers could quickly be taught to program themselves, given a broad description of the task to be accomplished. (This was also the age of the "General Problem Solver," an artificial-intelligence program which hoped to solve any and all problems that could be posed in logical form.) By the early 1970s, researchers had discovered their error. Many problems could not comfortably be stated logically. Programs which, like the General Problem Solver, tried to search methodically through all possible solutions to logical problems often required a few millennia of computing to find answers.

Some boffins decided that the way ahead lay in building assistants rather than gurus. Two young researchers at the Massachusetts Institute of Technology, Mr. Charles Rich and Mr. Richard Waters, decided to build such an assistant for computer programmers. Called the "Programmer's Apprentice," it would help programmers, rather than replace them. Like an efficient secretary, the machine would suggest ways of coping with familiar problems, point out inconsistencies in the work, and generally try to make itself useful. This new role, however, required a different approach to design. To work with people, the computer's ability to explain what it was doing became as important as its ability to do the job.

Messrs. Rich and Waters have not always found it easy to give their creation the ability to explain itself. Two ideas have helped. One is that the system should be organised around a collection of "clichés." The phrase "quicksort" describes commonly used procedures to programmers in much the same way that "sauté" works as a shorthand for chefs. Because it is part of the human programmer's vocabulary, a phrase should also be part of his mechanical assistant's. As well as sharing the human's language, it should also be able to share his thought processes. That means that it should at least be able to explain its workings in the sort of "if . . . then" rules that humans understand—even if its actual workings are more arcane.

Several developments make it easier for such ideas to be adopted in a variety of systems. One is simply that there are a lot more clichés around than there used to be. With each year that goes by, more technical problems in computing get solutions that an expert can refer to in shorthand, and take largely for granted. Many are also understood by the non-technical. While X.400, the worldwide electronic-mail standard, might not be a phrase on everyone's lips, most people now understand what is meant by "word-processor," "spreadsheet," and "database." And they can use those tools as an *entrée* into more complicated systems.

Meanwhile, some of the more complicated systems are coming to meet humans halfway. Cheaper computers mean that more processing power can be devoted to making the machines easy to use. Increasingly, companies are organising their machines to do just that. Huge databases are stored on mainframes. Smaller databases reside on minicomputers, which also provide serious computing muscle for heavy jobs like running computer models of bridges or markets. But people gain access to such big machines through desktop personal computers which, helped by easy-to-use graphical interfaces, can hide the complication of composing a query for a database or of analysing the results of a computer simulation.

Better still, computer technology itself has become more predictable. Relational databases, commercialised in the 1980s, are much less fussy about how their data are organised. Such capabilities, had they been available when banks first automated in the 1960s, could have saved many pin-striped folk the pain of discovering that questions concerning individual customers could be excruciatingly hard to answer on databases organised by account number. But databases are not the only area where progress is being made. Experience with communications standards steadily make it easier to link computers across both local-area networks and telephone lines.

And new technologies are making computers both more capable and easier to understand. So-called expert systems can seem very familiar to humans. Their programs come in the form of "if . . . then" rules: "If the engine won't start, then check the battery." Programs called "expert system shells"—like Inference's Corporation's ART and Teknowledge's KEE—then combine rules and data to deduce what can be learned from the data.

Expert systems let computers do new jobs. The Carnegie Group, a firm of consultants in Pittsburgh which is expert in the real-world applications of artificial intelligence, has built a system for Reuters which automatically classifies news stories coming over the news wire—and so decides which stories should be sent over which specialised news services. Another expert system built by Carnegie Group for Emerson Motor, a builder of electric motors, translates into manufacturable plans and diagrams orders saying simply "just like the last one except we want it to work at 220 volts."

Nearly all of those now working with expert systems have also learned a new way of working with the machines. No expert system is right all of the time. Most can handle only two thirds of the work they encounter. That is useful. By taking over the routine bulk of people's work, they can free up humans for the really tricky questions. But this means that humans and machines must work side by side—each handing over to the other the parts of the job he or it can do best. That takes some getting used to. It also places a premium on the skills needed to build both reliable, flexible systems and comprehensible, flexible organisations.

TOOLS FOR THE TRADES

Systems development—particularly if it involves writing software—provides some of modern business's most lurid horror stories. Tales of projects only one-third finished but already costing double or triple their budgets are common. So are tales of systems which never work. Building systems is hard work, and sometimes things just go wrong. But companies often make things harder for themselves by throwing common sense out the window.

Take the following history, from a company which, for obvious reasons, wishes to remain nameless. It had planned to buy software off the shelf for $2m. Because the off-the-shelf product did not work exactly the same way the company did, it then planned to spend another $2m and two years adapting its business practices to the software. It bought the software for $2m. Then some bright spark convinced the company that it would be better if they converted the software to run on the same "operating system'' as its existing software. That cost $8m. So long as it was adapting the software to a new operating system, the company decided to adapt the software to its business practices, too. That cost $10m. Eight years later, when the project was finished—five times over budget and four times over schedule—it had become irrelevant.

There are ways of doing better. One is to buy packaged software and use it as it was meant to be used. After all, companies do not feel compelled to rebuild their photocopiers or their computers; why should they feel the compulsion to do so with their software? With the rise of ''open systems'' based on the Unix operating system, it is becoming increasingly easy to buy a collection of software tools which can be linked together to do even the biggest jobs. Each tool does only a step of the job, and passes the result on to the next. So, by mixing and matching tools, a user can create exactly the system he wants. Microsoft's OS/2 operating system is developing similar capabilities. Mr. Roger Pavitt, head of Price Waterhouse's British information technology practice, says that his clients are becoming increasingly interested in open systems. Though neither Unix nor OS/2 applications can yet do everything that packages built for big mainframes can, such disadvantages can be outweighed by the ease with which changes can be made in systems built of a collection of small, interconnected pieces.

But taking advantage of open systems usually requires changes in the way information technology is managed. Having in the 1980s decentralised decisions about computers to take advantage of the opportunities created by personal computers, many companies are now recentralising part of the job. The idea is that a small, central information-services group should lay down a corporate ''architecture'' to ensure that everybody's new automation project will work with everybody else's. But the work of systems design and implementation typically remains decentralised, to tap the enthusiasm and expertise of those doing the jobs with which the system is meant to help.

Creating flexibility also requires changes in the way individual systems are designed and built. The traditional way of looking at systems design, called the ''waterfall model,'' held that, like a tangible machine, software evolved through several stages of design and implementation until, one day, it was ''finished'' (see Figure 1). Work done after that to fix, update, or improve the system was called ''maintenance.'' Companies discovered that their information services were spending up to 80 percent of their time on maintenance, while the backlog for even the simplest new systems stretched out for years.

Part of the solution to this problem lies in admitting that systems evolve—and that software maintenance is not really, as the name implies, as simple as keeping your car running. Instead of the ''waterfall model'' of development, some are adopting the ''spiral model'' (see Figure 2). Implicit in this model is the idea that a system is never really finished; it

FIGURE 1   Conventional Waterfall

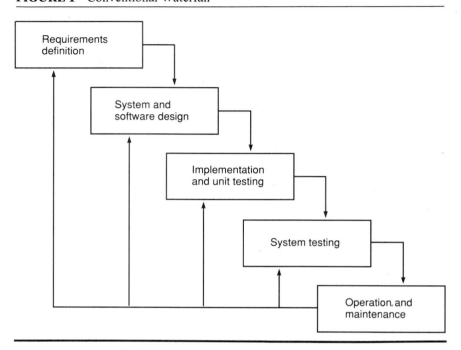

merely passes though successive cycles of design, implementation, testing and improvement.

Experience has evolved several techniques to help make systems evolution more efficient. So-called computer-aided software engineering (CASE) tools automate part of the process of programming, and so speed changes. "Structured" and "object-oriented" design methods help designers to get a grip on the complexity of systems, and so make change more manageable. Together with "layered architectures," such design methodologies can, cleverly used, enable systems to be built in modules so that some functions can be ripped out and rewritten without changing anything else. But even the best design methods and technical expertise can help only with the question of how to change, not decide what changes to make.

One obvious idea here is to involve the users of the system in design, implementation, and improvement. If anyone knows how to make a system better, it must be those that use it. Though this admonition appears constantly in textbooks and lectures, a recent study by the Kobler Unit at London's Imperial College found that only about half of the (British) firms in its sample actually did so. And many of those that do not are still surprised—and blame the computer—when users do not work well with new systems.

FIGURE 2 Virtuous Spiral

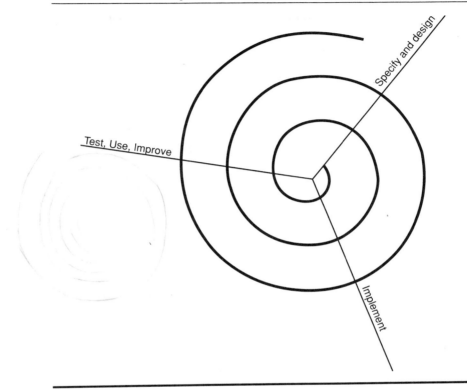

Specify and design

Test, Use, Improve

Implement

Electronic suggestion boxes would be a huge step forward for many firms. But some companies have already gone far beyond this. They are trying to use information technology to create new forms of organisation in which learning is part of the daily round of going about one's business.

A CURRICULUM FOR CHANGE

Anyone who tells you that it is easy to change the way groups of people do things is either a liar, a management consultant, or both. Change is hard for individuals; for groups it is next to impossible. That said, information technology is going to force most organisations to change over the next few years. Those who have some control over the process will find it less painful.

Mr. Patrick Jeffries of McKinsey, a management consultancy which admits that change can be difficult even if you can afford its fees, argues that two simple questions should be the starting point for thinking about change. The first concerns commitment: Why should the change be made? The second concerns skills: What is it that must be done to meet the new goals? Neither question is ever as simple as it sounds.

For change created by information technology, the question "why change" should first be answered by explaining how the new computer system supports a company's overall strategy. The sad truth is that many managers are not terribly clear on this point. There is often an unbridge-able gap between general managers and their colleagues in information services. One group lives in a world of return on equity, JIT, TQC and LIBOR; the other talks of bits, bytes, CASE and COBOL. Worse, companies give them no incentive to work together to thrash out a common language. The two groups often have different performance standards and career paths.

Some companies, however, are striving at least to bridge the gap—if not close it completely. Safeway has given its information-services employees the same two goals as the rest of the business: improve margins and increase market share. Their projects and performances are judged on these, just like the marketing department. IBM, like many Japanese companies, rotates general managers through information-services assignments. The present head of information services, Mr. Larry Ford, had marketing and general-management experience with IBM before he took over IBM's internal automators.

For its big information technology projects, Ford Motor Company has devised a three-tier system of management which forces information services and general managers to work side by side on committees at several levels. At the top, divisional vice presidents set broad goals: the system's strategic purpose and its links to overall, corporate information systems. One level down, middle managers thrash out more detailed plans covering the sorts of information that will go into the system, how it will change responsibilities between departments, and so on. Finally, the users-to-be of the system sit down with systems analysts to sort out what they would like to see on the screen and other exact details of how the system will work.

Unfortunately, the "what change" questions raised by automation can often make the "whys" seem easy. The problem is that automation changes many things at once. Even with the best motivation, learning how to do your old job in a new way, with a machine, is hard enough. Learning how to do a new job with new technology is even harder. Yet that is exactly what automation often forces people to do.

Morgan Stanley, for example, experimented with centralising responsibilities when it set up a state-of-the-art trading room to try to find new opportunities in computerised stock arbitrage. Though on-the-spot decision making is required in much share trading, experienced equity traders lacked discipline in executing arbitrage opportunities identified by the computer. They could not resist second-guessing the machines. Though the machines were indeed often wrong, the lack of consistency made it impossible to carry out computer-guided arbitrage, or even to judge new arbitrage ideas. So the firm hired bookkeepers to execute trades—and set experienced share traders and theoreticians the task of serving them, particularly by trying to make sure that the recommendations which came up on their screens would be profitable.

Frito-Lay, an American snack-food producer, moved decisions in the opposite direction. It had traditionally run a centralised system of sales and distribution, but wanted to decentralise to enable local promotions, and to allow local distributors greater flexibility in dealing with customers ranging from mom-and-pop stores to giant supermarket chains. Attempts to do this without computers flopped. The key to success, points out Miss Lynda Applegate of the Harvard Business School, turned out to be a little handheld computer terminal on which each delivery and sale could be logged. Not only did this free up distributors' time and improve efficiency, it also created a pool of timely sales information that could be doled out as and where it could be used most effectively.

The simple lesson, well drawn by Mr. Paul Strassman in his book *The Information Payoff*, is that training costs—both to learn the new technology and the new ways of doing things—are likely to be the most expensive and time-consuming parts of automation. But training is only part of the answer. Harvard's Miss Applegate reckons that many companies have muffed the opportunities offered by information technology to change the ways in which they make decisions. Instead of simply automating the status quo, companies today have a unique opportunity to reassess where and how decisions should be taken. Only a few have even begun to grasp it.

So far, even those furthest advanced in this endeavour are still struggling with parts of the puzzle—nobody has yet worked out the big picture. But interesting experiments include:

- *Knowledge management.* Companies are building up curricula of the skills and knowledge which their employees need, and are devising ways, both formal and informal, of teaching them. Management consultants at Arthur Andersen are, as part of their normal career progression, expected to spend some time teaching their peers. Computer programmers at Microsoft are building a vast database of software know-how. Its software-developing customers can electronically query the database, and the answers to their questions add to the overall body of knowledge. Similarly, management consultants at McKinsey are building a database which will help consultants with a problem get in touch with a colleague whose specialised knowledge might help solve it.
- *Planning.* Xerox uses computers to help executives co-operate in planning the future. The machine combines individual forecasts and budgets so that each individual can see how his plans affect the group and vice versa. Royal Dutch/Shell is experimenting with a yet more ambitious

technique. It is involving executives in planning as a sort of do-it-yourself computer game. Instead of "scenarios"—thick books which detail what might happen to Shell if oil prices do this and interest rates do that—Shell is trying to bring scenarios to life inside the computer. Ideally, however, it would like executives to create their own models of how Shell might react to various events, and play them out on the computer to test and improve their ideas.

- *Groupware.* Lotus Development, a company famous for the 1-2-3 spreadsheet, has developed a product to help people work together in groups. It monitors electronic mail and work in progress, handles ad hoc correspondence and maintains informal databases. If a client calls a salesman working with Lotus's "Notes," he can immediately call up all his colleagues' contacts with the client, check the status of his order on the manufacturing computer, and leave a note recording his conversation with the client for whoever contacts him next. Other firms have worked out other forms of computerised social lubricants. One common trick is to use computers to keep track of the various versions of a plan or drawing as engineers modify it.
- *Responding to customers.* Computers allow tailor-made products where previously only off-the-shelf had been economic. Rocky Mountain Log Homes, a builder of prefabricated housing, now lets its customers play architect on-screen. Previously customers had had to content themselves with one of a few predesigned homes. Now the computer can feed the customer's own design straight to the factory. British Telecom, among others, is building systems to improve the handling of customers' queries. By bringing all relevant information to screen while the customer is on the telephone, it hopes to resolve queries with less cost and frustration.

But huge challenges face those who would use information technology to improve their ability to learn. One problem that crops up time and again in Western companies' experiences with computers is the failure to communicate. Learning, as any teacher will tell you, is a moving target. Curricula have to be revised continually to reflect advances in knowledge or changes in students' abilities. That requires several sorts of dialogue. Companies are often fairly good at measuring employees' performance against a fixed standard. Sometimes they can help teach workers the skills they need to do better. And some firms can use feedback from workers to modify what the standard or performance can be. But only a handful can put all these skills together to create the sort of dialogue that keeps a good university faculty evolving in step with its discipline.

On the contrary, an anecdote from General Motors exemplifies the current state of affairs. In GM's Hamtramck Cadillac factory, all the welding robots are linked to a computer which prints out their performance daily for maintenance engineers. Unfortunately, maintenance engineers could not understand the stream of numbers which emerged from the machines. Their work suffered while they had to wade through reams of printouts to try to decipher which machines needed to be tuned. Eventually, some bright spark noticed that charting the data made it possible to tell at a glance which machines were in trouble. But the problem should never have arisen in the first place. As the Western world's experience with computers has shown, however, it is depressingly common. Look at progress towards the three goals of automation: productivity, competitive advantage, and responsiveness.

WORKING HARDER, DOING LESS

Productivity is the *raison d'être* of automation. Even those companies who admit to other uses for information technology often justify their investments by productivity-generated savings. Some companies can boast. IBM (which has no excuse for not making a success of automation) reckons that it averages a $4 return on each $1 invested in information technology. But plenty of IBM's customers must be very disappointed. Using statistics from America's Commerce Department, Mr. Stephen Roach, an economist at Morgan Stanley, calculates that the average output of an American information worker has not budged since the early 1960s—despite huge growth in both the number of information workers and the average technology investment sitting on each one's desk.

Mr. Roach's studies make sobering reading. They indicate that computers have so far failed to boost productivity even on the most generous measure, output per worker. Including capital costs, as any truly accurate measure should, would make the picture look even worse.

Part of the problem is simply that so many Americans joined the managerial ranks in the 1980s. Between 1978 and 1986 annual growth in white-collar employment was almost five times that of production workers. In manufacturing, employment of production workers declined while that of white-collar workers grew unabated. Much was invested in these decision makers. Analysts at DRI, a firm of economic forecasters, estimate that the share of office equipment in American's stocks of fixed capital (excluding property) has climbed from 3 percent in 1980 to 18 percent in 1990. All to no avail.

Though separating the contributions of white-collar and blue-collar workers is not easy, Mr. Roach calculates that by 1986 the average white-collar worker's output had declined to nearly 7 percent below his average level in the 1970s (back to the average of the early 1960s, before the high-tech investment boom began). Financiers performed particularly badly, with a 10 percent drop in average output. Production workers, by contrast, boosted output by nearly 17 percent from the 1970s to 1986.

There are three sorts of reaction to this depressing picture. One far too common group holds that the answer to white-collar productivity problems lies in "an action committee to reprioritise the managerial matrix and its links to corporate culture" (or some similar nonsense) . . . in other words, that the cure for too many unproductive managers is more managers. Leaving aside these members of the cult of management—who seem more part of the problem than its solution—the world divides into optimists, who believe that information technology investments have already planted the seeds for future productivity growth, and pessimists, who reckon that a cure requires full-scale managerial revolution.

One point for the optimists is that Mr. Roach's national averages hide some smaller successes. Studies of the effects of information technology on individual bits of the economy paint a rosier picture of productivity. Mr. Paul Osterman, of MIT, analysed 40 American industries, mostly in manufacturing. He found that from 1972 to 1978, on average, each 10 percent growth in computer processing power translated into a 1 percent reduction in the number of managers employed and a 2 percent reduction in clerks.

Mr. Thomas Steiner, a consultant who studies banking for McKinsey, reckons that productivity-boosting forces are now making themselves felt in banking. In his book, *Technology in Banking*—which is one of the best studies of the effects of information technology yet written—Mr. Steiner argues that employment in American banking peaked in 1986, and will decline steadily in the 1990s.

Though bank spending on information technology has been climbing steadily since the 1960s, two factors delayed its effect on productivity. One was that banks have for many years run paper systems alongside automated ones, lest a computer glitch wipe out the business. As experience with computers and computer security grows, those paper systems are being dismantled. More fundamentally, however, it also took time for the banks to discover how information technology—and, in many countries, deregulation—would change their ability to add value and profit to their activities.

Take funds transfer, the movement of large sums of money from one bank to another. At the beginning of the 1980s, New York's eight biggest banks made about $1 billion a year from funds transfer, a third of their total profits. Internally, funds transfer was pretty well automated. So efficiency was high. But inertia and ignorance meant that the banks could still charge many customers pre-automation prices for pre-automation service. No longer. Customers now know that transfers will reliably go through in a day—so they will no longer allow the banks to rack up four or five days' worth of interest on their money. Similarly, many customers now initiate transfers from terminals in their own offices. So they will not pay the banks a fee for doing that. This year, New York's eight biggest banks will make less than $100m on funds transfer, and the pressure on back-office employment is increasing.

This is only the beginning of change for the banks. The real efficiency-boosting potential, as Mr. Steiner points out, lies in eliminating more of the

50 billion cheques which American homes and businesses write each year. Banks have a strong incentive to do this. Each cheque costs nearly $1 to process. They have made a start with automated cash dispensers, and they hope to go further by installing the machinery for direct-debit cards at supermarkets, petrol stations, and convenience stores (which between them account for about two thirds of America's 60 billion retail transactions a year).

Unfortunately for the banks, progress with direct-debit cards, automated cash dispensers, and other innovations like home-banking has been consistently slower than they had hoped. People simply do not like to change. Nor do they have much incentive to do so. Price, the traditional capitalist incentive, is only slowly being brought to bear because the banks know that it would be competitive suicide to try to pass on to the customer the full cost of cheque handling. In many other industries, there is even less hope of achieving efficiency-boosting changes because companies do not know how much their products and services really cost to provide—let alone how they should price them.

Herein lies the nub of the pessimists' argument that a managerial revolution will be needed to tap the productivity gains offered by information technology. Many of the productivity gains of the early 20th century, they note, were achieved with the help of new ways of defining and costing work, notably Frederick Jackson Taylor's "time and motion" studies. Taylorism is viewed with some horror by most modern managers—who quite rightly point out that choreographing a worker's movements, limb by limb, minute by minute is oppressive, alienating, and usually counterproductive. But without some renewed job discipline, some of today's "enlightened" management structures are in danger of collapsing under their own weight.

One part of this task is simply getting a handle on costs in increasingly capital-intensive industries. As Mr. Thomas Johnson of Pacific Lutheran University and Mr. Robert Kaplan of the Harvard Business School point out in their damning analysis of management accounting, "Relevance Lost," many, if not most, companies get misleading information from their cost accountants. The problem is "overheads," general costs incurred by the business as a whole rather than by any specific product—like many information systems and almost all general management.

As businesses become more service-minded and more capital-intensive, overheads' share of total costs increases. In banks Mr. Steiner reckons the fixed cost of computers is now 50–60 percent of the cost of providing some products. Messrs. Johnson and Kaplan cite a "typical" cost-breakdown for a manufactured product in which overheads are 60 percent of total cost, materials 29 percent, and direct labour 11 percent. Apportioning overheads thus becomes crucial to product costing. Unfortunately many companies, following the prevailing wisdom of accounting textbooks, apportion overheads according to direct labour costs. This vastly exaggerates the benefits to managers of further reducing what is already the smallest component of their costs, direct labour. In some cases it can even make cost increases look like reductions. "Outsourcing" of components, for example, raises the overhead cost of administering contracts and quality while it reduces direct labour. But because the overheads are shared across a range of products, it is difficult to compare costs and benefits— nor do individual product managers have any incentive to do so.

Messrs. Johnson and Kaplan offer no easy solution to this problem. They simply urge each company to try to work out for itself what drives the cost of its products, and how to measure and control them. Some progress is being made. Information technology, which conquers the complexity of building customised measurement and control systems, helps greatly. But many managers, particularly in service industries, face an even more basic problem than working out the costs of their products: they have to work out exactly what their products are in the first place.

Information technology changes the things which banks and other service industries sell as well as the cost of creating them. A favourite example of business-school textbooks is Merrill Lynch's cash-management account, which, by each day sweeping the cash balances of its brokerage accounts into interest-bearing securities, brought brokerages into competition with banks—and helped to set in train forces which forced banks, in turn, to offer interest on chequeing accounts. It is only human, after all. Rather like the executive who wanders down the corridor to poke into other people's business while his personal computer cranks out his latest sales report, some companies have taken advantage of the resources freed—and new capabilities created—by information technology to poke into other companies' businesses. From their innovations have come some of the most startling success stories of the past 20 years.

MAGIC CIRCLES

What Mr. Marshall McLuhan called "the global village" modern businessmen may prefer to see as "the global office suite." Information technology's ability to overcome distance enables companies to work more closely together in a variety of ways. One of the neatest tricks is for a company to put its computer system on a customer's desk—so that the first name he sees when it is time to make a purchase is . . . you guessed it.

American business-school professors call this sort of thing "using information technology to gain competitive advantage." Strictly, that seems a misnomer—every use of information technology should be aimed at gaining competitive advantage. But the phrase often proves a useful shorthand for describing the ways in which a company can use its information technology capabilities to alter the behaviour of those around it. Some influence customers by building information technology into new products, like banks' cash dispensers or Merrill Lynch's cash-management account. Others are building electronic links to suppliers to create relationships which are at once more flexible, more efficient, and more exclusive.

It is an ironic testimony to the power of corporate inertia that, in using information technology, companies have often had better initial results from trying to change the behaviour of others than from improving themselves. Airlines, banks, air conditioners, drugs, linen, and a host of other industries provide examples of products that have succeeded in large part because the vendors' information technology has made their wares the most productive for customers to buy. These systems provide the initials which dot textbooks on information technology. The question, however, is how many companies today can duplicate successes like:

- *SABRE.* American Airlines' seat-reservation system helped revolutionise the airline business. By making it easiest for travel agents to buy seats on American, it boosted the airline's market share. It provided the information on customers needed to create innovative and complex fare structures aimed at filling every seat. In 1984, 11 rival airlines paid American the compliment of bringing an antitrust suit against it on the grounds that SABRE had become an "essential facility" to which they were unfairly denied equal access. More recently American has been trying to run SABRE as a general travel-reservations service—with equal access for all willing to pay its fees. As such, SABRE has in some years made more money than the airline which spawned it.
- *OTISLINE.* Otis Elevators decided in the early 1980s that one of the things that would give its customers most satisfaction is the prompt service of ailing lifts. So it built an automated system to dispatch repairmen. When something starts going wrong with Otis's newer lifts, they automatically call in their complaints to the computer—without human intervention. Otis's rivals suddenly had to compete on quality of service as well as on the price and quality of lifts themselves.
- *Thomson Holidays.* Thomson was one of the first firms to let British travel agents reserve package holidays from a computer screen—which was usually much quicker and cheaper than telephoning the tour operator. Thomson still has the easiest-to-use system, offering the broadest range of packages. Travel agents often turn to Thomson first.
- *Federal Express.* To grow huge in parcel-delivery, Federal Express backed up its skills in moving packages about with a computer system that can tell a customer exactly where his shipments are at any given moment. This ability has won new kinds of business. Federal Express now manages much of IBM's spare-parts inventory. Its system also creates a barrier to competition.

- *ASAP.*   American Hospital Supply provided quicker, cheaper delivery of medical odds and ends by encouraging customers to tap their orders directly into its computer system. Market share grew dramatically.

Inspiring as these examples may be to young executives, they are dicey role models. The opportunities for computer-powered success are more limited today. Companies have already built many of the obvious ideas for systems which could change consumer preferences at a stroke—including many which looked like obvious winners but in practice fell flat. One such was the system built by ICI agrichemicals to provide farmers with the latest research on plant diseases while they placed electronic orders for pesticide: farmers, it seems, would rather talk to the neighbours about bugs.

Worse, competitors have learnt to blunt the impact of systems that do provide something the customers want. The trick is simply to copy them. Most effective of all is when companies band together to copy a successful system because each then gets its capabilities for a fraction of the price paid by an innovator. So New York retail banks joined together to build a network of cash dispensers to compete with the lead that Citicorp, New York's biggest retail bank, had gained in the size and convenience of its cash-dispenser network. America's smaller insurance companies have joined together through a trade association to build a network that can eliminate much of the paperwork which independent agents must wade through in filing a policy or a claim. Their collective system counters much of the advantage garnered by the proprietary networks build by industry giants like Aetna.

Some of the most resourceful, and luckiest, innovators may find new ways to make money out of their systems. Baxter Health Care is offering to use the ASAP system built by its American Hospital Supply subsidiary to provide hospitals with a complete supplies-management service. Baxter says that it will order whatever brand of supplies the hospitals want. With its expertise in inventory management and automation, Baxter reckons it can make a big saving for the hospital and still have profit left for itself. Similarly, McKesson, which earned its automating credentials with the "Economost" system to supply drug stores (chemists, in English English), is offering to use the system to provide pharmacists with direct reimbursement for drugs covered by health insurance. The pharmacist can offer his customer the convenience of not having to reclaim drug costs on his own, and the health insurers, McKesson hopes, will welcome a chance to get more direct control of their drug costs.

But some industries do not enjoy even the slimmest of chances of creating instant success with automation. They are simply too complex. No single system could matter that much to a customer. And here the process of change is a painful groping indeed. Look, for example, at motor cars.

A GAME EVERYONE CAN PLAY

Information technology promises to help solve two of the most crucial problems facing Western carmakers. One is product-delivery time. Walk into a showroom and order a car that is not already on the lot, and you will probably have to wait six weeks for delivery—yet it takes only about 36 hours to build a car, and no more than a week to deliver it to most places. The second, bigger problem tackled by carmakers' computers is the time it takes to create a new product. Western companies take six or seven years from drawing board to product launch; the Japanese take half that. For both problems, the solution lies in improving the flow of information. Carmakers' efforts to use information technology to make those improvements are transforming their industry.

The interesting part of this process of change is that the carmakers cannot automate just on their own. Ford, for example, buys in from outside suppliers about two thirds of a car's parts. Those suppliers, too, must be brought into the carmaker's electronic networks. In a generation or so, those networks will be ubiquitous. Using them will confer no more competitive advantage than posting a letter today. But in the transition, suppliers will rise and fall not just on the price and quality of their parts but also on their ability to deliver them using the new techniques.

At Nissan's British factory in Sunderland, for example, the plant computer each morning calls up the computer of its seat-supplier, Akeda Hoover, to schedule Hoover's daily production. Seats of each colour and style are scheduled so that they can roll straight out of Hoover's door and into a car waiting on Nissan's assembly line. Similarly, Ford reckons that it now does daily production scheduling with about half of the 1,000 European suppliers with electronic links to it.

As Ford changes the way in which deliveries are scheduled, it also changes the way in which it pays for them. Instead of trading several bits of paper—each of which must be matched with physical parts or payment—the goal is a simple two-step process which Ford calls "push-button receiving." Ford's computer sends an order to its supplier, and payment is sent electronically as soon as that order appears at the receiving dock.

Achieving this wondrous simplicity requires some complicated changes in the relationship between supplier and customer. At the least, customers must be able to take quality for granted. But a superefficient link between buyer and seller also highlights the inefficiencies of each. Ford, though efficient by the standards of Western carmakers, could not deliver to its own customers as quickly as it is asking its suppliers to do. Some of the problems lie in the size of the necessary information systems. Building a system just to keep track of which parts Ford engineers use around the world—so that the company can begin to rationalise its parts purchasing—took several years and nearly $100m. The finished system handles over 500,000 queries daily from 20,000 users, and tracks over 1m parts.

But the technology is only part of the problem. Part of the delay in delivering a Ford car is caused by the need to draw up and reconcile two production schedules. The marketing department does one production schedule, which concentrates on sharing out best-selling cars in short supply. Then production does a second schedule, which concentrates on sharing out production facilities in short supply. Doing one schedule would, Ford admits, be simpler and quicker. Someday, soonish, it will. But building an organisation that knows about both demand and production—and can balance the two—takes time.

Suppliers face similar problems, at all sorts of levels. One problem is simply how much to invest in information technology. At a recent meeting of the Index Interchange—a group of European information-services directors organised by consultants at the Index Group to promote discussion of mutual problems—many said they saw little point in replacing paper with electronic systems to swap data and orders without making other changes. Just going "paperless" does not provide a big enough payoff. Yet many of the changes companies would most like to make require the ability to swap orders and data electronically.

Ford and other big customers have already broken the deadlock for some suppliers. Ford suppliers have been told to adopt its electronic ordering and payment systems. Some suppliers of key parts have been told exactly which computer-aided design system to buy so that Ford engineers can load new designs straight into suppliers' computers (which in turn will automatically instruct the appropriate machine tools). But even those who have decisions made for them must now decide what to do with their own suppliers, and so on.

As they automate, companies must also learn to manage the new trading relationships which information technology creates. Ford, like many others, is dramatically reducing the number of suppliers it deals with. And it measures those it does keep by different criteria. Simple price becomes less important than quality and the ability to evolve new products in harmony with Ford's own evolution. The new emphasis on flexibility and design skills often highlights new weaknesses.

Mr. Ramchandran Jaikumar of the Harvard Business School studied American metalworking companies with advanced "flexible manufacturing systems" capable of switching quickly from the production of one type of part to another. Compared with their Japanese counterparts, the Westerners barely used the capability of their technology. The average "flexible" American plant turned out 10 parts, with an average production volume of 1,727 of each. The average Japanese plant turned out 93 parts with an average production volume of 258. Worst of all, the Japanese introduced 22 new parts for every one introduced in America.

It is tempting to diagnose such findings as another failure of communication. Having set up automated systems, many in the West then seem to want to forget them, to let them chug away at the same jobs people have always done, rather than discussing with those around them ways in which all might change to take most advantage of the technology. This can make automation downright self-destructive. There are few things more wasteful than the expense and complication of automating business as usual—and few firms more vulnerable than a giant company which has expensively replaced its paper-shufflers with printout-shufflers.

SCHOOL, INC.

No wonder Western managers are growing disenchanted with information technology. It promises wonderful things. But when companies work those wonders for their customers, they are quickly copied. Those that innovate up the supply chain typically find that each bottleneck eliminated simply shows up a new blockage elsewhere. True, automation creates islands of efficiency. True, islands of automation are gradually linking up to form archipelagos. But with each "success" companies seem to find themselves running harder just to stay in the same place.

Some businessmen, however, have eased their disappointment simply by taking it to its logical conclusion. Instead of looking to information technology to provide answers to competitive problems, they are using it to ask better questions—like "what do our customers really want?" Instead of the "best" way of doing things, they are looking for better ways of changing in harmony with their customers' changing needs.

Some see a military analogy. One of the first uses for computers on the battlefield was to shoot down aircraft. Computer brains extrapolated the course of a moving aeroplane, and helped guide anti-aircraft guns along that track. Wonderful theories and technologies were created to build such systems. But much of the work was wasted. Aeroplanes changed course in the seconds between the time a shell left the gun and when it arrived at its target. So weapons designers changed tack. They built a "shell" that could change course, too—called the Sidewinder missile. Instead of the vast electronic brain which guided the gun, they imbued it with a wonderfully simple control system. The missile simply identified a target, and then kept turning towards it.

Some companies are similarly shifting the emphasis of their automation strategies towards responsiveness. It is not easy. At the least, the change requires the humility to listen to customers—no matter how bright your own people are. Achieving responsiveness also often requires handing some routine decisions over to the computer to make sure they are done quickly and predictably. Mr. John Thompson—head of the European part of the Computer Sciences Corporation, a firm of consultants on information technology—argues that some firms will have to be run more like the spreadsheets on which their results are modelled: change one number and others dependent on it adjust automatically.

So far, most of those who have successfully made this transition have simply had no other choice. Take Digital Equipment (DEC), a computer maker. In the early 1980s DEC decided to let its customers choose for themselves which options they wanted with their computers. Combined with the technical advances of DEC's VAX range of computers, so-called *à la carte* computers proved wonderfully popular. This popularity nearly killed DEC. DEC's staff simply found it impossible to keep abreast of the possible premutations of components. Computers arrived without crucial bits of cable, or with parts that did not fit together. As DEC did not collect payment until the computer worked, the mounting piles of misspecified machines were as expensive for DEC as they were irksome for its customers.

With great effort, DEC automated the process by which orders from the sales force were translated into schedules for the factory and lists of parts to be delivered to the customer. Unfortunately, this did not solve the problem. Some of the orders were simply wrong to start with. Salesmen had not read technical changes to the product line, or had not understood the original technical specifications. So DEC went back to the drawing board. It came up with a collection of automated systems to manage the whole process of ordering, configuring, and building computers—from product catalogue to shop floor.

Because DEC's product catalogue is kept on-line, it can be updated at a stroke—so salesmen do not specify out-of-date equipment. The computer maintains the rules by which computers are configured: "if you have a whizzo-wonder super-attachment, you will need a whizzo-wonder cable." An "expert system" called XCON automatically applies those rules to the task of making up orders. Other, related expert systems schedule production, help take orders from salesmen and so on.

DEC calls this sort of automation "knowledge-based systems." The key is that the computer helps with the whole business process—both organising data (like a product catalogue) and administering some of the simpler decisions taken from the data (e.g., applying rules about how computers are made up). By so doing, the machines enable people to overcome complexity in order to respond quickly to new challenges.

Inevitably, DEC is now selling its expertise in building knowledge-based systems. Mr. Themis Pappageorge, head of the marketing effort, reckons that some of the most successful customers have been those faced with challenges as severe as DEC's configuration problem. However good their intentions, those taking a rational approach cannot as readily break down the barriers to the new ways of doing business.

One company whose experience supports Mr. Pappageorge's observation is Phillips 66, the product-marketing arm of Phillips Petroleum. After fending off two attacks by corporate raiders, Phillips was deep in debt and deep in trouble. To help revive its fortunes, it reorganised the way in which it sold refined-oil products. Instead of setting petrol prices over three broad regions (defined by which of Phillip's three big pipelines fed them), it started setting prices in 240 smaller regions, defined more rationally according to market. Prices were changed daily, if need be. Both local managers, who set regional prices, and national managers, who coordinated the regions, got information on inventories and sales just as fast. Competitors, who were still working largely according to the old time-scales and the old geography, were flummoxed.

Some of the most ambitious, and best articulated, plans to use information technology to build a more responsive company come from the mother ship of computing, IBM. IBM reckons that it will be increasingly hard to maintain a competitive edge in the technical brilliance of its computers and software. There are simply too many bright, innovative companies out there. By its sheer size and scope, however, IBM may well be able to get ahead in the amount and quality of its information about what customers really want. IBM is now building information systems to gather that information and to deliver it to the people who should respond to it.

IBM's internal information strategy was the subject of its annual conference of top executives last year. The conference compared IBM's information systems with those of its customers and its competitors and found room for improvement. What IBM did was excellent, but too often irrelevant. So IBM's chairman, Mr. John Akers, and his colleagues decided to shift the focus of IBM's internal information services. Instead of being charged with providing information processing—as measured by lines of program code delivered, capacity of networks, and the millions or billions of instructions which its computers can execute each second—IBM is now asking its information services to provide the company with information itself.

To begin the task of providing food for his colleagues' thoughts, Mr. Larry Ford, head of IBM's internal information services, came away from the meeting with his colleagues' backing for three broad initiatives:

- Create competitive advantage from information about customers and markets. In practical terms, this means building up huge "warehouses" of that information, which can be got at by any part of the company, anywhere.
- Define internal information needs and fill them. One result of this has been a proliferation of "executive information systems" designed to give each IBM executive access to up-to-the second information on results and performance from around the world. So far, says Mr. Ford, the question of who gets what information has proved relatively uncontroversial. But the discussions could grow more interesting as IBM tries to shift the emphasis of both business and systems from internal functions (e.g., manufacturing or marketing) to market segments (e.g., American computer-aided design of European personal computers).

- Create new measures of performance for information services. Instead of rewarding information services for technical excellence, IBM is trying to link their rewards to business goals. In practice, this often means creating new goals for each project. Measurements which would track changes in customer satisfaction in computer-aided design markets—to judge the performance of the builders of an IBM system designed to do that—would have little relevance to the satisfaction of personal-computer customers, for example.

Mr. Ford's 27,000 employees (7 percent of IBM's total work force) are generally enthusiastic about the new initiatives, and confident. They mostly find it more satisfying, he reports, when they can try to make sure that their systems are used to their full potential to benefit the business—not just to the limits of the technology. Besides, the systems staff get more varied work. As part of the deal, IBM is encouraging its systems people to spend a bit of their time doing consulting work for outside clients, both to make money and to learn how others do things.

To help in their new endeavours, Mr. Ford is training his folk with a variety of new skills. Some of the most important are tricks for under-standing how organisations work and how they can be helped to change. The same lesson, in a different form, will be brought home to many managers—and indeed to whole corporations. Information is slippery stuff. As men and machines work more closely to take advantage of it, the world will, at a minimum, become a faster-changing place. To cope with that change, managers may have to rewrite the curricula of skills needed to prosper in the capitalist world, and to keep rewriting it.

THE SEARCH FOR KNOWLEDGE

If time is money, then so must information be. Both fit into the equations with which every business-school student is taught to value an investment. Value, say the textbooks, is the expected payoff discounted by the time an investor has to wait for his money back and the risk that that money will not come back. Information, say other textbooks, is data that reduce uncertainty, and thus risk. But information technology may subtly change the role played by information in the business world.

One of the ironies of the "information revolution" is that so few of those involved can give any definition of what information is. Starting point for most who would try to do that is still the theory of information published in 1948 by Mr. Claude Shannon in the *Bell Systems Technical Journal*. Information, argued Mr. Shannon, reduces uncertainty. If a piece of data convinces you of something you had previously thought very unlikely, then there is a great deal of information in it. If it merely tells you what you know, then there is no information in it.

Mr. Shannon built from this insight a detailed mathematical definition of information. Though his intent was to quantify the information-carrying capacity of telephone lines, his theory can also describe most uses of computers. Most of what computers do is to reduce uncertainty in one way or another. As number-crunchers they can distill answers from data about sales or inventory levels; as databases they store complete libraries of information; enhanced with the technology of expert systems they can dispense scarce human expertise to whoever needs it; and as communicators they can send the information they hold across the world.

This does not mean that computers—however advanced they may be—can work with information in anything like the way people do. The distinction between people's information-handling skills and those of machines will largely determine which of today's human activities are duplicated by computers—and thus devalued. A big part of it is computers' sheer predictability.

Given the same inputs a thousand times, a computer will produce the same outputs a thousand times. It will not get bored, make mistakes, or have a flash of inspiration that enables it to see the problem in a new light. That predictability is what makes computers so useful. It is also their greatest weakness.

Given any well-defined question, information technology is making it increasingly easy to get answers. "What were our sales last month?" "What does it mean when the engine goes 'chunk-a-lunk thump thump'?" The machines cannot, however, do much to help provide questions in the first place. But if answers are easier to come by, good questions become all the more valuable.

People seldom seem to have any shortage of questions. Individuals move from job to job, learning new skills and ways of looking at the world at each step. Groups, by contrast, get stuck. Many is the company which churns out similar products or services year after year, doing the same business in the same way. Information technology will make such firms increasingly easy to copy—when copying is worthwhile. But it may also make it easier for groups to learn new tricks.

The technology can show all workers the same overview of the company—so that they can see why this year the emphasis should be on, say, speeding delivery while last year it was on quality in manufacturing. The technology can show each worker, day-to-day, month-to-month how his actions affect the group. And it can broadcast his bright ideas to the company as a whole.

Building such learning organisations is a vast challenge. It requires new skills, clever people, and capable machines. It requires both high standards and a commitment to keep learning. Many, particularly in the West, do not want to learn.

At Toyota's factories, one of the main measures of performance looked at by management is the number of suggestions for improvements submitted each day by workers. Compare that with the history of automation in the West where time and again managers have taken great trouble and expense to install information technology whose purpose is to enable workers to do their jobs more effectively—without bothering to consult the workers or to ask them whether or not the machines really help. Workers are no better. Britain is particularly full of examples of workers clinging to dangerous, boring, and low-paid jobs despite all efforts at convincing them to change their ways.

Information technology will not sweep away the legacy of years of suspicion or inertia overnight. But it will expose to increasing competition those firms not adept at change and self-improvement. The developing world is full of cheap and willing workers. Sit still long enough, and some competitor will piece-by-piece duplicate, with computers' help, much of your information gathering and decision making. The ability to learn as a group will become increasingly important for firms looking to avoid being dragged down by hordes of copycat competitors. Learning from and with fellow workers helps to keep a step ahead of the competition. Helping customers to learn can inspire them to keep buying your product. Learning from customers helps to pay attention to their changing needs. Learning is still something that humans do best, and being more human is the best way for men to work with machines.

II Computer Hardware and Software

It is through computer hardware and software that information systems function. The hardware provides the required equipment, while the software provides the required processing instructions. There continue to be dramatic advances in hardware and software, and even more impressive developments are certain to occur in the next few years. In this part of the book we present five articles that should advance your knowledge of hardware and software technology and applications. The primary emphasis of these articles will be on software, while at the same time references to present and developing hardware will form the backdrop for these discussions.

The initial reading in this section is "Computing Is the Medium for the Message." Michael Antonoff, the author, focuses on the extent to which personal computers (PCs) are becoming our necessary partners in communications. In the realm of hardware, Antonoff provides coverage of developments in PCs, laptop computers, time-sharing, optical fiber, printers, fax machines, and modems. In the realm of software, he addresses word processing, electronic spreadsheets, telecommuting, and E-mail. Most important, he shows how hardware and software merge to create enhanced, integrated forms of communications.

Jeremy Main, a writer for *Fortune* magazine, presents "At Last, Software CEOs Can Use." This reading presents an enlightening and timely discussion of how executives now have access to software that can be used to create executive information systems. In particular, the author focuses on software developed by Comshare and Pilot Executive Software, two chief suppliers of software systems designed to support senior executives.

Article 4, by Louis Richman, continues the discussion of software in "Software Catches the Team Spirit." The particular subject of his reading is specialized software, often called "groupware," which supports teams of people in their efforts to work smarter and more efficiently. It is argued that, as the commercial software firms have perfected word processing and financial spreadsheet programs, they are now turning more to systems which facilitate group decision making. Some discussion addresses the increasing use of electronic conference rooms, which try to integrate meetings with the work that individuals do independently.

"Telecommunications in the 1990s" by Randall Tobias is Reading 5. This reading presents an insightful overview of the blurring boundaries between computing and communications. One major example of this is how today computers communicate and telecommunications networks compute. He then argues that businesses in the 1990s will have to manage computing and communications as total, integrated information systems. He provides detailed discussion of telecommunications networks in the 1990s, the integrated services digital network (ISDN), and specific services, such as home services, messaging, call redirection and handling, mobile communications, fax, telemarketing, multimedia teleconferencing, and private networks.

The final selection in this part of the book is "Corporate Videotex: A Strategic Business Information System" by Gene Kusekoski. Videotex is a general term for an easy-to-use and consistent approach to locating and selectively viewing information on a video screen. Though developed for such consumer applications as telephone directory services, teleshopping, and telebanking, it is now being used by corporations to electronically distribute document-based information to their many worldwide locations. Using Digital Equipment Corporation as a case study, the author describes the considerations for implementing a corporate videotex utility and the benefits that can be realized from this approach.

2 *Computing Is the Medium for the Message**

Michael Antonoff

What a difference a decade makes. In 1979 phone messages were scribbled on pink forms by receptionists; today, the "receptionist" is as likely to be a hard disk. Back then, memos and reports all looked the same; now, we worry about fancy fonts and graphics. The fastest way to get a document across the country used to be via overnight pouch; that document can now be faxed coast to coast in 15 seconds. In the 1970s, we discovered citizens band radio, chatting with callers miles away; with cellular car phones, we now can dial up a specific person in Tokyo while gliding along the freeway. Meanwhile, "CB" has been reborn as a chat mode offered by on-line services like CompuServe.

Ten years ago, we first put on the headphones of a Sony Walkman. The term *yuppie* was coined to define the largest demographic group ever to fight its way to the front of the counter at Bloomingdale's. This generation believed in its inalienable right to have consumer electronics—phones, videocassette recorders, and CD players—become better, smaller, and cheaper every season.

It was the same story with office equipment. Big, noisy impact printers yielded to quiet desktop machines called "laser printers." Bulky and expensive dedicated word-processing systems gave way to personal computers that indeed were better, smaller, and cheaper. And the new PCs had an added value—they could run that most important legacy of the 1970s, the electronic spreadsheet.

---

* Source: Michael Antonoff, "Computing Is the Medium for the Message," *Personal Computing*, October 1989.

David Liddle, chairman of Metaphor Computer Systems, Mountain View, California, declares that the modern PC was heralded by the arrival of VisiCalc on the Apple II. "The conceptual model underlying VisiCalc is one of the brilliant things to come out of the second half of the 20th century," he says. The spreadsheet put in the hands of a broad range of users a power not even mainframes offered. Its rows and columns of numerical data can be manipulated easily and presented to others. With spreadsheets, individuals are better able to understand complex numerical information—and share the results.

Liddle is by no means the only visionary who sees the spreadsheet as a turning point. Arno Penzias, vice president of research at AT&T's Bell Laboratories, Murray Hill, New Jersey, shared the 1978 Nobel Prize in Physics for his work in refining the big-bang theory on the origin of the universe. In his recent book, *Ideas and Information: Managing in a High-Tech World,* he emphasizes that spreadsheet technology has stream-lined communication to make us better competitors in business. "It could be the CFO of a half-billion-dollar corporation down to somebody running a grocery store who has had a better insight into their costs and financial matters because of spreadsheets than was ever possible," he says. "That's an example of communication between machine and person. Once that information has been digested, people can better communicate it with each other. In some cases people didn't understand it themselves until they finally visualized it."

Before there were spreadsheets on personal computers, there was time-sharing on costly mainframes. Analysis could take days or weeks, and computer specialists were integral to the process. Considering the expenditure of resources and the slow turnaround, what-if analyses were rarely done. Today, managers can obtain instant projections on all sorts of plans—as long as they can be represented numerically.

Time-sharing is still a fact of life on mainframes; but as a model for how we handle information, it has given way to time-shifting. The concept got its start with answering machines and videocassette recorders: You no longer had to be present to get your messages or receive a TV program. A decade after the demise of extraordinarily powerful programming chieftains like NBC's Fred Silverman, Americans sit in their respective time zones watching the offerings from three major television networks less and viewing programs of their own choosing more.

While this ability to time-shift is convenient in the home, in the work-place it is becoming indispensable. In the global village, people we need to talk to are sleeping when we are working. Even when their hours roughly match ours, all too often they are unavailable the moment we need to communicate. Time-shifting devices come to the rescue in the form of computer-run voice mail systems. Alternatively, a computer bulletin board system (BBS), electronic mail service, or fax machine can receive messages without anyone being present.

"People are spending their lives in meetings," says Penzias. "The notion of calling people on the phone, while it's not totally broken down yet, is at risk because people are no longer at their desks. Everyone is off at meetings—or they're already on the phone."

Something else has happened in the last decade that gives us more individual control. For the increasingly large class of information workers —people who "manufacture" words or process numbers for a living—the office can be anywhere. In Woody Allen's 1969 film *Play It Again, Sam,* a businessman named Mr. Christie constantly calls in for his messages, leaving phone numbers where he can be reached. Today, he'd be carrying a display pager in his pocket and a cellular mobile phone in his car. Similarly, powerful laptop computers are helping make the office truly portable. The only desk that traveling executives get to call their own during the course of the workday may be the tray on an airplane seat.

Commuting is less and less measured by distance as by time. Not only is the electronic cottage, forecast in the '70s by futurists like Alvin Toffler in his book, *The Third Wave,* a reality today, but it is also being increasingly viewed as a way to ease traffic congestion, reduce air pollution and energy use, free up office space, and attract and retain qualified workers. The state of California has taken the lead with an experimental telecommuting project in which some 150 employees go to work by staying at home.

Futurist Jack Nilles was a professor at the University of Southern California, Los Angeles, in 1973 when he coined the term *telecommuting.* He now heads a private consulting firm called Jala Associates in Los Angeles and is monitoring California's telecommuting program. According to Nilles, an interim report released this summer concludes that permitting selected volunteers to telecommute raises their output as much as 5 percent while improving the quality of their work and keeping some key employees from leaving.

Like any organization, says Nilles, "the state needs to be able to attract, retain, and develop able staff and not necessarily worry about where they live." He cites the example of a skilled actuary who would have had to quit his job in Sacramento because of an allergy to pollen. Instead, he moved to the seaside community of Marina Del Rey, where he telecommutes by phone and computer most of the time. He flies to the state capital every two weeks. Nilles estimates that, counting the underground telecommuters who have made informal agreements with their bosses to work at home on a part-time basis, there may be a million telecommuters across the United States.

One increasingly vital link in the communications chain is the facsimile machine. The word *fax* has joined *Xerox* as both a noun and a verb in the public lexicon. Some radio stations now accept faxed play requests ("Fax it to me, baby," as one disk jockey put it), and some delicatessens in New York now take handwritten orders via fax. The rise in junk fax, unsolicited advertising that costs the recipient paper and ties up the machine, inspired legislation around the nation to have it banned. Events in China demonstrated how fax could be used to spread the concepts of democracy and freedom of the press as students abroad received faxed requests for supplies and responded, in one case, with thousands of garbage bags for Tiananmen Square. Even after the crackdown, newspaper accounts of the government's attack were sent to fax machines throughout China.

According to CAP International, a Norwell, Massachusetts, market research firm, some 1.5 million stand-alone fax machines and 92,000 computer-based fax boards will be sold in the United States this year. Driven by the success of fax machines, the use of fax and fax/modem boards is increasing rapidly. With these, personal computer users who don't own dedicated fax machines can exchange text and graphics with people who don't necessarily have computers. According to a study by market researcher Venture Development Corporation of Natick, Massachusetts, unit shipments of fax boards are expected to reach 450,000 in 1993.

Communication can be enhanced by a nice-looking report or newsletter. In this realm, laser printers are changing publishing to the same degree that PCs have changed computing. Laser printers were actually invented in the '70s, but it took the introduction of Hewlett-Packard's LaserJet in 1984 and Apple's LaserWriter in 1985 to turn them into general office printers. Even then, easy-to-use software lagged behind, and it is only in the last couple of years that a wide range of desktop publishing, word processing, and laser utility programs have emerged.

In the early '80s, there were three general terms for describing the output printed from a personal computer: "letter quality" (just as good as a typewriter) was produced by daisywheel printers, and "draft" or "near letter quality" rolled out of dot matrix printers. With the coming of laser printers, the terminology shifted to "near typeset quality." Instead of inserting type wheels into mechanical printers, users downloaded scalable fonts from disks to their electronic printers. While dot matrix printers, unlike daisywheels, printed graphs and line art, desktop lasers boosted the resolution from as little as 72 dots per inch to as much as 300dpi, a fourfold improvement. "Staircases" disappeared from headlines and tiny typefaces became readable. In the world of office politics, where form often counts as much as substance, those with access to laser printers had a decided edge over those who didn't. Executives in the games division of one computer company complained that their 1989 budget didn't receive proper attention—because the proposal from the productivity division, printed on lasers, made their presentation look shabby.

Professional publishing has over the last decade turned from an industry of manufacturers' proprietary standards to one that increasingly is taking its marching orders from personal computers. In April, Cal Bauer, whose Bauer Enterprises is creating printer drivers for Presentation Manager, provoked the professional publishing crowd at the Seybold Seminars, a publishing conference, when he said that standards in the publishing world are now being driven by what people are doing on the desktop in the average office. (Microsoft acquired Bauer Enterprises in July.)

The danger of putting the power of the printing press into the hands of the many, of course, is that a deluge of good-looking and sometimes not-so-good-looking documents is probably cascading into your office in-box even now. In addition to that pile, there is information coming at you in the form of voice mail (''You have 18 messages,'' intones a synthetic voice) and ASCII text mail from the company BBS or on-line services like MCI Mail.

''Because we have a much greater ability to generate information than we do to store and retrieve it, we're drowning in undigestible material,'' observes Arno Penzias. ''The problem is the categorization bottleneck. As you move into the future and life becomes more complicated, the number of interdependencies always goes up. It makes the filing task much harder.''

One of the great failings of the modern age is that we've kept the old filing cabinet model around too long, Penzias says. ''You can't put things in isolated places. One of the reasons we keep so much on the desk is that it's the only place where we think we'll be able to find it again. But we're using up our most precious commodity: our own memory. To remember a lunch date at 3 o'clock tomorrow instead of writing it down is stupid. But it's futile to think that if there's a great pile of paper in the corner of my desk, I'll remember it. That corner of the desk keeps getting more and more stuff, and then you get to the point where you can't find your calendar anymore.''

Penzias is hopeful that the ability to search across a storage disk for keywords, a technology already finding its way into full-featured word processors and programs like Gofer and Dragnet, will help alleviate the problem. ''Once you get [error-free] optical character readers that can scan the paper and create an ASCII file and you get information back with a keyboard search, you won't be spending all this time sorting through stuff,'' he says.

Andrew Lippman, associate director of the Media Lab at the Massachusetts Institute of Technology, even suggests that one day your computer will be programmed to serve as a surrogate reporter that will search remote databases for information you formerly gleaned only by scanning the media yourself. A personally tailored electronic newspaper could result.

Corporations are increasingly tying their employees together through systems that can be accessed from their personal computers or terminals in their offices or homes or portable computers in their hotel rooms. This can be an efficient and even paper-free way to disseminate company-wide policies and reports and allow employees around the globe to communicate among themselves without playing phone tag.

A phenomenon that companies tend to discourage is something called

E-mail wars, a situation in which someone address a message—often not work-related—to everyone, and replies and counterreplies then snowball. Debates on topics from abortion rights to diet plans have raged on company E-mail.

Those exchanges aren't necessarily counterproductive, however. "Some companies are predisposed against the social use of electronic mail," observes William Dutton, an associate professor at the University of Southern California's Annenberg School of Communications. "They think that anything not strictly task-related is somehow wasteful or inefficient. It's because they're transferring from the use of telegrams and older mail systems. But they're making the wrong analogy. They should be more attuned to the analogy of face-to-face encounters, where communications that are not directly task-related are very functional in forging relationships and accomplishing tasks."

Private distribution lists are another phenomenon of corporate culture E-mail. Rather than addressing a message to one person or to everyone, this allows the sender to dispatch messages to a particular set of recipients. Thus, a gripe group or a social group may coalesce. When it comes to communicating thoughts without the usual prejudices associated with age, sex, or appearance, E-mail can be the greater equalizer.

Eventually, though, people do want to meet in person. A group that had been communicating regularly via E-mail recently got together for lunch at the California Cafe. "I was amazed how good-looking the guys turned out to be," said a woman who attended. "Working for a computer company, you expect nerds."

Home videotex, once written off as a costly failure, was never so visible as in 1989 thanks to TV and direct-mail advertising for Prodigy, a service owned by IBM and Sears. Some 21 local calling areas are expected to be on-line by the end of the year. New York City, Miami, and Denver were added this spring. Speaking at a videotex conference in San Francisco in June, David Waks, Prodigy's director of technology, said that more than 75,000 households were paying a flat fee of $9.95 a month to subscribe to the advertiser-supported service and that membership "will be into six digits soon."

Meanwhile, the regional Bell holding companies, including Nynex Corporation, with its Info-Look service, are beginning to provide gateways into on-line data banks. Customers typically use their own communication software and modems to access the regional phone company's general menu listing all the services available. Once a particular service is chosen, the call is routed to the information provider's database. As a convenience, users can pay for everything in their monthly phone bills.

If the future is brighter for videotex, it's partly because the definition has been changing. Where once videotex conjured colorful graphics delivered over the phone, now the definition covers any easy-to-use data service aimed at the individual, even those services providing text alone.

On the eve of this century's final decade, there is an anticipation that the way members of society interact will undergo rapid change as computers become better integrated into global communications. Ian Ross, president of AT&T Bell Laboratories, predicted last year that by the middle of the next decade, data transmission—machines talking to people and machines talking to machines—might well account for as much traffic on AT&T's U.S. telecommunications network as voice conversations.

The number of consumer and business E-mail messages have been growing steadily. According to Electronic Mail & Micro Systems, a New Canaan, Connecticut, newsletter that covers communications technology, in 1985 some 8 million messages were sent each month to 450,000 mailboxes; in 1989, those figures were projected at 31 million monthly messages and 1.6 million mailboxes.

Much of the hardware for this change is already in place. At the beginning of the '80s, there were zero miles of optical fiber laid; today, a million miles of the cable is in place. The advantage of fiber optics over copper wire is the much greater bandwidth. One fiber, thinner than a human hair, can transmit 24,000 simultaneous calls at the speed of light. This capacity is expected to double soon. One challenge in the coming decade will be to write the software that will enable computers to address, route, and bill all those calls. More than half the technical staff at Bell Labs is now working on software.

The greater bandwidth can be used to carry live video along with conversation. The "picture phones" unveiled at the 1964 World's Fair in New York never materialized, but Penzias says there is a critical difference between a business conference application and one-to-one communication. In the latter case, voice-only transmissions are just fine. But office workers in the future will be able to remain in their offices and put video windows on their PCs to see other participants in a conference. In fact, one of the windows might contain a document, such as a spreadsheet or a legal contract, that everyone at remote sites could peruse simultaneously.

The emerging ISDN (Integrated Services Digital Network) standard for telecommunications, developed by AT&T and well on its way to international recognition, may help make this scenario possible. ISDN allows several channels on a single phone line. Two of the three channels are capable of medium-resolution video.

The on-screen image suggested by Penzias is right out of the ABC News program, "Nightline," in which three or four people, each of whom can be located anywhere in the world, are seen in real time talking and reacting to each other's comments. While only a TV network or very large corporation can afford videoconferencing now, ISDN will eventually allow the multistation videoconference at a relatively low price. "You'll have the ability to stay in your own office instead of being totally meeting-driven, and you'll be able to look through that video window when you have to and get some work done the rest of the time," says Penzias. "And if you need somebody's input during a meeting, you call them into a window instead of holding yet another meeting or making a lousy decision."

An indication of the computer's impact on communications is its effect on the English language. The *Random House Dictionary of the English Language, Second Edition,* published last year, contained hundreds of new terms spawned in the computer age. Even more interesting were the new meanings for common words, such as "backup," "escape," "icon," "mouse," "prompt," and "window." Two trends are occurring regarding the way our language is changing: We use terms of animation to describe machines, and we increasingly describe ourselves using mechanical terms.

Says Penzias, "People say things like 'Sorry for giving you a core dump' [for giving you too much information at once] or 'I went nonlinear' or 'I blew my circuit' [for not making sense]." Penzias finds the trend disturbing, particularly when people start identifying themselves as machines. "Machines make wonderful tools, but they make lousy role models," he says.

A critical challenge of the '90s will be to adopt broad standards so that data can be exchanged between all kinds of computers. ISDN will provide an international standard for linking phones and computers in a high-speed digital system. And other standards are emerging. Though ASCII has become a standard for sending text messages, various E-mail systems may still be incompatible with each other. This is very frustrating, especially if two companies that do business want to access each other's systems. One standard being proposed for international mail is the X.400 protocol. The Aerospace Industry Association, a trade association representing the nation's aircraft manufacturers, earlier this year demonstrated the interconnection of major providers of E-mail services, including MCI Mail, AT&T Mail, and GE Information Services Quickcomm, with eight member companies of the association using X.400.

"The ability to communicate through a single service provider, in much the same way we use the telephone, demonstrates the tremendous capability of electronic mail," declared AIA member Steven York, who manages information exchange for Hughes Aircraft Company. The goal of the project is to interconnect all 51 AIA companies so that they can communicate with their suppliers, partners, and customers.

On the personal computing level, bridges are being built between diverse applications like communications, spreadsheets, and word processing. Thus, using a combination of programs that incorporate a protocol like Microsoft's Dynamic Data Exchange (DDE), fluctuating numbers can flow from a mainframe to a spreadsheet, to a graph, and to a report automatically. Word-processing programs are increasingly including conversion utilities so that files created in competitors' products can be imported, and vice versa.

As for communication between man and machine, there is still a long way to go on the interface; but the use of icons, pointers, scroll bars, dialog boxes, and windows—the kind of things popularized by the Macintosh—are rapidly eclipsing archaic command codes. Even the documentation is improving, with much of it now on-line and the printed manuals including many more graphics.

The merging of computing and telecommunications has been under way for some time. This trend will accelerate in the decade ahead as time and distance become almost incidental in a world where computers and individuals work together in a single system with unified standards.

3 At Last, Software CEOs Can Use*

Jeremy Main

Early one day last year, Duracell CEO C. Robert Kidder decided to spend his first hour at work browsing through a computer system designed for the company's top executives. This time he was curious about productivity. By manipulating a mouse attached to his workstation, he got his computer to search the company's mainframe memory for data comparing the performance of the Duracell hourly and salaried work forces in the United States and overseas. Within seconds the computer produced a crisp, clear table in colors showing that the U.S. salaried staff produced more sales per employee. He asked the computer to "drill down" for more data, looking for reasons for the difference. By the time he finished browsing, he had determined that Duracell, the world's largest alkaline battery maker, had too many salespeople in Germany wasting time calling on small stores. That information helped explain profit problems there. As a result, Duracell cut the German sales staff and signed up distributors to cover the mom and pop stores.

Kidder acknowledges that the same information could have been available on paper. But the computer gave it to him faster and better, making the comparisons clearer, all without sending aides scurrying around asking questions that would upset the troops. "The system has been useful," says Kidder, "and we are a long way from getting the most out of it."

Decades after they transformed backoffice operations, years after they started helping middle managers, computers are finally arriving on top

---

* Source: Jeremy Main, "At Last, Software CEOs Can Use," *Fortune*, March 13, 1989, pp. 77-78, 80, 83.

executives' desks. Why the delay? Until recently, no system possessed the combination of sophistication and simplicity that corporate chiefs demanded. A few buffs persevered anyway. Former Northwest Industries chief Ben Heineman, who loves to write programs the way other people love to solve crossword puzzles, created a $4 million system—which was scrapped after he retired. But most top managers won't allot much time for training themselves, and they recoil from a keyboard as if just touching one might demote them to the typing pool.

In the mid-1980s the right ingredients finally came together: powerful PCs and workstations that could shape masses of numbers into simple, colorful tables and charts; the touch screen and the mouse; interconnections that could weave a single network out of a company's different hardware and databases; and the software to turn it all into a system. Now any fumble-fingered chairman can use these systems to make faster and better, or at least better-informed, decisions. Many functions are represented on the screen by icons—pictures of wastebaskets, printers, files, and so forth—and he has only to touch them or point at them to make the computer do what the picture represents.

The whole thing is usually called an executive information system or executive support system, and it can do more than just help an executive. Users say it can transform their work. Xerox President Paul Allaire pushed for a system that forced executives to change the way they reported, planned, and ran meetings. Paul Lego, chairman-designate of Westinghouse, says, "This hasn't completely changed the way I manage, but I feel a lot more comfortable with the decisions I have made." He has more information and gets it faster.

The sudden success of these systems is evident in the sales of the two chief suppliers, Comshare and Pilot Executive Software. Although the market remains small, it grew last year by 45 percent, to $32 million, according to a market research firm, International Data. Comshare, based in Ann Arbor, Michigan, says its clients increased in 1988 from 120 to 220, almost all of them major corporations. Pilot, a Boston firm, claims its client list grew from 98 to 153 last year. Both companies say no clients have canceled.

Pilot and Comshare began to market their systems in the mid-1980s, confusingly naming them Command Center and Commander, respectively. Although superficially alike, the two are technically quite different. Comshare's is a "distributed" system, meaning that each executive's PC works with data stored in its memory. By contrast, Pilot's "coprocessing" system stays on-line with the mainframe. Pilot gives each user the memory and computing power of the mainframe, but if the mainframe is overloaded, Pilot can get sluggish. Comshare has the high speed of a PC, but its database must be refreshed frequently. How? In some early distributed systems before Commander, a sneaker brigade ran around the office early each morning sticking updated floppy disks into each PC. The sneaker brigades have been retired because Comshare systems can be updated automatically overnight by the mainframe.

Comshare's clients include Citizens & Southern, GE, Grumman, Kraft, John Hancock, Metropolitan Life, Motorola, Oscar Mayer, and New England Mutual Life Insurance. Pilot has signed up the Bank of Boston, Boeing, Duracell, Marine Midland, Monsanto, Public Service Electric & Gas of New Jersey, Unum Life, and Westinghouse, among many others. Several companies, including ConAgra, Johnson & Johnson, Phillips Petroleum, and Xerox, have created their own systems. Du Pont recently signed up with Comshare, while GTE rejected both off-the-shelf systems and instead devised a network based on Hyper-Card, the software Apple provides with every new Macintosh. Marine Midland dropped an early sneaker brigade model as too clumsy but has since adopted a Pilot system. Who uses an executive information system, and how, varies in each company. A CEO whose duties are broad and public won't even need the system, so the chief operating officer will be the top executive using it. And each user has particular likes.

Ted Athanassiades, executive vice president for pensions at Metropolitan Life, no longer says "I'll have to get back to you on that" when the chairman calls to find if the CEO he is meeting for lunch is a client. Instead, while on the phone he gets Comshare to skim silently through its records of Met Life's 3,200 pension clients. Athanassiades can find out instantly who handles an account, without sending a query down through layers of bureaucracy. Robert Shafto, president of insurance and personal financial services for New England Mutual Life Insurance, likes to track and compare the performance of the 87 general agency offices that represent his company. Instead of being scattered among many pieces of paper, the information is all in one easily accessible package that can be thrown on the screen. Shafto can manipulate the information to answer specific questions—for example, what's the difference in turnover among new vs. experienced salespeople in each agency? The answers are keys to the agencies' quality.

Xerox wanted more than just information from its system. When he became president in 1986, Paul Allaire said, "We want to change the way we run our business." Chairman David Kearns brought Allaire back from Europe in 1983 to be chief of staff and asked him to figure out how to apply Xerox's technological experience to running the company better. The resulting "executive support system," probably the most far-reaching in any company, goes to the heart of management. Ken Soha, who oversees the system, relates that when the company's 20 strategic business unit chiefs used to gather for annual meetings with the top half-dozen executives at headquarters in Stamford, Connecticut, torrents of paper would rush back and forth in the preceding few days. Senior executives would get a fat black briefing book of documents, only partly read and little digested before the meeting, with no consistent format or terminology. Two similar units might have different definitions of a basic term like revenue. Much of a meeting would be spent trying to agree on facts.

As in many companies, devising the new computer system forced Xerox to rationalize and discipline reporting. Now when a business unit makes a presentation in Stamford, no papers fly to and fro. Instead, says Soha, each unit must submit its plan electronically five days in advance, compressed to a five-page format with standard definitions of terms. Each top executive should have read the plan on the screen of his Xerox 6085 workstation before the meeting, and business unit heads should not waste time going over basic facts. They can focus on issues. As Allaire said in a Harvard business school case study, "Our management process is becoming inseparable from the technology which supports it."

An executive information system almost inevitably expands—once it's running, more people want it and get it. At Xerox the net has spread from the top 15 people to about 100 managers, and Soha is thinking about expanding it to 500.

Other companies may not have been as shaken up as Xerox by these systems, but they certainly notice a difference. Gathering and sorting data faster has become an important competitive weapon. Bob Kidder reports that at Duracell he gets his monthly detailed financial statements a week earlier than he did before. At Westinghouse the monthly figures come in two or three days faster. Like Xerox, others find meetings go better. William Jeffery, senior vice president at United Research, a consulting firm, says sharing information and just trying to agree on facts take 80 percent of a typical business meeting. But with a good executive information system furnishing participants the same facts, time spent planning, solving problems, and making decisions can be 80 percent instead of only 20 percent.

Requiring staffers or computer whizzes to figure out which facts the boss needs dooms a system, because they have no idea how his mind works. So system designers try to find out what he considers the so-called critical success factors—the few key things that must go right if a business is to flourish. John Rockart, a senior lecturer at MIT and co-author of a book called *Executive Support Systems,* says that at Microwave Associates one critical factor was simplicity itself—current sales. Another, a little more sophisticated, was sales of technically advanced products. An even more refined factor was customers' perception of the quality of Microwave's engineering staff.

Making all this timely, focused, critical information thoroughly useful to a busy senior executive requires one more element: a simple graphic color representation that makes anomalies leap off the screen. For instance, the system might be programmed to show sales figures in red if they are 10 percent below plan. Executives like to see trends highlighted and projected over long periods, say five years. Robert Wallace, recently retired president of Phillips 66, the refining and marketing arm of Phillips Petroleum, likens using an executive information system to his experience as a Navy antiaircraft gunner during World War II. With practice he could scan enormous reaches of sky and quickly identify an enemy plane when it was a speck on the horizon. Looking at his screen, he says, ''I can see trends in seconds. I can't do that if I'm scanning a lot of tables on paper.''

There's no gain without pain, as the coaches say, and the adoption of an executive information system can make managers uneasy. Some higher-ups just don't want computers in their offices, and some down below find such a system menacing. ''You should anticipate organizational resistance because an executive information system is inherently political,'' says David De Long, co-author with Rockart of *Executive Support Systems* and a researcher at the Harvard Business School. ''After all, you are changing information flows and access. That's very threatening.'' A middle manager spends up to 80 percent of his time collecting, analyzing, and passing on information. He might be spooked by knowing the chairman or president can probe into his work without leaving a trace. To allay that fear, some companies have put a limit on how far the boss can ''drill down'' with his computer. At Xerox he can't go below three layers: He can get figures for the corporation, for a major business unit, and for a subdivision of the unit—its U.S. sales, for example. But if he wants to go deeper and get, say, New England sales, then the computer tells him to mind his own business. He'll have to pick up the phone for that information.

While executive information systems alter the roles of middle managers, they needn't diminish them. Says Harvard Business School professor Lynda Applegate: ''People think an EIS centralizes decision and control, but what happens is that it can allow you to push decisions down while giving management a clearer view of what is happening.'' Since the boss can more easily check results all over the company, he can afford to let subordinates make more important decisions. At Phillips 66, price information from 240 motor fuel terminals, formerly available on various bits of paper, now appears on the screens of top executives at headquarters in Bartlesville, Oklahoma. They monitor trends but let local managers set prices. ''The system has increased our profits from oil trading by $30 million to $50 million a year,'' says Wallace. Applegate adds that if the system relieves middle managers of routine work, then an innovative company should use them on more demanding problems.

These systems can be expensive. With all the needed hardware and software, plus training and development costs, prices go as high as $1 million. Annual running expenses will include the salaries of three to six staff specialists. For its Commander system, Comshare charges between $100,000 and $280,000 for software to run 10 stations. Each additional station adds $1,500. Comshare also charges an annual ''maintenance and enhancement'' fee amounting to 15 percent of the original price. Pilot charged an average installation fee of $138,000 in 1988, with no limit on the number of users. Economy is the great appeal of Apple's HyperCard, which comes free with every Macintosh. HyperCard is not an executive information system but software that helps users develop customized systems easily and quickly. GTE spent only $14,000 creating a system based on HyperCard. Laurence Chait, an Arthur D. Little consultant, calls HyperCard "an infant version of what we will see in the next 5 or 10 years."

Comshare Chairman Richard Crandall has a personal answer to clients who complain you can travel with a briefing book but not with a work-station. Crandall travels with a laptop computer and loads its hard disk just before leaving. He can update the memory by phone line in a hotel room. Other innovations in this fast-changing field include sound and video recording capabilities in Apple's Macintosh line of computers. Douglas Neal, senior vice president of Decision Resources, a consulting firm in Washington, D.C., shows clients how to add voice annotations to charts and tables so a vice president can hear as well as see what the president wants to know. Neal also urges executives to use remote controls, like those for a TV set, rather than a mouse or a touch screen. A remote control lets the executive lean back in a thoughtful, relaxed posture, rather than toil hunched tensely over his computer. Sounds like a nice way to work.

4

Software Catches the Team Spirit*

Louis S. Richman

A commercial real estate broker in Boston pops a compact disk into a player. She taps a few keys on her computer terminal. The floor plan and pictures of an office tower in Dallas pop up on her client's screen a continent away in Los Angeles. The broker's man in Dallas comes on line to take the client on a video "tour" of the building. With a few more commands, the computer produces a spreadsheet outlining the building's costs and revenues. The buyer taps in an offer for the building and the numbers appear on the broker's screen. Broker and buyer agree. Deal closed.

From the fertile, science fiction-soaked imaginations of computer software engineers is springing a dazzling new vision of a futuristic office environment where the 21st-century TV cartoon character George Jetson might feel at home. Software that will enable people to collaborate across barriers of space and time is one of today's hottest frontiers of computer research. Like an electronic sinew that binds teams together, the new "groupware" aims to place the computer squarely in the middle of communications among managers, technicians, and anyone else who interacts in groups, revolutionizing the way they work.

Groupware boosters make breathtaking, if extravagant-sounding, claims for what this new technology will do. Linked desktop terminals running the new software will coordinate schedules and route messages.

---

* Source: Louis S. Richman, "Software Catches the Team Spirit," *Fortune,* June 8, 1987, pp. 125, 129, 132, 136.

Novel products will emerge as networks of computer work stations guide teams of workers through large shared databases; a pharmaceutical company, for example, might search a database of organic chemicals for possible new drugs. Managers will confer with colleagues, suppliers, and customers via wallsize video screens as cameras connected to computers record and store their conversations. And—hold on to your space helmets—even *meetings* will become more effective as today's low-tech conference rooms turn into multimedia "war rooms" controlled by software that helps keep everything on course.

Software that supports group work may not be as far out as it sounds. Advanced prototypes are already in use at a handful of research labs around the country; the first commercial products are beginning to reach the market. Says Jerry Wagner, a professor of management information systems at the University of Texas Business School in Austin: "This technology could be one of the most important contributions to management effectiveness in business history."

In the new effort to develop software that helps teams of people work smarter, necessity is running in tandem with opportunity. Software engineers need better ways to manage teams of programmers writing vastly more complicated computer codes; as programs grow more intricate, the risk increases that the work of engineers collaborating on one of dozens of subsystems will distort the work of other teams. At the same time, companies are looking for opportunities to transform their huge investment in office automation equipment into tools that actually, finally, pay off in productivity gains.

Engineers at the Microelectronics & Computer Technology Corporation (MCC) research consortium in Austin, Xerox's Palo Alto Research Center (PARC), and Tektronix Laboratories in Beaverton, Oregon, have made groupware a priority for their research. "We've reached the limits of what individuals can do," says Laszlo Belady, director of MCC's software research program. "The biggest problem we face isn't so much a technical problem as a human coordination problem." Belady is quick to add that solving the problem casts software designers in a new role: "As hard scientists, we've found it uncomfortable dealing with the messy, ambiguous relationships that exist among people in groups."

Says Benn Konsynski, a professor of management information systems at Harvard Business School: "Coordinating people is *the* business problem managers want to solve." Thomas Malone, who teaches the same subject at MIT's Sloan School, thinks companies will benefit most from software that helps quicken their "information metabolism," the speed with which they digest and respond to information. A team Malone heads has been working for over two years on a program called Information Lens, with funding from GM, Wang, and Xerox.

Information Lens blends into the office like a supercompetent servant with a team of scattered masters. It draws on an artificial intelligence programming tool that allows each user to tailor the system to his personal needs. The computer can be instructed to discriminate among electronic messages—recognizing the difference, say, between a routine announcement of a new pencil procurement policy and an urgent reminder that your boss wants your group's report before the end of the day. And it can cull information from other computers' databases that relates to the projects a group is working on, routing it speedily to each group member's terminal and automatically updating his files. Malone thinks commercial versions of the system designed to work on personal computers could be ready in two to three years.

Transforming groupware from an engineers' plaything into user-friendly programs for business poses formidable problems. "The pace of acceptance of these new tools will be determined by the abilities of the most technophobic member of a work group to use it," says George P. Huber, a professor at the University of Texas Business School. Commercial software developers, having perfected word processing and financial spreadsheet programs to a market-saturating fare-thee-well, have a powerful incentive to try to solve the problem. Among the biggest new markets for business applications software are the roughly 280,000 networks that companies have bought to link their computers together but so far have discovered few ways to use. Microsoft and Lotus Development are making software that supports group work a major focus of their research, but both estimate that they are about three years away from launching products.

Pride of place for bringing the first easy-to-use programs to market belongs to two California companies, Action Technologies and Brøderbund. At its start-up in January 1985, Action Technologies introduced a product called the Coordinator that is based on a stunningly simple theory of human communication. It is the brainchild of a cerebral Chilean émigré named Fernando Flores, who served as finance minister in the government of Salvador Allende.

Business, according to Flores, is essentially the completion of a set of action-oriented conversations, such as requests, offers, counteroffers, and promises. The trick to effective team coordination, he says, is having work groups label their conversations accordingly. The Coordinator lets a user compose a message on a personal computer, assign it to one of Flores's conversation categories, and transmit it via standard telephone lines to other users. The system tracks each user's conversations, reminds him of his pending commitments, and keeps a record of the status of a group project.

Gtel, a California-based seller of telephone equipment, uses the Coordinator to track inventory at its 20 retail outlets and four warehouses, assemble daily store management reports, and communicate between headquarters and the field. Denise Schubert, Gtel's personal computer manager, estimates that the new system yields better data and costs $4,500 a month less than the electronic-mail system it replaced. But Schubert is most impressed with the fact that Gtel's store clerks, most of them aged 17 to 24, were able to start using the system after just a day's training. The Coordinator is winning converts among managers at General Motors' EDS subsidiary, whose account managers are using the system at GM offices in Dayton. It is also being tested at Aetna Life, where Bonnie Johnson, a corporate technical planning manager, says, "This is the first effective group communications tool I've seen."

Brøderbund introduced a program called *For Comment* last November. It enables a team of up to 16 members to collaborate on writing, reviewing, and editing documents that can contain up to 236 single-spaced pages. Users relay a common document they are working on—a business plan, for example—through their network of personal computers, suggesting revisions and adding up to five levels of comments and comments on comments.

The software tracks and saves each draft revision as well as all the commentators' contributions, creating a record of the ideas that influenced the group decision process. To prepare a finished document, the author simply moves suggested changes from the comment block into the main text almost as easily as a crazed teenager in a video game arcade zaps a space invader. "Our background developing computer games gives us a big advantage in understanding how to make software easy to use," says Joanne Bealy, For Comment's product manager.

In the research labs, software engineers are taking two approaches to create programs that will transform networks of computers into more advanced collaboration tools. The first, called hypertext, allows groups working in the same building or at a distance to use their linked computer screens as a shared work space, something like a common desk. The second, using electronic meeting rooms, harnesses the computer to increase the amount of information that can be brought to bear in face-to-face meetings. The computer is at the heart of both approaches, capturing the communication among team members, tracking and updating the information exchanged, and rendering it back precisely to all of its users.

The term *hypertext* was coined in the 1960s by Ted Nelson, an exuberant Stanford University computer scientist who had the extraordinary idea of creating a computer-linked global information source he called *Xanadu,* after the mythic palace in Coleridge's "Kubla Khan." Today researchers at Xerox PARC, MCC, and Tektronix are plucking hypertext from the realm of fantasy and trying to shape it into a focused research tool. Working with networks of powerful Xerox and Sun work stations equipped with large display screens that can be divided into windows, hypertext programmers segment data into interconnected idea-size chunks called nodes.

Hypertext pulls together data from disparate sources and prompts the user to check information that may bear on what he's doing. In a simple commercial application, a toy company's market researcher checking a node called *Frisbee sales* might confirm that adolescent males are the toy's biggest buyers. Searching another node called *population trends—Minneapolis,* he might discover that the city's male population aged 12 to 18 is decreasing far faster than the national average. By linking the two nodes, the researcher could conclude that his company should reduce its Frisbee distribution to the Twin Cities.

Individual hypertext users can navigate freely among nodes, following established links. As they roam, they can add new nodes and link them to the existing network, enriching the foundation of associated ideas and creating a sort of nonlinear electronic encyclopedia. More limited systems that allow users to browse through data without adding new information or creating new links are beginning to find commercial applications. This summer Ford plans to automate its repair manuals, using a browsing system called *Guide* to help mechanics service its 1988 models. Sold by Owl International, a year-old company based in Bellevue, Washington, the software will run on Hewlett-Packard computers connected to touch screens at mechanics' work stations. Instead of having to leave the repair bay to leaf through volumes of grease-stained manuals, a mechanic using Guide will simply touch symbols on the computer screen to search through servicing instructions stored on compact disks in the computer's memory.

Software developers are also aiming to crack business's last computer-free inner sanctum, the conference room. For all the time managers spend in meetings, the process remains more a tribal rite than a structured, scientific process. After much talking and little listening, decisions too soon forgotten emerge by a process that no participant can describe. Armed with powerful work stations, researchers are mounting an assault on the meeting room and trying to integrate meetings with the work that individuals do independently. "We use computers in every other aspect of our work," says Mark Stefik, a lean, intense engineer who designed an electronic meeting room called *Colab* at Xerox PARC. "Yet each time we came to meetings, we had to leave them behind in our offices and resort to flip charts."

The Colab room in Palo Alto accommodates eight participants seated around a U-shaped table at computers linked by cables. Facing the table at the front of the room stands a glowing 4-foot-by-8-foot projection screen that serves as an electronic chalkboard. Unconventional as the room looks, what goes on inside it is positively bizarre. A meeting moves through three stages, beginning with "idea generation," proceeding to "idea structuring," and ending with evaluation. In the generation stage, participants hammer away at keyboards, creating a frenzied staccato as they simultaneously enter their thoughts into computer memory. As new ideas are entered, they pop up automatically on other participants' screens and on the electronic chalkboard.

Moving to the structuring stage, participants abandon their keyboards and shift ideas into related groups by using a mouse to shove a block of text across the screen and click it into place. Once the ideas are grouped to everyone's satisfaction and the clicking subsides, the group settles down to evaluate its work, supplementing the sorted thoughts with additional information drawn from members' personal databases. Colab's developers think all this chatterless clatter brings far greater cohesiveness to meetings. The computer records each participant's comments and displays them for all to see as the meeting progresses, a process Stefik describes as "what-you-see-is-what-I-see," or WYSIWIS (pronounced "whizzy-whiz"). The problems are equally obvious. Speed, unshakable concentration, and acute manual dexterity help a lot in getting one's point across.

Like latter-day Dr. Jekylls, the researchers at Xerox PARC and MCC, which is building its own electronic meeting room, are studying computer-coordinated meetings by experimenting on themselves. At the University of Arizona's College of Business and Public Administration, researchers headed by Jay Nunamaker are investigating how ordinary executives adjust to this new idea. Arizona built a Decision and Planning Laboratory in 1985 and tested it on over 200 planning executives from such organizations as IBM and the U.S. Army. The lab lets users enter their comments anonymously. Managers like the candor the process allows, and the test groups have been uniformly enthusiastic.

The work groupers' ultimate strategy is to marry the computer's memory with video and audio equipment. A small team of researchers headed by Robert Stults is exploring that far-out edge of technology at Xerox PARC in an experiment called *Media Spaces*. Last May, Stults and his team equipped a half dozen offices at Xerox's Palo Alto labs and four Xerox offices in Portland, Oregon, with video cameras, monitors, microphones, and speakers, and wired them together with recording gear—all controlled by computers. They even wired the coffee lounges to capture all the creative chitchat that goes on during what employees used to think of as breaks.

Media Spaces allows group members using these multimedia offices to see each other as they confer; the camera projects each user's image on television monitors in his colleagues' offices. Tapping into the computer's database, Media Spaces conferees can swap text and graphic data back and forth and exhibit them in windows on each other's screens.

In time a new participant in the system will be able to command his computer to search a vast library of meetings recorded on video disks, zero in on a specific conversation, and play it back to reconstruct the rationale for a decision that the group made before he joined it. Stults thinks advanced versions of Media Spaces may emerge by the end of the century. "Right now we may look like a bunch of over-age kids playing at a funny farm in Palo Alto," says Stults. "But when this technology is ready, it could take off fast."

CHAPTER

5

*Telecommunications in the 1990s**

Randall L. Tobias

It is an early morning in December 1999, and Dr. Anna Wright, a Chicago-based surgeon, is in trouble. What should have been a routine operation has developed nasty complications. No one on staff can help—no one except "Mike."

"Mike, quick, get me a list of the 10 top cardiovascular specialists." As she speaks, a large screen on the wall lights up.

"Yes, Anna," Mike's electronic voice replies. "In the U.S. or the world?"

"World, of course," she snaps.

A list appears. "Get me number one, Dr. Uno, wherever she is." At that, a remarkable sequence of events occurs. Within minutes, Anna gets her specialist on screen. With the help of intelligence in the telecommunications network, Mike has tracked her down. Dr. Uno happens to be in her rental car, on the way back to her hotel from St. Andrews Golf Club in Scotland. But the network could have found her almost anywhere.

Neither doctor speaks the other's language very well, so they ask the network to perform simultaneous translation. Luckily, Dr. Uno has almost reached her hotel, so they are able to use the more powerful information systems available there.

---

* Source: Reprinted from *Business Horizons*, January–February 1990, pp. 81-86. Copyright 1990 by the Foundation for the School of Business at Indiana University. Used with permission.

Anna has Mike transfer a copy of the patient's records, including x-rays and motion pictures of the last few minutes of the operation (recorded not on film but electronically). Incidentally, the pictures are displayed on large, flat, high-definition screens that are now widespread. They exhibit colors, shades, and textures with a sharpness and clarity that could be found only in movie theaters 10 years before.

Dr. Uno's expert advice helps Anna save the patient. And Mike records everything—both words and pictures—for the education of other medical people at Anna's hospital.

This scenario is not as futuristic as it may seem. In fact, it almost certainly does not do justice to the more exotic applications of information technology that will appear over the next 10 years in scientific research, engineering, and manufacturing.

But for business managers concerned about the challenges of the next decade, the point here is not whether all aspects of my scenario could really come true by the end of the century. Not all of them will. The point is to see them as logical extensions of powerful trends that are already at work today. One of the first trends to recognize is how much the boundaries between computing and communications are blurring. Today, computers communicate and telecommunications networks compute. It is impossible to consider one and exclude the other.

In what follows, I will focus more on the communications side of the equation, but it should be clear that in the 90s most businesses will need to manage computing and communications as total information systems. How well they manage these systems is certain to become more and more important. Information systems are becoming pervasive and global. They are advancing rapidly, reshaping our home and work environments, and transforming our markets. It is no accident that last year, computers and communications equipment accounted for at least 35 percent of all private investment in the United States—double what it was just 10 years ago.

Increasingly, information systems are becoming strategic. That is, the skill and insight with which they are applied will fundamentally determine a company's performance in the marketplace—by changing its production economics, for example, or its relationships with suppliers, distributors, and customers, or the very nature of its products and services.

THE DRIVERS OF CHANGE

The development of computing and communications will be driven by the interaction of two sets of forces—the forces created by technological advances and by the needs, principally, of business users and their customers. (I will mostly ignore here the impact of defense markets.)

The Technological Forces

The technological forces result from the pace of progress in three fields: microelectronics, fiber optic transmission, and software. In microelectronics, industry has been doubling the number of components on a chip each year for more than 30 years. As a result, the cost per circuit has fallen more than a millionfold. Today a single microprocessor developed by AT&T and Intel concentrates within it the power of the first Cray supercomputer.

The breakneck rate of progress has slowed somewhat—but the industry is still doubling the number of components per chip every 18 months. New generations of computer hardware will come in rapid order, each delivering much more processing power than the previous one for about the same price.

Machine intelligence will continue to become more affordable and ubiquitous. In addition, computing will become much more decentralized, because the economics of this process favor shifting computing loads away from mainframes to mini- and microcomputers networked together.

Fiber optic technology, which transmits information as pulses of laser light through ultrapure glass fibers, will furnish the transmission systems of choice for the 1990s. Industry has doubled fiber capacity each year since it was introduced in the late 1970s, and this rate shows no signs of diminishing through the 1990s. The most advanced system today can transmit information at the rate of 3.4 billion bits per second, or the equivalent of 48,000 telephone conversations on a single pair of fibers. Of course, fiber optics will be important not so much for its role in accommodating voice traffic as for its role in accommodating the explosively growing traffic generated by facsimile, computer networking, and video.

In software, productivity growth has advanced at a much slower rate than in the other two fields. Nevertheless, important advances are occurring. Industry continues to develop more advanced algorithms for solving specialized problems. For example, the Karmarkar algorithm, recently developed at AT&T Bell laboratories, readily solves linear programming problems so huge that they could not even be attempted before on the biggest computers in the world. Other important advances are continually improving the algorithms that enable information systems to recognize images and spoken words. And expert systems are becoming more widely developed and applied; systems that, in well-defined knowledge domains, can make every employee perform nearly as well as the best employee doing a job. And beyond expert systems we are beginning to see software advances enable information systems to learn and think for themselves. This is perhaps the key definition of artificial intelligence. However, as limited as this intelligence may be, it is already proving very useful for specialized tasks like managing the resources in telecommunications networks.

Interestingly, one of the more important uses of artificial intelligence may be in making our information systems less artificial; that is, making them more human, and easier to use. Computers can already recognize a limited vocabulary of spoken words, and sometime this decade they will improve to the point that we will be able to command them and input information more accurately by talking than by keyboarding. But we will need artificial intelligence before machines actually converse with us in natural language and perform simultaneous translation—that is, machines that can go beyond our words and know what we mean, not just what we say.

Achieving this will stretch our abilities, but by the mid-to-late 1990s we will probably see machines that can perform simultaneous translation of vocabularies limited to a few hundred words. A machine with the abilities of HAL, the fully conversational computer in *2001,* could well be possible about the year predicted there or a little later.

Business Needs

Technology almost creates more possibilities than industry can ever pursue. The path that a technology actually takes is determined by customer needs. In the 1990s, one of the most critical of these needs will be to increase the productivity of the information workers who make up an ever-increasing share of the work force. These workers are deluged with information, and they contribute to the deluge at their own desks day after day. In fact, according to the U.S. Department of Labor, they file away some 200 billion documents per year in this country at a cost of 55 cents apiece. And they only use about 10 percent of those documents ever again. We all need better ways to exchange, process, and retrieve information.

Businesses also need to exploit ways not only for automating work but also for optimizing the work process. This means creating "just-in-time" environments that minimize inventories and maximize the use of labor, capital equipment, and cash. It means unremitting attention to quality. It means a much more intense and coordinated use of information. This in turn carries with it a need to link disparate information "islands" to form tighter electronic relationships among different parts of the organization and with suppliers and customers. Finally, businesses need more flexibility, control, and reliability. They cannot afford any longer to have information systems inhibit their ability to adapt rapidly to the fast-changing markets that will characterize the 1990s. They will need computing and communications systems that conform to internationally accepted standards, so they will have the freedom to incorporate the latest technologies into their networks without making their present investments obsolete. And, as information systems become so much more central to the day-to-day running of their businesses, they will need systems that seldom or never fail, but that recover quickly if they do.

TELECOMMUNICATIONS NETWORKS IN THE 1990s

Telecommunications service providers will work hard to meet these needs, not least in the highly competitive long distance market in the United States. The biggest challenge will come in meeting their customers' data needs. On AT&T's network alone, data traffic is increasing at the rate of 15 to 20 percent per year; by mid-decade it could account for half of AT&T's traffic. Such growth explains why business customers in the long distance market have signalled their strong preference for digital facilities. Digital facilities deliver higher quality, particularly for data, and they greatly simplify the provisioning of advanced services. What is more, they cost less to operate and maintain, so they contribute to lower pricing. The transition from analog to digital systems has been under way for several years, but business customers' demands have accelerated the process. AT&T, for example, dramatically stepped up its own conversion timetable in 1988, writing down $6.7 billion worth of analog equipment. By 1990, AT&T will carry all of its domestic switched traffic digitally.

The digital revolution has facilitated a steady rise in the intelligence of telecommunications networks. As I indicated, modern switching machines are actually special-purpose digital computers (operating these days on several million lines of code). Yet these switchers represent only the first tier of network intelligence. The switchers can and do interact with other computers in the network and on the customers' premises. This has allowed telecommunications companies to offer a steady stream of new services, including toll-free calling, software-defined voice and data networking, and other services that customers can control for themselves.

As noted, fiber is the digital transmission system of choice for the 1990s and beyond (supplemented importantly by cellular radio in local exchange networks and by digital radio and satellite in long-distance networks). Fiber optic cables already lace the United States, and in the last two years telecommunications companies have laid fiber across both the Atlantic and Pacific. Users now have continuous fiber optic connectivity from Zurich to Tokyo. And that is only the beginning. Many more fiber optic cables are being considered and planned. There is only one segment of telecommunication networks where fiber does not usually exhibit a clear economic advantage—namely, the last mile or so extending from the substation to the residence. However, my scenario assumes that fiber will reach a large number of homes by the late 1990s, driven by soaring demand for High Definition Television (HDTV) services.

HDTV will be a superb entertainment medium—indeed, its advocates say the quality differences between TV and HDTV are at least as great as between black and white and color TV. The entertainment industry has learned again and again that people will gladly pay for such quality improvements. HDTV will probably be introduced in the U.S. around 1992, and if it does in fact take off, fiber to the home is almost a sure thing. With its immunity to electromagnetic interference and its large transmission capacity, fiber is by far the best way to distribute the huge amounts of digital information in HDTV signals. So great is the carrying capacity of fiber that—if a telecommunications company were foolish enough—it could run all its traffic between major population centers on a single cable and have room to spare. But this would only increase the risk of service interruptions at a time when telecommunications has become vital to the everyday health and safety of our society.

As the decade advances, service providers will be competing in many dimensions. Quality will be one of the most important. It can be defined in several critical ways, including transmission clarity, call setup times, and call processing (getting through the first time). But, for more and more businesses, none of these quality dimensions is likely to be more important than reliability. Modern technology is making it possible to build self-healing networks that, for all practical purposes, can make service interruptions a thing of the past. For example, the AT&T network already relies on switching and computing systems that are both redundant and geographically dispersed. If there is a catastrophe in one center, the load moves to the other center without interrupting service. AT&T has a computer-controlled dynamic routing system that instantaneously provides up to 21 alternative routes for calls when a cable is cut or when unexpected volume builds on a primary route. The fiber optic cable routes are configured in a series of interlocking circles that permit easy routing around a failure. Also, restoration switches are deployed that can sense breaks and divert circuits around failed facilities. Users are rapidly coming to expect precautions like these, and, barring Armageddon, they see no reason why they should have to endure the interruption of a single call or data session. Nor should they.

THE INTEGRATED SERVICES DIGITAL NETWORK

One of the most powerful trends in computing and communications today is the trend toward common international standards. The highly integrated services described in the opening scenario will surely prove impossible unless such standards continue to be developed and implemented during the 90s.

For the telecommunications industry in the decade, the most directly important group of these standards is known as the integrated services digital network, of ISDN. Despite its name, ISDN is not a network or service. It is an internationally agreed-upon set of standards for building digital telecommunications networks and delivering integrated voice and data services over them, whether those networks are private or public. ISDN standards will continue to evolve as technology advances. But ISDN services are already a reality. ISDN "islands" exist throughout the

United States, and as these become more interconnected, ISDN will be nearly ubiquitous by the turn of the century.

For most users, one of the greatest beauties of ISDN is that it offers them a way to simplify and unify their networks. Business users have typically built multiple special-purpose computer networks. Every time they had a new function, they tended to build a new network. The problem worsened if they happened to choose computers that were incompatible with their existing systems.

By creating an authentic multivendor environment based on international standards, ISDN in most cases eliminates the need for multiple networks, multiple access lines and multiple desktop terminals. It serves all the communications options: voice, electronic mail and other messaging, facsimile, video conference, and PC-to-PC or terminal-to-host data transmission. Users can exercise these options at the same time—for example, they can carry on a telephone conversation while looking at the same computer screen. Moreover, the ISDN signaling system provides a superb means for tying together the machine intelligence on the customers' premises with the intelligence in the telecommunications network. This can in turn be the basis for an array of powerful new services.

ISDN has been a living, evolving reality in the United States since at least December 1986, when McDonald's began a pioneering application of ISDN at its corporate headquarters location in Oak Brook, Illinois. Linked to a switch in an Illinois Bell central office, McDonald's ISDN services were initially used for digital telephones, voice/data terminals, facsimile, and modem pooling. Along with several other kinds of data applications, McDonald's is using ISDN lines to access IBM hosts from 3270-type terminals, which eliminates the need to string costly coaxial cable. One of the most attractive aspects of ISDN for McDonald's is that it will permit consolidation of all or nearly all its 20-odd networks onto a single network. ISDN rollout applications are underway with more than 20 local telephone companies in the United States. AT&T began offering ISDN service last year in the long distance network. Users began snapping up the service so fast that AT&T sped up its timetable and now offers ISDN in virtually every metropolitan area in the country. Outside the United States, ISDN applications are under way or planned in some 20 countries. We are well on the way to delivering globally consistent ISDN services to multinational business.

NEW TELECOMMUNICATIONS SERVICES

We live in a service economy that is certain to create demand for a vast number of new telecommunications services in the 1990s. The telecommunications industry will create these services—but so will business users, who will vie to develop new services for themselves or their customers as a way to achieve an edge in the marketplace. Entrepreneurs will get into the act, too. In fact, ISDN's open architecture could ignite a boom of entrepreneurial activity as great as the PC boom set off when IBM introduced the open MS-DOS operating system in 1980. Here is a sampler that includes services that may emerge, as well as services that exist today but that are likely to become much more widespread in the 1990s.

Home Services. Poor results with videotext and in the home-computer market may seem to indicate that Americans do not yet see a great need for home information services. Nevertheless, if HDTV and fiber-to-the-home do materialize, a general-purpose HDTV terminal/entertainment/information center could be the next step. This would be a two-way communications system that could spur dramatic, synergistic growth in pictorial communications, multimedia database services, home shopping, educational services, and the trend toward working at home.

Messaging. Users will be able to create, send, store, forward, receive, file, encrypt, decrypt, and broadcast messages as data, text, fax, or voice. One form will convert readily into another, and natural languages will be translated into another, both for voice and test. For example, people might call their electronic mailboxes and have a speech synthesizer "read" aloud their electronic mail messages. Or they might dictate messages to be broadcast, translated where necessary, and printed out through an international network of fax machines. They will be able to do such things from anywhere in the world, including their vehicles.

Call Redirection and Handling. Users will be able to forward all calls to wherever they are, and, if they happen to change their plans without informing the network, the network will likely develop the intelligence for searching them out (with permission!).

Users will be able to sort and process incoming calls intensively. To facilitate call screening, with ISDN the callers' telephone numbers, and thus their likely identities, can arrive with the call. A brokerage house might use this feature to trigger retrieval of its caller's portfolio and trading records, and use this information to give its best customers preference before sending both the file and call to designated brokers. Or in a telemarketing center, the procedure might be reversed. Thus, only after an outgoing call to a potential customer is completed would the file and the call be sent to a free agent, relieving agents of the drudgeries of entering call numbers, unanswered calls, and busy signals. Systems such as these already exist today.

Mobile Communications. Cellular radio systems will go digital, making mobile communications even more affordable and versatile. Users will be able to receive not just voice and fax, but advanced messaging services and relatively high-speed data.

Fax.   Facsimile machines have proven themselves to be tremendously versatile; in combination with the messaging services outlined earlier, that versatility can only grow. People are using fax machines to fill prescriptions, submit insurance claims, place orders, distribute product information to sales forces, and publish newsletters. It will be a very rare location that does not have a fax machine as the next decade advances. And with ISDN, advanced fax machines will print out faster than they do now, on ordinary paper, and with quality that is every bit as good as with the best copying machines. In effect what has happened is that fax standards have created a universal language for transmitting images (''fax Esperanto''). Building on these standards, systems now exist for fax-to-computer and computer-to-fax communications, as do systems for sending paperless fax messages from computer to computer and from computer to file server on a local area network. In this way, messages can be captured, viewed, shared, and filed electronically without the need for paper copies.

Telemarketing.   Businesses will use telecommunications to tighten their relationships with customers—both for sales and service. As noted earlier, telemarketers will use sophisticated call-handling techniques to raise the productivity of their agents and reduce lost calls. Speech recognition systems will increasingly take orders and instruct callers to give more information—such as credit card numbers. Business-to-business telemarketing could involve using a central computer to generate price lists, product descriptions, discounts, and promotions. The computer would send this information to a customer's fax or PC and receive orders back from it for processing.

Multimedia Teleconferencing.   Businesses will have the opportunity to reduce travel costs dramatically with the development of inexpensive and convenient teleconferencing tools. By decade's end, many employees will be able to send video pictures, computer files, and graphics freely to screens at each others' desktop workstations. They will have the ability to open and control windows on their screens that will let them view speakers and graphics simultaneously, or zoom in on either one.

Private Networks.   Many services I have described will be offered on both public and private network facilities. However, many businesses will discover less need for truly private networks. They will discover that software-defined services will give them virtual private services that combine the flexibility and control of private networks with the economies and reliability of shared public networks. And they will find that they can set up, tear down, and reconfigure their services with less and less delay. They will pay for what they want only when they use it. For example, AT&T's ISDN service already allows users to select among different services—such as data, WATS, and 800 Service—on a call-by-call basis.

Whatever they do, companies can expect better tools for what is now called *network management*. Network management is a complex task that includes not only the ability to manage failures but also provisioning, billing, least-cost routing, and security. Network management standards under development now will play an important role in giving users the unified systems they need to do these jobs in all three domains their networks traverse: the local-exchange network, the long-distance network, and their own multivendor private facilities.

Communications in the 1990s will be dynamic and rich in opportunity. To be sure, the details are impossible to predict. In many cases, it will be hard to tell the sizzle from the fizzle. But if history is any guide, we can look forward to surprises at least as great as the PC and fax revolutions of the 1980s. And we have good reason for expecting that the broad trends I have outlined will persist. Demand for services and transmission capacity ("band-width") will continue to burgeon, as computers exchange larger and larger amounts of information at higher speeds and users rely more and more on graphics and video.

In the last years of our century, such demands will be driving our ISDN networks to evolve toward what AT&T has called an era of "Universal Information Services." In this era, our telecommunications networks will achieve even higher degrees of intelligence. Users will tap into the networks through a small family of universal ports in much the same way we now plug appliances into standard electrical outlets. They will have instant access to a huge range of network resources, because the time lag between ordering and getting services will simply disappear. Users will be able to send and receive information anytime, anywhere, and in any form—voice, data, image, or video.

Using these telecommunications resources effectively will continue to pose complex challenges to business. Equipment vendors, service providers, and users will have to work more closely together than ever before. But together they will have an unprecedented power to make their employees and customers more efficient, productive, and creative.

6 Corporate Videotex: A Strategic Business Information System*

Gene Kusekoski

INTRODUCTION

The use of corporate videotex at Digital is producing significant cost savings and increased operating efficiencies. Employees around the world use videotex to quickly and easily access up-to-date information that allows them to make better business decisions. There are numerous groups within Digital that prepare and distribute information to internal audiences. Many of these groups are using videotex to save thousands of dollars in document production and distribution costs while eliminating months of labor from their administrative processes. Aggregated across the corporation, this results in yearly savings of millions of dollars. The use of videotex within the sales force extends well beyond cost savings. It is helping Digital maintain its competitive edge in today's dynamic marketplace.

Digital is not unique in its need to distribute information to its employees. Most large corporations produce, receive, and distribute huge quantities of document-based information. Studies have shown that the life-cycle

---

* Source: Reprinted by special permission from the *MIS Quarterly,* vol. 13, no. 4, December 1989. Copyright 1989 by the Society for Information Management and the Management Information Systems Research Center at the University of Minnesota.

costs of this information may comprise 10–15 percent of total corporate operating expenses. For a multinational Fortune 30 corporation like Digital, this results in an expense in excess of $1 billion per year. By adopting the use of videotex to distribute information throughout the corporation, Digital is better able to control these costs and address the evolving needs of the business.

TODAY'S BUSINESS NEEDS

While the paperless environment remains an elusive and perhaps unattainable goal, Digital is working to make several thousand new pages of information available for internal videotex distribution each year. This strategy has evolved over the last five years as Digital business managers realized that paper documents were no longer meeting the needs of an increasingly competitive environment.

In the period of weeks normally required to format, print, and distribute a document, changing conditions rendered the contents invalid. Despite the inestimable cost of making a bad business decision based on outdated information, use of the latest revision of a hardcopy document could not be ensured. As the company doubled in size to over 100,000 employees, the yearly cost of distributing a single document to an audience like the U.S. field began to exceed $1 million per year (see Table 1). While converting paper-based documents to on-line information does not completely eliminate these costs, they are significantly reduced when the on-line information is made available over the existing corporate network.

To address these problems, pioneers in engineering, sales communications, legal, and training groups began to experiment with electronic mail distribution and reference systems custom-coded in third or fourth generation languages. These were somewhat successful in enhancing information delivery, but there were limitations:

• *Connectivity.* Central applications required users to connect to a single system. This limited access to the number of interactive users the host system could support.

TABLE 1 Typical Field Support Documents

Document	Distribution	Issues	Size	Cost/Yr.*
Product reference	10,000	4	300pp	$360–600K
Product announcement	18,000	26	100pp	$1,404–2,340K

* Based on an estimated 3–5¢ per page for production and distribution only, exclusive of editorial and preparation costs.

• *Reusability.* Custom applications could not be easily redeployed to address analogous needs in other parts of the corporation. Users had to adapt to the unique characteristics of a variety of implementations.

• *Applicability.* Electronic mail is ideal for interpersonal communications. For corporate information distribution, it is a compromise (see Figure 1). People often received more information than they required, and delivery that was not synchronized with an immediate need created filing and retrieval problems.

Despite their drawbacks, these early applications clearly demonstrated the promise of on-line information delivery. What was needed was a standardized solution to the "one-to-many" communications model of published information (see Figure 1). Such a solution would:

• Effectively use the global wide-area network that Digital has developed over the last 10 years to interconnect all parts of the corporation.

FIGURE 1   Business Communications Models

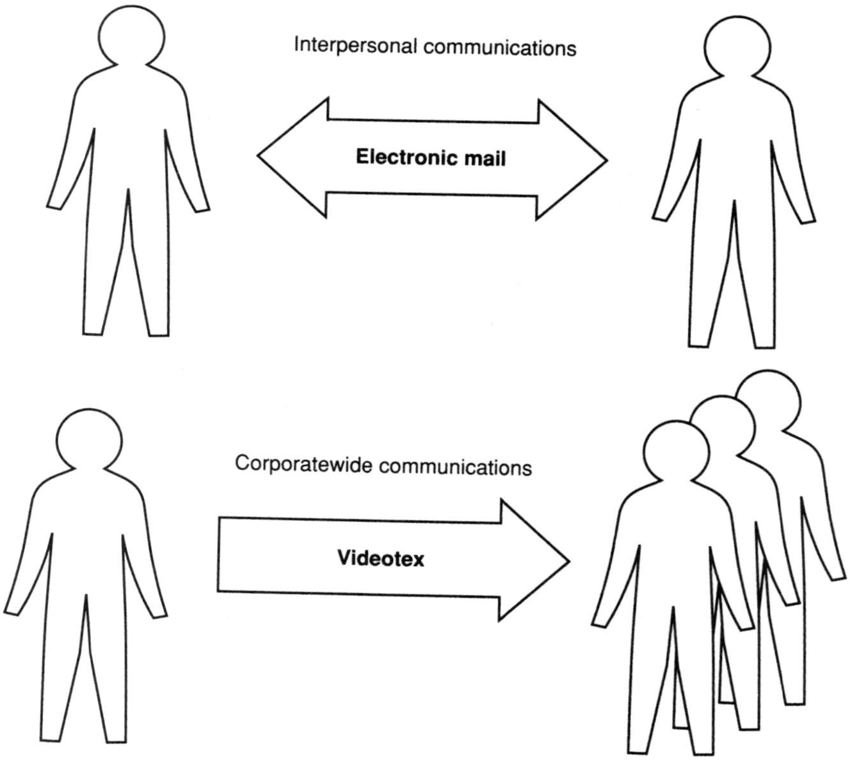

• Provide a superior alternative to paper document distribution just as corporate electronic mail had provided a superior replacement for paper memos within Digital several years earlier.

• Be easily deployed across the corporation to address a wide variety of business needs with a standardized architecture.

• Be highly responsive while placing a minimal drain on system resources.

• Be consistent and intuitive to use, allowing employees to remain focused on their activities in finance, sales, or engineering, rather than on technology.

The introduction of a corporate videotex product by Digital in 1984 provided just such a solution. Developed with input from our Information Management and Technology (IM&T) group, this product was immediately put to use in addressing key business information needs. Today, organizations throughout Digital make their information available through a corporatewide videotex utility that provides responsive, consistent access to the information employees need to support their business activity.

WHAT IS VIDEOTEX?

Videotex is a generic term for an easy-to-use, consistent approach to locating and selectively viewing information on a terminal screen (see Figure 2). Content is organized into a tree structure of pages that are

FIGURE 2   Information Retrieval Using Videotex

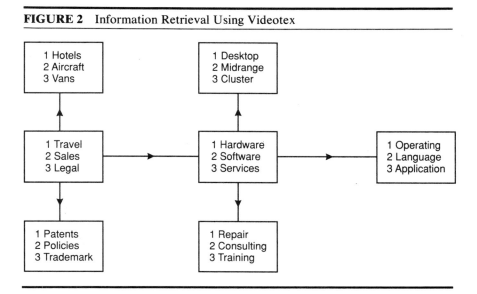

selected from a series of menus. Videotex was developed in Europe in the late 1970s for consumer applications, such as telephone directory services, teleshopping, telebanking, and personal news. Today, public videotex kiosks that provide information on shopping, restaurants, and entertainment can be seen in the lobbies of hotels in large cities throughout the United States.

As a consumer information service, videotex has received mixed reviews. Original examples were based on special purpose hardware that supports elaborate color artwork and even simulated animation. Display frames were designed by graphic artists to attract the attention and the money of the consumer. The lack of a public network of standard, inexpensive hardware that supports the unique characteristics of consumer videotex has been one factor that has impeded its growth.

Because of its consumer origins, however, videotex excels at delivering information to untrained or casual users in any environment. While business managers may find it hard to relate the technology they have seen in hotel lobbies to corporate business needs, the work at Digital has demonstrated that beneath the artwork of commercial applications lies a valuable tool for corporate information management.

In corporate videotex, pages are designed primarily to convey information efficiently. Although complex color graphics and images can be supported, many of the most effective solutions within Digital are based on pages composed by software applications from simple ASCII text. Information is deployed across the network of standard terminals and work stations already in place to support other business computing functions.

VIDEOTEX WITHIN DIGITAL

Digital's worldwide network of over 43,000 computer systems is integrated via site servers and routers into a single seamless utility. Corporate videotex is designed to make the most effective use of this network by segmenting applications into client and server components (see Figure 3).

Videotex information bases are distributed throughout the network, rather than centralized in a single information center. Each information base is located within the group responsible for that particular segment of Digital's business and is managed by standard videotex server software. IM&T developers have created a set of applications that allow business personnel to enter information into the videotex system without the involvement of a programming and technical support staff.

Within this standard framework, it is both possible and desirable to tailor applications to meet specific business needs. Some examples at Digital are:

• *Searching*. Product information bases include a term search capability that minimizes menu navigation.

FIGURE 3   Distributed Client-Server Model

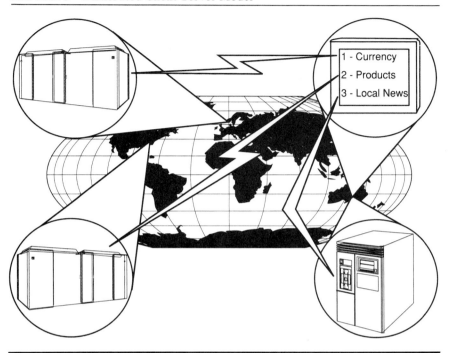

• *Interactivity.*   Course catalogs contain a component that allows an employee who finds a session of interest to instantly register on-line.

• *Ordering.*   Electronic "card catalogs" allow ordering of a typographically formatted document to be delivered via electronic mail for demand printing at the requester's location.

Because these applications are all based on the standard videotex architecture, developers can adapt a solution created for one group to meet the needs of another in a matter of weeks. Experience at Digital has shown that videotex allows new information to be brought on-line from two to five times faster than would be possible with custom-coded applications and with a uniform level of consistency across all applications that serve similar needs.

To provide access to the information within the videotex servers, a client software module is installed on every major system on the Digital corporate network. The client module is responsible for interacting with local users of the system on which it is installed. Where older applications required a direct connection to a specific information base, videotex protocols use the network only to request and deliver pages between the client system and the remote information server. In this way, server systems can support hundreds of remote users efficiently and responsively.

Best of all, the videotex client-server model allows a menu to be organized according to business topics without regard for where the information is actually located. The items on a single menu might point to a local CDROM, a site server, and a server on another continent. Users are not aware of where the information is coming from, only that it is available to meet their business needs.

Internally generated information distributed with videotex includes:

- Product and services information.
- Hazardous materials bulletins.
- Corporate standards, policies, and procedures.
- Internal job postings.
- Internal equipment procurement.

Like most large companies, Digital acquires external information in both on-line and magnetic tape forms. This information is integrated into the videotex utility to ensure that employees can access the information they need in a consistent manner regardless of its source. Closed user groups restrict confidential information access to authorized employees located anywhere within our worldwide network. Copyrighted information is controlled in the same way to ensure that purchase agreements are respected.

BENEFITS

Videotex capitalizes on Digital's investment in technology by distributing document-based information across the same corporatewide network we have built for electronic mail, transaction data, and all other business functions. It reduces paper production, storage, and distribution, a multimillion dollar yearly expense in a corporation the size of Digital. The time and cost of locating and scrapping obsolete documents is eliminated.

With videotex, an "electronic document" can be updated or taken out of circulation instantly, reducing the risk of bad business decisions based on incorrect information. With mass distribution of paper documents or even electronic mail, information providers often find it hard to determine whether all copies have been correctly delivered, let alone used. With videotex, accounting features determine what information is being used and by whom. Underutilized information can either be eliminated from the system or revitalized to increase its value.

Corporate videotex is making one of its greatest contributions in helping the Digital sales organization to compete in today's dynamic marketplace. In the past, sales representatives have found searching through a large variety of printed and on-line sources for the information they need to be a time-consuming and frustrating experience. The ACCESS Sales Information System addresses this problem by providing a standard method for retrieving information from 16 separate databases, ranging from numeric data to product information and external market intelligence.

Because ACCESS is organized in terms of sales functions, not data elements, sales representatives find locating information to be an intuitive and natural process. Users of ACCESS have indicated that they can now retrieve information in about a fifth of the time previously required, allowing each of them to spend several more hours per week actively closing sales. Videotex helps the Digital sales force to be better informed on their products, the competition, and customer needs, thereby increasing the overall effectiveness of the entire organization.

Employees across the corporation enjoy similar benefits. Because videotex applications at Digital are a natural extension of the end-user computing environment, the content of information bases can be readily integrated into other documents and messages. This extends the ability to access information into the ability to use information in the business process.

With videotex, the time delays and expenses involved with training people on new applications have been virtually eliminated. Learning to use videotex is more like learning to read than learning to operate a computer. Regardless of their level of technical knowledge, Digital employees can use videotex across a wide range of information categories and job functions throughout the corporation.

LESSONS LEARNED

As with all good things, the benefits of videotex do not come without some effort. Information providers, information consumers, and systems designers and operators must commit resources to ensure success of the business solution. Experience has shown that there are several critical areas to watch.

• *Stale or incorrect information.*   While videotex can instantly deliver accurate and timely information to thousands of people around the world, it can also do the same for inaccurate information. Information providers must commit to maintaining the timeliness and accuracy of their information. The continued presence of inappropriate information in a videotex information base will quickly kill off the use of that application and can undermine the viability of the entire system.

• *Response time and availability.*   Providing information on-line changes expectations among information consumers. People previously satisfied with a weekly or monthly paper document become irate with display updates that take more than a few seconds. They also expect the information to be there whenever they need it and have little patience with "That information is currently unavailable" messages. System designers and operators must ensure that server systems and their network links can accommodate the normal demand for videotex information. Failover and backup servers must be installed for critical information to ensure that users can get what they need when they need it.

• *Replacing paper.*   For many people in both the information provider and information consumer communities, the paper habit is hard to break. Information providers must define and follow a plan for phasing over from paper to on-line information. This plan must include provisions to ensure good response time and availability as mentioned above. If paper is not displaced by on-line information, corporate costs will simply increase and the benefits of videotex will not be realized. A compromise solution that has been successful at Digital is using videotex to deliver information that is printable by users on their local laser printers. While paper is not eliminated in this case, significant savings are realized when people print only the information of interest to them instead of an entire catalog or journal. For volatile information, however, information consumers must discipline themselves to continually go back to the on-line source to ensure they are not using demand-printed information that has become obsolete.

• *Pull/push models.*   By nature, videotex is a passive medium. That is, information consumers must assume responsibility for the act of retrieving new information. As people get busy, this can be easily forgotten or pushed aside. When the availability of new information must be immediately known, a short announcement or synopsis can be sent to information consumers via electronic mail to alert them to the update. This can be handled on the basis of functional or site distribution lists, as determined by the scope of the information. Results of such a strategy used within Digital's IM&T group have shown that a marked increase in videotex access occurs immediately following the announcement of new information.

• *Applications development.*   Today, virtually anyone can send electronic mail to a large distribution list. The same can be done with paper documents by using desktop publishing and conventional mail or even fax. In contrast, videotex requires development of an application, the complexity of which may vary with the desired outcome. The need for applications development may scare away some information providers who are used to working in a more ad hoc manner. In these cases, a business needs analysis should be performed to determine the potential benefits of using videotex over other distribution methods. Such a study will ensure that videotex is being applied to the appropriate business areas and that the benefits are understood by both information providers and consumers.

THE MIS CONTRIBUTION

Digital's corporate videotex solutions represent a new phase in the contribution of the IM&T group to corporate business operations. Embedded within the text, graphics, and images of corporate documents are the strategic business concepts that give a company the competitive advantage in today's marketplace. The strategic management of this information is every bit as critical as the management of corporate transaction data with which MIS has historically been involved. Through the deployment of corporate videotex solutions, IM&T is helping its business partners to control costs and improve productivity.

Digital believes it is appropriate for MIS to become involved with document-based information for the following reasons:

• *A precedent.* Many years ago, corporate data was in a chaotic state. Redundant, missing, and conflicting information made a corporatewide view of the business impossible. With sound data management principles, MIS organized and standardized corporate data and made it available to those who needed it. MIS now has the opportunity to perform a similar service for document-based information using videotex.

• *A corporate focus.* Corporate videotex solutions must cross organizational and geographical boundaries. The sales organization needs to reference customer lists maintained by accounting. A marketing group in France needs to reference engineering specifications in Massachusetts. An application developed for a purchasing group may form the basis for a similar application for marketing. MIS is the only organization that can effectively cross these boundaries to provide the enterprisewide integration needed by today's corporations.

The successful implementation of corporate videotex requires a close working relationship between MIS and corporate business managers. Business managers need to understand the value of videotex solutions in terms of increased sales or decreased costs. Digital IM&T groups are involved from the feasibility study through final deployment to determine the ways in which videotex can return the greatest benefit to the business.

In the planning stage, life-cycle costs of various approaches are studied and compared. Capital equipment, staffing implications, and cross-functional dependencies are identified. After deployment, videotex solutions are monitored and refined to ensure that the business actually realizes the benefits identified in the planning process.

As critical information is committed to videotex form, system designers must specify and maintain failsafe systems to ensure that a single point of failure will not prevent a sales representative from accessing the customer reference account information that could help close a key sale. Information that is heavily used at remote sites can be segmented out and placed on CDROM to provide independence from telecommunications overloads or failures. MIS development groups must also begin to extend their skills beyond traditional areas into library sciences and human factors considerations.

Digital has often stated the case for managing corporate telecommunications resources as a single pervasive utility, similar to electricity and water. The Digital Telecommunications Group provides a strong foundation of communications resoures and establishes standards for connection, guidelines for usage, and procedures for measurement and troubleshooting. These services allow Digital business organizations to effectively use the network to support their business needs.

A similar approach has been taken with the establishment of the Digital Corporate Videotex Program Office. This group maintains a corporate videotex menu into which all of the distributed videotex services within Digital are linked. The program registers information bases and their owners, establishes guidelines and minimum standards for information services, and provides assistance with problems. The Corporate Videotex Program and the IM&T groups that develop new videotex applications provide the foundation that enables Digital business personnel to effectively address their business information needs with corporate videotex (see Figure 4).

REALIZING THE POTENTIAL

The distribution of final form information with corporate videotex has already returned many benefits to Digital. Greater savings and increased productivity will result as the scope of the program is expanded. Yet, there are many more areas to be addressed in strategically managing document-based information within the corporation. Publishing can be represented

FIGURE 4   The IM&T Foundation

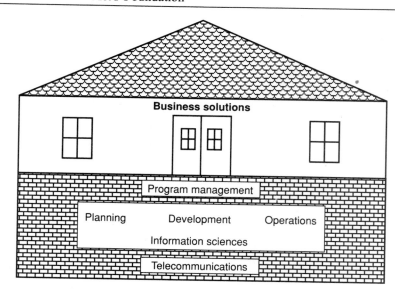

as a four-stage model that begins with the collection of information and ends with the distribution of a final form "information product" (see Figure 5). In this model, videotex distribution, like desktop page layout, is only part of a much larger process. The greatest benefits will be realized as MIS assumes an active role in all facets of document-based information management, just as it has done for corporate data. In this scenario, MIS will provide standardized, easy-to-use systems for collecting unique information across the corporation. This modular information collection will be organized and managed in distributed databases, irrespective of document or videotex screen formats. From this formless collection of revisable content, a wide variety of on-line applications and paper-based publications will be produced to meet changing business needs. With this end-to-end focus, the entire business process can be streamlined and improved. Several efforts are under way at Digital that exemplify this approach.

The purchasing organization has compiled a database of software vendors and products from which videotex reference services, printed catalogs, and CDROMs are being produced. Work is being done to produce price books and internal telephone directories in a similar manner.

FIGURE 5 Strategic Corporate Publishing Model

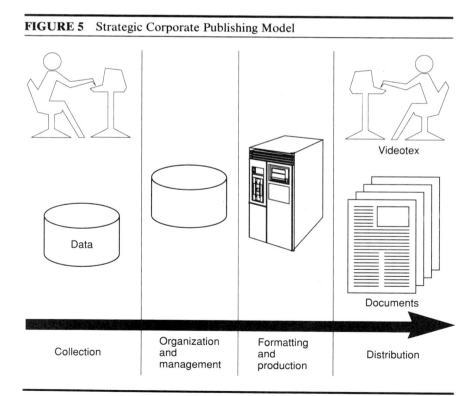

| Collection | Organization and management | Formatting and production | Distribution |

Digital's Internal Symposium Management Group is one of the many small groups that can contribute to a potential yearly savings in excess of a million dollars across the corporation. This group has improved both their own operations and their level of service to the corporation by replacing their old paper-based submissions and program publications with a combination of videotex and electronic publishing applications:

• An on-line session submissions process has been implemented using interactive videotex. The old hardcopy "call for participation" documents have been eliminated, along with their associated production and distribution costs of several thousand dollars. More importantly, a labor-intensive paper management nightmare has been replaced with an automated process that directly builds the database of submissions from information entered through the videotex application. This has improved the group's administrative process as well as the job satisfaction of individual group members.

• From the database of on-line submissions, preconference programs are made available only via videotex, saving another $6,000 in yearly printing expenses. The added cost of distributing printed programs to a large number of employees, only a small percentage of whom actually attended each conference, has been eliminated.

• Paper programs are produced from the submissions database, but only in quantities sufficient to meet the needs of those who actually attend each event. Attendees print only the information they need from the complete conference program.

The symposium management group could have realized some savings by simply using desktop publishing to produce their old paper documents. However, by including on-line information management and videotex in the solution, much greater savings were realized and all aspects of the process were improved. Extrapolating the economies and benefits achieved by this one group across all the organizations within Digital that produce and distribute internal information points out the opportunity for multimillion dollar yearly savings with a corporatewide strategy for document-based information management.

CONCLUSION

The experience at Digital has proven the effectiveness of videotex in distributing information throughout a large corporation. Fortune 100 companies are among the world's largest publishers. In today's business environment, it is this information that often makes the difference between lost opportunities and closed sales.

When measured against the business benefits, the investment in the strategic deployment of corporate videotex is easily justified and quickly recovered. Corporate MIS organizations are now in an excellent position to use this technology to extend their expertise in data management and access into the world of document-based information.

III Information Systems and Their Applications

Information systems and their applications are used to process data and to generate information to support decision making. Such systems do not appear overnight, but rather evolve through the coordinated efforts of data processing specialists, users, and management. In this section we present readings that should enhance your knowledge and ability to work with information systems. Since many readers of this text will be users, rather than computer specialists, we focus our attention on applications that are most likely to affect managerial performance: management information systems (MIS), decision-support systems (DSS), executive information systems (EIS), and expert, or knowledge-based systems (ES). Attention also is given to prototyping as a systems development methodology. And finally, a wide range of computer applications are discussed.

Management information systems are covered in the first selection. G. Anthony Gorry and Michael Scott Morton, in their CLASSIC, "A Framework for Management Information Systems" (Reading 7), provide a framework for conceptualizing a management information system. They also set the stage for understanding decision support systems.

Reading 8, another CLASSIC, "A Framework for the Development of Decision Support Systems," by Ralph H. Sprague, Jr., provides a framework for understanding and developing decision support systems. He also discusses the computer hardware and software and people who might become involved in creating a DSS.

Executive information systems are targeted at the occupants of mahogany row. Only recently have systems been developed to serve this very special group of users. George Houdeshel and Hugh J. Watson in Reading 9, "The Management Information and Decision Support (MIDS) Systems at Lockheed–Georgia," describe the highly successful EIS at Lockheed–Georgia.

An expert system captures in a computer program the training, experience, and judgment of a seasoned professional. Reading 10, "Expert

Systems: The Next Challenge for Managers,'' by Fred L. Luconi, Thomas W. Malone, and Michael Scott Morton, describes what expert systems are, what they do, their component parts, and how they can be developed and used in organizations.

Information systems do not magically appear; rather, data processing specialists, users, and managers must work together on systems developments. Justus D. Naumann and A. Milton Jenkins, in Reading 11, ''Prototyping: The New Paradigm for Systems Development,'' provide a comprehensive review of one of the newer systems development methods. Prototyping has become an even more important and effective method since the development of fourth-generation languages.

Computers are being used for a variety of applications. In Reading 12, ''Computers of the World, Unite!'' Jeremy Main discusses the emergence of the computer-integrated business. In this environment, major business functions can exchange operating information quickly and constantly through the computer. Main describes how this is taking place in several leading-edge companies. Computers and communications technology are changing how people and companies communicate. William R. Ruffin in Reading 13, ''Wired for Speed,'' describes how global companies communicate internally and with suppliers and customers. In Reading 14, ''The Compleat Angler,'' B. G. Yovovich describes how some firms are providing their sales force with computers and the kind of information needed to support the sales effort. Firms would like to improve customer service while controlling the growing cost of providing service. Jerry Kanter, Stephen Schiffman, and J. Faye Horn in Reading 15, ''Let the Customer Do It,'' explore a number of examples of customers using computer technology to complete transactions, rather than interacting with humans.

7 *A Framework for Management Information Systems**

G. Anthony Gorry
Michael S. Scott Morton

A framework for viewing management information systems (MIS) is essential if an organization is to plan effectively and make sensible allocations of resources to information systems tasks. The use of computers in organizations has grown tremendously in the 1955 to 1971 period, but very few of the resulting systems have had a significant impact on the way in which management makes decisions. A framework that allows an organization to gain perspective on the field of information systems can be a powerful means of providing focus and improving the effectiveness of the systems efforts.

In many groups doing MIS work, this lack of perspective prevents a full appreciation of the variety of organizational uses for computers. Without a framework to guide management and systems planners, the system tends to serve the strongest manager or react to the greatest crisis. As a result, systems activities too often move from crisis to crisis, following no clear path and receiving only *ex post facto* justification. This tendency inflicts an

---

* Source: Reprinted from "A Framework for Management Information Systems" by G. Anthony Gorry and Michael S. Scott Morton, *Sloan Management Review*, Spring 1989, pp. 49–61, by permission of the publisher. Copyright 1971 by the Sloan Management Review Association. All rights reserved.

unnecessary expense on the organization. Not only are costly computer resources wasted, but even more costly human resources are mismanaged. The cost of systems and programming personnel is generally twice that of the hardware involved in a typical project, and the ratio is growing larger as the cost of hardware drops and salaries rise.[1] Competent people are expensive. More important, they exist only in limited numbers. This limitation actively constrains the amount of systems development work that can be undertaken in a given organization, and so good resource allocation is critical.

Developments in two distinct areas within the last five years offer us the potential to develop altogether new ways of supporting decision processes. First, there has been considerable technological progress. The evolution of remote access to computers with short turnaround time and flexible user interfaces has been rapid.

Powerful minicomputers are available at low cost, and users can be linked to computer resources through inexpensive typewriter and graphical display devices. The second development has been a conceptual one. There is emerging an understanding of the potential role of information systems within organizations. We are adding to our knowledge of how human beings solve problems and of how to build models that capture aspects of the human decision-making processes.[2]

The progress in these areas has been dramatic. Entirely new kinds of planning and control systems can now be built—ones that dynamically involve the manager's judgments and provide support with analysis, models, and flexible access to relevant information. But to realize this potential fully, given an organization's limited resources, there must be an appropriate framework within which to view management decision making and the required systems support. The purpose of this article is to present a framework that helps us to understand the evolution of MIS activities within organizations and to recognize some of the potential problems and benefits resulting from our new technology. Thus, this framework is designed to be useful in planning for information systems activities within an organization and for distinguishing between the various model-building activities, models, computer systems, and so forth that are used for supporting different kinds of decisions. It is, by definition, a static picture, and it is not designed to say anything about how information systems are built.

In the next section we shall consider some of the general advantages of developing a framework for information systems work. We shall then propose a specific framework that we have found to be useful in the analysis of MIS activities. We believe that this framework offers us a new way to characterize the progress made to date and offers us insight into the problems that have been encountered. Finally, we shall use this framework to analyze the types of resources required in the different decision areas and the ways in which these resources should be used.

FRAMEWORK DEVELOPMENT

The framework we develop here is one for managerial activities, not for information systems. It is a way of looking at decisions made in an organization. Information systems should exist only to support decisions, and hence we are looking for a characterization of organizational activity in terms of the type of decisions involved. For reasons made clear later, we believe an understanding of managerial activity is a prerequisite for effective systems design and implementation. Most MIS groups become involved in system development and implementation without a prior analysis of the variety of managerial activities. This situation has, in our opinion, prevented them from developing a sufficiently broad definition of their purpose and has resulted in an inefficient allocation of resources.

In attempting to understand the evolution and problems of management information systems, we have found the work of Robert Anthony and Herbert Simon particularly useful. In *Planning and Control Systems: A Framework for Analysis,* Anthony addresses the problem of developing a classification scheme that will allow management some perspective when dealing with planning and control systems.[3] He develops a taxonomy for managerial activity consisting of three categories and argues that these categories represent activities sufficiently different in kind to require the development of different systems.

The first of Anthony's categories of managerial activity is *strategic planning*: "Strategic planning is the process of deciding on objectives of the organization, on changes in these objectives, on the resources used to attain these objectives, and on the policies that are to govern the acquisition, use, and disposition of these resources."[4] Certain things can be said about strategic planning generally. First, it focuses on the choice of objectives for the organization and on the activities and means required to achieve these objectives. As a result, a major problem in this area is predicting the future of the organization and its environment. Second, the strategic planning process typically involves a small number of high-level people who operate in a nonrepetitive and often very creative way. The complexity of the problems that arise and the nonroutine manner in which they are handled make it quite difficult to appraise the quality of this planning process.

The second category defined by Anthony is *management control*: "The process by which managers assure that resources are obtained and used effectively in the accomplishment of the organization's objectives."[5] He stresses three key aspects of this area. First, the activity involves interpersonal interaction. Second, it takes place within the context of the policies and objectives developed in the strategic planning process. Third, the paramount goal of management control is the assurance of effective and efficient performance.

Anthony's third category is *operational control,* by which he means "the process of assuring that specific tasks are carried out effectively and efficiently."[6] The basic distinction between management control and operational control is that operational control is concerned with tasks (such as manufacturing a specific part) whereas management control is most often concerned with people. There is much less judgment to be exercised in the operational control area because the tasks, goals, and resources have been carefully delineated through the management control activity.

We recognize, as does Anthony, that the boundaries between these three categories are often not clear. In spite of their limitations and uncertainties, however, we have found the categories useful in the analysis of information system activities. For example, if we consider the information requirements of these three activities, we can see that they are very different from one another. Further, this difference is not simply a matter of aggregation but one of fundamental character of the information needed by managers in these areas.

Strategic planning is concerned with setting broad policies and goals for the organization. As a result, the relationship of the organization to its environment is a central matter of concern. Also, the nature of the activity is such that predictions about the future are particularly important. In general, then, we can say that the information needed by strategic planners is aggregate information, and obtained mainly from sources external to the organization itself. Both the scope and variety of the information are quite large, but the requirements for accuracy are not particularly stringent. Finally, the nonroutine nature of the strategic planning process means that the demands for this information occur infrequently.

The information needs for the operational control area stand in sharp contrast to those of strategic planning. The task orientation of operational control requires information of a well-defined and narrow scope. This information is quite detailed and arises largely from sources within the organization. Very frequent use is made of this information and it must, therefore, be accurate.

The information requirements for management control fall between the extremes for operational control and strategic planning. In addition, it is important to recognize that much of the information relevant to management control is obtained through the process of human interaction.

In Table 1 we have summarized these general observations about the categories of management activity. This summary is subject to the same limitations and uncertainties exhibited by the concepts of management control, strategic planning, and operational control. Nonetheless, it does underscore our contention that, because the activities themselves are different, the information requirements to support them are also different.

This summary of information requirements suggests the reason that many organizations have found it increasingly difficult to realize some of their long-range plans for information systems. Many of these plans are

---

TABLE 1 Information Requirements by Decision Category

Characteristics of Information	Operational Control	Management Control	Strategic Planning
Source	Largely internal ⟶		External
Scope	Well defined, narrow ⟶		Very wide
Level of aggregation	Detailed ⟶		Aggregate
Time horizon	Historical ⟶		Future
Currency	Highly current ⟶		Quite old
Required accuracy	High ⟶		Low
Frequency of use	Very frequent ⟶		Infrequent

---

based on the "total systems approach." Some of the proponents of this approach advocate that systems throughout the organization be tightly linked, with the output of one becoming the direct input of another, and that the whole structure be built on the detailed data used for controlling operations.[7] In doing so, they are suggesting an approach to systems design that is at best uneconomic and at worst based on a serious misconception. The first major problem with this view is that it does not recognize the ongoing nature of systems development in the operational control area. There is little reason to believe that the systems work in any major organization will be complete within the foreseeable future. To say that management information systems activity must wait "until we get our operational control systems in hand" is to say that efforts to assist management with systems support will be deferred indefinitely.

The second and perhaps most serious problem with this total systems view is that it fails to represent properly the information needs of the management control and strategic planning activities. Neither of these *necessarily* needs information that is a mere aggregation of data from the operational control database. In many cases, if such a link is needed, it is more cost effective to use sampling from this database and other statistical techniques to develop the required information. In our opinion, it rarely makes sense to couple managers in the management control and strategic planning areas directly with the masses of detailed data required for operational control. Not only is direct coupling unnecessary but it can also be an expensive and difficult technical problem.

For these reasons it is easy to understand why so many companies have had the following experience. Original plans for operational control systems were met with more or less difficulty, but as time passed it became increasingly apparent that the planned systems for higher management were not being developed on schedule, if at all. To make matters worse, the systems developed for senior management had relatively little impact on the way in which the managers made decisions. This last problem is a direct result of the failure to understand the basic information needs of the different activities.

We have tried to show how Anthony's classification of *managerial* activities is a useful one for people working in information systems design and implementation; we shall return later to consider in more detail some of the implications of his ideas.

In *The New Science of Management Decision,* Simon is concerned with the manner in which human beings solve problems regardless of their position within an organization. His distinction between "programmed" and "nonprogrammed" decisions is a useful one:

> Decisions are programmed to the extent that they are repetitive and routine, to the extent that a definite procedure has been worked out for handling them so that they don't have to be treated *de novo* each time they occur. . . . Decisions are nonprogrammed to the extent that they are novel, unstructured, and consequential. There is no cut-and-dried method of handling the problem because it hasn't arisen before, or because its precise nature and structure are elusive or complex, or because it is so important that it deserves a custom-tailored treatment. . . . By nonprogrammed I mean a response where the system has no specific procedure to deal with situations like the one at hand, but must fall back on whatever *general* capacity it has for intelligent, adaptive, problem-oriented action.[8]

We shall use the terms *structured* and *unstructured* for programmed and nonprogrammed because they imply less dependence on the computer and more dependence on the basic character of the problem-solving activity in question. The procedures, the kinds of computation, and the types of information vary depending on the extent to which the problem in question is unstructured. The basis for these differences is that in the unstructured case the human decision maker must provide judgment and evaluation as well as insights into problem definition. In a very structured situation, much if not all of the decision-making process can be automated. Later in this article we shall argue that systems built to support structured decision making will be significantly different from those designed to assist managers in dealing with unstructured problems. Further, we shall show that these differences can be traced to the character of the models relevant to each of these problems and the way in which these models are developed.

This focus on decisions requires an understanding of the human decision-making process. Research on human problem solving supports Simon's claim that all problem solving can be broken down into three categories:

> The first phase of the decision-making process—searching the environment for conditions calling for decision—I shall call *intelligence* activity (borrowing the military meaning of intelligence). The second phase—inventing, developing, and analyzing possible courses of action—I shall call *design* activity. The third phase—selecting a course of action from those available—I shall call *choice*

activity. . . . Generally speaking, intelligence activity precedes design, and design activity precedes choice. The cycle of phases is, however, far more complex than the sequence suggests. Each phase in making a particular decision is itself a complex decision-making process. The design phase, for example, may call for new intelligence activities; problems at any given level generate subproblems that in turn have their intelligence, design and choice phases, and so on. There are wheels within wheels. . . . Nevertheless, the three large phases are often clearly discernible as the organizational decision process unfolds. They are closely related to the stages in problem solving first described by John Dewey: "What is the problem? What are the alternatives? Which alternative is best?"

A fully structured problem is one in which all three phases—intelligence, design, and choice—are structured, that is, we can specify algorithms, or decision rules, that will allow us to find the problem, design alternative solutions, and select the best solution. An example here might be the use of the classical economic order quantity (EOQ) formula on a straightforward inventory control problem. An unstructured problem is one in which none of the three phases is structured. Many job-shop scheduling problems are of this type.

In the ideas of Simon and Anthony, then, we have two different ways of looking at managerial activity within organizations. Anthony's categorization is based on the purpose of the management activity, whereas Simon's classification is based on the way in which the manager deals with the existing problems. The combination of these two views provides a useful framework within which to examine the purposes and problems of information systems activity. The essence of this combination is shown in Figure 1. The figure contains a class of decisions we have called "semi-structured"—decisions with one or two of the intelligence, design, and choice phases unstructured.

Decisions above the dividing line in Figure 1 are largely structured, and we shall call the information systems that support them "Structured Decision Systems" (SDS). Decisions below the line are largely unstructured, and their supporting information systems are "Decision Support Systems" (DSS). The SDS area encompasses almost all of what *has* been called "Management Information Systems" in the literature—an area that has had almost nothing to do with real managers or information but has been largely routine data processing. We exclude from consideration here all of the *information-handling* activities in an organization. Much computer time in many organizations is spent on straightforward data handling with no decisions, however structured, involved. Payroll, for example, is a data-handling operation.

In Figure 1, we have listed some examples in each of the six cells. It should be stressed, however, that these cells are not well-defined categories. Although this may sometimes cause problems, the majority of important decisions can be classified into their appropriate cell without difficulty.

FIGURE 1   Information Systems: A Framework

	Operational Control	Management Control	Strategic Planning
Structured	Accounts receivable	Budget analysis- Engineered cost	Tanker fleet mix
	Order entry	Short-term forecasting	Warehouse and factory location
	Inventory control		
Semi-Structured	Production scheduling	Variance analyis- Overall budget	Mergers and acquisitions
	Cash management	Budget preparation	New product planning
Unstructured	PERT/ COST systems	Sales and production	R&D planning

---

DECISION MAKING WITHIN THE FRAMEWORK

Planning and Resource Allocation Decisions.   An immediate observation can be made about the framework. Almost all the so-called MIS activity has been directed at decisions in the structured half of the matrix, specifically in the "operation control" cell. On the other hand, most of the areas of greatest concern to managers, areas where decisions have a significant effect on the company, are in the lower half of the matrix. That is, managers deal for the most part with unstructured decisions. This implies, of course, that computers and related systems that have so far been largely applied to the structured operational control area have not yet had any real impact on management decision making. The areas of high potential do not lie in bigger and better systems of the kind most companies now use. To have all the effort concentrated in only one of the six cells suggests at the very least a severe imbalance.

A second point to be noted on the planning question is the evolutionary nature of the line separating structured from unstructured decisions. This line is moving down over time. As we improve our understanding of a particular decision, we can move it above the line and allow the system to take care of it, freeing the manager for other tasks. For example, in previous years the inventory reordering decision in most organizations was made by a well-paid member of middle management. It was a decision that involved a high degree of skill and could have a significant effect on the profits of the organization. Today this decision has moved from the unstructured operational control area to the structured. We have a set of decision rules (the EOQ formula) that on average do a better job for the standard items than most human decision makers. This movement of the line does not imply any replacement of managers, since we are dealing with an almost infinite set of problems. For every one we solve, there are 10 more demanding our attention.

It is worth noting that the approach taken in building systems in the unstructured area hastens this movement of the line because it focuses our analytical attention on decisions and decision rules. We would, therefore, expect a continuing flow of decisions across the line, or at least into the "gray" semistructured decision area.

Through the development of a model of a given problem-solving process for a decision in one of the cells, we can establish the character of each of the three phases. To the extent that any of these phases can be structured, we can design direct systems support. For those aspects of the process that are unstructured (given our current understanding of the situation), we would call on the manager to provide the necessary analysis. Thus, a problem might be broken down into a set of related subproblems, some of which are "solved" automatically by the system and the remainder by the user alone or with varying degrees of computational and display support. Regardless of the resulting division of labor, however, it is essential that a model of the decision process be constructed *prior* to the system design. It is only in this way that a good perspective on the potential application of systems support can be ascertained.

Structured/Unstructured Decisions.   Information systems ought to be centered on the important decisions of the organization, many of which are relatively unstructured. It is, therefore, essential that models be built of the decision process involved. Model development is fundamental because it is prerequisite for the analysis of the value of information, and because it is the key to understanding which portions of the decision process can be supported or automated. Both the successes and failures in the current use of computers can be understood largely in terms of the difficulty of this model development.

Our discussion of Structured Decision Systems showed that the vast majority of the effort (and success) has been in the area of structured operational control, where there is relatively little ambiguity as to the goals sought. For example, the typical inventory control problem can be precisely stated, and it is clear what the criterion is by which solutions are to be judged. Hence, we have an easily understood optimization problem. This type of problem lends itself to the development of formal "scientific" models, such as those typical of operations research.

Another important characteristic of problems of this type is that they are to a large extent "organization independent." By this we mean that the essential aspects of the problem tend to be the same in many organizations, although the details may differ. This generality has two important effects. First, it encourages widespread interest and effort in the development of solutions to the problem. Second, it makes the adaptation of general models to the situation in a particular organizational setting relatively easy.

The situation with regard to areas of management decision making is quite different. To the extent that a given problem is semistructured or unstructured, there is an absence of a routine procedure for dealing with it. There is also a tendency toward ambiguity in the problem definition because of the lack of formalization of any or all of the intelligence, design, or choice phases. Confusion may exist as to the appropriate criterion for evaluating solutions, or as to the means for generating trial solutions to the problem. In many cases, this uncertainty contributes to the perception of problems of this type as being unique to a given organization.

In general, then, we can say that the information systems problem in the structured operational control area is basically that of implementing a given general model in a certain organizational context. On the other hand, work in the unstructured areas is much more involved with model development and formalization. Furthermore, the source of the models in the former case is apt to be the operations research or management science literature. In the latter case, the relevant models are most often the unverbalized models used by the managers of the organization. This suggests that the procedure for the development of systems, the types of systems, and the skills of the analysts involved may be quite different in the two areas.

Although the evolution of information systems activities in most organizations has led to the accumulation of a variety of technical skills, the impact of computers on the way in which top managers make decisions has been minimal. One major reason for this is that the support of these decision makers is not principally a technical problem. If it were, it would have been solved. Certainly there are technical problems associated with work in these problem areas, but the technology and the technological skills in most large organizations are more than sufficient. The missing ingredient, apart from the basic awareness of the problem, is the skill to elicit from management its view of the organization and its environment, and to formalize models of this view.

To improve the quality of decisions, a systems designer can seek to improve the quality of the information inputs or to change the decision process, or both. Because of the existence of a variety of optimization models for operational control problems, there is a tendency to emphasize improvement of the information inputs at the expense of improvement in the decision-making process. Although this emphasis is appropriate for structured operational control problems, it can retard progress in developing support for unstructured problem solving. The difficulty with this view is that it tends to attribute low quality in management decision making to low-quality information inputs. Hence, systems are designed to supply more current, more accurate, or more detailed information.

While improving the quality of information available to managers may improve the quality of their decisions, we do not believe that major advances will be realized in this way.[10] Most managers do not have great informational needs. Rather, they have need of new methods to understand and process the information already available to them. Generally speaking, the models that they employ in dealing with this information are very primitive, and, as a result, the range of responses that they can generate is very limited. For example, many managers employ simple historical models in their attempts to anticipate the future.[11] Further, these models are static in nature, although the processes they purport to represent are highly dynamic. In such a situation, there is much more to be gained by improving the information-processing ability of managers in order that they may deal effectively with the information that they already have, than by adding to the reams of data confronting them, or by improving the quality of that data.[12]

If this view is correct, it suggests that the decision support systems area is important and that these systems may best be built by people other than those currently involved in the operational control systems area. The requisite skills are those of the model building based on close interaction with management, structuring and formalizing the procedures employed by managers, and segregating those aspects of the decision process that can be automated. In addition, systems in this area must be able to assist the evolution of the manager's decision-making ability through increasing understanding of the environment. Hence, one important role of a DSS is educative. Even in areas in which we cannot structure the decision process, we can provide models of the environment from which managers can develop insights into the relationship of their decisions to the goals they wish to achieve.

In discussing models and their importance to systems in the DSS area, we should place special emphasis on the role managers assume in the process of model building. To a large extent they are the source upon which the analyst draws. That is, although a repertoire of "operations research" models may be very valuable for analysts, their task is not simply to impose a model on the situation. These models may be the building blocks. The analyst and the manager in concert develop the final structure. This implies that the analyst must possess a certain empathy for the manager, and vice versa. Whether the current systems designers in a given organization possess this quality is a question worthy of consideration by management.

This approach in no way precludes normative statements about decision procedures. The emphasis on the development of descriptive models of managerial problem solving is only to ensure that the existing situation is well understood by both the analyst and the manager. Once this understanding has been attained, various approaches to improving the process can be explored. In fact, a major benefit of developing descriptive models of this type is the exposure of the decision-making process to objective analysis.

In summary, then, we have asserted that two sets of implications flow from our use of this framework. The first set centers on an organization's planning and resource allocation decision in relation to information systems. The second set flows from the distinction we have drawn between structured and unstructured types of decisions. The focus of our attention should be on the critical *decisions* in an organization and on explicit modeling of these decisions prior to the design of information systems support.

The second major point in relation to the structured/unstructured dimension that we have raised is that the kinds of implementation problems, the skills required by the managers and analysts, and the characteristics of the design process are different above and below the dashed line in Figure 1. In discussing these differences, we have tried to stress the fundamental shift in approach that is required if decision support systems are to be built in a way that makes them effective in an organization. The approach and technology that have been used over the last 15 years to build information systems in the structured operational control area are often inappropriate in the case of decision support systems.

IMPLICATIONS OF THE FRAMEWORK

System Design Differences.   The decision categories we have borrowed from Anthony have a set of implications distinct from those discussed in connection with the structured and unstructured areas. The first of these has to do with the systems design differences that follow from supporting decisions in the three areas.

As was seen earlier, information requirements differ sharply among the three areas. There are few occasions in which it makes sense to connect systems directly across boundaries. Aggregating the detailed accounting records (used in operational control) to provide a base for a five-year sales forecast (required for a strategic planning decision) is an expensive and unnecessary process. We can often sample, estimate, or otherwise obtain data for use in strategic planning without resorting to the operational control database. This statement does not imply that we should *never* use such a database, merely that it is not necessarily the best way of obtaining the information.

This point is also relevant in the collection and maintenance of data. Techniques appropriate for operational control, such as the use of on-line data collection terminals, are rarely justified for strategic planning systems. Similarly elaborate environmental sampling methods may be critical for an operational control decision. In looking at each of the information characteristics in Table 1, it is apparent that quite different databases will be required to support decisions in the three areas. Therefore, the first implication of the decision classification in our framework is that the "totally-integrated-management-information-systems" ideas so popular in the literature are a poor design concept. More particularly, the "integrated" or "companywide" database is a misleading notion, and even if it could be achieved it would be exorbitantly expensive.

Information differences among the three decision areas also imply related differences in hardware and software requirements. On the one hand, strategic planning decisions require access to a database that is used infrequently and may involve an interface with a variety of complex models. Operational control decisions, on the other hand, often require a larger database with continuous updating and frequent access to current information.

Differences in Organizational Structure.   A second distinction is in the organizational structure and the managerial and analytical skills that will be involved across the three areas. The managerial talents required, as well as the numbers and training of the managers involved, differ sharply for these categories. The process of deciding on key problems that might be worth supporting with a formal system is a much smaller, tighter process in the strategic-planning area than in the operational control area. The decision to be supported is probably not a recurring one and will normally not involve changes in the procedures and structure employed by the remainder of the firm. Because it is a relatively isolated decision in both time and scope, it need not involve as many people. However, the process of defining the problem must be dominated by the managers involved if the right problem and hence the best model formulation are to be selected. Similarly, the implementation process must be tightly focused on the immediate problem. The skills required of the managers involved are analytical and reflective, rather than communicative and procedural. In the strategic-planning case, the manager must supply both the problem definition and the key relationships that make up the model. Doing this requires an ability to think logically and a familiarity with models and computation. In the case of operational control, the particular solution and the models involved are much more the concern of the technical specialist. This is not to say that in unstructured operational control the manager's judgment will not be involved in the process of solving problems. However, the manager's role in *building* that model can be much more passive than in the strategic area.

The decision process, the implementation process, and the level of analytical sophistication of the managers (as opposed to the staff) in strategic planning all differ quite markedly from their counterparts in operational control. The decision makers in operational control have a more constrained problem. They have often had several years in which to define the general nature of the problem and to consider solutions. In addition, to the extent that these managers have a technical background, they are more likely to be familiar with the analysis involved in solving structured and unstructured problems. In any event, the nature of the operational control problem, its size, and the frequency of the decision all combine to produce design and implementation problems of a different variety. The managers involved in any given problem tend to be from the decision area in question, be it strategic planning, management control, or operational control. As a result, their training, background, and style of decision making are often different. This means that the types of models to be used, the method of elucidating these from the managers, and the skills of the analysts will differ across these three areas.

As the types of skills possessed by the managers differ, so will the kinds of systems analysts who can operate effectively. We have already distinguished between analysts who can handle structured as opposed to unstructured model building. There is a similar distinction to be made between the kind of person who can work well with a small group of senior managers (on either a structured or unstructured problem) and the person who is able to communicate with the various production personnel on an unstructured job-shop scheduling problem, for example.

In problems in the strategic area, the analyst has to be able to communicate effectively with the few managers who have the basic knowledge required to define the problem and its major variables. The skills required to do this include background and experience which are wide enough to match those of the line executives involved. Good communication depends on a common understanding of the basic variables involved, and few analysts involved in current MIS activity have this understanding.

A breadth of background implies a wide repertoire of models with which the analyst is familiar. In the operational control area, an analyst can usefully specialize to great depth in a particular, narrow problem area. The depth, and the resulting improvement in the final system, often pays off because of the frequency with which the decision is made. In the strategic area the coverage of potential problems is enormous and the frequency of a particular decision relatively low. The range of models with which the analyst is familiar may be of greater benefit than depth in any one type.

In addition to the managerial and analyst issues raised above, there is a further difference in the way the information systems group is organized. A group dealing only with operational control problems would be structured differently and perhaps report to a different organizational position than a group working in all three areas. It is not our purpose here to go into detail on the organizational issues, but the material above suggests that, on strategic problems, a task force reporting to the user and virtually independent of the computer group may make sense. The important issues are problem definition and problem structure; the implementation and computer issues are relatively simple by comparison. In management control, the single user, although still dominant in that one application, has problems of interfacing with other users. An organizational design that encourages cross-functional (marketing, production, distribution, etc.) cooperation is probably desirable. In operational control, the organizational design should include the users as a major influence, but they will have to be balanced with operational systems experts, and the whole group can quite possibly stay within functional boundaries. These examples are merely illustrative of the kind of organizational differences involved. Each organization has to examine its current status and needs and make structural changes in light of them.

Model Differences. The third distinction flowing from the framework is among the types of models involved. Again looking at Table 1 and the information differences, it is clear that model requirements depend, for example, on the frequency of decisions in each area and their relative magnitude. A strategic decision to change the whole distribution system occurs rarely. It is significant in cost, perhaps hundreds of millions of dollars, and it therefore can support a complex model, but the model need not be efficient in any sense. An operational control decision, however, may be made frequently, perhaps daily. The impact of each decision is small but the cumulative impact can involve large sums of money. Models for the decision may have to be efficient in running time, have ready access to current data, and be structured so as to be easily changed. Emphasis has to be on simplicity of building, careful attention to modularity, and so forth.

The sources of models for operational control are numerous. There is a history of activity, the problems are often similar across organizations, and the literature is extensive. In strategic planning, and to a lesser extent management control, we are still in the early stages of development. Our models tend to be individual and have to come from the managers involved. It is a model creation process as opposed to the application of a model.

In summary, then, we have outlined implications for the organization that follow from the three major decision categories in the framework. We have posed the issues in terms of operational control and strategic planning, and with every point we assume that management control lies somewhere between the two. The three major implications we have discussed are the advisability of following the integrated database path; the differences in managerial and analyst skills, as well as the appropriate forms of organizational structure for building systems in the three areas; and differences in the types of models involved. Distinguishing among decision areas is clearly important if an organization is going to be successful in its use of information systems.

SUMMARY

The information systems field absorbs a significant percentage of the resources of many organizations. Despite these expenditures, there is very little perspective on the field and the issues within it. As a result, there has been a tendency to make incremental improvements to existing systems. The framework we suggest for looking at decisions within an organization provides one perspective on the information systems issues. From this perspective, it becomes clear that our planning for information systems has resulted in a heavy concentration in the operational control area. In addition, there is a series of implications for the organization that flows from the distinction between the decision areas. Model structure and the implementation process differ sharply between the structured and unstructured areas. Database concepts, types of analysts and managers, and organizational structure all differ along the Strategic Planning to Operational Control axis.

We believe that each organization must share *some* common framework among its members if it is to plan and make resource allocation decisions that result in effective use of information systems. We suggest that the framework presented here is an appropriate place to start.

RETROSPECTIVE COMMENTARY

In looking back over the 18 years since the publication of this article, we find much that has changed. Information technology is used more and more in dealing with semistructured managerial problems, and our call for decision support systems has been productively answered in many corporate settings. The remarkable development of information technology has enabled this change. The mainframe computer of the early 1970s, surrounded by ranks of systems analysts using rigid methods, was an uncongenial host for the growth of decision support systems. Now the computational power of that old mainframe is embodied in the ubiquitous personal computer. The mainframe itself has assumed power that exceeds all but the most wildly optimistic forecasts of that day, and a range of general-purpose and specialized computers span the computational range between the mainframe and the personal computer. Highly developed networks of computers within and across organizations are further evidence of the technical progress made in these years. And while programming is still a demanding task, new information management and analysis tools facilitate the creation of decision support systems. Business leaders, faced with an increasingly turbulent environment, see with greater clarity the role information technology can play in enhancing organizational effectiveness. So today it is a rare organization that is not permeated by computers and in which most vital challenges of organizational life are not mediated by some form of computation.

While the broad thrust of our analysis remains valid today, with the advantage of hindsight we would make some modifications. We still adhere to our basic premise—that a decision-centered view of an organization provides the best basis for information technology development. We argued against a narrow perspective on the range of decisions made in organizations, noting that the data and processing as well as the styles of the decision makers differed across the three major decision categories. This argument remains sound. Today, however, we would change some of the terminology. We would use the phrase *tactical planning* in place of *management control,* and we would emphasize that planning and control are two sides of the same coin. Thus, there is a need for planning and control systems at the strategic, tactical, and operational levels.[13]

We should have written in a more contingent, less declarative manner. Part of our new-found caution comes from 20 years of research, teaching, consulting, and practice. Another part comes from the seemingly greater complexity of the world in which organizations find themselves. Had we seen matters more clearly in the early 1970s, we would have acknowledged that the "rational actor" model of decision making does not properly reflect the vagaries of the management setting. To improve on practice there, we need to accommodate the complexities of multiple goals, different organizational cultures, and varying personal styles described by Schein, Mason and Mitroff, Mintzberg, Weick, and others.[14] Further, task complexity often demands that highly integrated groups carry projects forward. These teams must often solve difficult problems of task coordination and information integration; deficiencies in information management support diminish the progress they could otherwise achieve. Advanced information technology, with its enormous capabilities for transmitting and storing information, would seem to hold considerable promise for these groups. But our discussion was generally concerned with facilitating the work of individuals, and we ignored the collective nature of many undertakings, where the coordination of specialized efforts is of utmost importance.[15]

Again, with the advantage of hindsight, we would have put more stress on implementation and evaluation. Innovations such as "decision support systems" are much more likely to succeed if these issues are squarely addressed. The best implementation strategy can be very different in the different cells of our original framework, but in all cases a business need, rather than a fascination with technology, should drive the process. A technological imperative often creates an understandable backlash that stifles change. We should not have ignored the challenge of motivating users to take ownership of a new systems-based way to do their jobs. Such motivation will be even more important as users become the front-line troops in organizational change in the years ahead.

Perhaps most important, we glossed over the distinction between "structured" and "unstructured" problems. While we did spell out Simon's view of the decision-making phases (intelligence, design, and choice), we did not offer alternatives or elaborate on his views. It would have been useful to bring in Alan Newell's robust model of problem solving. (Newell was Simon's collaborator on many projects.)

The distinction between *decision making* and *problem solving* is more than just semantic. "Decision making" suggests a clarity that does not correspond with the real world; much of the time (perhaps most of the time) managers engage (often in groups) in problem solving over extended periods of time. The five components of problem solving as Newell saw them were as follows: specification of the problem space and its states; definition of the appropriate operators; identification and setting of goals; identification and understanding of path constraints; and specification of the relevant search control knowledge.

Such a view adds richness to the decision-making perspective by recognizing the crucial learning that takes place during the complex iterative process of moving toward a solution in anything but the simplest situation. In particular, Newell's view allows us to more easily incorporate the idea of heuristics. These "rules of thumb" used by knowledgeable practitioners are too important to be hidden behind the simple intelligence, design, and choice view.

A related enrichment of our framework would have emphasized the amount and diversity of knowledge that often matters in semistructured problems. Indeed, it was partly the problem of casting this knowledge in the limited representational framework of the time that led us to classify certain problems as semistructured and to consider them only briefly. With the fruits of research in artificial intelligence and cognitive science, we are now in a better position to address such problems as "candidates for decision support." The technology represented by expert systems often can be productively applied to organizing the range of knowledge and procedures necessary for such problems. Work of this kind points to the next stage in the evolution of decision support systems.[16]

LOOKING FORWARD

Productivity in the manufacturing sector of the United States has been poor relative to that of our trading partners. Productivity in the service sector is even worse than it is in manufacturing. "Services" in this case includes workers in banking, insurance, education, government, retail, and so on. Falling logically in this same group, although *not* included in the statistics, are the knowledge workers in the manufacturing sector—

designers, accountants, marketing specialists, lawyers, and so forth. For decision support systems to significantly improve the performance of skilled service sector workers and manufacturing sector knowledge workers, these systems must move beyond what we conventionally construe as data processing. The highly structured approach of data processing—its reliance on algorithms and quantitative data—is generally insufficient to meet the needs of these workers. More quantitative and heuristic approaches will be needed.

It is for this reason that the recently developed knowledge-based systems (or expert systems) are adding significantly to the classical decision support system view. This approach uses the concepts and tools that have emerged from the field of artificial intelligence. For example, American Express has had considerable economic success using a knowledge-based system to improve the quality of its credit authorization decisions. When requests for credit approval come in over the phone lines, the new system leverages the credit analyst by providing a powerful set of heuristics culled from their most experienced personnel. These heuristics analyze and filter the data, ultimately giving the analyst the important facts on which to base a final judgment. This is one example of an expert support system that is enhancing the productivity of knowledge workers. One of the challenges of the 1990s is to expand and continue such work.

NOTES

1. J. W. Taylor and N. J. Dean, "Managing to Manage the Computer," *Harvard Business Review,* September–October 1966, pp. 98–110.
2. M. S. Scott Morton, *Management Decision Systems* (Boston: Harvard Business School Press, 1971); P. O. Soelberg, "Unprogrammed Decision Making," *Industrial Management Review* (now *Sloan Management Review*), Spring 1967, pp. 19–30.
3. R. N. Anthony, *Planning and Control Systems: A Framework for Analysis* (Boston: Harvard Business School Division of Research Press, 1965).
4. Ibid., p. 24.
5. Ibid., p. 27.
6. Ibid., p. 69.
7. J. L. Becker, "Planning the Total Information System," in *Total Systems,* ed. A. D. Meacham and V. B. Thompson (New York: American Data Processing, 1962).
8. H. A. Simon, *The New Science of Management Decision* (New York: Harper & Row, 1960), pp. 5–6.
9. Ibid., pp. 2–3.
10. *See* R. Ackoff, "Management Misinformation Systems," *Management Science* 11 (December 1967), pp. B-147–B-156.

11. *See* W. F. Pounds, "The Process of Problem Finding," *Industrial Management Review* (now *Sloan Management Review*), Fall 1969, pp. 1–20.

12. *See* G. A. Gorry, "The Development of Managerial Models," *Sloan Management Review,* Winter 1971, pp. 1–16.

13. P. Lorange, M. S. Scott Morton, and S. Ghoshal, *Strategic Control* (St. Paul, Minn.: West Publishing, 1986).

14. R. O. Mason and I. I. Mitroff, *Challenging Strategic Planning Assumptions: Theory, Cases, and Techniques* (New York: John Wiley & Sons, 1981);   H. Mintzberg, *The Nature of Managerial Work* (New York: Harper & Row, 1973);   E. H. Schein, *Organizational Culture and Leadership* (San Francisco: Jossey-Bass, 1985);   K. E. Weick, *The Social Psychology of Organizing,* 2d ed. (Reading, Mass.: Addison-Wesley, 1979).

15. D. L. Gladstein, "Groups in Context: A Model of Task Group Effectiveness," *Administrative Science Quarterly* 29 (December 1984), pp. 499–517;   J. C. Henderson, "Managing the IS Design Environment: A Research Framework" (Cambridge, Mass.: MIT Sloan School of Management, working paper 1897–87, May 1987);   T. W. Malone, "Modeling Coordination in Organizations and Markets," *Management Science* 33 (October 1987), pp. 1317–32.

16. F. L. Luconi, T. W. Malone, and M. S. Scott Morton, "Expert Systems: The Next Challenge for Managers," *Sloan Management Review,* Summer 1986, pp. 3–14.

8 A Framework for the Development of Decision Support Systems*

Ralph H. Sprague, Jr.

INTRODUCTION

We seem to be on the verge of another "era" in the relentless advancement of computer based information systems in organizations. Designated by the term *decision support systems* (DSS), these systems are receiving reactions ranging from "a major breakthrough" to "just another buzz word."

One view is that the natural evolutionary advancement of information technology and its use in the organizational context has led from EDP to MIS to the current DSS thrust. In this view, the DSS picks up where MIS leaves off. A contrary view portrays DSS as an important subset of what MIS has been and will continue to be. Still another view recognizes a type of system that has been developing for several years and "now we have a name for it." Meanwhile, the skeptics suspect that DSS is just another buzz word to justify the next round of visits from the vendors.

The purpose of this article is to briefly examine these alternative views of DSS and present a framework that has proven valuable in reconciling them. The framework articulates and integrates major concerns of several "stakeholders" in the development of DSS: executives and professionals who use them, the MIS managers who manage the process of developing

---

and installing them, the information specialists who build and develop them, the system designers who create and assemble the technology on which they are based, and the researchers who study the DSS subject and process.

Definition, Examples, Characteristics

The concepts involved in DSS were first articulated in the early 70s by Michael S. Scott Morton under the term *management decision systems* [32].* A few firms and a few scholars began to develop and research DSS which became characterized as *interactive* computer-based systems which *help* decision makers utilize *data* and *models* to solve *unstructured* problems. The unique contribution of DSS resulted from the key italicized words. That definition proved restrictive enough that few actual systems completely satisfied it. Recently loosened by some authors to include any system that makes some contribution to decision making, the term can be applied to all but transaction processing. A serious definitional problem is that the words have a certain "intuitive validity." Any system that supports a decision (in any way) is a decision support system—obviously!

Unfortunately, neither the restrictive nor the broad definition help much, because they do not provide guidance for understanding the value, the technical requirements, or the approach for developing DSS. A complicating factor is that people from different backgrounds and contexts view a DSS quite differently. A manager and computer scientists seldom see things in the same light.

Another way to get a feeling for a complex subject like DSS is to examine examples. Several specific examples were discussed in The Society for Management Information Systems (SMIS) Workshop on DSS in 1979 [35]. Alter examined 56 systems which might have some claim to the DSS label and used this sample to develop a set of abstractions describing their characteristics [1, 2]. More recently, Keen has designated about 30 examples of what he feels are DSS and compares their characteristics [26].

The "characteristics" approach seems to hold more promise than either definitions or collections of examples in understanding DSS and its potential. More specifically, a DSS may be defined by its capabilities in several critical areas; capabilities which are required to accomplish the objectives which are pursued by the development and use of a DSS. Observed characteristics of DSS which have evolved from the work of Alter, Keen, and others seem to include the following:

> They tend to be aimed at the less well-structured, underspecified problems that upper level managers typically face.

---

* Bracketed numbers cite the references at the end of this chapter.

They attempt to combine the use of models or analytic techniques with traditional data access and retrieval functions.

They specifically focus on features which make them easy to use by noncomputer people in an interactive mode.

They emphasize flexibility and adaptability to accommodate changes in the environment and decision-making approach of the user.

A serious question remains. Are the definitions, examples, and characteristics of DSS sufficiently different to justify the use of a new term and the inference of a new era in information systems for organizations? Or are the skeptics right? Is it just another buzz word to replace the fading appeal of MIS?

DSS versus MIS

Much of the difficulty and controversy with terms like *DSS* and *MIS* can be traced to the difference between an academic or theoretical definition and "connotational" definition. The former is carefully articulated by people who write textbooks and articles in respectable journals. The latter evolves from what actually is developed and used in practice, and is heavily influenced by the personal experiences that the user of the term has had with the subject. It is this connotational definition of EDP-MIS-DSS that is used in justifying the assertion that DSS is an evolutionary advancement beyond MIS.

This view can be articulated using Figure 1, a simple organizational chart, as a model of an organization. EDP was first applied to the lower operational levels of the organization to automate the paperwork. Its basic characteristics include:

- A focus on data, storage, processing, and flows at the operational level.
- Efficient transaction processing.
- Scheduled and optimized computer runs.
- Integrated files for related jobs.
- Summary reports for management.

In recent years, the EDP level of activity in many firms has become a well-oiled and efficient production facility for transactions processing.

The MIS approach elevated the focus of information systems activities, with additional emphasis on integration and planning of the information systems function. In *practice,* the characteristics of MIS include:

- Information focus, aimed at the middle managers.
- Structured information flows.
- Integration of EDP jobs by business function (production MIS, marketing MIS, personnel MIS, etc.).
- Inquiry and report generation (usually with a database).

FIGURE 1   The Connotational View

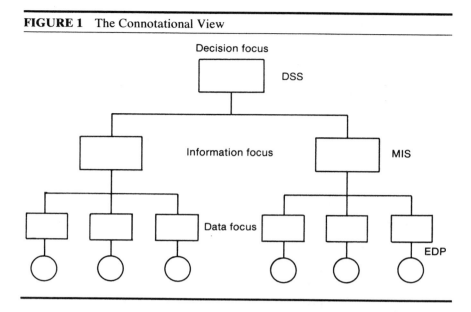

The MIS era contributed a new level of information to serve management needs but was still very much oriented to and built on information flows and data files.

According to this connotational view, DSS is focused still higher in the organization, with an emphasis on the following characteristics:

- Decision focused, aimed at top managers and executive decision makers.
- Emphasis on flexibility, adaptability, and quick response.
- User initiated and controlled.
- Support for the personal decision-making styles of individual managers.

This connotational and evolutionary view has some credence because it does roughly correspond to developments in practice over time. A recent study found MIS managers able to distinguish the level of advancement of their application systems using criteria similar to those above [27]. Many installations with MIS-type applications planned to develop applications with DSS-type characteristics. The "connotational" view has some serious deficiencies, however, and is definitely misleading in the further development of DSS.

It implies that decision support is needed only at the top levels. In fact, decision support is required at all levels of management in the organization.

The decision making which occurs at several levels frequently must be coordinated. Therefore, an important dimension of decision support is the communication and coordination between decision makers across organizational levels as well as at the same level.

It implies that decision support is the only thing top managers need from the information system. In fact, decision making is only one of the activities of managers that benefit from information systems support.

There is also the problem that many information systems professionals, especially those in SMIS, are not willing to accept the narrow connotational view of the term MIS. To us, MIS refers to the entire set of systems and activities required to manage, process, and use information as a resource in the organization.

The Theoretical View

To consider the appropriate role of DSS in this overall context of information systems, let us characterize the broad charter and objectives of the information systems function in the organization as follows:

Dedicated to improving the performance of knowledge workers in organizations through the application of information technology.

1. Improving the performance is the ultimate objective of information systems—not the storage of data, the production of reports, or even "getting the right information to the right person at the right time." The ultimate objective must be viewed in terms of the ability of information systems to support the improved performance of people in organizations.
2. Knowledge workers are the clientele. This group includes managers, professionals, staff analysts, and clerical workers whose primary job responsibility is the handling of information in some form.
3. Organizations are the context. The focus is on information handling in goal-seeking organizations of all kinds.
4. The application of information technology is the challenge and opportunity facing the information systems professional for the purposes and in the contexts given above.

A triangle was used by Robert Head in the late 60s as a visual model to characterize MIS in this broad comprehensive sense [22]. It has become a classic way to view the dimensions of an information system. The vertical dimension represented the levels of management and the horizontal dimension represented the main functional areas of the business organization. Later authors added transactional processing as a base on which the entire system rested. The result was a two-dimensional model of an MIS in the broad sense—the total activities which comprise the information system in an organization. Figure 2 is a further extension of the basic triangle

FIGURE 2   The Complete View

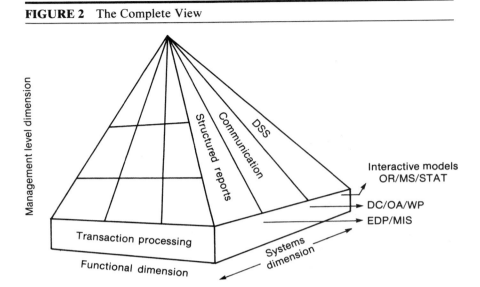

to help conceptualize the potential role of DSS. The depth dimension shows the major technology "subsystems," which provide support for the activities of knowledge workers.

Three major thrusts are shown here, but there could be more. The structured reporting system includes the reports required for the management and control of the organization, and for satisfying the information needs of external parties. It has been evolving from efforts in EDP and MIS (in the narrow sense) for several years. Systems to support the communication needs of the organization are evolving rapidly from advances in telecommunications with a strong impetus from office automation and word processing. DSS seems to be evolving from the coalescence of information technology and operations research/management science approaches in the form of interactive modeling.

To summarize this introductory section, DSS is not merely an evolutionary advancement of EDP and MIS, and it will certainly not replace either. Nor is it merely a type of information system aimed exclusively at top management, where other information systems seem to have failed. DSS is a class of information system that draws on transaction processing systems and interacts with the other parts of the overall information system to support the decision-making activities of managers and other knowledge workers in the organizations. There are, however, some subtle but some significant differences between DSS and traditional EDP or so-called MIS approaches. Moreover, these systems require a new combination of information systems technology to satisfy a set of heretofore unmet needs. It is not yet clear exactly how these technologies fit together, or which important problems need to be solved. Indeed, that is a large part of the purpose of this article. It is apparent, however, that DSS have the potential to become another powerful weapon in the arsenal of the information systems professional to help improve the effectiveness of the people in organizations.

THE FRAMEWORK

The remainder of this article is devoted to an exploration of the nature of this "thrust" in information systems called DSS. The mechanism for this exploration is another of the oft-maligned but repeatedly used "frameworks."

A framework, in the absence of theory, is helpful in organizing a complex subject, identifying the relationships between the parts, and revealing the areas in which further developments will be required. The framework presented here has evolved over the past two years in discussions with many different groups of people [1]. It is organized in two major parts. The first part considers (*a*) three levels of technology, all of which have been designated DSS (with considerable confusion), (*b*) the development approach that is evolving for the creation of DSS, and (*c*) the roles of several key types of people in the building and use of DSS. The second part of the framework develops a descriptive model to assess the performance objectives and the capabilities of DSS as viewed by three of the major stakeholders in their continued development and use.

Three Technology Levels

It is helpful to identify three levels of hardware/software which have been included in the label DSS. They are used by people with different levels of technical capability and vary in the nature and scope of task to which they can be applied.

Specific DSS. The system which actually accomplishes the work might be called the *Specific DSS*. It is an information systems "application," but with characteristics that make it significantly different from a typical data-processing application. It is the hardware/software that allows a specific decision maker or group of them to deal with a specific set of related problems. An early example is the portfolio management system [20] also described in the first major DSS book by Keen and Scott Morton [23]. Another example is the police beat allocation system used on an experimental basis by the City of San Jose, California [9]. The latter system allowed a police officer to display a map outline and call up data by geographical zone showing police calls for service, activity levels, service time, etc. The interactive graphic capability of the system enabled the officer to manipulate the maps, zones, and data to try a variety of police beat alternatives quickly and easily. In effect, the system provided tools to *amplify* his managerial judgment. Incidentally, a later experiment attempted to apply a traditional linear programming model to the problem; the solution was less satisfactory than the one designed by the police officer.

DSS Generator. The second technology level might be called a *DSS Generator*. This is a "package" of related hardware and software which provides a set of capabilities to quickly and easily build a Specific DSS. For example, the police beat system described above was built from the Geodata Analysis and Display System (GADS), an experimental system developed at the IBM Research Laboratory in San Jose [8]. By loading different maps, data, menu choices, and procedures (command strings), GADS was later used to build a Specific DSS to support the routing of IBM copier repairmen [42]. The development of this new "application" required less than one month.

Another example of a DSS Generator is the Executive Information System (EIS) marketed by Boeing Computer Services [6]. EIS is an integrated set of capabilities which includes report preparation, inquiry capability, a modeling language, graphic display commands, and a set of financial and statistical analysis subroutines. These capabilities have all been available individually for some time; the unique contribution of EIS is that they are available through a common command language which acts on a common set of data. The result is that EIS can be used as a DSS Generator, especially for Specific DSS to help in financial decision-making situations.

Evolutionary growth toward DSS Generators has come from special-purpose languages. In fact, most of the software systems that might be used as Generators are evolving from enhanced planning languages or modeling languages, perhaps with report preparation and graphic display capabilities added. The Interactive Financial Planning System (IFPS) marketed by Execucom Systems of Austin, Texas [18], and EXPRESS available from TYMSHARE [44] are good examples.

DSS Tools. The third and most fundamental level of technology applied to the development of DSS might be called *DSS Tools*. These are hardware or software elements which facilitate the development of a Specific DSS *or* a DSS Generator. This category of technology has seen the greatest amount of recent development, including new special purpose languages, improvements in operating systems to support conversational approaches, color graphic hardware and supporting software, and so on. For example, the GADS system described above was written in FORTRAN using an experimental graphics subroutine package as the primary dialogue handling software and a laboratory enhanced raster-scan color monitor.

Relationships. The relationships between these three levels of technology and types of DSS can be illustrated by Figure 3. The DSS Tools can be used to develop a Specific DSS application directly as shown on the left half of the diagram. This is obviously the same approach used to develop most traditional applications with tools such as a general purpose language, data access software, and subroutine packages. The difficulty with this approach for developing DSS applications is the constant change and flexibility which characterize them. DSS change character not only in response to changes in the environment, but to changes in the way managers want to approach the problem. Therefore, a serious complicating factor in the use of basic tools is the need to involve the user directly in the change and modification of the Specific DSS.

APL was heavily used in the development of Specific DSS because it proved cheap and easy for APL programmers (especially the APL enthusiasts) to produce "throw-away" code which could be easily revised or discarded as the nature of the application changed. Except for the few

FIGURE 3 Three Levels of DSS Technology

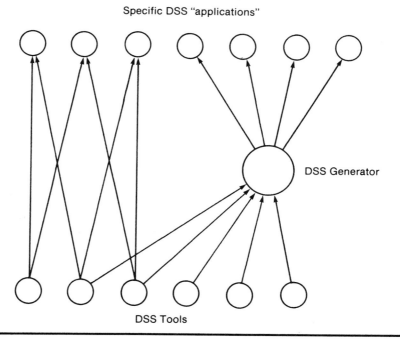

Specific DSS "applications"

DSS Generator

DSS Tools

users who became members of the APL fan club, however, that language *did not* help capture the involvement of users in the building and modification of the DSS. The development and use of DSS Generators promise to create a "platform" or staging area from which Specific DSS can be constantly developed and modified with the cooperation of the user, and without heavy consumption of time and effort.

Evolving Roles in DSS

All three levels of technology will probably be used over time in the development and operation of DSS. Some interesting developments are occurring, however, in the roles that managers and technicians will play.

Figure 4 repeats part of the earlier diagram with a spectrum of five roles spread across the three levels.

1. The *manager or user* is the person faced with the problem or decision— the one that must take action and be responsible for the consequences.
2. The *intermediary* is the person who helps the user, perhaps merely as a

FIGURE 4   Three Levels of DSS with Five Associated Roles for Managers and Technicians

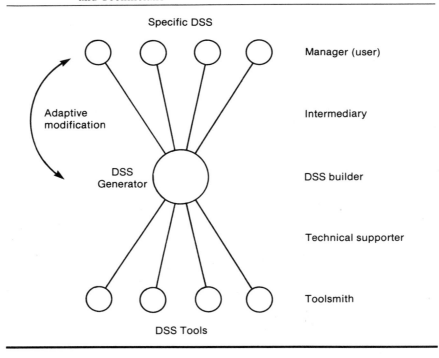

clerical assistant to push the buttons of the terminal, or perhaps as a more substantial "staff assistant" to interact and make suggestions.

3. The *DSS builder* or facilitator assembles the necessary capabilities from the DSS Generator to "configure" the specific DSS with which the user/intermediary interacts directly. This person must have some familiarity with the problem area and also be comfortable with the information system technology components and capabilities.

4. The *technical supporter* develops additional information system capabilities or components when they are needed as part of the Generator. New databases, new analysis models, and additional data display formats will be developed by the person filling this role. It requires a strong familiarity with technology and a minor acquaintance with the problem or application area.

5. The *toolsmith* develops new technology, new languages, new hardware and software, improves the efficiency of linkages between subsystems, etc.

Two observations about this spectrum of roles are appropriate. First, it is clear that they do not necessarily align with individuals on a one-to-one basis. One person may assume several roles, or it may require more than one person to fill a role. The appropriate role assignment will generally depend on:

- The nature of the problem, particularly how narrow or broad.
- The nature of the person, particularly how comfortable he or she is with the computer equipment, language, and concepts.
- The strength of the technology, particularly how user-oriented it is.

Some managers do not need or want an intermediary. There are even a few chief executives who take the terminal home on weekends to write programs, thereby assuming the upper three or four roles. In fact, a recent survey of the users of IFPS shows that more than one third of them are middle and top level managers [45]. Decisions which require group consensus or systems design (builder) teams are examples of multiple persons per role.

Second, these roles appear similar to those present in traditional system development, but there are subtle differences. The top two are familiar even in name for the development of many interactive or on-line systems. It is common practice in some systems to combine them into one "virtual" user for convenience. The user of the DSS, however, will play a much more active and controlling role in design and development of the system than has been true in the past. The builder/technical supporter dichotomy is relatively close to the information specialist/system designer dichotomy discussed in the ACM curriculum recommendations [3]. Increasingly, however, the DSS builder resides in the functional area and not in the MIS Department. The toolsmith is similar to a systems programmer, software designer, or computer scientist, but is increasingly in the employ of a hardware or software vendor, and not the user's organization. The net result is less direct involvement in the DSS process by the information system professional in the EDP/MIS Department. (Some implications of this trend are discussed later.) Moreover, the interplay between these roles is evolving into a unique development approach for DSS.

The Development Approach for DSS

The very nature of DSS requires a different design technique from traditional batch (or on-line) transaction processing systems. Because there is no single comprehensive theory of decision making, and because of the rapidity of change in the conditions which decision makers face, the traditional approaches for analysis and design have proven inadequate. Designers literally "cannot get to first base" because no one, least of all the decision maker or user, can define in advance what the functional requirements of the system should be. DSS need to be built with short, rapid feedback from users to ensure that development is proceeding correctly. They must be developed to permit change quickly and easily.

Iterative Design. The result is that the most important four steps in the typical systems development process (analysis, design, construction, implementation) are combined into a single step which is iteratively repeated. Several names are evolving to describe this process including *breadboarding* [31], *L'Approache Evolutive* [14], and *middle out* [30]. The essence of the approach is that the manager and builder agree on a small but significant subproblem, then design and develop an initial system to support the decision making which it requires. After a short period of use (a few weeks), the system is evaluated, modified, and incrementally expanded. This cycle is repeated three to six times over the course of a few months until a *relatively* stable system is evolved which supports decision making for a cluster of tasks. The word *relatively* is important, because although the frequency and extent of change will decrease, it will never be stable. The system will always be changing, not as a necessary evil in response to imposed environmental changes but as a conscious strategy on the part of the user and builder.

In terms of the three-level model presented earlier, this process can be viewed as the iterative cycling between the DSS Generator and the Specific DSS (Figure 4). With each cycle, capabilities are added to or deleted from the Specific DSS from those available in the DSS Generator. Keen depicts the expansion and growth of the system in terms of adding verbs which represent actions managers require [24]. Carlson adds more dimension by focusing on representations, operations, control, and memories as the elements of expansion and modification [11]. In another paper, Keen deals substantively with the interaction between the user, the builder, and the technology in this iterative, adaptive design process [25].

Note that this approach requires an unusual level of management involvement or management participation in the design. The manager is actually the iterative designer of the system; the systems analyst is merely the catalyst between the manager and the system, implementing the required changes and modifications.

Note also that this is different from the concept of "prototyping"; the initial system is real, live, and usable, not just a pilot test. The iterative process does not *merely* lead to a good understanding of the systems performance requirements, which are then frozen. The iterative change-ability is actually *built in* to the DSS as it is used over time. In fact, the development approach *becomes the system.* Rather than developing a system which is then "run" as a traditional EDP system, the DSS development approach results in the installation of an adaptive process in which a decision maker and a set of information system "capabilities" interact to confront problems while responding to changes from a variety of sources.

The Adaptive System. In the broad sense, the DSS is an adaptive system which consists of all three levels of technology in place and operating with the participates (roles) and the technology adapting to changes over time. Thus, the development of a DSS is actually the development and installation of this adaptive system. Simon describes such a system as one that adapts to changes of several kinds over three time horizons [34]. In the short run, the system allows *search* for answers within a relatively narrow scope. In the intermediate time horizon, the system *learns* by modifying its capabilities and activities (the scope or domain changes). In the long run, the system *evolves* to accommodate much different behavior styles and capabilities.

The three level model of DSS is analogous to Simon's adaptive system. The Specific DSS gives the manager the capabilities and flexibility to *search,* explore, and experiment with the problem area (within certain boundaries). Over time, as changes occur in a task, the environment, and the user's behavior, the Specific DSS must *learn* to accommodate these changes through the reconfiguration of the elements in the DSS generator (with the aid of the DSS builder). Over a longer period of time, the basic tools evolve to provide the technology for changing the capabilities of the Generators out of which the Specific DSS are constructed (through the efforts of the toolsmith).

The ideas expressed above are not particularly new. Rapid feedback between the systems analyst and the client has been pursued for years. In the long run, most computer systems *are* adaptive systems; they are changed and modified during the normal system life cycle, and they evolve through major enhancements and extensions as the life cycle is repeated. However, when the length of that life cycle is shortened from three to five years to three to five months or even weeks, there are significant implications. The resulting changes in the development approach and the traditional view of the systems life cycle promises to be one of the important impacts of the growing use of DSS.

PERFORMANCE OBJECTIVES AND CAPABILITIES

Most of the foregoing discussion has dealt with some aspects of the technological and organizational contexts within which DSS will be built and operated. The second part of the framework deals with what the DSS must accomplish and what capabilities or characteristics it must have. The three levels of hardware/software technology and the corresponding three major "stakeholders" or interested parties in the development and use of DSS can be used to identify the characteristics and attributes of DSS.

At the top level are the *managers or users* who are primarily concerned with what the Specific DSS can do for them. Their focus is the problem-solving or decision-making task they face and the organizational environment in which they operate. They will assess the DSS in terms of the assistance they receive in pursuing these tasks. At the level of the DSS Generator, the *builders* or designers must use the capabilities of the Generator to configure a Specific DSS to meet the manager's needs. They will be concerned with the capabilities the Generator offers and how these capabilities can be assembled to create the Specific DSS. At the DSS tool level, the *"toolsmiths"* are concerned with the development of basic technology components and how they can be integrated to form a DSS Generator which has the necessary capabilities.

Let us now look more closely at the attributes and characteristics of the DSS as viewed from each level. From the manager's view, we can identify six general performance objectives for Specific DSS. They are not the only six that could be identified, but as a group they represent the overall performance of DSS that seems to be expected and desirable from a managerial viewpoint. The characteristics of the DSS Generator from the viewpoint of the builder is described by a conceptual model which identifies performance characteristics in three categories: Dialog handling (the man-machine interface), database and database management capability, modeling, and analytic capability. The same three-part model is used to depict the viewpoint of the "toolsmith" but from the aspect of the technology, tactics, and architecture required to produce those capabilities required by the builders.

Manager's View: Performance Objectives

The following performance requirements are phrased using the normative word *should*. It is likely that no Specific DSS will be required to satisfy all six of the performance requirements given here.

In fact, it is important to recall that the performance criteria for any Specific DSS will be entirely dependent on the task, the organizational environment, and the decision maker(s) involved. Nevertheless, the following objectives collectively represent a set of capabilities which characterize the full value of the DSS concept from the manager/user point of view. The first three pertain to the type of decision-making task which managers and professionals face. The latter three relate to the type of support which is needed.

1. A DSS should provide support for decision making, but with emphasis on semistructured and unstructured decisions. These are the types of decisions that have had little or no support from EDP, MIS, or management science/operations research (MS/OR) in the past. It might be better to refer to *hard* or *underspecified* problems because the concept of "structure" in decision making is heavily dependent on the cognitive style and approach to problem solving of the decision maker. It is clear from their expressed concerns, however, that managers need additional support for certain kinds of problems.

2. A DSS should provide decision-making support for managers at all levels, assisting in integration between the levels whenever appropriate. This requirement evolves from the realization that managers at *all* organizational levels face "tough" problems (as in 1 above). Moreover, a major need articulated by managers is the integration and coordination of decision making by several managers dealing with related parts of a larger problem.

3. A DSS should support decisions which are *inter*dependent as well as those that are *in*dependent. Much of the early DSS work implied that a decision maker would sit at a terminal, use a system, and develop a decision *alone*. DSS development experience has shown that a DSS must accommodate decisions which are made by groups or made in part by several people in sequence. Keen and Hackathorn [24] have identified three decision types as:

- *Independent:* A decision maker has full responsibility and authority to make a complete implementable decision.
- *Sequential interdependent:* A decision maker makes part of a decision which is passed on to someone else.
- *Pooled interdependent:* The decision must result from negotiation and interaction between decision makers.

Different capabilities will be required to support each type of decision (personal support, organizational support, and group support, respectively).

4. A DSS should support all phases of the decision-making process. A popular model of the decision-making process is given in the work of Herbert Simon [33]. He characterized three main steps in the process as follows:

- *Intelligence:* Searching the environment for conditions calling for deci-

sions. Raw data is obtained, processed, and examined for clues that may identify problems.
* *Design:* Inventing, developing, and analyzing possible courses of action. This involves processes to understand the problem, to generate solutions, and to test solutions for feasibility.
* *Choice:* Selecting a particular course of action from those available. A choice is made and implemented.

Although the third phase includes implementation, many authors feel that it is significant enough to be shown separately. It has been added to Figure 5 to show the relationships between the steps. Simon's model also illustrates the contribution of MIS and MS/OR to decision making. From the definition of the three stages given above, it is clear the EDP and MIS (in the narrow sense) have made major contributions to the intelligence phase, while MS/OR has been primarily useful at the choice phase. There has been no substantial support for the design phase which seems to be one of the primary potential contributions of DSS. There has been very little support from traditional systems for the implementation phase, but some early experience has shown that DSS can make a major contribution here also [42].

5. A DSS should support a variety of decision-making processes but not be dependent on any one. Simon's model, though widely accepted, is only one model of how decisions are actually made. In fact, there is no universally accepted model of the decision-making process, and there is no

FIGURE 5 Phases of Decision Making

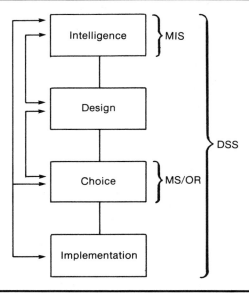

promise of such a general theory in the foreseeable future. There are too many variables, too many different types of decisions, and too much variety in the characteristics of decision makers. Consequently, a very important characteristic of a DSS is that it provide the decision maker with a set of capabilities to apply in a sequence and form that fits his or her cognitive style. In short, a DSS should be process-independent and user driven (or controlled).

6. Finally, a DSS should be easy to use. A variety of terms have been used to describe this characteristic including *flexibility, user-friendly,* and *nonthreatening.* The importance of this characteristic is underscored by the discretionary latitude of a DSS's clientele. Although some systems which require heavy organizational support or group support may limit the discretion somewhat, the user of a DSS has much more latitude to ignore or circumvent the system than the user of a more traditional transaction system or required reporting system. Therefore, the DSS must "earn" its users' allegiance by being valuable and convenient.

The Builder's View: Technical Capabilities

The DSS Builder has the responsibility of drawing on computer-based tools and techniques to provide the decision support required by the manager. DSS Tools can be used directly, but it is generally more efficient and effective to use a DSS Generator for this task. The Generator must have a set of capabilities which facilitate quick and easy configuration of a Specific DSS and modification in response to changes in the manager's requirements, environment, tasks, and thinking approaches. A conceptual model can be used to organize these capabilities, both for the builders and for the "toolsmith" who will develop the technology to provide these capabilities.

The old "black box" approach is helpful here, starting with the view of the system as a black box, successively "opening" the boxes to understand the subsystems and how they are interconnected. Although the DSS is treated as the black box here, it is important to recall that the overall system is the decision-*making* system consisting of a manager/user who uses a DSS to confront a task in an organizational environment.

Opening the large DSS box reveals a database, a model base, and a complex software system for linking the user to each of them. (See Figure 6). Opening each of these boxes reveals that the database and model base have some interrelated components and that the software system is comprised of three sets of capabilities: database management software (DBMS), model base management software (MBMS), and the software for managing the interface between the user and the system, which might be called the dialog generation and management software (DGMS). These three major subsystems provide a convenient scheme for identifying the

FIGURE 6   Components of the DSS

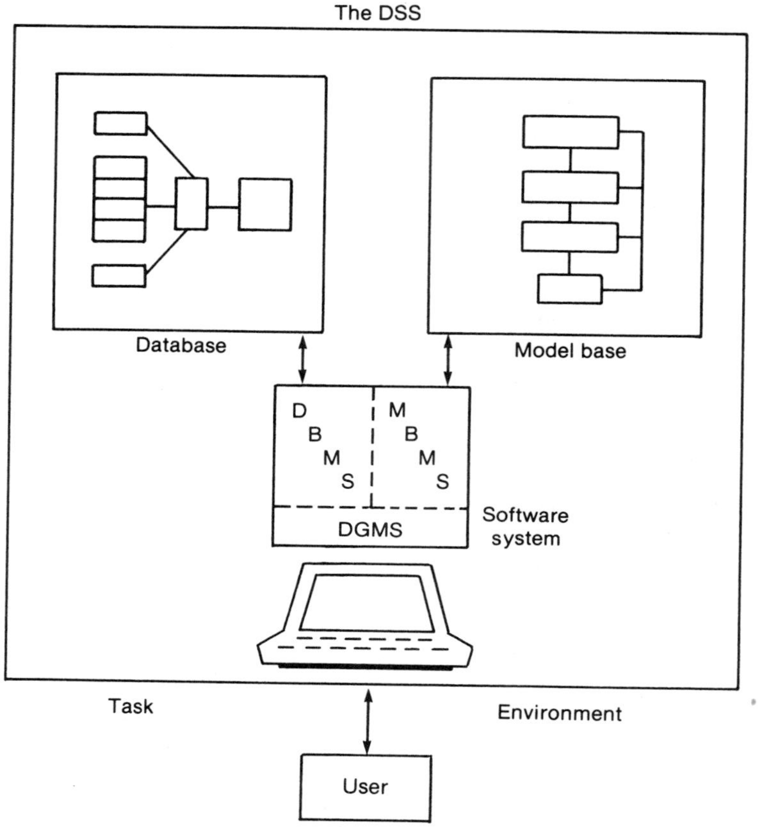

technical capability which a DSS must have. Let us consider the key aspects in each category that are critical to DSS from the Builder's point of view, and a list of capabilities which will be required in each category.

The Data Subsystem

The data subsystem is thought to be a well-understood set of capabilities because of the rapidly maturing technology related to databases and their management. The typical advantages of the database approach, and the powerful functions of the DBMS are also important to the development and use of DSS. There are, however, some significant differences between the Database/Data Communication approach for traditional systems and those applicable for DSS. Opening the Database box summarizes these key characteristics as shown in Figure 7.

First is the importance of a much richer set of data sources than are usually found in typical non-DSS applications. Data must come from external as well as internal sources, since decision making, especially in the upper management levels is heavily dependent on external data sources. In addition, the typical accounting-oriented transaction data must be supplemented with nontransactional, nonaccounting data, some of which has not been computerized in the past.

Another significant difference is the importance of the data capture and extraction process from this wider set of data sources. Most successful DSS have found it necessary to create a DSS database which is logically separate from other operational databases. The nature of DSS requires that the extraction process and the DBMS which manages it be flexible enough to allow rapid additions and changes in response to unanticipated user requests. A partial set of capabilities required in the database area can be summarized as follows:

Ability to combine a variety of data sources through a data capture and extraction process.

FIGURE 7   The Data Subsystem

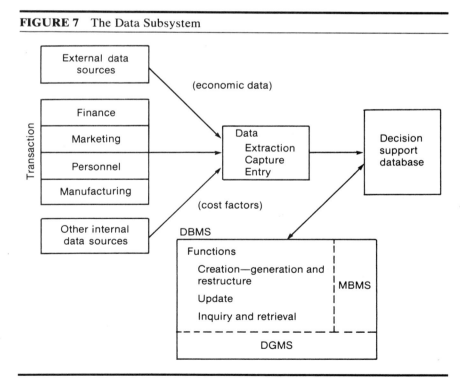

Ability to add and delete data sources quickly and easily.

Ability to portray logical data structures in user terms so the user understands what is available and can specify needed additions and deletions.

Ability to handle personal and unofficial data so the user can experiment with alternatives based on personal judgment.

Ability to manage this wide variety of data with a full range of data management functions.

The Model Subsystem

A very promising aspect of DSS is their ability to integrate data access and decision models. They do so by imbedding the decision models in an information system which uses the database as the integration and communication mechanism between models. This characteristic unifies the strength of data retrieval and reporting from the EDP field and the significant developments in management science in a way the manager can use and trust.

The misuse and disuse of models have been widely discussed [21, 28, 36, 39]. One major problem has been that model builders were frequently preoccupied with the structure of the model. The existence of the correct input data and the proper delivery of the output to the user was assumed. In addition to these heroic assumptions, models tended to suffer from inadequacy because of the difficulty of developing an integrated model to handle a realistic set of interrelated decisions. The solution was a collection of separate models, each of which dealt with a distinct part of the problem. Communication between these related models was left to the decision maker as a manual and intellectual process.

A more enlightened view of models suggests that they be imbedded in an information system with the database as the integration and communication mechanism between them. Figure 8 summarizes the components of the model base "box." The model creation process must be flexible, with a strong modeling language and a set of building blocks, much like subroutines, which can be assembled to assist the modeling process. In fact, there is a set of model management functions, very much analogous to data management functions. They key capabilities for DSS in the model subsystems include:

- Ability to create new models quickly and easily.
- Ability to catalog and maintain a wide range of models, supporting all levels of management.
- Ability to interrelate these models with appropriate linkages through the database.
- Ability to access and integrate model "building blocks."

FIGURE 8 The Model's Subsystem

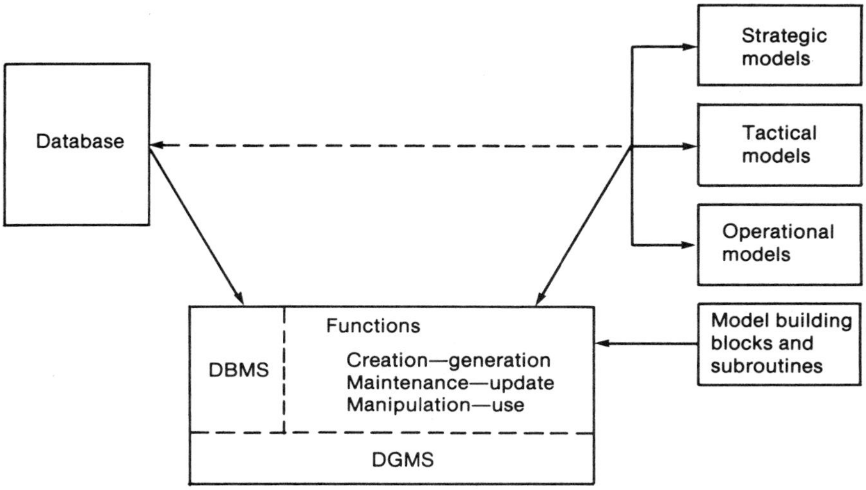

- Ability to manage the model base with management functions analogous to database management (e.g., mechanisms for storing, cataloging, linking, and accessing models).

(For a more detailed discussion of the model base and its management, see 37, 38, 46.)

The User-System Interface.   Much of the power, flexibility, and usability characteristics of a DSS derive from capabilities in the user-system interface. Bennett identifies the user, the terminal, and the software system as the components of the interface subsystem [5]. He then divides the dialog (interface) experience itself into three parts (see Figure 9):

1. The action language—what the user *can do* in communicating with the system. It includes such options as the availability of a regular keyboard, function keys, touch panels, joy stick, and voice command.
2. The display or presentation language—what the user *sees*. The display language includes options such as character or line printer, display screen, graphics, color, plotters, and audio output.
3. The knowledge base—what the user *must know*. The knowledge base consists of what the user needs to bring to the session with the system in order to effectively use it. The knowledge may be in the user's head, on a reference card or instruction sheet, in a user's manual, or in a series of "help" commands available on request.

FIGURE 9   The User-System Interface

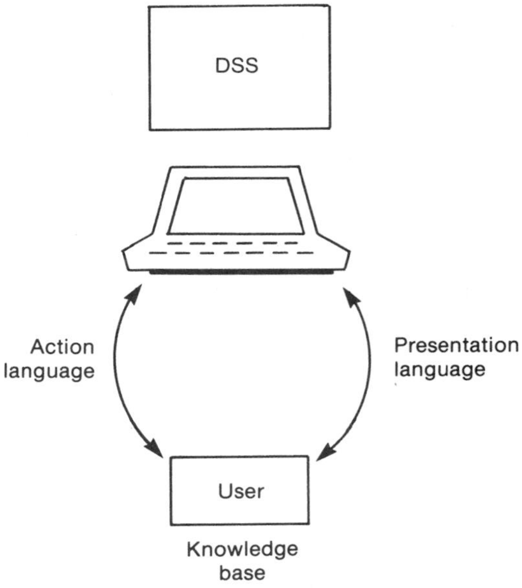

The "richness" of the interface will depend on the strength of capabilities in each of these areas.

Another dimension of the user-system interface is the concept of "dialog style." Examples include the questions/answer approach, command languages, menus, and fill-in-the-blanks. Each style has pros and cons depending on the type of user, task, and decision situation. [For a more detailed discussion of dialog styles see 13.]

Although we have just scratched the surface in this important area, a partial set of desirable capabilities for a DSS Generator to support the user/system interface includes:

- Ability to handle a variety of dialog styles, perhaps with the ability to shift among them at the user's choice.
- Ability to accommodate user actions in a variety of media.
- Ability to present data in a variety of formats and media.
- Ability to provide flexible support for user's knowledge base.

The Toolsmith View: The Underlying Technology

The toolsmith is concerned with the science involved in creating the information technology to support DSS and the architecture of combining the basic tools into a coherent system. We can use the same three-part model to describe the toolsmith's concerns because the tools must be designed and combined to provide the three sets of capabilities.

Each of the three areas (dialog, data handling, model handling) has received a fair amount of attention from toolsmiths in the past. The topics of DSS and the requirements they impose have put these efforts in a new light, revealing how they can be interrelated to increase their collective effectiveness. Moreover, the DSS requirements have revealed some missing elements in existing efforts, indicating valuable potential areas for development.

Dialog Management. There has been much theoretical and some empirical work on systems requirements for good man-machine interface. Many of these studies are based on watching users' behavior in using terminals, or surveying users or programmers to ascertain what they want in interactive systems [10, 16]. A recent study examines a series of interactive applications, many of which are DSS, to assess the *type* of software capabilities required by the applications [43]. This study led directly to some creative work on the software architecture for dialog generation and management systems (DGMS) as characterized in the model of the previous section [12]. This research uses a relation as a data structure for storing each picture or "frame" used in the system and a decision table for storing the control mechanism for representing the potential users' option in branching from one frame to another.

Data Management. Most of the significant work in the database management area during the past several years is aimed at transaction processing against large databases. Large DBMS generally have inquiry/retrieval and flexible report preparation capabilities, but their largest contribution has been in the reduction of program maintenance costs through the separation of application programs and data definitions. On the other hand, DBMS work has generally had a rather naive view of the user and his requirements. A DSS user will not be satisfied merely with the capability to issue a set of retrieval commands which select items from the database, or even to display those selected items in a report with flexible definition of format and headings. A DSS user needs to interact repeatedly and creatively with a relatively small set of data. He may only need 40–100 data variables, but they must be the *right ones;* and what is right may change from day to day and week to week. Required data will probably include time series data which are not handled comprehensively by typical DBMS. We will need better ways to handle and coordinate time series data as well as mechanisms for capturing, processing, and tagging judgmental and probabilistic data. We will also need better ways of extracting data from existing files and capturing data from previously noncomputerized sources. The critical area of data extraction with fast response, which allows additions and deletions to DSS database from the large transaction database was a major contribution of the GADS work [8, 29]. In short, the significant development in database technology needs to be focused and extended in some key areas in order to directly serve the needs of DSS.

Model Management. The area of model creation and handling may have the greatest potential contribution to DSS. So far, the analytic capability provided by systems has evolved from statistical or financial analysis subroutines which can be called from a common command language. Modeling languages provide a way of formulating interrelationships between variables in a way that permits the creation of simulation or "what if" models. As we noted earlier, many of the currently viable DSS Generators have evolved from these efforts. Early forms of "model management" seem to be evolving from enhancements to some modeling languages which permit a model of this type to be used for sensitivity testing or goal seeking by specifying target and flexibility variables.

The model management area also has the potential for bringing some of the contributions of artificial intelligence (AI) to bear on DSS. MYCIN, a system to support medical diagnosis, is based on "production rules" (in the AI sense) which play the role of models in performing analytic and decision guidance functions [15]. A more general characterization of "knowledge management" as a way of handling models and data has also been tentatively explored [7]. More recent work proposes the use of a version of semantic networks for model representation [17]. Though this latter work is promising, AI research has shown the semantic network approach to be relatively inefficient with today's technology. Usable capabilities in model management in the near future are more likely to evolve from modeling languages, expanded subroutine approaches, and in some cases, production rules.

ISSUES FOR THE FUTURE

At this stage in the development of the DSS area, issues, problems, and fruitful directions for further research/development are plentiful. At a task force meeting this summer, 30 researchers from 12 countries gathered to discuss the nature of DSS and to identify issues for the future. Their list, developed in group discussions over several days, was quite long [19]. The issues given here, phrased as difficult questions, seem to be the ones that must be dealt with quickly, lest the promise and potential benefits of DSS be diluted or seriously delayed.

What's a DSS? Earlier we noted that some skeptics regard DSS as "just another buzz word." This article has shown that there is a significant amount of content behind the label. The danger remains, however, that the bandwagon effect will outrun our ability to define and develop potential contributions of DSS. The market imperatives of the multibillion dollar information systems industry tend to generate pressures to create simple labels for intuitively good ideas. It happened in many cases (but not all, of course) with MIS. Some companies are still trying to live down the aftereffects of the over-promise-under-undelivery-disenchantment sequence from the MIS bandwagon of the late 60s. Eventually, there should evolve a set of minimal capabilities or characteristics which characterizes a DSS. In the short range, a partial solution is education—supplying managers with intellectual ammunition they can use in dealing with vendors. Managers should and must ask sharp, critical questions about the capabilities of any purported DSS, matching them against what is really needed.

What Is Really Needed?   After nearly two decades of advancement in information technology, the real needs of managers from an information system are not well understood. The issue is further complicated by the realization that managers' needs and the needs of other "knowledge workers" with which they interact are heavily interdependent. The DSS philosophy and approach has already shed some light on this issue by emphasizing "capabilities"—the ability for a manager to do things with an information system—rather than just "information needs," which too often implies data items and totals on a report.

Nevertheless, it is tempting to call for a hesitation in the development of DSS until decision making and related managerial activities are fully understood. Though logically appealing, such a strategy is not practical. Neither the managers who face increasingly complex tasks, nor the information systems industry, which has increasingly strong technology to offer, will be denied. They point out that a truly comprehensive theory of decision making has been pursued for years with minimum success.

A potential resolution of this problem is to develop and use DSS in a way that reveals what managers can and should receive for an information system. For example, one of Scott Morton's early suggestions was that the system be designed to capture and track the steps taken by managers in the process of making key decisions, both as an aid to the analysis of the process and as a potential training device for new managers.

The counterpart of the "needs" issue is the extent to which the system meets those needs, and the value of the performance increase that results. Evaluation of a DSS will be just as difficult—and important—as the evaluation of MIS has been. The direct and constant involvement of users, the ones in the best position to evaluate the systems, provides a glimmer of hope on this tough problem. Pursuit of these two tasks together may yield progress on both fronts with the kind of synergistic effect often sought from systems efforts. The iterative design approach and the three levels of technology afford the opportunity, if such a strategy is developed from the beginning.

Who Will Do It?   A series of organizational issues will revolve around roles and organizational placement of the people who will take the principal responsibility for the development of DSS. Initiative and guidance for DSS development frequently comes from the user area, not from the EDP/MIS area. Yet current technology still requires technical support from the information systems professional. The DSS builder may work for the vice president of finance, but the technical support role is still played by someone in the MIS department. To some extent, the demand for DSS supports the more general trend to distribute systems development efforts out of the MIS department into the user department. The difference is that many DSS software systems (generators) specifically attempt to directly reach the end user without involvement of the MIS group. The enlightened MIS administrator considers this a healthy trend and willingly supplies the required technical support and coordination. Less enlightened DP administrators often see it as a threat; the resulting political negotiation obviously limits the advancement of DSS development. Some companies have set up a group specifically charged with developing DSS-type applications. This strategy creates a team of "DSS Builders" who can develop the necessary skills in dealing with users, become familiar with the available technology, and define the steps in the development approach for DSS.

How Should It Be Done?   One of the pillars on which the success of DSS rests, is the iterative development or adaptive design approach. The 5–7 stage system development process and the system life-cycle concept have been the backbone of systems analysis for years. Most project management systems and approaches are based on it. The adaptive design approach, because it combines all the stages into one quick step which is repeated, will require a redefinition of system development milestones and a major modification of project management mechanisms. Since many traditional systems will not be susceptible to the iterative approach, we also need a way of deciding when an application should be developed in the new way instead of the traditional way. The outline of the approach described earlier is conceptionally straightforward for applications that require only personal support. It becomes more complicated for group or organizational support when there are multiple users. In short, DSS builders will need to develop a set of milestones, checkpoints, documentation strategies, and project management procedures for DSS applications, and recognize when they should be used.

How Much Can Be Done?   The final issue is a caveat dealing with the limitations of technical solutions to the complexity faced by managers and decision makers. As information systems professionals, we must be careful not to feel, or even allow others to feel, that we can develop or devise a technological solution to all the problems of management. Managers will always "deal with complexity in a state of perplexity"—it is the nature of the job. Information technology can, and is, making a major contribution to improving the effectiveness of people in this situation, but the solution will never be total. With traditional systems, we continually narrow the scope and definition of the system until we know it will do the job it is required to do. If the specification-design-construction-implementation process is done right, the system is a success, measured against its original objectives. With a DSS, the user and his systems capability are constantly pursuing the problem, but the underspecified nature of the problem insures that there will never be a complete solution. Systems analysts have always had a little trouble with humility, but the DSS process requires a healthy dose of modesty with respect to the ability of technology to solve all the problems of managers in organizations.

CONCLUSION

The Framework for Development described above has attempted to show the dimensions and scope of DSS in a way that will promote the further *development* of this highly promising type of information system.

1. The relationships between EDP, MIS, and DSS show that DSS is only one of several important technology substances for improving organizational performance, and that DSS development efforts must carefully integrate with these other systems.
2. The three levels of technology and the interrelationships between people that use them provide a context for organizing the development effort.
3. The iterative design approach shows that the ultimate goal of the DSS development effort is the installation of an *adaptive system* consisting of all three levels of technology and their users operating and adapting to changes over time.
4. The performance objectives show the types of decision making to be served by, and the types of support which should be built into DSS as it is developed.
5. The three technical capabilities illustrate that development efforts must provide the DSS with capabilities in dialog management, data management, and model management.
6. The issues discussed at the end of the paper identify some potential roadblocks which must be recognized and confronted to permit the continued development of DSS.

In closing, it should now be clear that DSS is more than just a buzz word, but we should be cautious about announcing a new era in information systems. Perhaps the best term is a "DSS Movement" as user organizations, information systems vendors, and researchers become aware of the field, its potential, and the many unanswered questions. Events and mechanisms in the DSS Movement include systems development experience in organizations, hardware/software developments by vendors, publishing activities to report experience and research, and conferences to provide a forum for the exchange of ideas among interested parties. With this article, *MIS Quarterly* contributes to the movement by launching a series of articles on DSS as announced in this issue by the senior editor, Gary Dickson.

It is clear that the momentum of the DSS Movement is building. With appropriate care and reasonable restraint, the coordinated efforts of managers, builders, toolsmiths, and researchers can converge in the development of a significant set of information systems to help improve the effectiveness of organizations and the people who work in them.

REFERENCES

1. ALTER, S. "A Taxonomy of Decision Support Systems." *Sloan Management Review,* Fall 1977, pp. 39–56.
2. _____. *Decision Support Systems: Current Practice and Continuing Challenges.* Reading, Mass.: Addison-Wesley Publishing, 1980.
3. ASHENHURST, R. L. "Curriculum Recommendations for Graduate Professional Programs in Information Systems." *ACM Communications,* May 1972, pp. 363–98.
4. BARBOSA, L. C., AND R. G. HIRKO. "Integration of Algorithmic Aids into Decision Support Systems." *MIS Quarterly,* March 1980, pp. 1–12.
5. BENNETT, J. "User-Oriented Graphics, Systems for Decision Support in Unstructured Tasks." In *User-Oriented Design of Interactive Graphics Systems,* ed. S. Treu. New York: Association for Computing Machinery, 1977, pp. 3–11.
6. BOEING COMPUTER SERVICES. c/o Mr. Park Thoreson, P.O. Box 24346, Seattle, Washington 98124.
7. BONEZEK, H.; C. W. HOSAPPLE; AND A. WHINSTON. "Evolving Roles of Models in Decision Support Systems." *Decision Sciences,* April 1980, pp. 337–56.
8. CARLSON, E. D.; J. BENNETT; G. GIDDINGS; AND P. MANTEY. "The Design and Evaluation of an Interactive Geo-Data Analysis and Display System." *Information Processing—74.* Amsterdam, Holland: North Holland Publishing Co., 1974.
9. CARLSON, E. D., AND J. A. SUTTON. "A Case Study of Non-Programmer Interactive Problem Solving." *IBM Research Report RJ1382.* San Jose, Calif., 1974.
10. CARLSON, E. D.; B. F. GRACE; AND J. A. SUTTON. "Case Studies of End User Requirements for Interactive Problem-Solving Systems." *MIS Quarterly,* March 1977, pp. 51–63.
11. CARLSON, E. D. "An Approach for Designing Decision Support Systems." *Proceedings, 11th Hawaii International Conference on Systems Sciences.* North Hollywood, Calif.: Western Periodicals Co., 1978, pp. 76–96.

12. CARLSON, E. D., AND W. METZ. "Integrating Dialog Management and Data Management." *IBM Research Report RJ2738.* San Jose, Calif., February 1, 1980.
13. CARLSON, E. D. "The User-Interface for Decision Support Systems." Unpublished working paper, IBM Research Laboratory, San Jose, Calif.
14. COURBON, J.; J. DRAGEOF; AND T. JOSE. "L'Approache Evolutive." *Information Et Gestion No. 103.* Grenoble, France: Institute d'Administration des Enterprises, January–February 1979, pp. 51–59.
15. DAVIS, R. "A DSS for Diagnosis and Therapy." *Data Base,* Winter 1977, pp. 58–72.
16. DZIDA, W.; S. HERDA; AND W. D. ITZFELDT. "User-Perceived Quality of Software Interactive Systems." *Proceedings, Third Annual Conference on Engineering (IEEE) Computer Society,* Long Beach, Calif., 1978, pp. 188–95.
17. ELAM, J.; J. HENDERSON; AND L. MILLER. "Model Management Systems: An Approach to Decision Support in Complex Organizations." *Proceedings, Conference on Information Systems.* Philadelphia: The Society for Management Information Systems, December 1980.
18. EXECUCOM SYSTEMS CORPORATION, P. O. Box 9758, Austin, Texas 78766.
19. FICK, G., AND R. H. SPRAGUE, JR., eds. *Decision Support Systems: Issues and Challenges.* Oxford, England: Pergamon Press, 1981.
20. GERRITY, T. P., JR. "Design of Man-Machine Decision Systems: An Application to Portfolio Management." *Sloan Management Review,* Winter 1971, pp. 59–75.
21. HAYES, R. H., AND R. L. NOLAND. "What Kind of Corporate Modeling Functions Best?" *Harvard Business Review,* May–June 1974, pp. 102–12.
22. HEAD, R. "Management Information Systems: A Critical Appraisal." *Datamation,* May 1967, pp. 22–28.
23. KEEN, P. G. W., AND M. S. SCOTT MORTON. *Decision Support Systems: An Organizational Perspective.* Reading, Mass.: Addison-Wesley Publishing, 1978.
24. KEEN, P. G. W., AND R. D. HACKATHORN. "Decision Support Systems and Personal Computing." Working Paper 79-01-03, Department of Decision Sciences, The Wharton School, The University of Pennsylvania, April 3, 1979.
25. KEEN, P. G. W. "Adaptive Design for DSS." *Database,* Fall 1980, pp. 15–25.
26. _____. "Decision Support Systems: A Research Perspective." In *Decision Support Systems: Issues and Challenges.* Oxford, England: Pergamon Press, 1981.
27. KROEBER, H. W.; H. J. WATSON; AND R. H. SPRAGUE, JR. "An Empirical Investigation and Analysis of the Current State of Information Systems Evolution." *Journal of Information and Management,* February 1980, pp. 35–43.
28. LITTLE, J. D. C. "Models and Managers: The Concept of a Decision Calculus." *Management Science,* April 1970, pp. B466–85.
29. MANTEY, P. E., AND E. D. CARLSON. "Integrated Geographic Data Bases: The GADS Experience." *IBM Research Report RJ2702.* IBM Research Division, San Jose, Calif. December 3, 1979.
30. NESS, D. N. "Decision Support Systems: Theories of Design." Presented at the Wharton Office of Naval Research Conference on Decision Support Systems, Philadelphia, Pa., November 4–7, 1975.

31. Scott, J. H. "The Management Science Opportunity: A Systems Development Management Viewpoint." *MIS Quarterly,* December 1978, pp. 59–61.

32. Scott Morton, M. S. *Management Decision Systems: Computer Based Support for Decision Making.* Cambridge, Mass.: Harvard University, Division of Research, 1971.

33. Simon, H. *The New Science of Management Decision.* New York: Harper & Row, 1960.

34. _____. "Cognitive Science: The Newest Science of the Artificial." *Cognitive Science* 4 (1980), pp. 33–46.

35. Society for Management Information Systems. *Proceedings of the Eleventh Annual Conference,* September 10–13, 1979, Chicago, pp. 45–56.

36. Sprague, R. H., and H. J. Watson. "MIS Concepts Part I." *Journal of Systems Management,* January 1975, pp. 34–37.

37. _____. "Model Management in MIS." *Proceedings, 7th National AIDS,* Cincinnati, Ohio, November 5, 1975, pp. 213–15.

38. _____. "A Decision Support Systems for Banks." *Omega—The International Journal of Management Science,* 1976, pp. 657–71.

39. _____. "Bit by Bit: Toward Decision Support Systems." *California Management Review,* Fall 1979, pp. 60–68.

40. Sprague, R. H. "Decision Support Systems—Implications for the Systems Analysts." In *Systems Analysis and Design: A Foundation for the 1980's.* New York: Elsevier North-Holland Publishing, 1980.

41. _____. "A Framework for Research on Decision Support Systems." In *Decision Support Systems: Issues and Challenges,* ed. G. Fick, and R. H. Sprague. Oxford, England: Pergamon Press, 1981.

42. Sutton, J. "Evaluation of a Decision Support System: A Case Study with the Office Products Division of IBM." *IBM Research Report FJ2214.* San Jose, Calif. 1978.

43. Sutton, J. A., and R. H. Sprague. "A Study of Display Generation and Management in Interactive Business Applications." *IBM Research Report No. RJ2392.* IBM Research Division, San Jose, Calif. November 9, 1978.

44. TYMSHARE. 20705 Valley Green Drive, Cupertino, California 95014.

45. Wagner, G. R. "DSS: Hypotheses and Interferences." Internal report. EXECUCOM Systems Corporation, Austin, Texas, 1980.

46. Will, Hart J. "Model Management Systems." In *Information Systems and Organizational Structure,* ed. E. Grochla and H. Szyperski. New York: Walter de Gruyter, 1975, pp. 467–83.

9 The Management Information and Decision Support (MIDS) System at Lockheed-Georgia*

George Houdeshel
Hugh J. Watson

INTRODUCTION

Senior executives at Lockheed-Georgia are hands-on users of the management information and decision support system (MIDS). It clearly illustrates that a carefully designed system can be an important source of information for top management. Consider a few examples of how the system is used:

- The president is concerned about employee morale which for him is a critical success factor. He calls up a display which shows employee contributions to company-sponsored programs such as blood drives, United Way, and savings plans. These are surrogate measures of morale, and, because they have declined, he becomes more sensitive to a potential morale problem.
- The vice president of manufacturing is interested in the production status of a C-5B aircraft being manufactured for the U.S. Air Force. He calls up a display which pictorially presents the location and assembly status of the plane and information about its progress relative to schedule. He concludes that the aircraft is on schedule for delivery.

* Source: Reprinted by special permission from the *MIS Quarterly*, vol. 11, no. 1, March 1987. Copyright 1987 by the Society for Information Management and the Management Information Systems Research Center at the University of Minnesota.

- The vice president of finance wants to determine whether actual cash flow corresponds with the amount forecasted. He is initially concerned when a $10 million unfavorable variance is indicated, but an explanatory note indicates that the funds are en route from Saudi Arabia. To verify the status of the payment, he calls the source of the information using the name and telephone number shown on the display and learns that the money should be in a Lockheed account by the end of the day.
- The vice president of human resources returns from an out-of-town trip and wants to review the major developments which took place while he was gone. While paging through the displays for the human resources area, he notices that labor grievances rose substantially. To learn more about the situation so that appropriate action can be taken, he calls the supervisor of the department where most of the grievances occurred.

These are not isolated incidents; other important uses of MIDS occur many times a day. They demonstrate that computerized systems can have a significant impact on the day-to-day functioning of senior executives.

The purpose of this article is to describe aspects of MIDS which are important to executives, information systems managers, and information systems professionals who are the potential participants in the approval design, development, operation, and use of systems similar to MIDS. As a starting point, we want to discuss MIDS in the context of various types of information systems (i.e., MIS, DSS, and EIS), because its positioning is important to understanding its hands-on use by senior Lockheed-Georgia executives. We will describe how it was justified and developed, because these are the keys to its success. While online systems are best seen in person to be fully appreciated, we will try to describe what an executive experiences when using MIDS and the kinds of information that are available. Any computer system is made possible by the hardware, software, personnel, and data used and these will be described. Then we will discuss the benefits of MIDS. An organization considering the development of a system like MIDS needs to focus on key factors of success, and we will describe those factors that were most important to MIDS' success. As a closing point of interest, future plans for the evolution of MIDS will be discussed.

MIDS IN CONTEXT

Management information systems (MIS) were the first attempt by information systems professionals to provide managers and other organizational personnel with the information needed to perform their jobs effectively and efficiently. While originators of the MIS concept initially had high hopes and expectations for MIS, in practice MIS largely came to represent an expanded set of structured reports and has had only a minimal impact on upper management levels [11].*

Decision support systems (DSS) were the next attempt to help management with its decision-making responsibilities. They have been successful to some extent, especially in regard to helping middle managers and functional area specialists such as financial planners and marketing researchers. However, their usefulness to top management has been primarily indirect. Middle managers and staff specialists may use a DSS to provide information for top management, but despite frequent claims of ease-of-use, top managers are seldom hands-on users of a DSS [4, 5].

With hindsight it is understandable why DSSs have not been used directly by senior executives. Many of the reasons are those typically given when discussing why managers do not use computers: poor keyboard skills, lack of training and experience in using computers, concerns about status, and a belief that hands-on computer use is not part of their job. Another set of reasons revolves around the tradeoff between simplicity and flexibility of use. Simpler systems tend to be less flexible while more flexible systems are usually more complex. Because DSSs are typically used to support poorly structured decision-making tasks, the flexibility required to analyze these decisions comes at the cost of greater complexity. Unless the senior executive is a "techie" at heart, or uses the system enough to master its capabilities, it is unlikely that the executive will feel comfortable using the system directly. Consequently, hands-on use of the DSS is typically delegated to a subordinate who performs the desired analysis.

Executive information systems (EIS), or executive support systems as they are sometimes called, are the least computerized attempt to help satisfy top management's information needs. These systems tend to have the following characteristics which differentiate them from MIS and DSS:

- They are used directly by top managers without the assistance of intermediaries.
- They provide easy online access to current information about the status of the organization.
- They are designed with management's critical success factors (CSF) in mind.
- They use state-of-the-art graphics, communications, and data storage and retrieval methods.

The limited reportings of EIS suggest that these types of systems can make top managers hands-on users of computer-based systems [2, 10, 12]. While a number of factors contribute to their success, one of the most important is ease of use. Because an EIS provides little analysis capabili-

---

* Bracketed numbers cite the references at the end of the chapter.

ties, it normally requires only a few, easy to enter keystrokes. Consequently, keyboard skills, previous training and experience in using computers, concerns about loss of status, and perceptions of how one should carry out job responsibilities are less likely to hinder system use.

MIDS is an example of an EIS. It is used directly by top Lockheed-Georgia managers to access online information about the current status of the firm. Great care, time, and effort goes into providing information that meets the special needs of its users. The system is graphics-oriented and draws heavily upon communications technology.

THE EVOLUTION OF MIDS

Lockheed-Georgia, a subsidiary of the Lockheed Corporation, is a major producer of cargo aircraft. Over 19,000 employees work at their Marietta, Georgia, plant. Their current major activities are production of the C-5B transport aircraft for the U.S. Air Force, Hercules aircraft for worldwide markets, and numerous modification and research programs.

In 1975, Robert B. Ormsby, then president of Lockheed-Georgia, first expressed an interest in the creation of an online status reporting system to provide information which was concise, timely, complete, easy to access, relevant to management's needs, and could be shared by organizational personnel. Though Lockheed's existing systems provided voluminous quantities of data and information, Ormsby thought them to be unsatisfactory for several reasons. It was difficult to quickly locate specific information to apply to a given problem. Reports often were not sufficiently current, leading to organizational units basing decisions on information which should have been the same but actually was not. This is often the case when different reports or the same report with different release dates are used. Little action was taken for several years as Ormsby and information services personnel waited for hardware and software to emerge which would be suitable for the desired type of system. In the fall of 1978, development of the MIDS system began.

The justification for MIDS was informal. No attempt was made to cost-justify its initial development. Ormsby felt that he and other Lockheed-Georgia executives needed the system and mandated its development. Over time, as different versions of MIDS were judged successful, authorization was given to develop enhanced versions. This approach is consistent with current thinking and research on systems to support decision making. It corresponds closely with the recommendation to view the initial system as a research and development project and to evolve later versions if the system proves to be successful [7]. It also is in keeping with findings that accurate, timely, and new kinds of information, an organizational champion, and managerial mandate are the factors which motivate systems development [6].

A number of key decisions were made early in the design of the system. First, an evolutionary design approach would be used. Only a limited number of displays would be created initially. Over time they would be modified or possibly deleted if they did not meet an information need. Additional screens would be added as needed and as MIDS was made available to a larger group of Lockheed-Georgia managers. Ease of use was considered to be of critical importance because of the nature of the user group. Most of the Lockheed-Georgia executives had all of the normal apprehensions about personally using terminals. In order to encourage hands-on use, it was decided to place a terminal in each user's office, to require a minimum number of keystrokes in order to call up any screen, and to make training largely unnecessary. Response time was to be fast and features were to be included to assist executives in locating needed information.

Bob Pittman was responsible for the system's development and he, in turn, reported to the vice president of finance. Pittman initially had a staff consisting of two people from finance and two from information services. The finance personnel were used because of their experience in preparing company reports and presentations to the corporate headquarters, customers, and government agencies. Their responsibility was to determine the system's content, screen designs, and operational requirements. The information services personnel were responsible for hardware selection and acquisition and software development.

Pittman and his group began by exploring the information requirements of Ormsby and his staff. This included determining what information was needed, in what form, at what level of detail, and when it had to be updated. Several approaches were used in making these determinations. Interviews were held with Ormsby and his staff. Their secretaries were asked about information requested of them by their superiors. The use of existing reports was studied. From these analyses emerged an initial understanding of the information requirements.

The next step was to locate the best data sources for the MIDS system. Two considerations guided this process. The first was to use data sources with greater detail than what would be included in the MIDS displays. Only by using data which had not already been filtered and processed could information be generated which the MIDS team felt would satisfy the information requirements. The second was to use data sources which had a perspective compatible with that of Ormsby and his staff. Multiple organizational units may have data seemingly appropriate for satisfying an information need, but choosing the best source or combination of sources requires care in order that the information provided is not distorted by the perspective of the organizational unit in which it originates.

The initial version of MIDS took six months to develop and allowed Ormsby to call up 31 displays. Over the past eight years, MIDS has evolved to where it now offers over 700 displays for 30 top executives and

40 operating managers. It has continued to be successful through many changes in the senior executive ranks, including the position of president. MIDS subsystems are currently being developed for middle managers in the various functional areas and MIDS-like systems are being implemented in several other Lockheed companies.

MIDS FROM THE USER'S PERSPECTIVE

An executive typically has little interest in the hardware or software used in a system. Rather, the dialog between the executive and the system is what matters. The dialog can be thought of as consisting of the command language by which the user directs the actions of the system, the presentation language through which the system provides the response, and the knowledge that the user must have in order to effectively use the system [1]. From a user's perspective, the dialog *is* the system, and, consequently, careful attention was given to the design of the dialog components in MIDS.

An executive gains access to MIDS through the IBM PC/XT on his or her desk. Entering a password is the only sign-on requirement, and every user has a unique password which allows access to an authorized set of displays. After the password is accepted, the executive is informed of any scheduled downtime for system maintenance. The user is then given a number of options. He can enter a maximum of four keystrokes and call up any of the screens that he is authorized to view, obtain a listing of all screens that have been updated, press the "RETURN/ENTER" key to view the major menu, access the on-line keyword index, or obtain a listing of all persons having access to the system.

The main menu and keyword index are designed to help the executive find needed information quickly. Figure 1 shows the main menu. Each subject area listed in the main menu is further broken down into additional menus. Information is available in a variety of subject areas, including by functional area, organizational level, and project. The user can also enter the first three letters of any keywords which are descriptive of the information needed. The system checks these words against the keyword index and lists all of the displays which are related to the user's request.

Information for a particular subject area is organized in a top-down fashion. This organization is used within a single display or in a series of displays. A summary graph is presented at the top of a screen or first in a series of displays, followed by supporting graphs, and then by tables and text. This approach allows executives to quickly gain an overall perspective while providing backup detail when needed. An interesting finding has been that executives prefer as much information as possible on a single display, even if it appears "busy," rather than having the same information spread over several displays.

FIGURE 1 The MIDS Main Menu

```
┌─────────────────────────────────────────────────────────┐
│                                                           │
│  OMNVO          MIDS MAJOR CATEGORY MENU                  │
│             ■  TO RECALL THIS DISPLAY AT ANY TIME         │
│                HIT 'RETURN-ENTER' KEY.                    │
│             ■  FOR LATEST UPDATES SEE S1.                 │
├───────────────────────────────┬───────────────────────────┤
│  A   MANAGEMENT CONTROL       │  M   MARKETING            │
│       MSI'S OBJECTIVES;        │       ASSIGNMENTS;        │
│       ORGANIZATION CHARTS;     │       PROSPECTS; SIGN-UPS;│
│       TRAVEL/AVAILABILITY/     │       PRODUCT SUPPORT;    │
│       EVENTS SCHED.            │       TRAVEL              │
│    CP CAPTURE PLANS INDEX      │                           │
│                                │                           │
│  B   C-58                      │  O   OPERATIONS           │
│       ALL PROGRAM ACTIVITIES   │       FACILITIES;         │
│                                │       MANUFACTURING;      │
│  C   HERCULES                  │       MATERIEL; PRODUCT   │
│       ALL PROGRAM ACTIVITIES   │       ASSURANCE & SAFETY  │
│                                │                           │
│  E   ENGINEERING               │  P   PROGRAM CONTROL      │
│       COST OF NEW BUSINESS;    │       FINANCIAL & SCHEDULE│
│       R&T                      │       PERFORMANCE         │
│                                │    MS MASTER SCHEDULING MENU│
│  F   FINANCIAL CONTROL         │                           │
│       BASIC FINANCIAL DATA;    │  S   SPECIAL ITEMS        │
│       COST REDUCTION; FIXED    │       DAILY DIARY; SPECIAL│
│       ASSETS; OFFSET;          │       PROGRAMS            │
│       OVERHEAD; OVERTIME;      │                           │
│       PERSONNEL                │                           │
│                                │                           │
│  H   HUMAN RESOURCES           │  U   UTILITY              │
│       CO-OP PROGRAM,           │       SPECIAL FUNCTIONS   │
│       EMPLOYEE STATISTICS      │       AVAILABLE           │
│       & PARTICIPATION          │                           │
└───────────────────────────────┴───────────────────────────┘
```

Executives tend to use MIDS differently. At one extreme are those who browse through displays. An important feature for them is the ability to stop the generation of a display with a single keystroke when it is not of further interest. At the other extreme are executives who regularly view a particular sequence of displays. To accommodate this type of system use, sequence files can be employed which allow executives to page through a series of displays whose sequence is defined in advance. Sequence files can either be created by the user, requested by the user and prepared by the MIDS staff, or offered by MIDS personnel after observing the user's viewing habits.

All displays contain a screen number, title, when it was last updated, the source(s) of the information presented, and a telephone number for the source(s). It also indicates the MIDS staff member who is responsible for maintaining the display. Every display has a backup person who is responsible for it when the primary person is on leave, sick, or unavailable for any reason. Knowing the information source and the identity of the responsible MIDS staff member is important when an executive has a question about a display.

Standards exist across the displays for the terms used, color codes, and graphic design. These standards help eliminate possible misinterpretations of the information provided. Standard definitions have also improved communications in the company.

The importance of standard definitions can be illustrated by the use of the word *signup*. In general, the term refers to a customer's agreement to buy an aircraft. However, prior to the establishment of a standard definition, it tended to be used differently by various organizational units. To marketing people, a signup was when a letter of intent to buy was received. Legal services considered it to be when a contract was received. Finance interpreted it as when a down payment was made. The standard definition of a signup now used is "a signed contract with a nonrefundable down payment." An on-line dictionary can be accessed if there is any question about how a term is defined.

Color is used in a standard way across all of the screens. The traffic light pattern is used for status: green is good, yellow is marginal, and red is unfavorable. Under budget or ahead of schedule is in green, on budget or on schedule is in yellow, over budget and behind schedule is in red. Bar graphs have a black background and yellow bars depict actual performance, cyan (light blue) is used for company goals and commitments to the corporate office, and magenta represents internal goals and objectives. Organization charts use different colors for the various levels of management. Special color combinations are used to accommodate executives with color differentiation problems, and all displays are designed to be effective with black and white hard copy output.

Standards exist for all graphic designs. Line charts are used for trends, bar charts for comparisons, and pie or stacked bar charts for parts of a whole. On all charts, vertical wording is avoided and abbreviations and acronyms are limited to those on an authorized list. All bar charts are zero at the origin to avoid distortions, scales are set in prescribed increments and are identical within a subject series, and bars that exceed the scale have numeric values shown. In comparisons of actual with predicted performance, bars for actual performance are always wider.

Comments are added to the displays to explain abnormal conditions, explain graphic depictions, reference related displays, and inform of pending changes. For example, a display may show that signups for May are three less than forecasted. The staff member who is responsible for the display knows, however, that a down payment from Peru for three aircrafts is en route and adds this information as a comment to the display. Without added comments, situations can arise which are referred to as "paper tigers," because they appear to require managerial attention though they actually do not. The MIDS staff believes that "transmitting data is not the same as conveying information" [8].

The displays have been created with the executives' critical success factors in mind. Some of the CSF measures, such as profits and aircrafts sold, are obvious. Other measures, such as employee participation in company-sponsored programs, are less obvious and reflect the MIDS staff's efforts to fully understand and accommodate the executives' information needs.

To illustrate a typical MIDS display, Figure 2 shows Lockheed-Georgia sales as of November 1986. It was accessed by entering F.3. The sources of the information and their Lockheed-Georgia telephone numbers are in the upper right-hand corner. The top graphs provide past history, current, and forecasted sales. The wider bars (in yellow) represent actual sales while budgeted sales are depicted by the narrower, (cyan) bars. Detailed, tabular information is provided under the graphs. An explanatory comment is given at the bottom of the display. The R and F in the bottom right-hand corner indicate that related displays can be found by paging in a reverse or forward direction.

Executives are taught to use MIDS in a 15-minute tutorial. For several reasons, no written instructions for the use of the system have ever been prepared. An objective for MIDS has been to make the system easy enough to use so that written instructions are unnecessary. Features such as menus and the keyword index make this possible. Another reason is that senior executives are seldom willing to take the time to read instructions. And most importantly, if an executive has a problem in using the system, the MIDS staff prefers to learn about the problem and to handle it personally.

FIGURE 2 Lockheed-Georgia Sales

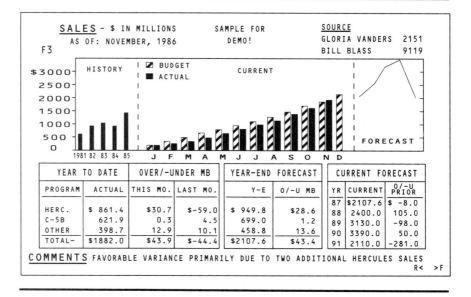

The IBM PC/XT on the executive's desk is useful for applications other than accessing MIDS displays. It can be used offline with any appropriate PC software. It is also the mechanism for tying the user through MIDS to other computer systems. For example, some senior executives and even more middle managers want access to outside reference services or internal systems with specific databases. Electronic messaging is the most common use of the IBM PC/XT's for other than MIDS displays. The executive need only request PROFS from within MIDS and the system automatically translates the user's MIDS password to a PROFS password and transfers the user from the DEC 780 VAX host to the IBM mainframe with PROFS. After using PROFS' electronic mail capabilities, the transfer back to MIDS is a simple two keystroke process.

THE COMPONENTS OF MIDS

A number of component parts are essential to the functioning of MIDS: hardware, software, MIDS personnel, and data sources.

Hardware

A microcomputer from Intelligent Systems Corporation was used for the initial version of MIDS. Each day MIDS personnel updated the floppy disks which stored the displays. As more executives were given access to MIDS, it became impractical to update each executive's displays separately, and the decision was made to store them centrally on a DEC 11/34 where they could be accessed by all users. Executives currently interact with MIDS through IBM PC/XT's tied to a DEC 780 VAX. Next year MIDS will be migrated to an IBM 3081 as part of Lockheed's plan to standardize around IBM equipment. Because an objective of MIDS was to reduce the amount of paper, the generation of hard copy output has always been minimized. The only printers are in the MIDS office and include four Printronix 300 (black and white, dot matrix) and Xerox 6500 (color copier, laser unit, with paper and transparencies) printers.

Software

At the time that work on MIDS began, appropriate software was not commercially available. Consequently, the decision was made to develop the software in-house. Even though commercial EIS software such as Command Center and Metaphor are now available, none of it has justified a switch from what has been developed by the MIDS staff.

The software is used for three important tasks: creating and updating the displays, providing information about the system's use and status, and maintaining system security.

Creating and Updating the Displays

Each display has an edit program tailored to fit its needs. Special edit routines have been developed for graph drawing, color changes, scale changes, roll-offs, calculations, or drawing special characters such as airplanes. These edit functions are then combined to create a unique edit program for each display. This approach allows MIDS personnel to quickly update the displays and differs from off-the-shelf software which requires the user to answer questions for all routines, regardless of whether they are needed.

The edit software has other attractive features. There are computer-generated messages to the information analyst advising of other displays which could be affected by changes to the one currently being revised. Color changes are automatically made to display when conditions become unfavorable. When the most recent period data is entered, the oldest period data is automatically rolled off of all graphs. The edit software has error checks for unlikely or impossible conditions.

Providing Information about the System's Use and Status

Daily reports are generated at night and are available the next morning for the MIDS staff to review. A daily log of system activity shows who requested what, when, and how. The log indicates everything but "why," and sometimes the staff even asks that question in order to better understand management's information needs. The log allows MIDS personnel to analyze system loads, user inquiry patterns, methods used to locate displays, utilization of special features, and any system and/or communication problems. Another report indicates the status of all displays, including the last time each display was updated, when the next update is scheduled, and who is responsible for the update. Yet another report lists all displays which have been added, deleted, or changed.

Weekly reports are generated on Sunday night and are available Monday morning for the MIDS staff. One report lists the previous week's users and the number of displays viewed by each executive. Another report lists the number of displays with the frequency of viewing by the president and his staff and others.

A number of reports are available on demand. They include an authorization matrix of users and terminals; a count of displays by major category and subsystem; a list of users by name, type of terminal, and system line number to the host computer; a list of displays in sequence; a list of display titles with their number organized by subject area; and a keyword exception report of available displays not referenced in the keyword file.

Maintaining System Security

Careful thought goes into deciding who has access to which displays. Information is made available unless there are compelling reasons why it should be denied. For example, middle managers might not be allowed to view strategic plans for the company. System access is controlled through a double security system. Users can call up only displays which they are authorized to view and then only from certain terminals. This security system helps protect against unauthorized users gaining access to the system and the unintentional sharing of restricted information. As an example of the latter situation, a senior executive might be allowed to view sensitive information in his office but be denied access to the information in a conference room or the office of lower management.

Personnel

The MIDS staff has grown from five to its current size of nine. Six of the staff members are classified as information analysts, two are computer analysts, and there is the manager of the MIDS group. The information analysts are responsible for determining the system's content, designing the screens, and keeping the system operational. Each information analyst is responsible for about 100 displays. Approximately 170 displays are updated daily by the MIDS staff. The computer analysts are responsible for hardware selection and acquisition and software development. While the two groups have different job responsibilities, they work together and make suggestions to each other for improving the system.

It is imperative that the information analysts understand the information that they enter into the system. Several actions are taken to ensure that this is the case. Most of the information analysts have work experience and/or training in the areas for which they supply information. They are encouraged to take courses which provide a better understanding of the users' areas. And they frequently attend functional area meetings, often serving as an important information resource.

Data

In order to provide the information needed, a variety of internal and external data sources must be used. The internal sources include transaction processing systems, financial applications, and human sources.

Some of the data can be transferred directly to MIDS from other computerized systems, while others must be rekeyed or entered for the first time. Access to computerized data is provided by in-house software and commercial software such as DATATRIEVE. External sources are very important and include data from external databases, customers, other Lockheed companies, and Lockheed's Washington, D.C., office.

MIDS relies on both hard and soft data. Hard data comes from sources such as transaction processing systems and provides "the facts." Soft data often comes from human sources and results in information which could not be obtained in any other way; it provides meaning, context, and insight to hard data.

BENEFITS OF MIDS

A variety of benefits are provided by MIDS: better information, improved communications, an evolving understanding of information requirements, a test-bed for system evolution, and cost reductions.

The information provided by MIDS has characteristics which are important to management. It supports decision making by identifying areas which require attention, providing answers to questions, and giving knowledge about related areas. It provides relevant information. Problem areas are highlighted and pertinent comments are included. The information is timely because displays are updated as important events occur. It is accurate because of the efforts of the MIDS staff, since all information is verified before it is made available.

MIDS has also improved communications in several ways. It is sometimes used to share information with vendors, customers, legislators, and others. MIDS users are able to quickly view the same information in the same format with the most current update. In the past, there were often disagreements, especially over the telephone, because executives were operating with different information. PROFS provides electronic mail. The daily diary announces major events as they occur.

Initially identifying a complete set of information requirements is difficult or impossible for systems which support decision making. The evolutionary nature of MIDS' development has allowed users to better understand and evolve their information requirements. Having seen a given set of information in a given format, an executive is often prompted to identify additional information or variations of formats that provide still better decision support.

The current system provides a test-bed for identifying and testing possible system changes. New state-of-the-art hardware and software can be compared with the current system in order to provide information for the evolution of MIDS. For example, a mouse-based system currently is being tested.

MIDS is responsible for cost savings in several areas. Many reports and graphs which were formerly produced manually are now printed from MIDS and distributed to non-MIDS users. Some requirements for special reports and presentation materials are obtained at less cost by modifying standard MIDS displays. Reports that are produced by other systems are summarized in MIDS and are no longer printed and distributed to MIDS users.

THE SUCCESS OF MIDS

Computer-based systems can be evaluated on the basis of cost/benefit, frequency of use, and user satisfaction considerations. Systems which support decision making, such as MIDS, normally do not lend themselves to a quantified assessment of their benefits. They do provide intangible benefits, however, as can be seen in the following example.

Lockheed-Georgia markets its aircrafts worldwide. In response to these efforts, it is common for a prospective buyer to call a company executive to discuss a proposed deal. Upon receipt of a phone call, the executive can call up a display which provides the following information: the aircraft's model and quantity; the dollar value of the offer; the aircraft's availability for delivery; previous purchases by the prospect; the sales representative's name and exact location for the week; and a description of the status of the possible sale. Such a display is shown in Figure 3. All of this

FIGURE 3 The Status of a Sale

```
M5  PERU                                   SOURCE  BUD LAWLER   5431
    REP: DICK SIGLER                               JIM CERTAIN  2265

          MON    TUE    WED    THR    FRI    SAT    SUN
REP LOCATION              CARACAS, VENEZUELA---------
IF AWAY

FORECAST - THREE L-100-30s          PREV. HERC. BUY---8

NEXT EVENT--                  AS OF TODAY: MEETINGS CONTINUE AMONG
  FINALIZE FINANCING          POTENTIAL LENDING INSTITUTIONS,
                              INSURERS, AND GELAC'S INTERNATIONAL
KEY PERSON -- CERTAIN         MARKETING/FINANCE/LEGAL TEAM TO
                              DISCUSS REQUIREMENTS AND CONDITIONS
SIGN UP -- NEXT MONTH         FOR FINANCING. GELAC REPRESENTATIVES
                              WILL BE IN LIMA MONDAY TO LAY
PROBABILITY -- GOOD           GROUNDWORK FOR FINAL NEGOTIATIONS. NO
                              PROBLEMS EXPECTED.
ROM VALUE -- $60M

A/C DELIVERY: 4TH QTR
```

information is available without putting the prospective customer on hold, transferring the call to someone else, or awaiting the retrieval of information from a file.

When a user can choose whether or not to use a system, frequency of use can be employed as a measure of success. Table 1 presents data on how the number of users and displays and the mean number of displays viewed per day by each executive has changed over time. The overall picture is one of increased usage; currently an average of 5.5 screens are viewed each day by the 70 executives who have access to MIDS. Unlike some systems which are initially successful but quickly fade away, the success of MIDS has increased over time.

Frequency of use can be a very imperfect measure of success. The MIDS group recognizes that a single display which has a significant impact on decision making is much more valuable than many screens which are paged through with passing interest. Consequently, frequency of use is used as only one indicator of success.

MIDS personnel have felt no need to conduct formal studies of user satisfaction. The data on system usage and daily contact with MIDS users provide ample information on how satisfied users are with MIDS. User satisfaction can be illustrated by the experience of Paul Frech who was vice president of operations in 1979. When MIDS was offered to him, he had little interest in the system because he had well-established channels for the flow of information to support his job responsibilities. Shortly afterward, Frech was promoted to the corporate headquarters staff in California. When he was again promoted to become the president of Lockheed-Georgia, MIDS had become a standard for executive information and he was reintroduced to the system. He has stated:

> I assumed the presidency of the Lockheed-Georgia Company in June 1984, and the MIDS system had been in operation for some time prior to that. The MIDS

TABLE 1   MIDS Users, Displays, and Displays Viewed

Year	Number of Users	Number of Displays	Mean Number of Displays Viewed, per User per Day
1979	12	69	*
1980	24	231	*
1981	27	327	*
1982	31	397	3.0
1983	31	441	4.0
1984	49	620	4.2
1985	70	710	5.5

* Figures not available

system enabled me to more quickly evaluate the current conditions of each of our operational areas and, although I had not been an advocate of executive computer systems, the ease and effectiveness of MIDS made it an essential part of my informational sources.

Because Frech and other senior executives have come to rely on MIDS, middle managers at Lockheed-Georgia and executives at other Lockheed companies want their own versions of MIDS. Within Lockheed-Georgia there is the feeling that "if the boss likes it, I need it." Currently, MIDS personnel are helping middle functional area managers develop subsystems of MIDS and are assisting other Lockheed companies with the development of similar systems.

KEYS TO THE SUCCESS OF MIDS

Descriptions of successful systems are useful to people responsible for conceptualizing, approving, and developing similar systems. Perhaps even more important are insights about what makes a system a success. We will identify the keys to MIDS' success here, but it should be remembered that differences exist among executive information systems, organizations, and possibly the factors that lead to success.

1. *A committed senior executive sponsor.* Ormsby served as the organizational champion for MIDS. He wanted a system like MIDS, committed the necessary resources, participated in its creation, and encouraged its use by others.

2. *Carefully defined system requirements.* Several considerations governed the design of the system. It had to be custom-tailored to meet the information needs of its users. Ease-of-use, an absolutely essential item to executives who were wary of computers, was critical. Response time had to be fast. The displays had to be updated quickly and easily as conditions changed.

3. *Carefully defined information requirements.* There has been a continuing effort to understand management's information requirements. Displays have been added, modified, and deleted over time. Providing information relevant to managements' CSFs has been of paramount importance.

4. *A team approach to systems development.* The staff that developed, operates, and evolves MIDS combines information systems skills and functional area knowledge. The computer analysts are responsible for the technical aspects of the system while the information analysts are responsible for providing the information needed by management. This latter responsibility demands that the information analysts know the business and maintain close contact with information sources and users.

5. *An evolutionary development approach.* The initial version of MIDS successfully addressed the most critical information needs of the company president and strengthened his support for the system. There is little doubt that developing a fully integrated system for a full complement of users would have resulted in substantial delays and less enthusiasm for the system. Over the years, MIDS has expanded and evolved as more users have been provided access to MIDS, management's information requirements have changed, better ways to analyze and present information have been discovered, and improved computer technology has become integrated into the system.

6. *Careful computer hardware and software selection.* The decision to proceed with the development of MIDS was made when good color terminals at reasonable prices became available. At that time graphics software was very limited and it was necessary to develop the software for MIDS in-house. The development of MIDS could have been postponed until hardware and software with improved performance at reduced cost appeared, but this decision would have delayed providing management with the information needed. Also affecting the hardware selection was the existing hardware within the organization and the need to integrate MIDS into the overall computing architecture. While it is believed that excellent hardware and software decisions have been made for MIDS, different circumstances at other firms may lead to different hardware and software configurations.

FUTURE PLANS FOR MIDS

MIDS continues to evolve along the lines mentioned previously: expansion through subsystems to lower organizational levels, expansion to other Lockheed companies, and hardware changes to make MIDS more IBM compatible. Improvements in display graphics are also planned through the use of a video camera with screen digitizing capabilities. A pilot program for voice input is currently being sponsored by the vice president of engineering.

A number of other enhancements are also projected. A future version of MIDS may automatically present variance reports when actual conditions deviate by more than user-defined levels. Audio output may supplement what is presented by the displays. The system may contain artificial intelligence components. There may be large screen projection of MIDS displays with better resolution than is currently available. The overriding objective is to provide Lockheed-Georgia management with the information they need to effectively and efficiently carry out their job responsibilities.

REFERENCES

1. BENNETT, J. "User-Oriented Graphics, Systems for Decision Support in Unstructured Tasks." In *User-Oriented Design of Interactive Graphics Systems,* ed. S. Treu., New York: Association for Computing Machinery, 1977, pp. 3–11.

2. DeLong, D. W., and J. F. Rockart. "Identifying the Attributes of Successful Executive Support System Implementation." *Transactions from the Sixth Annual Conference on Decision Support Systems,* J. Fedorowicz (ed.). Washington, D.C., April 21–24, 1986, pp. 41–54.

3. El Sawy, O. A. "Personal Information Systems for Strategic Scanning in Turbulent Environments: Can the CEO Go On-Line?" *MIS Quarterly* 9, no. 1 (March 1985), pp. 53–60.

4. Friend, D. "Executive Information Systems: Success, Failure, Insights and Misconceptions." *Transactions from the Sixth Annual Conference on Decision Support Systems,* J. Fedorowicz (ed.). Washington, D.C., April 21–24, 1986, pp. 35–40.

5. Hogue, J. T., and H. J. Watson. "An Examination of Decision Makers' Utilization of Decision Support System Output." *Information and Management* 8, no. 4 (April 1985), pp. 205–12.

6. Hogue, J. T., and H. J. Watson. "Management's Role in the Approval and Administration of Decision Support Systems." *MIS Quarterly* 7, no. 2 (June 1983), pp. 15–23.

7. Keen, P. G. W. "Value Analysis: Justifying Decision Support Systems." *MIS Quarterly* 5, no. 1 (March 1981), pp. 1–16.

8. McDonald, E. "Telecommunications." *Government Computer News,* February 28, 1986, p. 44.

9. Rockart, J. F. "Chief Executives Define Their Own Data Needs." *Harvard Business Review* 57, no. 2 (January–February 1979), pp. 81–93.

10 Expert Systems: The Next Challenge for Managers*

Fred L. Luconi
Thomas W. Malone
Michael Scott Morton

Winston defines artificial intelligence (AI) as "the study of ideas which enable computers to do the things that make people seem intelligent" [1].** AI systems attempt to accomplish this by dealing with qualitative as well as quantitative information, ambiguous and "fuzzy" reasoning, and rules of thumb that give good but not always optimal solutions. Another way to characterize artificial intelligence is not in terms of what it attempts to do, but in terms of the programming techniques and philosophies that have evolved from it. Specific AI techniques such as "frames" and "rules" allow programmers to represent knowledge in ways that are often much more flexible and much more natural for humans to deal with than the algorithmic procedures used in traditional programming languages.

There are at least three areas in which AI, in its current state of development, appears to have promising near-term applications: robotics, natural language understanding, and expert systems. In this article, we will focus on the realistic potential for the use of expert systems in business. To emphasize our main point about appropriate ways of using these systems, we will exaggerate a distinction between expert systems, as they are often

** Bracketed numbers cite the references at the end of the chapter.

conceived, and a variation of expert systems, which we will call expert support systems.

WHAT DO EXPERT SYSTEMS DO?

Preserve and Disseminate Scarce Expertise

Expert systems techniques can be used to preserve and disseminate scarce expertise by encoding the relevant experience of an expert and making this expertise available as a resource to the less experienced person. Schlumberger Corporation uses its "Dipmeter Advisor" to access the interpretive abilities of a handful of their most productive geological experts and to make it available to their field geologists all over the world [2]. The program takes oil well log data about the geological characteristics of a well and makes inferences about the probable location of oil in that region.

Solve Problems Thwarting Traditional Programs

Expert systems can also be used to solve problems that thwart traditional programming techniques. For example, an early expert system in practical use today is known as XCON. Developed at Digital Equipment Corporation in a joint effort with Carnegie-Mellon University, XCON uses some 3,300 rules and 5,500 product descriptions to configure the specific detailed components of VAX and other computer systems in response to the customers' overall orders. The system first determines what, if any, substitutions and additions have to be made to the order so that it is complete and consistent. It then produces a number of diagrams showing the electrical connections and room layout for the 50 to 150 components in a typical system [3].

This application was attempted unsuccessfully several times using traditional programming techniques before the AI effort was initiated. The system has been in daily use now for over four years and the savings have been substantial, not only in terms of saving the technical editor time, but also in ensuring that no component is missing at installation time—an occurrence that delays the customer's acceptance of the system [4].

WHAT ARE EXPERT SYSTEMS?

With these examples in mind, we define expert systems as *computer programs that use specialized symbolic reasoning to solve difficult problems well*. In other words, expert systems (1) use specialized knowledge about a particular problem area (such as geological analysis or computer configuration), rather than just general purpose knowledge that would apply to all problems; (2) use symbolic (and often qualitative) reasoning, rather than just numerical calculations; and (3) perform at a level of competence that is better than that of nonexpert humans.

Expert systems can, of course, include extensive numerical calculations; but a computer program that uses *only* numerical techniques (such as a complex optimization program) would not ordinarily be called an "expert system." The kinds of nonnumerical symbolic knowledge that expert systems use include component/subcomponent relationships and qualitative rules about causal factors.

One of the most important ways in which expert systems differ from traditional computer applications is in their use of heuristic reasoning. Traditional applications employ algorithms—that is, precise rules that, when followed, lead to the correct conclusion. For example, the amount of a payroll check for an employee is calculated according to a precise set of rules. Expert systems, in contrast, often attack problems that are too complex to be solved perfectly; to do this, they use heuristic techniques that provide good but not necessarily optimum answers.

In some ways, of course, all computer programs are algorithms in that they provide a complete set of specifications for what the computer will do. Heuristic programs, however, usually search through alternatives using "rules of thumb," rather than guaranteed solution techniques. A program might consider many different types of geological formations before deciding which type best explains the data observed in a particular case.

WHAT ARE EXPERT SUPPORT SYSTEMS?

While expert support systems and expert systems use the same technique, expert support systems help *people* (the emphasis is on people) solve a much wider class of problems. In other words, *expert support systems are computer programs that use specialized symbolic reasoning to help people solve difficult problems well.* This is done by pairing the human with the expert system in such a way that the expert system provides some of the knowledge and reasoning steps, while the human provides overall problem-solving direction as well as specific knowledge not incorporated in the system. Some of this knowledge can be thought of beforehand and made explicit when it is encoded in the expert system. However, much of the knowledge may be imprecise and will remain below the level of consciousness, to be recalled to the conscious level of the decision maker only when it is triggered by the evolving problem context.

COMPONENTS OF EXPERT SYSTEMS

To understand how expert systems (and expert support systems) are different from traditional computer applications, it is important to understand the components of a typical expert system (see Figure 1). In addition

FIGURE 1   Expert Systems Architecture

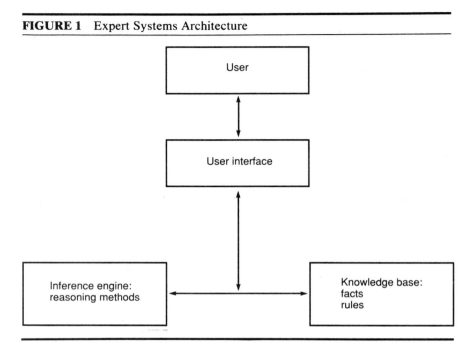

to the *user interface,* which allows the system to communicate with a human user, a typical expert system also has (1) a *knowledge base* of facts and rules related to the problem and (2) a set of reasoning methods—an *"inference engine"*—that interacts with the information in the knowledge base to solve the problem. As these two components are separate, it makes it much easier to change the system as the problem changes or becomes better understood. New rules can be added to the knowledge base in such a way that all the old facts and reasoning methods can still be used. Figure 1 shows in detail the elements of the expert systems architecture.

Knowledge Base

To flexibly use specialized knowledge for many different kinds of problems, AI researchers have developed a number of new "knowledge representation" techniques. Using these techniques to provide structure for a body of knowledge is still very much an art and is practiced by an emerging group of professionals sometimes called "knowledge engineers." Knowledge engineers in this field are akin to the systems analysts of data-processing (DP) applications. They work with the "experts" and draw out the relevant expertise in a form that can be encoded in a computer program. Three of the most important techniques for encoding this knowledge are (1) production rules, (2) semantic networks, and (3) frames.

Production Rules. Production rules are particularly useful in building systems based on heuristic methods [5]. These are simple "if-then" rules that are often used to represent the empirical consequences of a given condition or the action that should be taken in a given situation. For example, a medical diagnosis system might have a rule like:

> If: (1) The patient has a fever, and
> (2) The patient has a runny nose,
> Then: (3) It is very likely (.9) that the patient has a cold.

A computer configuration system might have a rule like:

> If: (1) There is an unassigned single port disk drive, and
> (2) There is a free controller,
> Then: (3) Assign the disk drive to the controller port.

Semantic Networks. Another formalism that is often more convenient than production rules for representing certain kinds of relational knowledge is called "semantic networks" or "semantic nets." To apply the rule about assigning disk drives, for example, a system would need to know what part numbers correspond to single port disk drives, controllers, and so forth. Figure 2 shows how this knowledge might be represented in a network of "nodes" connected by "links" that signify which classes of components are subsets of other classes.

FIGURE 2 Semantic Network

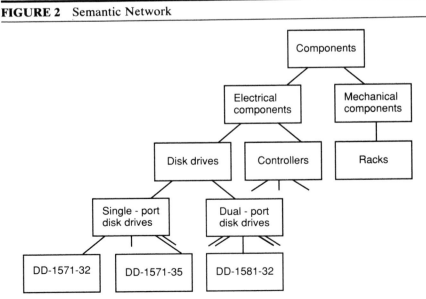

Frames.   In many cases, it is convenient to gather into one place a number of different kinds of information about an object. Figure 3 shows how several dimensions (such as length, width, and power requirements) that describe electrical components might be represented as different "slots" in a "frame" about electrical components. Unlike traditional records in a database, frames often contain additional features, such as "default values" and "attached procedures." For instance, if the default value for voltage requirement of an electrical component is 110 volts, then the system would infer that a new electrical component required 110 volts unless explicit information to the contrary was provided. An attached procedure might automatically update the "volume" slot, whenever "length," "height," or "width" is changed (see Figure 3).

These three knowledge representation techniques—production rules, semantic networks, and frames—have considerable power in that they permit us to capture knowledge in a way that can be exploited by the "inference engine" to produce good, workable answers to the questions at hand.

Inference Engine

The inference engine contains the reasoning methods that might be used by human problem solvers for attacking problems. As these are separate from the knowledge base, either the inference engine or the knowledge base can be changed relatively independently of the other. Two reasoning methods often employed with production rules are *forward chaining* and *backward chaining*.

FIGURE 3   Frame

Electrical Component	
Part no.	
Length	
Width	
Height	
Volume	
Voltage	

Forward Chaining.   Imagine that we have a set of production rules like those shown in Figure 4 for a personal financial planning expert system. Imagine also that we know the current client's tax bracket is 50 percent, his liquidity is greater than $100,000, and he has a high tolerance for risk. By forward chaining through the rules, one at a time, the system could infer that exploratory oil and gas investments should be recommended for this client. With a larger rule base, many other investment recommendations might be deduced as well.

Backward Chaining.   Now imagine that we want to know only whether exploratory oil and gas investments are appropriate for a particular client, and we are not interested in any other investments at the moment. The system can use exactly the same rule base to answer this specific question more efficiently by backward chaining through the rules (see Figure 4). With backward chaining, the system starts with a goal (e.g., "show that this client needs exploratory oil and gas investments") and asks at each stage what subgoals it would need to reach to achieve this goal. Here, to conclude that the client needs exploratory oil and gas investments, we can use the third rule (indicated in Figure 4) if we know that risk tolerance is high (which we already do know) and that a tax shelter is indicated. To conclude that a tax shelter is recommended, we have to find another rule

---

FIGURE 4   Inference Engine

Forward Chaining

If: Tax bracket = 50%
        and liquidity is greater than $100,000
Then: A tax shelter is indicated.

If: A tax shelter is indicated and risk tolerance is low
Then: Recommend developmental oil and gas investments.

If: A tax shelter is indicated and risk tolerance is high
Then: Recommend exploratory oil and gas investments.

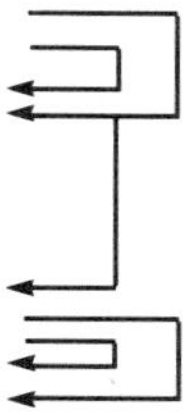

Backward Chaining (Subgoaling)

What about exploratory oil and gas?

If: Tax bracket = 50%
        and liquidity is greater than $100,000
Then: A tax shelter is indicated.

If: A tax shelter is indicated and risk tolerance is low
Then: Recommend developmental oil and gas investments.

If: A tax shelter is indicated and risk tolerance is high
Then: Recommend exploratory oil and gas investments.

(in this case, the first one) and then check whether its conditions are satisfied. In this case, they are, so our goal is achieved: we know we can recommend exploratory oil and gas investments to the client.

Keeping these basic concepts in mind, we now turn to a framework that puts expert systems and expert support systems into a management context.

THE FRAMEWORK FOR EXPERT SUPPORT SYSTEMS

The framework developed in this section begins to allow us to identify those classes of business problems that are appropriate for data processing, decision support systems, expert systems, and expert support systems. In addition, we can clarify the relative contributions of humans and computers in the various classes of applications.

This framework extends the earlier work of Gorry and Scott Morton [6], in which they relate Herbert Simon's seminal work on structured vs. unstructured decision making [7] to Robert Anthony's strategic planning, management control, and operational control [8]. Figure 5 presents Gorry and Scott Morton's framework. They argued that to improve the quality of

FIGURE 5   The Original Information Systems Framework

Information System: A Framework

	Operational Control	Management Control	Strategic Planning
Structured	Accounts receivable	Budget analysis-Engineered cost	Tanker fleet mix
	Order entry	Short-term forecasting	Warehouse and factory location
	Inventory control		
Semi -Structure	Production scheduling	Variance analyis-Overall budget	Mergers and acquisitions
	Cash management	Budget preparation	New product planning
Unstructured	PERT/ COST systems	Sales and production	R&D planning

decisions, the manager must seek not only to match the type and quality of information and its presentation to the category of decision but he or she must also choose a system that reflects the degree of the problem's structure.

In light of the insights garnered from the field of artificial intelligence, Figure 6 shows how we can expand and rethink the structured/ unstructured dimension of the original framework. Simon separated decision making into three phases: intelligence, design, and choice [9]. A structured decision is one where all three phases are fully understood and "computable" by the human decision maker. As a result, the decision is programmable. In an unstructured decision, one or more of these phases are not fully understood.

For business purposes, we can extend this distinction by taking Alan Newell's insightful categorization of problem solving, which consists of goals and constraints, state space, search control knowledge, and operators [10]. We relabel and regroup these problem characteristics into four categories (see Figure 6):

1. *Data.* The dimensions and values necessary to represent the state of the world that is relevant to the problem (i.e., the "state space");

FIGURE 6 Problem Types

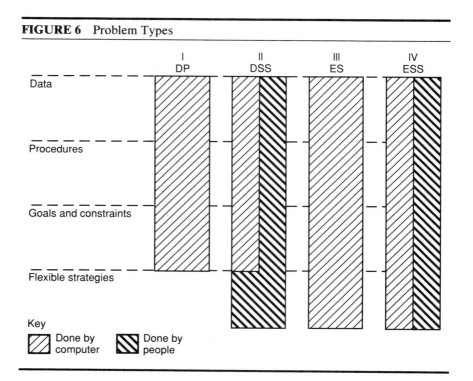

2. *Procedures.*   The sequence of steps (or "operators") used in solving the problem;

3. *Goals and constraints.*   The desired results of problem solving and the constraints on what can and cannot be done; and

4. *Strategies.*   The flexible strategies used to decide which procedures to apply to achieve goals (i.e., the "search control knowledge").

For some structured problems, we can apply a standard procedure (i.e., an algorithm or formula) and proceed directly to a conclusion with no need for flexible problem-solving strategies. For example, we can use standard procedures to compute withholding taxes and prepare employee paychecks, and we can use the classical formula for "economic order quantity" to solve straightforward inventory control problems.

In other less structured problems, no straightforward solution techniques are known. Here, solutions can often be found only by trial and error—that is, by trying a number of possibilities until an acceptable one is found. For instance, for a manager to determine which of three sales strategies to use for a new product, he or she might want to explore the probable consequences of each for advertising expenses, sales force utilization, revenue, and so forth. We will discuss the range of these different types of problems and the appropriate kinds of systems for each.

Type I Problems: Data Processing

A fully structured problem is one in which all four elements of the problem are structured: we have well-stated goals, we can specify the input data needed, there are standard procedures by which a solution may be calculated, and there is no need for complex strategies for generating and evaluating alternatives. Fully structured problems are computable and one can decide if such computation is justifiable given the amount of time and computing resources involved.

Such problems are well suited to the use of conventional programming techniques in that virtually everything about the problem is well defined. In effect, the expert (i.e., the analyst/programmer) has already solved the problem. He or she must only sequence the data through the particular program. Figure 6 represents pictorially the class of decision problems that can be solved economically using conventional programming techniques. This class is referred to as Type 1 Problems—that is, problems historically thought to be suited for data processing.

It is interesting to note that the economics of conventional programming are being fundamentally altered with the provision of new tools such as an "analyst's workbench" [11]. These tools include professional workstations used by the systems analyst first to develop flowchart representations of the problem and then to move automatically to testable running code. The more advanced stations use AI techniques, thereby turning these new techniques into tools to make old approaches more effective in classical DP application areas.

Type II Problems: Decision Support Systems

As we move away from problems that are fully structured, we begin to deal with many of the more complicated problems organizations have to grapple with each day. These are cases where standard procedures are helpful but not sufficient by themselves, where the data may be incompletely represented, and where the goals and constraints are only partially understood. Traditional data processing systems do not solve these problems. Fortunately, in these cases, the computer can perform the well-understood parts of the problem solving, while, at the same time, humans use their goals, intuition, and general knowledge to formulate problems, modify and control the problem solving, and interpret the results. As Figure 6 shows, human users may provide or modify data, procedures, or goals, and they may use their knowledge of all these factors to decide on problem-solving strategies.

In many of the best-known decision support systems [12], the computer applies standard procedures to certain highly structured data but relies on human users to decide which procedures are appropriate in a given situation and whether a given result is satisfactory. Investment managers, for instance, who used the portfolio management system (PMS) [13] did not rely on the computer for either making final decisions about portfolio composition or deciding on which procedures to use for analysis: they used the computer to execute the procedures they felt were appropriate, say for calculating portfolio diversity and expected returns. In the end, the managers themselves proposed alternative portfolios and decided whether a given diversification or return was acceptable. Many people who use spreadsheet programs today for what-if analyses follow a similar flexible strategy of proposing an action, letting the computer predict its consequences, and then deciding what action to propose next.

Type III Problems: Expert Systems

We call the problems where essentially all the relevant knowledge for flexible problem solving can be encoded Type III Problems: the systems that solve them are expert systems. Using AI programming techniques like production rules and frames, expert systems are able to encode some of the same kinds of goals, heuristics, and strategies that people use in solving problems but that have previously been very difficult to use in computer programs. These techniques make it possible to design systems that don't just follow standard procedures, but instead use flexible problem-solving strategies to explore a number of possible alternatives before picking a solution. A medical diagnosis program, for example, may consider many different possible diseases and disease combinations before finding one that adequately explains the observed symptoms.

For some cases, like the XCON system, these techniques can capture almost all of the relevant knowledge about the problem. As of 1983, less than 1 out of every 1,000 orders configured by XCON was misconfigured because of missing or incorrect rules. (Only about 10 percent of the orders had to be corrected for any reason at all and almost all of these errors were due to missing descriptions of rarely used parts [14].)

It is instructive to note, however, that even with XCON, which is probably the most extensively tested system in commercial use today, new knowledge is continually being added and human editors still check every order the system configures. As the developers of XCON remark: "There is no more reason to believe now than there was [in 1979] that [XCON] has all the knowledge relevant to its configuration task. This, coupled with the fact that [XCON] deals with an ever-changing domain, implies its development will never be finished [15]."

If XCON, which operates in the fairly restricted domain of computer order configuration, never contained all the knowledge relevant to its problem, it appears much less likely that we will ever be able to codify all the knowledge needed for less clearly bounded problems like financial analysis, strategic planning, and project management.

In all of these cases, there is a vast amount of knowledge that is *potentially* relevant to the problem solution: the financial desirability of introducing a proposed new product may depend on the likelihood and nature of a competitor's response; the success of a strategic plan may depend as much on the predispositions of the chief executive as it does on the financial merit of the plan; and the best assignment of people to tasks in a project may depend on very subtle evaluations of people's competence and motivation. While it is often possible to formalize and represent any *specific* set of these factors, there is an unbounded number of such factors that may, in some circumstances, become important. Even in what might appear to be a fairly bounded case of job-shop scheduling, often there are many continually changing and possibly implicit constraints on what people, machines, and parts are needed and available for different steps in a manufacturing process [16]. What this suggests is that for many of the problems of practical importance in business, we should focus our attention on designing systems that *support* expert users, rather than on replacing them.

Type IV Problems: Expert Support Systems

Even where important kinds of problem-solving knowledge cannot feasibly be encoded, it is still possible to use expert systems techniques. (This dramatically extends the capabilities of computers beyond previous technologies such as DP and DSS.) What is important, in these cases, is to design expert support systems with very good and deeply embedded "user interfaces" that enable their human users to easily inspect and control the problem-solving process (see Figure 6). In other words, a good expert support system should be both *accessible* and *malleable*. Many expert support systems make their problem solving accessible to users by providing explanation capabilities. For example, the MYCIN medical diagnosis program can explain to a doctor at any time why it is asking for a given piece of information or what rules it used to arrive at a given conclusion. For a system to be malleable, users should be able to easily change data, procedures, goals, or strategies at any important point in the problem-solving process. Systems with this capability are still rare, but an early version of the Dipmeter Advisor suggests how they may be developed [17]. The advisor is unable by itself to automatically detect certain kinds of complex geological patterns. Instead it graphically displays the basic data and lets human experts detect the patterns themselves. The human experts then indicate the results of their analysis, and the system proceeds using this information.

An even more vivid example of how a system can be made accessible and malleable is provided by the Steamer Program, which teaches people how to reason in order to operate a steam plant [18]. This system has colorful graphic displays of the schematic flows in the simulated plant, the status of different valves and gauges, and the pressures in different places. Users of the system can manipulate these displays (using a mouse pointing device) to control the valves, temperatures, and so forth. The system continually updates its simulation results and expert diagnostics based on these user actions.

SUMMARY OF FRAMEWORK

This framework helps clarify a number of issues. First, it highlights, as did the original Gorry and Scott Morton framework, the importance of matching system type to problem type. The primary practical points made in the original framework were that traditional DP technologies should not be used for semistructured and unstructured problems where new DSS technologies were more appropriate; and secondly that interactive human/computer use opened up an extended class of problems where computers could be exploited. Again, the most important practical point to be made is twofold: first, "pure" expert systems should not be used for partially understood problems where expert support systems are more appropriate; and second, expert systems techniques can be used to dramatically extend the capabilities of traditional decision support systems.

Figure 7 shows, in an admittedly simplified way, how we can view expert support systems as the next logical step in each of two somewhat separate progressions. On the left side of the figure, we see the DSS developed out of a practical recognition of the limits of DP for helping real human beings solve complex problems in actual organizations. The right side of the figure reflects a largely independent evolution that took place in computer science research laboratories. This evolution grew out of a recognition of the limits of traditional computer science techniques for solving the kinds of complex problems that people are able to solve. We are now at the point where these two separate progressions can be united to help solve a broad range of important practical problems.

THE BENEFITS OF ESS TO MANAGERS

The real importance of ESS lies in the ability of these systems to harness and make full use of our scarcest resource: the talent and experience of key members of the organization. There are considerable benefits in capturing the expert's experience and making it available to those in an organization who are less knowledgeable about the subject in question. As organizations and their problems become more complex, management can benefit from initiating prototypes ES and ESS. However, the questions now facing managers are when and where to start.

FIGURE 7 Progressions in Computer System Development

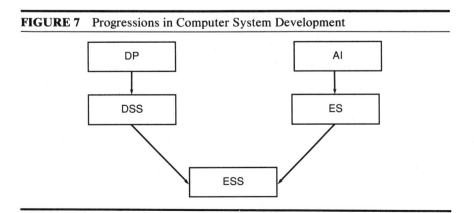

When to Start

The "when" to start is relatively easy to answer. It is "now" for exploratory work. For some organizations, this will be a program of education and active monitoring of the field. For others, the initial investment may take the form of an experimental low-budget prototype. For a few, once the exploration is over, it will make good economic sense to go forward with a full-fledged working prototype. Conceptual and technological developments have made it possible to begin an active prototype development phase.

Where to Start

The second question is "where" to start. A possible beginning may be to explore those areas in which the organization stands to gain a distinct competitive advantage. Schlumberger would seem to feel that their ES used as a drilling advisor is one such example. Digital Equipment Corporation's use of an expert system for "equipment configuration control" is another example. It is interesting that, of the more than 20 organizations that we know are investing in ES and ESS, almost none would allow themselves to be quoted. The reasons given basically boil down to the fact that they are experimenting with prototypes they think will give them a competitive advantage in making or delivering their product or service. Examples of where we can quote without attribution are cases in which an ESS is used to support the cross-selling of financial services products (e.g., an insurance salesman selling a tax shelter), or to evaluate the credit worthiness of a loan applicant in a financial services organization.

It is clear that there are a great many problem areas where even our somewhat primitive ability to deal with expert systems can permit the building of useful first generation systems. The development of expert support systems makes the situation even brighter: By helping the beleaguered "expert," the organization will get the desired leverage in the marketplace.

PROBLEMS, RISKS, AND ISSUES

It would be irresponsible of us to conclude without acknowledging that expert systems and expert support systems are in their infancy, and researchers and users alike must be realistic about their capabilities. Already there is an apparent risk that an expert system will be poorly defined and oversold: The resulting backlash may hinder progress.

There is also a danger of proceeding too quickly and too recklessly, without paying careful attention to what we are doing. We may very well embed our knowledge (necessarily incomplete at any moment in time) into a system that is only effective when used by the person who created it. If this system is used by others, there is a risk of misapplication: holes in another user's knowledge could represent a pivotal element in the logic leading to a solution. While these holes are implicitly recognized by the creator of the knowledge base, they may be quite invisible to a new user.

The challenge of proceeding at an appropriate pace can be met if managers treat artificial intelligence, expert systems, expert support systems, and decision support systems as a serious topic, one that requires management attention if it is to be exploited properly. To this end, managers must recognize the differences between Types I and II problems, for which the older techniques are appropriate, and the new methods available for Types III and IV.

CONCLUSION

Although there are some basic risks and constraints that will be with us for some time, the potential of AI techniques is obvious. If we proceed cautiously, acknowledging the problems as we go along, we can begin to achieve worthwhile results.

The illustrations used here are merely a few applications that have been built in a relatively brief period of time with primitive tools. Business has attempted to develop expert systems applications since 1980 and, despite the enormity of some of the problems, has succeeded in developing a number of simple and powerful prototypes.

The state of the art is such that everyone building an expert system must endure this primitive start-up phase to learn what is involved in this fascinating new field. We expect that it will take until about 1990 for ES and ESS to be fully recognized as having achieved worthwhile business results.

However, expert systems and expert support systems are with us now, albeit in a primitive form. The challenge for managers is to harness these tools to increase the effectiveness of the organization and thus add value for its stakeholders. Pioneering firms are leading the way, and, once a section of territory has been staked out, the experience gained by these leaders will be hard to equal for those who start later.

REFERENCES

1. WINSTON, P. H. *Artificial Intelligence*. 2nd ed. Reading, Mass.: Addison-Wesley, 1984, p. 1.
2. DAVIS, R. ET AL. "The Dipmeter Advisor: Interpretation of Geological Sig-

nals." *Proceedings of the 7th International Joint Conference on Artificial Intelligence.* Vancouver, 1981, pp. 846–49.

3. BACHANT, J., AND J. MCDERMOTT. "RI Revisited: Four Years in the Trenches." *AI Magazine,* Fall 1984, pp. 21–32.

4. MCDERMOTT, J. "RI: A Rule-based Configurer of Computer Systems." *Artificial Intelligence* 19 (1982).

5. WINSTON, 1984.

6. GORRY, G. A., AND M. S. SCOTT MORTON. "A Framework for Management Information Systems." *Sloan Management Review,* Fall 1971, pp. 55–70.

7. SIMON, H. A. *The New Science of Management Decision.* New York: Harper & Row, 1960.

8. ANTHONY, R. N. "Planning and Control Systems: A Framework for Analysis." Boston: Harvard University Graduate School of Business Administration, 1965.

9. SIMON, 1960.

10. NEWELL, A. "Reasoning Problem Solving and Decision Processes: The Problem Space as a Fundamental Category." In *Attention and Performance VIII,* ed. R. Nickerson. Hillsdale, N.J.: Erlbaum, 1980.

11. SHEIL, B. "Power Tools for Programmers." *Datamation,* February 1983, pp. 131–44.

12. KEEN, P. G. W., AND M. S. SCOTT MORTON. *Decision Support Systems: An Organizational Perspective.* Reading, Mass.: Addison-Wesley, 1978.

13. IBID.

14. BACHANT AND MCDERMOTT, 1984.

15. IBID., p. 27.

16. FOX, M. S. "Constraint-Directed Search: A Case Study of Job-Shop Scheduling." Pittsburgh. Carnegie-Mellon University Robotics Institute. Technical Report No. CMU-RI-TR-83-22, 1983.

17. DAVIS, 1981.

18. HOLLAN, J. D.; E. L. HUTCHINS; AND L. WEITZMAN. "Steamer: An Interactive Inspectable Simulation-based Training System." *AI Magazine,* Summer 1984, pp. 15–28.

11 *Prototyping: The New Paradigm for Systems Development**

Justus D. Naumann
A. Milton Jenkins

INTRODUCTION

A quiet revolution is taking place in the information systems industry. Trade publications, academic journals, and advertisements are filled with references to "prototyping" for systems development. Traditional systems development methods have become more complex and cumbersome as the industry attempts to incorporate new tools in new applications. The authors believe that the traditional methods—the old systems development paradigm—no longer fits the real world. Their research suggests that the new systems development paradigm is prototyping. However, the meaning of the method is not always clear in the published literature. To add to the problem of understanding, experiences and prescriptions that are very similar to prototyping have been called "heuristic development, infological simulation," or "middle-out design."

This article reports on the growing body of knowledge about prototyping. The authors synthesize fragments from the published discussions of this method into a consistent model of the prototyping process. The reasons for its emergence are discussed, and the roles of the system user and

* Reprinted by special permission from the *MIS Quarterly,* vol. 6, no. 3, September 1982. Copyright 1982 by the Society for Information Management and the Management Information Systems Research Center at the University of Minnesota.

system builder in the new paradigm are discussed. Several examples of prototype systems development are also described.

Webster's defines the word *prototype* as:

1. An original model on which something is patterned; an archetype, or
2. An individual that exhibits the essential features of a later type, or
3. A standard or typical example.

All three descriptions apply to systems development to some extent. Systems are developed as patterns or archetypes and are modified and enhanced for later distribution to multiple users. The first definition is closest to that of manufacturing, where a prototype frequently precedes the fabrication process. In information systems development, the familiar concept of a "pilot" system covers this sort of prototyping. The literature suggests that this is not an adequate view of the prototyping paradigm in information systems development.

The second definition—that is, a system that captures *the essential features* of a later system—is the most appropriate definition of an information system prototype. A prototype system, intentionally incomplete, is to be modified, expanded, supplemented, or supplanted.

THE PROTOTYPE MODEL IN MANAGEMENT INFORMATION SYSTEMS

The characteristics of completed information systems depend on the problem that was to be solved, the development process, and the resources employed for development. The parameters of the development process— problems to solve and available resources—are changing. Expectations of the resulting systems are also changing as individuals and organizations learn to interact with information systems. The process of systems development is changing too, in response to these changes in its environment.

Prototyping is a revolutionary[1]—rather than evolutionary—change in the development process. It is a way of responding to the types of changes mentioned above. This section describes changes that have taken place or are occurring in the problems to be addressed by information systems and in the resources available to the builder. The discussion presents the prototype model for systems development and describes its impact on system builders, system users, and organizations.

MIS Design Problems/Opportunities

As organizations gain experience and familiarity with computer data processing, they are able to recognize problems and opportunities which require the development of larger and more complex systems. Complexity

can increase in specific application areas, for example, material requirements planning supplants inventory accounting, in the level and amount of
systems integration, or in the organization's goals—"information resource management" replaces "applications processing." Many organizations have developed the data processing systems that automate previously manual applications; their system builders are *now* developing
systems to support decision making.

Users are also recognizing the potential benefits of new applications
which were not considered feasible without automation. Many such applications may not be well defined. Although users may see the potential
benefits, they may not be able to describe the necessary details of a
solution to analysts.

Gibson and Nolan [13]* classify these applications as stage 3 or stage 4
information systems. They are characterized by more than increased complexity; they may also be:

• *State-of-the-art:* they may be intended to perform a business function
  that could not be done without advanced technology.
• *Of very high potential value:* they may present a payoff potential far in
  excess of development and operation cost.
• *Integrative by nature:* they may necessitate a gathering together of many
  discrete applications processes, databases, models, and organization
  units.

Stage 3 and 4 applications require more systems development resources,
offer higher benefits, and carry higher risks.

The resources required by stage 3 and 4 information systems included
on-line systems, database management systems, higher level languages,
generalized transaction processors, report generators, and easy to use or
build models. New systems development opportunities plus advances in
hardware and software technology demand replacement of the traditional
paradigm. More of the knowledge and effort for the development process
must come from the functional area. Systems need to be tailored to individual users while remaining open to rapid, verifiable changes.

The traditional development paradigm does not respond well to increased complexity and uncertainty. The tendency is to increase controls
and to require more precise requirements definitions. This response conflicts with the characteristics of stage 3 and 4 information systems: more
complex systems, using a more diverse set of resources, and subject to
frequent changes, are much more difficult, costly, and time-consuming to
specify precisely. The prototyping paradigm provides the needed alternative approach.

---

* Bracketed numbers cite the references at end of this chapter.

The Prototype Model

Prototyping an information system is a four-step procedure (see Figure 1).

Identify the User's Basic Information Requirements. Two distinct emphases are suggested for this step: the "data abstracting approach" and the "process simulating approach." Data abstraction is the focus of Research Group CADIS [7], which suggests that "infological simulation" in the form of experiments with a database driven pilot system is appropriate. Konsynski [22] surveys the database literature and describes DBMS as a new system design paradigm. In this view, determining requirements means constructing a model of the relevant data. The thrust of more conventional techniques such as the Jackson Methodology [19] and Logical Construction of Programs [33] is that systems design begins with identification of entities, attributes, and data structures. Canning [9] suggests that the new systems development methodologies begin with data rather than process.

The other view is that the first step in prototyping is to model the process. Basili and Turner suggest iterative enhancement [6], that is, implementation of a skeletal solution to be enhanced during interaction with users. Berrisford and Wetherbe [8] propose "heuristic development" to replace the systems analysis phase of the traditional life cycle.

FIGURE 1 The Prototype Model

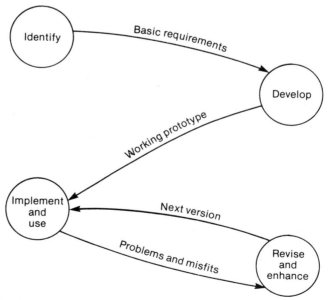

Prototyping is a four-step interactive process between user and builder. The initial version is defined, constructed, and used quickly; as problems and misfits are discovered, revisions and enhancements are made to the working system in its user's environment.

In both of these approaches, the emphasis is on identifying the essential features of a user's requirements. The data abstraction approach assumes that the essential features are *data* and *data relationships*. Processes are expected to be provided through the auxiliary features of generalized DBMS. In contrast, the process simulating approach assumes that *both data and process* must be identified in the first step. These two views agree that *completeness is not important at this stage.*[2]

Develop a Working Prototype. The initial prototype must be implemented in a very short time—almost "overnight." Hancock [18] suggests "half specified" requirements to produce a "first cut" and "breadboard" system in half the time usually devoted to requirements determination. Online Systems, Inc. [28], suggests that many first cut systems can be developed overnight or at most in two or three days. Donovan and Madnick suggest that prototyping or breadboarding is effective only if done in weeks, rather than months or years [11]. According to McCracken [24], delivery of a running prototype should not take more than a day or two, and, if it does, the user is not being served properly.

This time requirement serves both the user and the builder. The user has a tangible system to experience and criticize; the builder gets responses based on that experience. This requirement distinguishes prototyping from other approaches in two respects: the resources required by the builder and the initial analysis objectives. The initial prototype system is purposefully incomplete. It is a simulation, in the sense that it represents the essential elements desired by the user in a simplified form. Design and implementation of this system is accomplished not by completely documenting the user's information requirements but by building a working system.

Implement and Use the Prototype System. "Hands-on" use of the system provides experience, understanding, and evaluation. Earl [12], who emphasizes an organizational development view of systems development, suggests that under prototyping: "As it is a live and operational system, users cannot escape and opt out so easily. . . . Users and managers, once they realize that things can be changed and that they can exert influence, may in turn participate with more dedication."

The delivered prototype system meets a fundamental goal of design. According to one of the most quoted thinkers about design, Christopher Alexander [1]: "The process of achieving [a] good fit between two entities [is] a negative process of neutralizing the incongruities, or irritants, or forces, which cause misfit. The experiment of putting a prototype in the context itself is the real criterion of fit."

It should be apparent that an evaluation takes place whether the traditional or prototype model is used for system development. The users will find the incongruities and irritants which cause misfit whenever a new system is experienced. *The prototype model exploits, rather than deplores, this behavior.*

Revise and Enhance the Prototype System. Undesirable or missing features identified by the user must be corrected. Rapid turnaround remains important; therefore, the resources required to build the first prototype are necessary to the revision and enhancement process. The user is not likely to identify all the remaining problems in the system during a single evaluation step. Therefore, several iterations will undoubtedly be required. Steps 3 and 4 must be repeated until the user accepts the system as a good fit.

Principles Underlying Prototyping

The prototype model for information systems development specifies construction of a prototype system as a representation of a solution to a problem or opportunity. The prototype model is the most effective representation possible since it enables evaluation of the proposed design *in context*. According to Alexander [1]: "Every design problem begins with an effort to achieve fitness between two entities: the form in question and its context. The form is the solution to the problem; the context defines the problem. In other words, when we speak of design, the real object of discussion is not the form alone but the ensemble comprising the form and its context. Good fit is a desired property of this ensemble into form and context."

The prototype model is not just another among alternative representations such as written specifications. It is the representation that anticipates evaluation of the design in its operating environment.

Prototyping represents and parallels the dynamic process of growth, change, and evolution existing in any living system. It neither requires nor permits prolonged static specifications in development projects. Since any "freeze points" in the prototype design process are of only a very limited duration, prototyping accommodates changes in both the user and systems environments.

If the user environment is unstable or extremely dynamic, development iterations could continue indefinitely [29]. In such an environment the separate development and maintenance activities of traditional systems methodologies are integrated by the prototype model.

In a more static environment where a prototype meets the user's full needs, it may either serve as-is or be used as the design specification for a more efficient information system. In a stable environment, the decision to replace an operating prototype system with a traditional system can be made with a relatively simple breakeven analysis.

The prototype model is accommodating to instability in the builder's environment. With the introduction of new hardware and software technologies, operating prototypes may become inefficient. When dramatic changes in the technologies being utilized occur, an operating prototype may have to be replaced by a more efficient version. The operating prototype serves as the specification for its own replacement. Because the implementation of a prototype must be easy to change, the effects of systems changes can be largely transparent to the user.

Prototyping Resource Requirements

Current technologies, especially on-line transaction processing and natural language-based query-retrieval systems, have in many ways reintroduced a more personalized concept of transactions and accounts, and have reduced the apparent overriding concern for process control associated with earlier batch systems.

Evolution of the systems development process parallels the evolution of data processing methods. Technological capabilities and the "software problem" have impelled development of increasingly detailed and rigorous system development methodologies. This approach has reduced uncertainty about systems development *once information requirements have been determined*. That is, correctly specified systems can be built on budget and on schedule.

The prototype model differs from the traditional approach in the same way that new processing technology differs from batch data processing. The traditional approach adds steps to keep control of the development process; the prototype model reduces the need for process controls in favor of direct user-system interaction (see Figure 2).

Prototyping must be supported by on-line interactive systems, database management systems, very high level languages, generalized input and output software, and an accessible modeling facility.

Interactive Systems.   In the prototype model, both the builder and the system must respond rapidly to the user's needs. Some batch systems are capable of rapid response, but batch systems do not permit interaction and revision at a human pace. Interactive system capabilities extend computing resources, that is, information processing resources appear to be physically adjacent and immediately available. Interactive facilities extend the apparent power of information processing resources by reducing delays and by extending control over the resource to the user. User perception of rapid and efficient operation and revision helps speed evaluation.

Database Management Systems.   When coupled with interactive processing resources, the natural language-based query language of database management systems provides most of the auxiliary functions of managing data. A substantial portion of traditional systems design focuses on tasks and decisions to select access methods, design physical storage structures,

FIGURE 2   Prototyping Resources

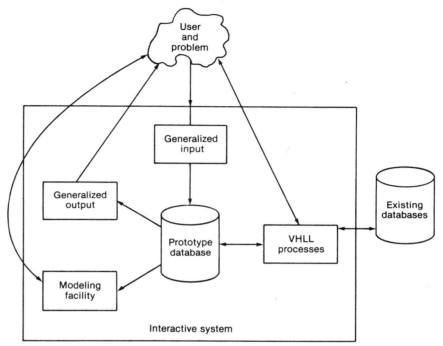

The prototype model requires a database populated through some generalized input processor and/or data obtained from existing databases using very high level languages. Prototype outputs are produced interactively through a generalized output processor, models from a model bank, or, for some uses, through programs and procedures developed in very high level languages.

provide for backup, security, and integrity, and define and create special data conversion programs. These procedure-oriented tasks have no direct value to the user. The supporting database system must provide for rapid and easy creation and revision and should include input and updating procedures and extensive reporting facilities. Berild and Nachmens [7] provide a list of the features that a prototyping database management system should include.

Database management systems are central to prototyping in two ways. Prototyping without use of database management software prohibits the design and programming of data handling facilities in the desired time frame. In addition, many of the other resources needed for prototyping are being developed as extensions to database management systems. Konsynski [22] surveys a number of database oriented research projects that point in this direction.

Generalized Input and Output Software.   Report generators, report writers, and query languages of varying capabilities have been in use for many years, and are frequently features of, or associated with, database management systems. An output package that uses default formats from very brief specifications is most useful in the initial prototype, while capability to accept more precise specification permits eventual tailoring of the prototype system.

Because editing, validation, error correction, and controls are more difficult to define in any general way for batch oriented processing systems, general input software has not been in widespread use. The adoption of on-line technology and source data capture has permitted editing, validation, and error correction on a single transaction basis at the point of data entry. Many source data entry systems are currently available, with capabilities ranging from simple field validation and correction to fairly complete editing and validation relative to a database definition. Generalized input software provides for database creation and update without construction of complex edit programs.

Very High Level Languages.   The traditional approaches seem to promote a single language view of information systems development (e.g., a COBOL shop or a PL/1 shop). Language resources of the designer must include more flexibility under the prototype model. Language selection criteria are different: self-documentation, ease of change, and coding and testing speed become far more important when operating efficiently is no longer a primary objective of program development. Languages need to be connected or connectable to the appropriate database management resource and should include provisions for rapid report specification and input processing specification. Languages like APL may have increasingly useful roles in prototype development as standard facilities for input and output of complex data structures are added to them. Emerging very high level languages, for example, BDL [17] are consistent with prototyping and may ultimately provide design primitives at or near the level of user-designer interaction. Query/update languages associated with database management systems may prove useful as very high level languages for prototyping.

Modeling.   Models that make decisions or support human decision making are integral to many systems. A model bank—a collection of potentially useful models—is an important prototyping resource. Inventory replenishment models that can be integrated in a transaction processing prototype, and simulation models used to assess outcomes of alternative decisions are examples. Montgomery and Urban [25] describe the relationship of such a model bank to the decision maker and the database.

Very high level languages facilitate the development of models. Under the prototyping paradigm, however, rapid application of reliable models favors the model bank.

Prototyping Roles and Results

Prototyping stresses the interactions between the user, builder, and system. This emphasis alters the critical user skills and abilities required for successful implementation of information systems. Similarly, the critical skills and abilities required of the builder are significantly different from those required for traditional systems development. Figure 3, adapted from Keen [20], illustrates the relationship of the user, system, and builder.

The User

Users play more active roles in prototyping than is possible with traditional development methods. In effect they are system designers who use and evaluate a system, and in the process, identify problems and suggest solutions. Users set the development pace by the time they spend using and evaluating the prototype. They decide when the cycle of evaluation and refinement ends.

The user's role requires understanding that along with the flexibility and responsiveness provided by the prototype model comes responsibility for the results. In the relationship established with the systems builder during the development of a prototype, the user will develop an understanding for and appreciation of the specific skills possessed by the builder. Certainly some features of an application will have been initiated by the builder rather than the user. Technical features, performance, and integration of the system with existing databases and processes is the builder's concern,

FIGURE 3 Prototyping Roles

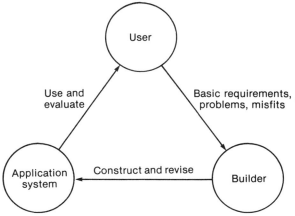

The user is responsible for the functions of the application system, beginning with definition of basic requirements. Through use and evaluation, the user detects problems and misfits and communicates to the builder. The builder constructs and revises the system in response to user feedback.

Source: This figure is adapted from P. G. W. Keen, "Adoptive Design for Decision Support Systems," *Database* 12, nos. 1, 2 (Fall 1980), pp. 15–25.

not the user's. While performance and system integration are important to the user, they are primarily builder-system concerns.

In many applications, multiple organizational units and multiple individuals are involved. Here, the user's role includes coordination and communication with other users. The designer cannot perform this key linking role without usurping the user's responsibility for functional systems design.

The Builder

The prototype builder constructs successive versions of the system, compromising and resolving conflicts between the context (i.e., user needs and desires) and the form, as constrained by technology and economics. This role more closely resembles that of the systems designer or programmer analyst than of the information analyst [4]. In addition to functional knowledge (e.g., understanding of the user's responsibilities) the builder must understand the available technology that can be used to support development of the prototype system.

In step one of the prototyping process, the builder works with the user to define essential features of the prototype systems. Under the data abstraction approach, the builder must identify the entities of interest, some of their attributes, and the relationships among them. Sufficient detail must be included to create a data-base definition. With the process simulating approach, the builder must identify those processes that are essential to the user. Finally, the builder must relate both data and processes to available data-bases, files, and models and decide how to quickly implement the first prototype.

In step two, the builder uses system resources to construct a working prototype. Initial prototype implementation may include report definition, screen generation, database definition, and population with existing or new data, model selection and integration, and user documentation.

In steps three and four, the builder works closely with the user, responding to perceptions of problems and misfits with rapid revisions. Use—and user learning and participation—require that the prototype system "keep up."

The builder, then, is responsive to user changing perceptions of need and keeps the prototype system responsive to those needs.

The Application

Using the Gorry and Scott Morton [14] model of an information system as a frame of reference, prototyping can be used in any functional area. It will be most useful at the tactical and strategic levels of applications. Managerial activities at these levels are less structured. Decisions are more open and less programmable. More uncertainty exists in the user environment and in design alternatives.

The most promising candidates for the prototype methodology are normally related to managerial functions. Typically, these tasks concern planning, direction, controlling, problem solving, and decision making. Often, these tasks within these areas will be exploratory in nature—probing more deeply and comprehensively into the nature of the problem as well as developing a solution.

Operational control systems and transaction systems are also candidates for prototyping. Lower level systems can be difficult to define as decision support systems. They need modification and enhancement just like higher level systems. The traditional approach is too inflexible and takes too long.

Selection of the best approach is contingent upon a number of factors including systems size, user knowledge, developer skill, and application stability. Naumann, Davis, and McKeen [26] discuss methodology selection as a function of such contingencies. They suggest that the determining factor is the level of certainty of a successful implementation. When certainty is low, an experimental approach, prototyping, is most effective.

Development Time

The total development time for any given application system may not be significantly changed by prototyping, but the time required to get a useful system in the hands of the user is greatly reduced. The prototype model focuses on quick delivery of an initial system. Both user and analyst time is minimized initially. The user will spend more time on design with the prototype model than with a traditional approach, but the user sets the pace for systems development. The builder is responsible for the rapid design and modification of the prototype. The authors have found no prototype procedures which tolerated over a month for developing the initial model, with much less time allowed for modifications and initial data conversions.

Economics of Prototyping

Anecdotal evidence [7, 16, 24, 27, 30, 31, 32] suggests an order of magnitude decrease in both development cost and time with the prototype model. No empirical comparisons have been published; such research is difficult for well-known reasons, not the least of which is determining the time when a prototype system is "finished."

Others [22, 30] have noted the additional costs that are or might be associated with the prototype model; expensive resources may have to be acquired to support prototyping; operating costs may be higher for a given system because of the inefficiency on generalized software.

Finally, there is the question of maintenance. Maintenance costs of a traditionally developed system are generally accepted to be the largest component of life cycle cost. Since flexibility is so fundamental to prototyping, maintenance cost should be much lower.

These five factors—development cost, development time, prototyping resource cost, operating cost, and maintenance—are parameters of any economic analysis of the prototype model. Figure 4 depicts the relationships of these parameters. In Figure 4a, life-cycle costs of a prototyped system include RA: the cost of acquiring additional resources to support prototyping; SD_p: the cost of systems development; and operating cost OP_p plus maintenance cost M_p. Figure 4b contrasts the costs associated with the traditional systems development paradigm. Systems development, SD_t, takes considerably longer. In addition to the much higher systems development cost, there is some opportunity cost, or cost for delayed use, DE. Over the operating life of the traditionally developed system, frequent and costly maintenance[3] M_t significantly increases life cycle cost.

Figure 4 highlights several relationships that must be considered in any comparison of the paradigms:

1. Resource acquisition (RA) may completely override all other cost considerations. But many organizations have already installed generalized database management systems and other resources needed to support prototyping. High initial resource costs may not be a significant part of life-cycle costs when amortized over a large number of systems.

2. The slope shown in Figure 4a, $OP_p + M_p$, for operating cost plus maintenance of a prototype is not well understood. Operating costs may be higher because of the overhead associated with generalized software, although the parallels with program code suggest otherwise. (Expert programmers can produce more efficient code than generalized software, but applications programmers generally do not do so.)

Prototype maintenance is assumed to cost much less than maintenance of traditionally developed systems because there is less to maintain and because maintenance takes place at a higher level. Prototype systems are designed with changeability in mind. Extending the change process into the operating life of a prototyped system should not greatly reduce the capacity for rapid and inextensive change.

3. The opportunity cost of traditional systems shown in Figure 4b, DE, is a critical parameter. The time from starting to completing development in the traditional paradigm means that the new system is not available for an extended period. Opportunity cost is not often included in life-cycle costs in part because it is difficult to estimate and in part because it is not directly charged to the development project. It needs to be considered because the new paradigm offers the opportunity for a significant reduction.

FIGURE 4   The Economics of Prototyping

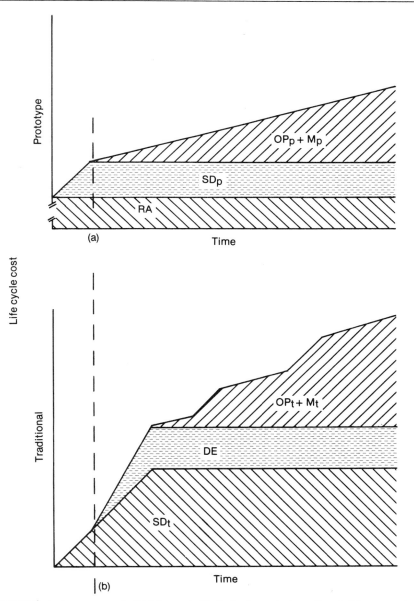

Prototyping resource costs (RA) may initially be large but are fixed. The opportunity cost (OC) of not having a system as rapidly, plus the continued cost of maintenance (M), may make the life-cycle cost of the traditional paradigm exceed prototyping.

4. Maintenance, under the traditional paradigm, may really be a sort of extended prototyping [10]. Much of maintenance is matching a system to new users' needs and to changes in the users' and system's environment. Regardless of the purpose, the cost of changing a traditionally developed system is assumed to be higher than that of a prototype.

At this state of understanding, each manager must provide the parameter values for this analysis. The authors believe that when a careful analysis is performed, prototyping will be economically preferable for many applications.[4]

The other side of prototyping economics is measurement of benefits. The cost comparison presented above is limited to a discussion of the choice of development paradigm once the decision to build a system has been made. The prototype model suggests two additional economic factors. First, as suggested by Naumann et al. [26], for some potential applications the level of uncertainty about successful implementation is too high to attempt development with a traditional approach. The "experimental discovery of requirements" provided by prototyping permits informed evaluation of benefits at an early stage. This implies that at least some beneficial systems that could not be developed under traditional methods will be implemented with prototyping.

Secondly, prototyping implies an incremental decision strategy; that is, the user can make an informed decision to drop a system, hold it stable, or continue development with each evaluate-refine cycle. Keen [21] suggests that value analysis is appropriate, at least for DSS, with prototypes. In this model, users establish a cost threshold by estimating the maximum benefits to be gained by a system development investment. Value analysis seems to apply to any prototype since investments can be made in relatively small increments.

PUBLISHED EXAMPLES OF PROTOTYPING

The term *prototype* appears with increasing frequency in journals, the trade press, and advertising. Users of these terms are each describing a nontraditional approach to systems development. This section surveys some of these references to prototyping.[5]

Small and Simple

Bally, Brittan, and Wagner [5] describe the development of a very simple application. The initial model in this system required no computer programming and simply produced computer printouts from cards; subsequent models introduced the computer to users. The system evolved from a listing of job transactions to experiments with job scheduling. The authors stress the importance of noting that *each step in this simple development sequence was undertaken only as a response to a clearly perceived user demand that was based on the practical experience gained in a previous step.*

This article illustrates the *iterative nature of the prototype* model and the *need for user learning to determine information requirements.* While the prototyping resources required in this application were minimal, the roles of the user and designer are clearly defined.

Changeability

Appleton [2] provides an unusual example of the application of the prototype model to a functioning system. A complex operational information system was plagued by continually changing requirements and high dissatisfaction with the inability of the systems development group to respond to the users' dynamic environment. The developers replaced a conventionally developed system with a prototype system. Following this conversion, which was entirely transparent to the users, enhancements and modifications were expeditiously handled and user dissatisfaction nearly disappeared. In this example an operational information system was converted to a prototype system to be able to respond to the user's changing needs. In this article, the *existing application system was used to determine basic user requirements. Users then evaluated and builders refined the prototyped systems.*

Large Multiple-User System

Groner, Hopwood, Palley, and Sibley [15] present a case study illustrating *the effectiveness of prototyping in conducting a thorough information requirements analysis.* The article describes the use of prototypes to deal with uncertainty in both the user and designer environments.

> Prototypes were required in the requirements analysis phase because users could not be sure that computer systems were needed, what functions they should perform, or how they would use them. [15]

The prototyping process described in this article appears to deviate from the prototyping model in the sense that the users played a minor role in specifying the initial systems requirements. This article provides a discussion of the prototyping resources, the level of documentation, and the perceived benefits of the prototyping approach. The builders provided a *tangible system to facilitate user understanding of both the problem and possible solutions.*

User Learning

Earl [12] provides a brief description of three prototype case studies. He focuses on *the behavioral aspects of prototyping—as a catalyst to participative design, learning, and organizational development.* A financial control system prototype forced managers, who had delegated design to an accountant and a designer, to particpate in the development of the system and to make critical design decisions.

Appropriate Tools

Read and Harmon [30] describe the development of an integrated reporting system supporting the U.S. Navy's Fleet Combat Direction System Support Activity. They describe the resources employed as "fourth generation language." *The system they describe collects data from the databases and files of many transaction systems and supports interactive user development of tabular and graphic outputs.* Read and Harmon state that a more traditional approach would have been futile for this application. In particular, they emphasize the improvement in systems development productivity with fourth-generation languages.

Quick and Clean

New software is available which appear to ease or eliminate many of the problems of long periods of definition or implementation, of uncertainty around system specifications and benefits, and of the high cost of frequent alterations. [31]

Scott suggests that a *database can be built in a day, reports can be produced in less than a day, and such systems can be both effective and efficient.* He describes a system that was estimated to cost $350,000 to develop, and the under $35,000 prototype that did the job instead. The managers who use the system have become eager and satisfied users as well as enthusiastic supporters of the Systems Division.

These application articles illustrate that systems are being implemented using the prototype model. The literature also presents several related design techniques, for example, heuristic development, iterative enhancement, systems sketching, evolutionary design, and pilot models. All of these techniques share with the prototype model the recognition that development of complete and correct information requirements specifications prior to implementation is both technically and behaviorally infeasible. However, all of these techniques differ from the prototype model in terms of the resources required, the roles of the users and designer, and in the nature of the resulting information system.

CONCLUSIONS

Builders and users of information systems continue to be dissatisfied with the traditional approach to systems development. Information requirements are very difficult to determine, and there is substantial risk that a system, when implemented, will not fit the user environment. Systems take a long time to implement; during that time, users and their environments change. Over the operational life cycle of a system, both environmental changes and user learning necessitate system modifications and enhancements.

More complex systems that must operate in less structured environments are demanded. Such systems must be designed to respond rapidly to user learning, user environment changes, and new technology.

Prototyping presents a different way of approaching information systems implementation. The prototype model requires extremely rapid construction of systems. The prototype builder's and user's paradigm accepts the uncertainty of information requirements statements and the certainty of continuing change. Prototype information systems are purposely incomplete and very changeable. Users interact with their system in its environment to specify their requirements more completely and correctly. System builders accept more costly technology and continual change in order to match changing user perceptions of need.

Prototyping, like any new paradigm, can be expected to introduce a new set of problems. The economics justifying prototyping in general seem clear, but the decision rules for specific organizations and applications are not.

Advances in technology have made prototyping feasible, but no integrated set of prototyping resources is yet available. Individual applications can be and are being developed under the prototype model. No one has studied the implications of a portfolio of prototypes. Issues such as developer training, management control, data integrity and security, and the behavioral implications of more frequent change must be studied and resolved.

Understanding of these issues and solutions to the problems of prototyping will require research. Applied research on prototyping is very expensive, the technology is costly, and experiments will need real users in their organizational environments.

It is not clear how much of system development can or should be done with prototyping. Certainly, many structured problems require it. The authors are convinced that this paradigm addresses the most critical issue facing MIS managers today: the organizational productivity gained if applications systems are put into operation when they are needed.

NOTES

1. While the use of prototyping as an approach to systems development is markedly different from the traditional phased life cycle approach, the prototyping *approach* is evolutionary.
2. In some respects, the first step is the same in the traditional systems development life-cycle model. Part of the feasibility study is certainly a high-level analysis of user requirements. The objectives are quite different, however; in the feasibility study the objective is to define requirements in broad terms with sufficient detail to assess technical, economic, and developmental feasibility. The goal affects the result; the traditional feasibility study does not result in enough detail to go on to step 2 of prototyping. See Keen [21, page 11] for a comparison of prototyping with feasibility study.
3. According to Lientz, Swanson, and Tompkins [23], maintenance consists of correction of errors, adaptation to change in environment and needs, and "perfective" maintenance to utilize new resources. In the prototype model, most maintenance is adaptive and perfective.
4. A caveat—an additional cost of prototyping does not appear in this model—that is, the cost of managing and controlling a large number of prototyped systems. Clearly, control procedures will be needed to avoid return to the profusion of uncoordinated application systems that characterized some organizations during the 1960s.
5. In each description, features that directly relate to principles, resources, or roles in prototyping have been highlighted.

REFERENCES

1. ALEXANDER, C. *Notes on the Synthesis of Form.* Cambridge, Mass.: Harvard University Press, 1964, pp. 21–24.
2. APPLETON, D. S. "System 2000 Database Management System." *Guide 37, Session No. IS-23,* Boston, Massachusetts, November 1–2, 1973.
3. ————. "What Data Base Isn't." *Datamation,* January 1977, pp. 85–92.
4. ASHENHURST, R. L., ED. "Curriculum Recommendations for Graduate Professional Programs in Information Systems." *Communications of the ACM* 15, no. 5 (May 1972), pp. 368–98.
5. BALLY, L.; J. BRITTAN; AND K. H. WAGNER. "A Prototype Approach to Information Systems Design and Development." *Information and Management* 1, no. 1 (November 1977), pp. 21–26.
6. BASILI, V. R., AND A. H. TURNER. "Iterative Enhancement: A Practical

Technique for Software Development." *IEEE Tutorial: Structured Programming,* #75CH1049-6, September 1975.

7. BERILD, S., AND S. NACHMENS. "CS4—A Tool for Database Design by Infological Simulation." Research Group CADIS Report TRITH-IBADB 3103, *IEEE Tutorial: Software Methodology,* #EHO 142-0, November 1978.

8. BERRISFORD, T. R., AND J. C. WETHERBE. "Heuristic Development: A Redesign of Systems Design." *Management Information Systems Quarterly* 3, no. 1 (March 1979), pp. 11–19.

9. CANNING, R. G. "The Production of Better Software." *EDP Analyzer* 17, no. 2, Canning Publications, Inc., (February 1979).

10. DODD, W. P. "Prototype Programs." *Computer* 13, no. 2 (February 1980), p. 81.

11. DONOVAN, J. J., AND S. E. MADNICK. "Institutional and Ad Hoc DSS and Their Effective Use." *Database* 8, no. 3 (Winter 1977), pp. 79–88.

12. EARL, M. J. "Prototype Systems for Accounting, Information and Control." *Accounting, Organizations and Society* 3, no. 2 (March 1978), pp. 161–70.

13. GIBSON, F., AND R. S. NOLAN. "Managing the Four Stages of EDP Growth." *Harvard Business Review* 52, no. 2 (January–February 1974), pp. 76–88.

14. GORRY, G. A., AND M. S. SCOTT MORTON. "A Framework for Management Information Systems." *Sloan Management Review* 13, no. 1 (Fall 1971), pp. 55–70.

15. GRONER, C.; M. D. HOPWOOD; N. A. PALLEY; AND W. SIBLEY. "Requirements Analysis in Clinical Research Information Processing—A Case Study." *Computer* 12, no. 9 (September 1979), pp. 100–08.

16. HALBRECHT, H. Z.; F. EDELMAN; D. J. PETERSON; E. F. BEDELL; AND G. M. PERRY. "Critical Perspectives on MIS: The MIS Executive Perspective." *Proceedings of the Eleventh Annual Conference of the Society for Management Information Systems,* September 1979, pp. 161–71.

17. HAMMER, M. W.; G. HOWE; V. J. KRUSKAL; AND I. WLADAWSKY. "A Very High Level Programming Language for Data Processing Applications." *Communications of the ACM* 20, no. 11 (November 1977), pp. 832–40.

18. HANCOCK, J. L. *Presentation to the Society for Management Information Systems.* Washington, D.C., May 1977.

19. JACKSON, M. A. *Principles of Program Design,* London, England: Academic Press, 1975.

20. KEEN, P. G. W. "Adoptive Design for Decision Support Systems." *Database* 12, nos. 1, 2 (Fall 1980), pp. 15–25.

21. ———. "Value Analysis: Justifying Decision Support Systems." *MIS Quarterly* 5, no. 1 (March 1981), pp. 1–16.

22. KONSYNSKI, B. R. "Data Base Driven System Design." *Proceedings of the First Conference on Systems Analysis and Design.* New York: Elsevier-North Holland, 1981.

23. LIENTZ, B. P.; E. B. SWANSON; AND G. E. TOMPKINS. "Characteristics of Application Software Maintenance." *Communications of the ACM* 21, no. 6 (June 1978), pp. 466–71.

24. MCCRACKEN, D. D. "A Maverick Approach to Systems Analysis and Design." *Proceedings of the First Conference on Systems Analysis and Design,* New York: Elsevier-North Holland, 1981.

25. MONTGOMERY, D. B., AND G. L. URBAN. "Marketing Decision-Information Systems: An Emerging View." *Journal of Marketing Research* 7, no. 2 (May 1980), pp. 226–34.

26. NAUMANN, J. D.; G. B. DAVIS; AND J. D. McKEEN. "Determining Information Requirements: A Contingency Method for Selection of a Requirements Assurance Strategy." *The Journal of Systems and Software* 1, no. 4. New York: Elsevier-North Holland, 1980, pp. 273–81.

27. NICHOLS, P. L. "The Radical Effect of Data Base on Systems Development." *Canadian Data Systems* 9, no. 3 (May–June 1977), pp. 64–65.

28. ON-LINE SYSTEMS, INC. *OLIVER Reference Manual,* Pittsburgh, Pa., 1973.

29. PODOLSKY, J. L. "Horace Builds a Cycle." *Datamation* 23, no. 11 (November 1977), pp. 162–68.

30. READ, N. S., AND D. L. HARMON. "Assuring MIS Success." *Datamation* 27, no. 2 (February 1981), pp. 109–20.

31. SCOTT, J. H. "The Management Science Opportunity: A Systems Development Management Viewpoint." *MIS Quarterly* 2, no. 4 (December 1978), pp. 59–61.

32. SPRAGUE, R. H. "Decision Support Systems: Implications for the Systems Analyst." *Proceedings of the First Conference on Systems Analysis and Design.* New York: Elsevier-North Holland, 1981.

33. WARNIER, J. *Logical Construction of Programs.* New York: Van Nostrand Reinhold, 1974.

C H A P T E R

12 *Computers of the World, Unite!**

Jeremy Main

"I don't know what you're talking about, but keep talking," said Edson
Gaylord, chairman of Ingersoll Milling Machine Company of Rockford,
Illinois. George Hess, his vice president for systems and planning, kept
talking. When Hess finished, he had persuaded Gaylord to launch Ingersoll, an extremely competitive machine tool producer, on a complex, risky
venture: turning itself into what is becoming known as a computer-
integrated business. That was in 1979. Today a lot of CEOs want to do the
same.

The computer-integrated business is a hot concept. The phrase describes an enterprise whose major functions—for example, sales, finance,
distribution, manufacturing—exchange operating information quickly and
constantly via computer. Product designers can send specifications
straight to machines on the factory floor. Salesmen—or even customers—
can find out which products are in stock and when they can be delivered,
and can place orders, which automatically cause new units to be manufactured. Accounting receives on-line all information about sales, purchases,
and prices. And high executives can get any of this information, and much
more, immediately. The computer system parallels the whole process of
producing and selling goods or services and makes it move faster—much
faster.

Speed is the compelling reason for computer integration. Old methods of
deploying a lot of different computer systems that couldn't talk to each
other, or could talk only through expensive translation programs, aren't
good enough anymore. Says John Rockart, head of the Center for Informa-

---

* Source: Jeremy Main, "Computers of the World, Unite!" *Fortune*, September 24, 1990.

tion Systems Research at MIT's Sloan School: "The buffers of space, time, people, and inventory are gone, so you have to have the lubrication of information to get the flow going." To react fast enough to customers' demands, corporations need a fast, seamless information network throughout the company. For example, Sony aims to use integration to cut the time it takes to make and distribute products from 50 days to 20.

It isn't easy. No large company is yet fully computer integrated. One company's network started in manufacturing and then grew to encompass management and sales. Another began on the sales side and is just now reaching into the factories. But even if a system falls short of the scale its planners envisaged, it can still dramatically improve performance.

Ingersoll's system, put in place by 1982 at a cost of $5 million and much elaborated since, has helped considerably. While half of America's machine tool companies have folded since the 1970s, Ingersoll's shipments of large tools multiplied tenfold to nearly $500 million last year. The company is just finishing what it believes to be the largest custom-built machine tool ever made, a monster the size of a three-story house to make large turbines and other parts for hydroelectric generators. The customer is Impsa, a maker of hydroelectric equipment in Argentina.

Companies much bigger than Ingersoll are following its example. Frito-Lay, PepsiCo's most profitable division, has a new network that joins the hand-held computers used by every one of its 10,000 route salespeople to the office of president Robert Beeby, with connections to area and division offices and to company plants. Saturn Corporation, the new General Motors small-car subsidiary, starts off fully computer integrated. Du Pont is committed to tying all its 80 businesses in 50 countries into a uniform information network. The effort will take at least five years, swallowing up about $200 million of Du Pont's $900 million annual spending on information systems.

If you're thinking of computer-integrating your operation, brace yourself: It won't be easy. No computer company sells a ready-made integrated system. Because of any large enterprise's vast complexity, each system must be specially created, a fact that provides fertile ground for consultants, business professors, and software and hardware firms.

Digital Equipment Corporation not only is turning itself into a computer-integrated enterprise but is also showing others how to do it. The large Tokyo office of Andersen Consulting (part of Arthur Andersen) works almost entirely on helping clients such as Sony create networks. The job is big enough that pessimistic experts, such as Brandt Allen of the University of Virginia business school, argue that big companies can never integrate themselves completely. Says he: "The effort is so gargantuan and takes so long that by the time you have finished, everything has changed and the champions of the project have long gone."

Giant conglomerates probably don't need to be fully integrated: The lawn equipment division doesn't require intimate communication with the life insurance division. In any case, argues MIT's Rockart, "total integration is not the issue—integration with the customer is the issue." He says that companies with distinct sets of clients might use a separate network for each, rather than try to tie the whole corporation into one giant network. Johnson & Johnson might have a network for hospitals, another for pharmacies, and a third for other retail stores. Competition to give the customer better and faster service will keep up the pressure to put more business on-line.

In achieving integration on any scale, the key obstacles are no longer technological; they are in management and organization. "Integration was inhibited in the past by cost and lack of technology, but that has changed in the past two or three years," says David Mengden, director of Du Pont's computing and networking services. Unit computing costs have dropped by a factor of 100,000 in 20 years, and telecommunications costs are falling by 10 to 15 percent a year. Fiber-optic cables can furnish the vast capacity that companies need when transmitting engineering drawings and other graphic material. Two such cables span the Atlantic, another crosses the Pacific, and two more will reach the Orient in the next two years.

So the machines are up to the job. The trouble comes from complicated, sometimes irrational, corporate organizations and procedures. For example, each division in a company often counts sales or profits differently. A computer network can't cope until they are counted the same way. Every process, whether in accounting or design or the CEO's office, needs to be rethought and simplified.

Small companies are easier to integrate than big ones, new companies easier than old ones. Lynda Applegate, a Harvard business school professor, says the companies having the hardest time integrating are the large ones that set up massive back-room computer systems in the 1960s and 1970s, such as banks and insurance companies. The systems are obsolete, but replacing them is difficult and costly. It's easier to computerize the operations of a brand-new company or of an existing company that wasn't heavily computerized, like Frito-Lay.

Ex-CEO Michael Jordan relates that Frito-Lay decided to reorganize its sales system in the mid-1980s because processing 100,000 sales documents a week by hand had become too cumbersome. Besides that, the business was getting more complex and fragmented. As a national company competing mostly with strong regional companies that are close to their markets, Frito-Lay was handicapped because news of competitive incursions took months to drift up to headquarters in Dallas. Says Jordan: "We needed instant actuals."

Frito-Lay anchored its new system to the hand-held Fujitsu computers issued to all its salespeople in 1987 and 1988. The computers are about as big and tough as a long brick. A salesman carries one into the store, punching in the code numbers and quantity of Fritos, Cheetos, Tostitos, and other snacks that need replacing, and the number of "stales" he removes because they have reached the end of their 35-day shelf life. When he attaches his hand-held, as Frito-Lay people call it, to a printer in his truck, it spits out an invoice for the day's deliveries to that store, which he hands over with the snacks.

At day's end, the 10,000 Frito-Lay salespeople hook their hand-helds to telephones and the sales information pours into the company's IBM 3090 mainframes in Dallas. They pull it all together and then redistribute it in appropriate chunks to the area and division offices; to marketing, purchasing, and transportation offices, and to top management.

For salesmen, the hand-helds eliminate four to five hours of paperwork a week. To a division sales manager like Paul Davis in Dallas they mean that every Monday he gets a summary of sales, crisp and clear, on his computer screen. He can break down the sales any way he wants—by product, type of store, or district—and he can get the results daily if he wants to follow a critical campaign closely. Bad news shows up in red. Davis recalls that he used to get sales figures six weeks after the fact, in a hard-to-analyze two-foot pile of computer printouts.

When Frito-Lay and Von's, a Los Angeles supermarket chain, recently ran a joint promotion, the daily report showed that sales were up, but, more important, that some stores in the chain were doing a lot better than others. A quick trip through the chain revealed a big variance in the displays. Then a call to the chain's headquarters—which didn't know that not all stores were cooperating—got the laggards revved up. The reaction time was two days. The old Frito-Lay would have noticed a slight increase in Los Angeles sales weeks later, and probably would never have known why the promotion didn't do better.

Frito-Lay keeps a product-by-product, store-by-store watch on competitors through its integrated system, although the information comes more slowly. Monthly reports from a market research firm, Information Resources, go into the database with the internal information. Competitors can buy the same information about Frito-Lay, but they can't pass it around the company in the same accessible and friendly graphic fashion. Frito-Lay finds that this use of competitive information has helped persuade store owners to give its products more shelf space. If you can show them that Frito-Lay's snacks move faster or produce a higher margin than the snacks of another brand that is getting bigger displays, says Jordan, you have a powerful argument for winning more space.

Integration certainly has produced results. Since 1988 Frito-Lay has added 400 routes without increasing its sales force of 10,000 and pushed revenues up by almost $1 billion, to $4.2 billion. Jordan, now CEO of PepsiCo World Wide Foods, says, "We couldn't manage the company today without this system." PepsiCo's soft-drink division is going to hand-held computers, and the restaurant division is considering a similar network tied to the cash registers.

How fast can a computer-integrated company move? Take a look at

Mayday, a sophisticated $5-million-a-year machine tool shop in Lewis-ville, Texas. Mayday manufactures bushings, the metal sleeves that protect some moving parts on aircraft, such as the wheel struts. They are often made of exotic metals to fine tolerances.

Jim Nelson, Mayday's president, says every company in the business uses the same type of production equipment. "What we need is time management," he says. "I'm selling time on the machines." He began by buying big automated Japanese lathes for the plant. But as the plant became more productive, he realized he needed to computerize the office to process more orders faster to keep up with the machines. Nelson bought some elements of the integrated system, like the bookkeeping software, off the shelf, which helped keep costs down. Others had to be designed by his own programmer.

Today, Nelson has an automated system for quoting prices when a customer calls in for an order. When the customer gives his specifications, Nelson's computers can figure the costs of materials and machine time and quote a delivery date and suggested prices within 30 seconds, even if the part has never been made before. If the client places the order, then the system itself sends him a confirmation by fax or mail, or both, and takes other steps to make the product, such as ordering materials and scheduling machine time. As the order flows through the plant, Nelson's computers can report its progress. At the end, the system produces the shipping labels and invoices.

Mighty Du Pont is far behind Mayday, but the imperatives are the same. Du Pont needs to develop, sell, and deliver products faster to remain competitive. If a Du Pont salesman in West Germany wants to sell O rings to an auto company today, he can look up the parts available in Germany in a catalog. But when Du Pont becomes computer integrated in the mid-1990s, he will be able to look into a worldwide database and find not only what O rings are available but also what products are being developed and when they should be ready for delivery.

Du Pont has a head start on building its system. Ten years ago the company told all divisions to standardize equipment, using IBM main-frames with Hewlett-Packard and DEC minicomputers. Du Pont also has a worldwide electronic mail network linking 80,000 of its 146,000 employ-ees. And last year it installed an executive information system that sup-plies some 300 top executives with key numbers and charts that can be updated daily.

Over the next five or six years, each of these Du Pont systems will be meshed into a much expanded network with the same basic hardware and software throughout. The system will grow and bend to accommodate new technologies and business needs, says Ray Cairns, vice president for information technology. The effort to simplify and rationalize the corpora-tion to give integration a chance to work has already caused major changes at Du Pont. For example, there used to be more than 40 kinds of distributed control systems corporatewide. They are the computer brains that run continuous processes like refining oil by manipulating valves, sensing pressures, and so forth. Du Pont cut the 40 types to seven and then to two.

In contrast to Du Pont, GM's Saturn started with a clean sheet since the division is brand new and was conceived as a computer-integrated enterprise. EDS, the data processing company that GM acquired from Ross Perot, supplies much of the expertise and equipment to tie all of Saturn into a single database. Michael Reed, the EDS group manager for Saturn, uses the slogan FROM ART TO PART, meaning that the pieces that make up a Saturn car are designed on computers, which tell purchasing, manufacturing, and other departments what they must do for that part to be made and then schedule production.

Saturn's system actually goes well beyond art to part. Top suppliers will link electronically with Saturn, so that the orders they get from GM, bills they send, and payments they receive will all move electronically. Once a car is built, a computer record will follow it to the dealer and through its life until it is scrapped, so long as the owners keep going to Saturn dealers anywhere for service. Each service visit or repair will go into the car's record. With this system plus good service at reasonable prices, Saturn hopes to hang on to two thirds of its customers for regular service and repairs after the warranty period instead of the usual one third.

By tracking sales and customer preferences closely and fine-tuning production, Saturn also hopes to run on slimmer inventories. Says Saturn vice president Donald Hudler: "Conventional wisdom holds that everybody should have a 60-day supply of cars. We want to operate on a 30- to 45-day supply. Nothing good happens to a car sitting in inventory." How well all this will work, of course, remains to be seen.

Creating the computer-integrated corporation remains chancy. How can you put into a computer the subtleties and intricacies of relationships in a big corporation? Even if you succeed, won't you create an overbearing centralized management at a time when business theorists are calling for more decision-making power down the line? Supporters of integration argue that, if the new networks give CEOs better knowledge of what even distant managers are doing, the CEOs will feel comfortable allowing the managers a freer hand—and the managers will have the knowledge to make good decisions.

At least, that is the goal. Reaching it is sure to be difficult. But like a number of other elusive goals, just pursuing it can make a company a lot stronger.

13 *Wired for Speed**

William R. Ruffin

It's Saturday, 9:00 A.M. Fresh from a morning jog, Westinghouse president Paul Lego takes his coffee into the den of his suburban Pittsburgh home to see what's happening in Taiwan, where it is still the middle of the night.

The information Lego needs is at his fingertips. With a few keystrokes, his computer becomes another point in a global communications network that delivers a world of facts, figures, and ideas. Satisfied with the data, he moves it on to marketing managers in Texas who need it.

It's a simple procedure. Routine, really. But it says volumes about life in the global marketplace, where time zones, oceans, and national borders just don't count any more.

It's a future that Westinghouse saw taking shape in the 1970s, at a time when the old-line manufacturing company was in dire straits. Totally lacking focus, the company was a grab bag of disparate businesses, including turbines, appliances, 7-Up bottlers, light bulbs, broadcasting, and low-income housing. Wracked by the 1974–75 recession and stiffened international competition in most of its major product lines, the company was hard put to turn a profit.

What happened, of course, is now the stuff of management case studies. In 1988, two up-through-the-ranks engineers, Lego and chairman John Marous, took over from previous chairman Douglas Danforth, who had gotten things rolling with a massive restructuring.

Since that time, the company has cut, built, and acquired its way to a lean, profitable collection of winners. Unlike the many companies that have restructured by zeroing in on a few core businesses, Westinghouse

---

* Source: William R. Ruffin, "Wired for Speed," *Business Month*, January 1990, pp. 56–58.

has remained diversified. The company's fold today still boasts 18 groups of businesses spread throughout the world.

Marous and Lego saw early on that the trick to managing a diverse group of international companies was a global information system that would give headquarters in Pittsburgh a detailed flow of instantaneous data. The system is used to make decisions, to sell products, and to keep customers happy. Says David Edison, executive vice president and one of the builders of the system: "We wanted a state-of-the-art network that could really become part of the business—a tool that is part of the product itself. We're selling more than turbines or refrigeration equipment. We're selling the information technologies to order them, to keep them running, to make sure they are doing what the customer needs them to do."

During the past decade, the Westinghouse Information Network (WIN) has been built into one of the largest integrated—meaning it carries both voice and data—networks in the world. It links more than 600 locations across Europe, Asia, and the Americas. Every day, it's used in one form or another by more than 90,000 people.

The internal electronic-mail system makes virtually every employee around the world instantly reachable. If they want to, employees can even tie their home phones into the network. Managers on the road can tap into it from laptop computers. And a global voice-mail system helps travelers keep track of messages. Leading-edge digital technology carries massive amounts of data, including complex technical drawings. A videoconferencing system ties operations together with the most advanced and flexible technologies.

What all this adds up to is a companywide intelligence and quality-control system. "We're not interested in finding and fixing mistakes," says Harlan Rosenzweig, president of Westinghouse Communications. "We build in checks and tests through every step of the operation so that we can see trouble coming long before it becomes an issue with the customer."

Many of those checks are delivered through network intelligence, which is the new frontier in network technology. The intelligence system is based on a combination of hardware and software that turns an inert bunch of cables and switches into what amounts to a large computer. With software deployed throughout the system, changing the network—to set a new data service for a plant, for example—isn't a matter of construction, just re-programming.

At a thousand points in the network, software-driven monitors sense, find, and report on trouble. Working from the Communications Systems Center in Pittsburgh, network managers can instantly reroute traffic while the problem is being fixed. With still newer technologies, if there is trouble along the network, alarms will be set off and traffic will be rerouted automatically. Meanwhile—and this is key—the customers are blissfully unaware that there has been a hiccup in the system.

The heavily traveled network is used by a wide-ranging group of businesses: defense and commercial electronic systems, environmental services, power generation, transport refrigeration, to name just a few. Even Westinghouse Credit, now one of the nation's largest financial companies, manages its global financial system over the network.

Customer service was once defined as delivering good products on time at a fair price. That's still important, of course. It's also not enough, at least not in the rough-and-tumble of international markets, where customer allegiance frequently has the life span of a mayfly.

Westinghouse management has dedicated the entire company to building the kind of customer relations that withstand the test of time—not to mention a competitor with a low-ball price. "There is only one scorecard that really counts," says chairman Marous. "It's the customer. When we make that scoreboard light up, all the rest of them will take care of themselves."

Increasingly, the ties that bind supplier and customer are electronic. For example, utilities that buy from Westinghouse's power-generation business can do their shopping on their own PCs; the software is supplied by Westinghouse.

If they need a part for a turbine, they just dial into the network and fill out the form on their computer screen. They can examine a detailed schematic of the part on the same system. The electronic purchase order goes into the system, which locates the equipment and issues an order to move it out.

So that fast maintenance and technical service may be provided, the whereabouts of key support staff is kept in a constantly updated database. If a customer needs a rush repair on a generator, Westinghouse can track down and dispatch the right technicians over the network. The company also uses the network to maintain communications links to its power equipment, so that it can monitor performance and spot potential problems.

From a monitoring point in Orlando, Florida, technicians keep tabs on the performance of Westinghouse turbine generators in the United States and three foreign countries, spotting small glitches before they become big ones. If they need to do some mega-numbers crunching, Westinghouse customers can even access the company's Cray supercomputers, which roar through 840 million calculations a second. That's about the workload of 30,000 PCs.

The network is also improving the sales process with such innovations as the EDGE advanced negotiations system, which automates pricing and order engineering. As complex negotiations progress, they involve far more than face-to-face jawboning on price and delivery. A major sale will involve the people who sell the product, as well as those who will price it, make it, and deliver it.

EDGE creates a database containing information on the product that all these groups can access over the network, so information flows quickly and smoothly from all points to the people who are actually closing the deal. "The system has cut the salesperson's negotiation time by 80 percent," says Jack Froggatt, manager of information systems for Westinghouse Distribution and Control.

An indication of just how much the customer is king at Westinghouse is the manner in which it treats Pacific Power. The Oregon-based utility asked Westinghouse for a data link that could speed orders and maybe shave costs by 10 percent. Instead, Westinghouse completely redesigned the utility's purchasing process. As a result, the time necessary to process an advanced order dropped from 14 days to six hours, while the cost plunged from $86 to $12.

That bit of wizardry was performed by the Productivity and Quality Center, an in-house technical team whose job is to assist any group in the company—or its customers—in using technology and advanced management systems to do its work better, faster, or less expensively.

Information technology also makes its mark on manufacturing efficiency. Thanks in large part to the network's ability to speed manufacturing data around the world, parts for, say, circuit breakers can be made in the Dominican Republic and fitted neatly into finished products in North Carolina. Orders are placed, parts configured, and shipments confirmed, all machine-to-machine over the network.

This kind of communications-based manufacturing synergy has helped power a highly efficient just-in-time inventory system that has opened up considerable plant floor space—so much that the company's industries group plans no new construction until well into the 1990s.

Videoconferencing has produced major savings in both executive time and travel costs. Videoconferencing, of course, is nothing new; it just works much better. Attribute that to higher-quality screen images and more compact and easier-to-use equipment that can be wheeled right into an executive's office. No more scheduling trips to centralized studios or need for a battalion of television technicians. As a result, videoconferencing has been elevated from a technology of last resort—when there wasn't time or budget for decision makers to travel—to a routine tool.

Last year, Westinghouse decided really to cash in on its telecommunications expertise by selling it to other companies. It is now offering a full menu of value-added telecommunications network and management services: data, voice, video, electronic mail, and others. Westinghouse will also provide the management help to configure and run a client's communications system. It has set up shop in a Pittsburgh suburb and is already expanding. A joint venture with Harbinger Computer Service and the acquisition of Communications Design Corporation will bring new software and network-management capabilities into the operation.

MCI, a longtime supplier that has worked closely with the company in building the network, and Northern Telecom have both been signed up to help prepare for expected increases in demand. The focus: still newer and more advanced network technologies. The network will provide more digital equipment and additional service features. Much of the new equipment will be housed on premises around the country owned by MCI. But they will be controlled by Westinghouse from the Westinghouse Network Management Center in Pittsburgh.

By luring outside clients, Westinghouse has already achieved a one-third increase in its network volume. "We're consumers of telecommunications service," says Rosenzweig, "as well as sellers. We know what people are looking for in telecommunications, because we look for it ourselves. We've been on the other side of the desk."

14 *The Compleat Angler**

B. G. Yovovich

A word of warning to companies rushing to outfit their sales forces with laptop computers and to provide sales reps with the benefits of information technology: Applying computers to the sales function is likely to be a lot different from computerizing an accounting system or automating manufacturing.

In fact, say the experts, the key to a successful sales-force-automation project is, paradoxically, to make sure that you don't approach it as an automation effort.

"The term *sales-force automation* doesn't capture the essence of what is going on," said Fred D. Wiersema, a principal with the Index Group, a consulting firm based in Cambridge, Massachusetts. "Any effort that does nothing more than streamline the way things are done today is basically working at the margins and is not going to have the big payoff. The big payoff comes from those things that can really change the job of a salesperson—really change the way that he goes about the job and help him do it in a far more productive manner."

To Larry Loop, district manager of marketing information systems at Southwestern Bell Telephone in St. Louis, making salespeople more productive means giving them information that can help them sell or give customers some added value. "What is important is not automation of call reporting, or providing a word-processing capability, or electronic mail to send in expense reports if you are on the road. It is great if you can make it easier to do the paperwork and the typical administrative functions, but what you want is not really automation, but more along the lines of a decision support system. What salespeople really want is to be able to get

* Source: B. G. Yovovich, "The Compleat Angler," *CIO*, May 1989, pp. 16–18, 20–22. Copyright CIO Publishing, Inc., © 1989 by CIO Publishing, Inc., Framingham, Mass. All rights reserved.

the kind of information that will help them do what they need to do, whether that is how to address the competition, how to deal with the customer, or any of the other decisions they have to make.''

Several factors have prompted a surge in efforts to bring the benefits of IT to the sales force. In part, the increased interest has been spurred by a drop in the prices of laptop computers and improvements in their capabilities, including better-quality displays, expanded memory and the availability of such peripherals as portable printers.

Another factor that has stimulated efforts to apply computer technology to the sales function—a function long-neglected by IS operations—is the growing recognition that sales applications now offer a greater payback potential than any other information technology investment. According to Rowland Moriarty, associate professor at the Harvard Business School in Cambridge, computerization and automation have already been used to cut sharply the costs of engineering and manufacturing a product. At a time when ''wringing yet more cost reductions from production labor is increasingly difficult,'' he said, opportunities to use computer technology to streamline marketing and sales are becoming more alluring. Moriarty has compiled figures that indicate that marketing and sales currently represent an average of 15 percent to 35 percent of total corporate costs, and that ''investments in marketing- and sales-automation systems hold tremendous potential for productivity improvements.''

Despite the promise, however, there are important reasons why the sales force has been among the last functions to which information technology has been applied. For one thing, the sales function is a highly complex endeavor, one for which successful computer applications can be difficult to design. Even sales managers are likely to misjudge the types of capabilities that will be most useful, and have the most appeal, to the sales force.

According to Ken Dulaney, marketing manager for GRiD Systems Corporation in Fremont, California, ''Sales managers often have misconceptions regarding what the salespeople need, or they make the big mistake of looking at sales-force automation in terms of their own selfish needs'' and end up designing systems that focus on such features as having call reports entered into a laptop computer rather than submitted on paper.

Nor do good intentions always work out. Systems that try to help sales forces computerize their time-management efforts or expense-reimbursement process, for example, have not proven particularly successful. ''In most cases they can do it faster [with] pencil and paper,'' said Dulaney. ''Committing your schedule to a computer is much less convenient than using something like [an appointment book], and even with expense reporting, paper is pretty hard to beat. The last thing that salespeople want to do is to put an expense report on the computer. They know they can do it much faster on a piece of paper.''

Computerizing one's calendar and appointment information can have other shortcomings as well. "We [attempted] to have my group use the calendar on the system," recalled Jerry Griggs, a sales manager with Southwestern Bell in Mission, Kansas. The idea was that "they would save on the paper they would turn in to me each week—things like the weekly planning and the results tracking. But it just didn't work out." Not only did the sales representatives find the system inconvenient—for example, they would have to boot up the computer every time they wanted to enter a change—but "one time we lost some of it, and the guys got a little paranoid," said Griggs.

Sales personnel are more likely to resist changes in which they see no benefit than are employees in other functions, according to Jayashree Mahajan, Ph.D., an assistant professor of marketing at the University of Arizona in Tucson. "A lot of salespeople are paid partly or completely on commission, and they are used to a direct link between effort and salary, which is not true of people working on the shop floor or of people working behind a desk and printing out an accounting ledger," he said. Mahajan has conducted in-depth interviews at 15 companies that have implemented sales-support systems. "They see the [sales-support system] training sessions as taking valuable time during which they could be selling. And if all you are doing is automating the call reports or things like that, they see it as simply adding new responsibilities that are of no benefit to them."

"The only way to make a sales-force-automation effort succeed is to convince the guy at the end of the line—the salesman—that this is going to help them," added Dulaney.

One way to win over the sales force is to use information technology to expand its competitive arsenal. The specific type of information system capabilities that a sales force would treasure depends greatly on the selling environment in which the salespeople operate. For example, the system designed to support the sales force at the Sara Lee Hosiery Group's Hanes operations in Winston-Salem, North Carolina, doesn't include expense-accounting, call-management, or call-reporting capabilities. Instead, the system provides the members of Hanes sales force with improved capability to customize sales presentations and to give them better access to account information than was available in the mainframe.

According to John Owens, vice president of IS for the Sara Lee Hosiery Group, "Over the years, we have become more committed to information management and have concentrated on giving the sales force information to do a thorough and professional job of managing our relationship with the trade. The laptops [provided to the Hanes sales force] are just an extension of that. The system has a word processing and a spreadsheet capability, but those are really secondary."

In particular, Owens said, the thrust of the Hanes sales support system is to help sales personnel "analyze our [products'] performance for the retailer regarding all the traditional things that the retailer worries about."

This includes offering retailers such information as gross-margin performance and inventory turns of Hanes products—a variety of hosiery brands. The system also enables Hanes salespeople to call up information that shows how Hanes products are selling in stores similar to the customer's outlet and what mix of Hanes products is likely to produce optimal profits for the retailer.

Moreover, Hanes new sales support system was designed not only to provide sales reps with more information, but also to help them sort through that information, according to Jim Collins, who oversees Hanes hosiery sales in the Northeast. "We try to manage 3,000 [different items] for our retailers," said Collins, "and obviously there is a lot of analysis and reviewing of numbers. With the number of [items] we have, and the number of stores, there are reams and reams of data."

As a result, when the new system was being designed, Hanes included a capability to "build in our goals and objectives and to flag those [products] where we are turning too slow or too fast, where we are stocking out, where our best business opportunities are likely to be. It takes a lot of the pain out of the analytic process and enables our people to be more productive with their time."

Likewise, one of the features built into the sales support system at Chevron USA, Inc., in San Francisco, makes it possible for the sales rep to use sales figures provided by Chevron dealers to help point the dealers toward enhanced productivity. "[We] plug in those figures and show them which profit centers are not working too well for them," said Sandy Anderson, a Chevron territory manager based in Salinas, California. Armed with results that pinpoint the weak links in their businesses, dealers can concentrate on improving them.

Some of the most useful information a sale force could want concerns order entry and status. Increasingly demanding customers, especially in the retail industry, want up-to-date order information, and a sales force can profit by providing it quickly and easily. "For example," said Dulaney, "in the apparel industry it is important to know whether or not an order is in stock. So a high-leverage, 'home-run' application could be one that enables a salesperson to know that what he is selling is actually available, and to reserve that product."

For other sales forces, the winning feature might be the ability to access information that compares one's product with that of competitors. The new sales support system at Southwestern Bell has this capability, according to Loop.

"We have a certain amount of competitive analysis going on now in each one of our market-segment groups," he said, "and we have created the capability of taking that competitive information and bringing it into a videotex environment or a database environment where it can be retrieved and accessed by anyone who is on the system." Thus a salesman would be able to look at the competitive alternatives to a central-office switching system that is sold by Southwestern Bell, for example, and compare the advantages and disadvantages of the various products.

"It would equip the salesperson to say, 'This is what we offer you, and here are the advantages we have over product X and product Y,' " said Loop. "We are not there yet. We have not fully implemented and begun to populate these environments with competitive information, but we now have the ability to make that kind of data and information available."

In some cases, the sales force can get excited by capabilities that have long been available to other parts of the company. At Mercedes-Benz of North America, Inc., in Montvale, New Jersey, the members of the field force were particularly enthusiastic about being hooked up, via electronic mail, to the same information network that the company uses to provide dealers with the latest corporate information, including major announcements such as management changes and shifts in company policies or strategies.

"The members of our field force are well educated and aggressive, and when they go into a dealership, they want to have their facts together," said James Bersig, manager of systems services. Because the members of the field force are on the road a great deal, it was difficult to get information to them in a timely manner before the electronic-mail service was implemented. Not only is the E-mail system informative, it also helps combat the isolation from company doings that salespeople are frequently prey to. "If we can keep them current on what is going on, they feel like they are with it. This way they are plugged into the system and know the party line, and that is very important."

Electronic mail was a similarly popular feature with the Chevron sales force, and "turned out to be our biggest win" with salespeople, said Larry Martin, manager of information systems for the marketing department. "Electronic mail turned out to be the hook that made people really use the laptops. One of the key things we did was that we trained the managers and the reps at the same time, and when the managers saw what the potential was, they instructed their salespeople to get on the system once or twice a day to check [their E-mail]." Now, he said, "instead of playing telephone tag or mailing notes and memos back and forth," the sales force can communicate efficiently and effectively across a wide geographic area.

"There is an urgency that is associated with electronic mail," he added. "If someone sends a salesperson [an E-mail] note, it is there right away, and everyone knows that it is there—and they are supposed to take care of it.

"It works the other way when the salesperson sends a note. There is a little bit of pressure to keep up with electronic mail; whereas [with] paper mail, you can let it slide. The E-mail, and the fact that they jumped in and used it right away, meant that we had a leg up" with the users that helped stimulate use of other features in the system.

Identifying key applications is no simple task and generally requires help from the sales force. "It is important to involve the sales organization at an early stage in the development of the business objectives of the system," said Hanes's Owens. "If you only have a group of headquarters people or systems types trying to do it in a vacuum, you are going to have some critical mismatches."

If Owens's group hadn't sought the input of the Hanes sales force before designing their system, he said, "we probably would have gone in there with certain assumptions about time management and the productivity of the sales force, and we could have had it all wrong." However, armed with user recommendations, they instead focused on "the quality of information and analytical capabilities, and assessing performance of specific retail [outlets]. I think we would have missed some of that had we not had that involvement of sales early in the project."

The importance of such insights can scarcely be overstated. Argued Wiersema of the Index Group, "We're talking about transformation of the sales job, making it a totally different job by giving [salespeople] choosing machines . . . ordering machines . . . configuration tools . . . [and] databases that enable them to zero in on the right people. If you [only] tinker at the margins, it takes an awful lot of your time and effort and is rife with frustration."

A HARD SELL

Early Adopters Jumped in Feet First, but Most Companies Now Demand Some Cost Justification

Not only do sales support systems confront IS executives with knotty problems concerning design, implementation, and support, they can also present difficult cost-justification challenges.

Sales-force-automation efforts tend to be held to standards not applied to other IS projects. "If you were going to start a company today, you would never give a second thought as to whether you would computerize the accounting function; there would be absolutely no hesitation," said Ken Dulaney of GRiD Systems. "Sales is as big or bigger than accounting, and it has very little computerization. But a lot of people doing sales-force automation today . . . have to go through an intense justification process and try to figure out what percent increase in sales they can get."

In part, the emphasis on cost justification is an indication that a new wave of organizations is beginning to get interested in implementing sales support systems.

"The early adopters of these systems did it on the basis of vision and faith," said Rowland Moriarty. "We are now over 15 percent penetration and are moving past those innovators to people who need more formal mechanisms" to convince them to implement such systems.

This insistence on cost-justification raises significant problems because of the complexity of the sales function and the consequent difficulty of calculating the bottom-line impact of supporting technology. "The hard measures are not there," said Jayashree Mahajan. He has found that "most companies are collecting softer measures," including such indicators as system-usage rates and sales-force satisfaction with the system.

According to Fred Wiersema, other measurements—"such as increases in the proportion of time spent with customers [or] increases in the success rate in calls on new customers—provide an indication of a streamlining of the sales process.

"If you are putting these systems together and are only looking for the ultimate payoff," said Wiersema, "and [you] don't have the intermediate milestones to tell you if you are on track, you are not likely to stay on track."

BIG BROTHER IN A LAPTOP?

Your Company's Sales Force May not Fully Appreciate the Wonders of Its New Sales Support System

Companies implementing sales support systems are often faced with strong resistance from their sales staff. These systems can do more than just automate a function; they can change the very nature of the sales role. As a result, sales personnel are apt to feel—often justifiably—that their territory is being encroached upon and their identity is being threatened. But companies can take steps to make the transition go more smoothly.

According to Professor Mahajan, "Salespeople often are described as 'boundary spanners.' They work at the boundary of the organization, and they work very autonomously." Because of their independent nature, they don't always respond well to sales support systems that gather large amounts of information about their activities. "It can give salespeople the notion of someone looking over their shoulder—foster a Big Brother Syndrome," he explained.

Likewise, it is not surprising that sales reps feel they are losing some of their autonomy when a sales information system is installed. According to Michael Hammer, of Hammer and Company, Inc., in Cambridge, "It would be foolish to make a universal statement for all companies, but for many companies, one of the main objectives in using information technology will be a tighter integration of the sales function with the rest of the company." Hammer, whose consulting firm organizes an annual conference on marketing and technology, said that properly explaining the benefits a sales force is likely to reap from a system will generally help minimize difficulties.

Another factor that can interfere with smooth implementation is that salespeople often regard the systems as having the potential to endanger their jobs—not without some justification. For one thing, the goal of using information technologies to transform sales from an "order-oriented" to a "consultative" function (using salespeople's expertise to add value for the customer rather than simply move a product) poses a direct threat to many sales reps. Hammer cited the example of a chemical company currently developing such a system. "They expect [that] half the salespeople will not survive—not because the computer will replace them, but because they do not have the skills to adapt to a really consultative selling environment."

Even when jobs are not threatened, a sales support system can cause concern. Unanswered questions about changes the new technology will bring—especially changes in compensation—can foster resistance, which, if strong enough, could very well scuttle a system that in the long run would have benefited both the company and the sales reps.

To minimize the danger of such opposition, companies should take steps to make it less likely that "people will worry about the short-term issues, about short-term compensation changes, about short-term changes in quota," advised Hammer. "I know of one organization that—short-term— kept the normal commission structure for orders that came in on the EDI system, even if the salesman was not involved. Short-term, the salesmen were very happy about it. Later on, you can start changing the rules.

"There may be some costs connected with this in the short-term," Hammer said, "but you look at it as a cost [that is necessary] to get some things established."

15 *Let the Customer Do It**

Jerry Kanter
Stephen Schiffman
J. Faye Horn

Remember the scene in *The Adventures of Tom Sawyer* in which Tom gets his friends to do his whitewashing chore by convincing them that it's a privilege? Today, companies are exercising that same approach by using technology to get customers to do their work for them.

Maturing technologies, such as personal computers, networking, and electronic data interchange, hold the promise of improving customer service while managing the growing labor cost of customer transactions. The new approach? Let the customer do it.

Examples of do-it-yourself point-of-sale (POS) technology are becoming more common each day: In addition to using the ubiquitous automated teller machine (ATM), travelers can now do self-ticketing of airline flights and use self-actuated kiosks to buy insurance policies and mortgage options. You can also design your own deck or price a new car, all by keying in your requirements.

In certain areas, fully automatic gas stations enable you to pump your own gas and pay by credit card—without a human attendant. Citicorp has developed a telephone with a built-in screen to facilitate banking at home. Home buying services, such as Compuserve, Inc.'s Compuserve, which has been in business for years, are being joined by new competitors.

Yet the idea of letting the customer do transaction processing is not new. Users have been dialing telephone calls without operator assistance since the 1920s.

Today, two major factors are driving the rapid growth of self-service

---

* Source: Jerry Kanter, Stephen Schiffman, and J. Faye Horn, "Let the Customer Do It," *Computerworld,* August 27, 1990, pp. 75–78.

systems: improved technology and business pressures. Until recently, transaction processing was handled exclusively by large mainframe systems. The advent of minicomputers and PCs, along with better, more reliable networks, has changed all that. Tied to bar-code scanning and other POS devices, these electronic links have been extended from the retail store directly to customers.

The bottom line is that today's technology allows the capture of transactions at the point of sale, integrating them electronically with a company's billing and order-replenishment systems.

And organizations everywhere are under great pressure to make technology investments pay off.

NOT JUST AN OPTION

Letting the customer do it may be more than just an option. Research company American Demographics points out that a fast-growing elderly population, declining numbers of young adults, and a record low population growth rate will put the nation in a demographic vise in the 1990s. Nationally, the 20 to 29 age group is projected by the U.S. Census Bureau to drop 12.5 percent during the next decade. With the continued growth of a service-oriented economy, there may not be enough people to satisfy the demand for retail clerks and service attendants.

These demographic shifts are forcing retailers, financial service providers, and other firms that deal directly with consumers to take a hard look at customer self-service systems. The approach could become a key determinant of survival for some industries.

Beyond survival, many businesses implement self-service systems for other reasons. Cost leadership, product differentiation, bigger market share, or strategic advantage are among the possibilities.

For example, an ATM can help a bank reduce its labor expenses and thus provide a cost leadership position in the industry. As a technology, ATMs can help distinguish a bank's services from its competitors. Sears, Roebuck and Company, for instance, may support Prodigy Services Company's Prodigy to exploit a market niche not currently addressed through catalog or showroom sales channels.

Self-service systems can also help customers with various stages of the buying cycle. Weyerhauser Company's design-a-deck system, for example, helps the customer establish requirements. Prodigy allows the customer to select, order, pay for, and acquire a product. ATMs let customers acquire cash and monitor their accounts. Avis, Inc.'s ATM-like machines allow customers to expedite car-rental returns. The biggest payoffs come from applications that support many buying steps.

However, it is clear today that competitive advantage gained through information technology is not necessarily sustainable. Even small banks eventually responded to the ATM challenge and joined regional and national bankcard networks. This in turn forced leading banks to evolve their ATM services in order to stay ahead of the competition. Baybanks, Inc., for instance, has introduced a service that allows the customer to keep an eye on which of their checks have cleared most recently.

Looking at three technologies—ATMs, automatic checkout machines, and the Prodigy home buying service—provides a good insight into the current state of the do-it-yourself movement.

ATMs: MORE FOR THE MONEY

In the 20 years since their introduction, money machines, or ATMs, have become an accepted method of convenient access to cash. Financial institutions originally intended ATMs to provide customers with convenient banking services at lower costs than tellers' salaries. By 1988, approximately 65,000 ATMs were in use in the United States, handling nearly half a *trillion* transactions. Nearly half of all cash withdrawals are made from ATMs. In fact, ATMs are so common today that, for most of the United States, automated banking is no longer a differentiator between financial institutions. ATMs have become a commodity service as common as telephone booths.

As a result, banks are looking at two major strategies to increase ATM profitability. One is to join nationwide network systems, such as Cirrus, that permit users to access cash outside of the bank's regional area. The other is to increase the range of services and their attractiveness to ATM users and generate revenue from new fees.

The new challenge for bankers is twofold: Offer profitable services and convince customers that automation is the most effective way to conduct their financial affairs. Some innovative options are within one or two years of implementation. These will require rethinking the role of automation in financial institutions, and, in some cases, the nature of the banking business itself. Institutions will probably rely heavily on frequent use bonuses and other use incentives.

Dale L. Reistad, president of the Electronic Funds Transfer Association, predicts that ATM cards will evolve eventually into "supersmart cards" with key pads, readouts, and a small battery. These cards will be used not only for personal banking but also for stock transactions, worldwide special-interest electronic mail systems, and accessing a variety of databases.

Reistad suggests that the end result in the United States will be that customers will have their own "individual bank" custom-designed to meet their personal banking, investment, and transactional needs.

CHECKROBOTS: NEW WAVE MARKET

A different twist on customer self-service systems has less to do with dollars than with doughnuts. The Automated Checkout Machine (ACM) System, a product of Florida-based Checkrobot, Inc., enables shoppers to check out their own merchandise before paying a centrally located cashier. It incorporates a security system to ensure that each item departing the store has been scanned and paid for. Laser scanning, local-area networks, and database management systems are combined to produce a user interface with the store's central computer.

Checkrobot claims that ACM System offers the perception of improved customer service because the automated checkout machine is easy to use, decreases shopping time, and increases customers' control over their shopping environment. It also says the system provides a high return on investment, primarily because of decreased labor costs. While the current target market is supermarkets, the company plans to expand to retail organizations in general.

ACM System consists of automated checkout machine stations, a central computer linked to the stations, and a POS computer. The automated stations are made up of five parts: a laser scanner, which reads bar-code labels; a color video touch screen, which displays a complete description of the items being purchased, along with their prices and a running subtotal; a produce key pad and produce video screen for handling produce and other variable-weight bulk items; a proprietary and patented merchandise security system; and a conveyer belt that moves through the merchandise security system to the bagging area.

Checkrobot developed ACM System as a response to the evolving retail market and shrinking labor pool. The company claims that automated checkout machines can not only cut down on staffing needs but also lower costs and increase profitability. Checkrobot estimates that one cashier is needed for every three to four automated checkouts, plus one optional bagger (usually working for a lower wage than checkout operators) for every one to two checkouts.

Beyond cost savings, the system also offers the promise of a competitive advantage. Increasingly, customer service in supermarkets is becoming a big differentiator in a competitive industry. By far the most important factor is efficient, speedy checkout.

Customers seem to think that automated checkout machines work. Independent research found that more than half of the users surveyed said that the systems were "much faster" than conventional checkouts; two thirds preferred the automated checkout machine to a conventional checkout, perceived self-scanning as an additional service offered by the store, thought overall service was better than in stores without automated checkout, and thought their overall checkout time was shorter than prior to the installation of the machines. In addition, five sixths of the respondents labeled the automated checkout machines as easy to use.

Why does this high-tech system cause a perceived improvement in a low-tech area such as customer service? In general, it is because customers judge service quality perceptually, not quantitatively. There are four possible reasons for this perception.

First, autoscanning responds to shoppers' No. 1 complaint: waiting in line. Automatic checkout machine-equipped lines are always open, regardless of the number of checkout operators working at the time. (The actual time spent scanning is longer, however.) Customers do not operate the scanning system as fast as trained employees. But the longer real time does not affect their perception of faster checkout.

Second, customers perceive autoscanning as more accurate than staff-operated scanning systems. As they scan, the customer can see the item listed with its price on the video screen and then verify its accuracy.

Third, customer research indicates that automatic checkout machines are readily accepted across demographic lines of age, sex, or income.

If the financial benefits of ACM System are firmly established, autoscanning may become a familiar everyday part of life—just like ATMs.

SELF-SERVE SUCCESS

What makes some self-service systems become part of everyday life quickly, while others never seem more than expensive, awkward monstrosities?

- *A perception of benefit:* Customers are willing to operate a transaction processing system if they perceive a benefit greater than the effort of doing it themselves. Prodigy may not shorten delivery time, but customers may still view it as a sales aid. If transaction processing does not appeal to some buyers' purchase criteria in a meaningful way, it may well fail to gain acceptance.
- *Rapid response and a good interface:* High bandwidth is key here. Transaction speeds—and thus satisfaction—are affected by communications between the customer's input device and the rest of the transactional system.

  High bandwidth allows for both rapid response time and the use of a user friendly graphical or video interface, such as the one currently found in Checkrobot's ACM System.

  There are limitations, though. Prodigy's user interface certainly yields much higher bandwidth than text-oriented videotex systems, which have faired poorly in the past, yet Prodigy still cannot compete with the high-bandwidth environment of a glitzy, live display of merchandise in a store or even with television advertisements.

- *Ease of use:* Beyond a good interface, ease of use also depends on the complexity of information exchanged between the customer and the transaction processing system. For example, when a customer wants cash, he decides to withdraw an amount—say $50—and tells the ATM.

  Compare this with a novice ordering a fly-fishing rod through Prodigy. A good salesperson would know that certain rods are suitable for salt-water fishing, others for river fishing and still others for lake fishing. If the customer is not prompted for specific requirements, he could well end up with the wrong rod.

- *Native intelligence:* Built-in artificial intelligence or other "smart" capabilities can make self-service systems more useful, because such systems can aid in the interchange of complex information between the customer and the system. For example, the leading producer of elevators, Otis Elevator Company, provides its customers with PCs and the required software to guide them in selecting, ordering and scheduling the construction of elevators.

NEW IDEAS FOR SELF-SERVICE

Several promising technologies are emerging that will allow customers to handle more of the ordering burden:

- *Multimedia:* A host of devices now coming to market will transmit video, voice and even three-dimensional pictures to potential customers. For example, a real estate office can simulate a walk through a house, or an architect can superimpose a home or garden addition to an existing property.

- *Automatic scanning devices:* In a Milan, Italy bank, for example, a customer can stack his U.S. bills in a device that returns lire and an itemized record of the transaction. The device handles 16 different currencies. And the scanner reportedly does a much better job than the human eye of detecting counterfeit bills.

- *Voice recognition:* Like optical scanning, this is another powerful option. It works on the premise that most people are more comfortable speaking than keying or typing. A few working applications are in the field, and research continues. One system employs a chip in an ATM card that will verify the voice of the cardholder. This can be considered a "voice print" and offers voice withdrawals as opposed to the current method of using a key pad.

- *Handwriting recognition:* Akin to optical scanning are machines that can read printed writing. Their use would allow office workers and customers to record information in the same way they always have—by filling in the blanks and checking off boxes. The potential also exists for processing handwriting in foreign languages with automatic translation.

PRODIGY: A PROMISING INFANT

Prodigy Services, a joint venture combining IBM's technological expertise and Sears' retailing expertise, offers PC owners an "on-line electronic mall of information and shopping services." Operating from telephone networks connecting 22 minicomputer centers around the country, Prodigy provides shopping, banking, news, and database access to an estimated 160,000 subscribers.

Prodigy's launch in October 1988 was greeted with skepticism because of the earlier failures of similar ventures. In particular, home banking services were expected to be widely accepted when they first became available in the mid-1980s. But earlier technology was not user-friendly, and applications were not geared to the mass market. Thus, those systems disappeared.

Prodigy faces stiff competition. Not only do 1.3 million computer owners subscribe to similar systems, such as Compuserve, but telephone companies are also starting information ventures of their own. However, according to Sears chairman Edward Brennan, Prodigy's edge is that it is broader and less expensive than its competitors.

To meet mass-market appeal, Prodigy is menu-driven and friendly and costs $9.95 per month for unlimited use. Subscribers can order from Sears, J.C. Penney Company, and 45 other direct-mail retailers. They can also bank with more than a dozen affiliates, including Manufacturers Hanover Corporation, and make plane reservations through American Airline's Sabre system. A wide range of news, financial and entertainment sources are also available.

The deliberate mass nature of Prodigy's marketing appeal has another advantage: It provides an attractive advertising medium. Almost 200 companies, including American Express and J.C. Penney, pay Prodigy every time an advertisement is accessed, a lead is generated or a product is sold.

Edward Papes, Prodigy's chief executive, says he doesn't expect Prodigy to break even for another few years. However, IBM and Sears say they consider Prodigy a long-term project. If Prodigy continues to upgrade its electronic package for a growing market, it could change how Americans acquire a wide variety of goods and services.

Letting the customer do transaction processing is not a fad. It is driven by such factors as population demographics and industry competition.

As with the introduction of any new technology, some will fail, and some will succeed. Technological improvements in computing hardware and software and in the telecommunications infrastructure will allow for the introduction of new customer-driven systems. The successful ones will provide a perceived benefit to customers by convincing them, as Tom Sawyer did, that "it's a privilege."

IV Management of Information Systems

The management of information systems (IS) is a critical topic. In addition to their development and evolution, information systems must be managed by those in the organization who understand their importance and the key role that they play in achieving organizational goals. Knowledge about information systems must be integrated with knowledge about management and organizational processes. Vital management processes include, but are not limited to, planning, facilitating, integrating, measuring, controlling, and implementing. Two other dominant concerns are managing end-user computing and using information systems for competitive and strategic advantage. Both topics are of growing importance in the contemporary business world.

Strategic planning is a logical starting point for the study of the management of information systems. William R. King in his CLASSIC, "Strategic Planning for Management Information Systems," Reading 16, discusses strategic planning for the organization, the need for the information systems plan to support the business plan, and a process for making the two compatible.

The management of information systems is too important to be left to technical specialists. John F. Rockart in "The Line Takes the Leadership —IS Management in a Wired Society," Reading 17, argues that system conception and implementation requires line management leadership. The reasons for and implications of these important role changes are discussed.

End users are increasingly developing and using computer applications. Thomas P. Gerrity and John F. Rockart in Reading 18, "End-User Computing: Are You a Leader or a Laggard?" first discuss the benefits of end-user computing. Then they discuss three general approaches to its management—monopolist, laissez-faire, and the information center. They conclude that each approach is lacking and suggest that end-user computing should be managed as a free economy.

Reading 19, "Creating Competitive Weapons from Information Systems," by Charles Wiseman and Ian C. MacMillan, shows how a business can use modern information technologies to create a competitive edge by adding value to present products and services. This is a logical outgrowth of intensified competition and the recognition that information systems are emerging as critical new weapons in the battle to gain an advantage over competitors.

American Airlines is often cited as an example of a firm that has used information systems for competitive advantage. Max D. Hopper is the senior vice president for information systems at American Airlines and he argues, in Reading 20, "Rattling SABRE—New Ways to Compete on Information," that information systems is entering a new era and that its new challenge is to build a technology platform that supports applications that allows individuals and groups to do their jobs smarter, better, and more creatively.

Reading 21, "Managing the Introduction of Information Systems Technology in Strategically Dependent Companies," by James I. Cash, Jr., and Poppy L. McLeod, proposes that modern organizations, strategically dependent on computer and communications technology, must establish an organizational unit with specific responsibilities for these processes and use a contingency framework for the design of the administrative infrastructure to effectively manage the new technology.

Should organizations centralize their information systems resources for economies of scale or decentralize them to provide proximity to users? Robert F. Morison in Reading 22, "The Shape of IS to Come," concludes that information systems organizations need not trade off the advantages of a centralized group over a centralized one. He provides strategies for gaining the benefits of both.

Organizations often spend millions of dollars on information systems but are uncertain of the returns. Reading 23, "Measuring Information Systems Performance: Experience with the Management by Results System at Security Pacific Bank," by John P. Singleton, Ephraim R. McLean, and Edward N. Altman, discusses the performance measure problem and how it has been handled effectively at the Security Pacific Bank.

16 Strategic Planning for Management Information Systems*

William R. King

The literature of management information systems (MIS) concentrates largely on the nature and structure of MISs and on processes for designing and developing such systems. The idea of "planning for the MIS" is usually treated as either one of developing the need and the general design concept for such a system, or in the context of project planning for the MIS development effort.

However, *strategic* planning for the informational needs of the organization is both feasible and necessary if the MIS is to support the basic purposes and goals of the organization. Indeed, one of the possible explanations [6]‡ for the failure of many MISs is that they have been designed from the same "bottom up" point of view that characterized the development of the data processing systems of an earlier era. Such design approaches primarily reflect the pursuit of *efficiency,* such as through cost savings, rather than the pursuit of greater organizational *effectiveness.* "Efficiency" may be thought of in terms of a ratio of output to input. "Effectiveness" relates output to the goals which are being sought.

The modern view of MIS as an organizational decision support system is inconsistent with the design/development approaches which are appro-

---

* Source: Reprinted by special permission from the *MIS Quarterly,* vol. 2, no. 1 March 1978. Copyright 1978 by the Society for Information Management and the Management Information Systems Research Center at the University of Minnesota.
‡ Bracketed numbers cite the references at the end of the chapter.

priate for data processing. The organization's operating efficiency is but one aspect for consideration in management decision making. The achievement of greater organizational *effectiveness* is the paramount consideration in most of the management decisions which the MIS is to support; it also must be of paramount importance in the design of the MIS.

There is an intrinsic linkage of the decision-supporting MIS to the organization's purpose, objectives, and strategy. While this conclusion may appear to be straightforward, it has not been operationalized as a part of MIS design methodology. There are those who argue that the MIS designer cannot hope to get involved in such things as organizational missions, objectives, and strategies, since they are clearly beyond his domain of authority.

This article describes an operationally feasible approach for identifying and utilizing the elements of the organization's "strategy set" to plan for the MIS. Whether or not written statements of these strategic elements (e.g., missions, objectives, etc.) exist, it still often will be necessary to perform the identification phase of the analysis, since such written statements are frequently outdated or may be of the variety that are commonly produced for public relations purposes, rather than for strategic management purposes. If credible statements of organizational purpose and strategy do exist, only that portion of the process which deals with *transforming* organizational strategy into MIS strategic parameters need be implemented.

MIS STRATEGIC PLANNING—AN OVERVIEW

Figure 1 abstractly shows the overall process for performing MIS strategic planning. This figure shows a "MIS Strategic Planning" process, which transforms an "Organizational Strategy Set," made up of organizational mission, objectives, strategy, and other strategic organizational attributes, into an "MIS Strategy Set," made up of system objectives, constraints, and design principles.

Figure 1 describes an information-based approach to strategic planning for the MIS, in that it identifies an information set—the "MIS Strategy Set"—which will guide the design and development of the MIS. While the elements of this MIS Strategy Set—system objectives, constraints, and design principles—are not usually thought of in this context, they are generally recognized to be the guiding considerations in developing the MIS design (e.g., [10]).

However well recognized the elements of the MIS Strategy Set are, Figure 1 shows the MIS Strategy Set as emanating directly from another information set, the "Organizational Strategy Set." This direct relationship between the two information sets is neither well recognized nor operationalized. It is this linkage which is the province of MIS Strategic

---

FIGURE 1   Overall MIS Strategic Planning Process

ORGANIZATIONAL
STRATEGY SET

MIS
STRATEGY SET

Mission
Objectives
Strategy
Other strategic organizational
attributes

MIS
Strategic

Planning
Process

System objectives
System constraints
System design strategies

Planning and it is on the operationalizing of the transformation process between these two information sets that this article focuses.

It will prove useful to describe both the "Organizational Strategy Set" and the "MIS Strategy Set" in some detail, before describing an operational process for accomplishing the MIS Strategic Planning function, which is described conceptually in Figure 1.

THE ORGANIZATIONAL STRATEGY SET

The "Organizational Strategy Set" is composed of those elements of organizational purpose and direction which are developed as a result of the organization's strategic planning process—the organization's mission, objectives, and strategy—as well as certain other strategic organizational attributes which are of particular relevance to the MIS.

Since the terminology which is applied to these strategic planning outputs generally varies from company to company and between business firms and public agencies, it is useful to define and illustrate the elements of the organizational strategy set used in this article. No inference should be drawn that these are proposed as the "correct" descriptions, or that the definitions used here are universally appropriate; rather, the delineations are useful for fully developing the MIS Strategic Planning process.

The Organization's Mission

The broadest strategic planning which must be done by an organization is that of its *mission*. An organization's *mission statement* tells what it is, why it exists, and the unique contribution it can make. The mission answers the organization's basic question: "What business are we in?" Some people consider such questions idle academic nonsense; to them, their mission—the business that they are in—is clear: "We make widgets," or "We run railroads."

It became increasingly apparent during the 1960s that such thinking was too limited. Organizations which felt that they knew their business disappeared in vast numbers from the scene. Today's business, however bright its growth prospects may appear, may not exist in its current form in only a few years.

Conversely, during the 1970s, it also became apparent that firms which slavishly followed expansive views of their mission could encounter serious problems. Broad mission statements were open invitations to get into new businesses solely on the criterion of *"potential profitability."* Such a criterion does not take into account vital factors such as expertise—technological, market, and otherwise; neither does it take into account the uncertainty which is inherent in potential profit. Many of the companies which got into new "growth" businesses on this basis in the 1960s found themselves in the position of selling off unprofitable ventures in the 1970s [12]. These problems have led to the conclusion that *the mission statement for an organization must carefully define what it does not do, as well as what it does.*

The values of such a clearly defined mission statement can be illustrated with the "business statement" of one medium-sized firm:

> We are in the business of supplying system components and services to a worldwide, nonresidential air conditioning market. Air conditioning is defined as heating, cooling, cleaning, humidity control, and air movement.

While such a statement may at first seem to be the same as "We make widgets," it clearly specifies by exclusion many things that the firm does not do: it does not supply air conditioning *systems*—rather, it focuses on system *components;* it does not address itself to the residential market for air conditioners; and so on.

The Organization's Objectives

Once the organization's mission has been determined, its objectives—desired future positions or "destinations" that it wishes to reach—should be selected. These destinations may be stated in either quantitative or qualitative terms; but they should be *broad and timeless statements,* as opposed to specific, quantitative goals, or targets.

For instance, among the stated objectives of PPG Industries are:

> 1. . . . to increase earnings per share to attain a continuing return of 14.5 percent or more on stockholder's equity and to provide consistently increasing dividends [the prime objective].

2. . . . to employ the least number and highest quality of people necessary to accomplish the prime objective and to provide them with the opportunities to develop and apply their fullest abilities.

3. . . . to have the company accepted as a dynamic, responsible, professionally managed, profit oriented corporation engaged in exciting and important fields of business, with the ability to meet successfully the economic and social challenges of the future. [5]

While such statements may at first appear to be "motherhood and sin," they say very important things about the company. For instance, the "image" objective, 3, says that PPG cares greatly how it is thought of in society. This serves to clearly constrain other choices which must be made in the planning process (e.g., strategies which may be followed to attain the prime objective).

The Organization's Strategy

The organization's strategy is the *general direction* in which it chooses to move in order to achieve its goals and objectives. For instance, one company has stated that it:

. . . has heavy investment, a good reputation, great skills and experience, a viable organization, and, in some instances, a special situation in the . . . industries.

And that it will:

. . . exploit these strengths and, . . . not diversify at the present time, into unrelated industries.

A more detailed strategy for another firm includes the following:

. . . increase U.S. market penetration through the development of a regional manufacturing capability and the development of secondary distribution channels.

Another company's strategy calls for a:

. . . low-price, low-cost product achieved through product standardization . . . together with:

. . . the development of new products on a similar basis in a posture of defensive innovation against the technological progress of competitors.

Again, as with a mission statement, the strategy is as important for what it does not say as what it does say. By excluding numerous, possibly valid ways of achieving a stated objective, it ensures a focusing of organizational resources and precludes a "scatter-gun" approach, which is likely to be ineffective, and which is likely to result if numerous managers are permitted to make decisions without strategy guidance.

Other Strategic Organizational Attributes

Other strategic attributes of the organization should also influence the strategic planning for the MIS. These "miscellaneous" attributes are difficult to categorize, but they may be extremely important. For instance, if the sophistication of management is low and their familiarity with computers, models, and interactive systems is limited, such factors must obviously be explicitly taken into account in planning for the MIS. If they are not accounted for, an MIS better suited for sophisticated computer-skilled managers might be developed by technicians who naturally desire the systems that they develop to be as "modern" and sophisticated as is possible.

Admittedly, such organizational attributes as the sophistication of management, the readiness of the organization to accept change, and the familiarity of management with the values and limitations of computer systems are difficult to measure. However, if strategic MIS planning is to be performed, such strategic organizational attributes must be incorporated into the organizational strategy set and used as a basis for developing the MIS strategy set.

THE MIS STRATEGY SET

The MIS strategy elements, which are the substance of strategic planning for the MIS, are system objectives, system constraints, and system design strategies.

System Objectives

System objectives define the *purpose* which the MIS is to serve. For instance, system objectives may be stated in terms that are similar to, but much more specific than, organizational objectives (e.g., "to permit the payment of 98 percent of invoices by the due date" is a system objective stated in *activity* terms). Also, system objectives may be stated in direct *information and communication terms* (e.g., "to collect, and process all routing and cost information and provide it in a timely fashion to the dispatcher"). The most sophisticated variety of system objectives are stated in decision-oriented terms (e.g., "to permit the determination of the best routing no more than one hour after the tentative routing choice has been implemented").

System Constraints

Both internal and external constraints must be identified if MIS planning is to be effective. These constraints will emanate both from outside and within the organization.

The most obvious forms of external MIS constraints are government and industry reporting requirements and the need for the MIS to interface with other systems, such as the ordering and billing systems of suppliers and customers.

Internal constraints emanate from the nature of the organization, its personnel, practices, and resources. The most obvious internal constraint is the MIS budget; however, many other organizational characteristics serve to limit the MIS's scope and nature. For instance, the degree of complexity with which the system is incorporated may be constrained because of the limited sophistication of management, the lack of experience within the management group with computers, or demonstrated distrust of sophisticated information systems.

System Design Strategies

The strategies which guide the MIS design effort are important MIS strategy elements, as are the organizational strategies which guide its progress. While many design strategies appear to be of the "motherhood and sin" variety, their value may be demonstrated by virtue of the number of unsuccessful systems which have been developed in the absence of such underlying strategic principles.

Among the strategies which might guide a MIS design effort is one dealing with *parsimony* (e.g., "the system should be designed so that the user is provided with the minimum amount of relevant information which is necessary to achieve his managerial objective"). Another often useful design strategy deals with the nature of the system (e.g., "the system should operate primarily in an exception-reporting mode in accomplishing its credit monitoring objective"). Other possible design strategies have to do with the criteria which will be used to evaluate the system (e.g., "the system will be evaluated both in terms of its perceived utility to users as well as its technical capability" [9].

THE MIS STRATEGIC PLANNING PROCESS

The process for MIS strategic planning is one of transforming the Organizational Strategy Set into an appropriate, relevant, and consistent MIS Strategy Set.

Explicating the Organization's Strategy Set

The first step in MIS strategic planning is the identification and explication of the organizational strategy set. Some elements of the organizational strategy set may exist in written form. The organization's strategic, or long-range, plan is the most obvious source of such material. So, too, are various pronouncements made by chief executive officers in reporting to their various constituencies: stockholders, unions, government, and the like.

However, existing plans may be deficient if the planning process is not a sophisticated one which explicitly gives consideration to such broad choices as that of the organization's objectives. Other documentary evidence may be deficient in that it is prepared for a "public relations" purpose, rather than for the purpose of guiding managerial choice. If so, an explicit process of identifying strategy set elements will be required of the MIS designer.

Such a process may be thought of in terms of a number of steps:

1. Delineating the claimant structure of the organization.
2. Identifying goals for each claimant group.
3. Identifying the organization's purposes and strategy relative to each claimant group.

Delineating the Organization's Claimant Structure.   The organization's purpose, objectives, and strategy must necessarily relate to its various clientele, or claimants—those who have a claim on it. These claimants, sometimes referred to as "stakeholders" to distinguish them from the legal owners of corporations, have a stake in the activities and future of the organization. Thus, most business firms will delineate its owners, managers, employees, suppliers, customers, and creditors as claimant groups. Other claimants whose views and desires will form a basis for the organization's purpose and strategy may be local governments, local communities, competitors, other firms in the same industry, and the general public.

Identifying the Goals for Claimants.   The goals of each claimant group must be accounted for in the organization's mission, objectives, and strategy. King and Cleland [8] have shown an approach for doing this which involves the qualitative description of the nature of each claimant's claim and the specification of measures, direct or proxy, of the degree to which the claim is being satisfied.

Identifying the Organization's Goals and Strategies for Each Claimant Group.   Once the nature of each claimant group's claim has been identified, the organization's goals and strategies relative to each group must be identified. Sometimes these linkages will be quite simple, as in linking a desire for a 15 percent ROI to the stockholders' desire for investment return. "Per share earnings" objectives relate to the goals of stockholders as well as to those of creditors, who wish the firm to remain financially stable. "Social responsibility" objectives can be traced directly to the goals of the general public and local communities, as can strategies involving the construction of pollution-free production facilities and the employment of minority group members. "Product quality" objectives and strategies are traceable directly to the interests of customers, government regulatory agencies, and the industry.

Methodologies for Further Explication and Validation of the Organization's Strategy Set

Once tentative statements of organizational mission, objectives, and strategy have been developed either from written documents, an analytic process such as that just described, or more commonly some combination of the two, the organization's top managers may be asked to critique the statement. This feedback step essentially says, "Here is what MIS analysts can infer about the organization's MIS-relevant missions, objectives, and strategies. Please give us your opinion as to the validity of these inferences."

These queries may be presented to top management either as overall statements on which to comment or in the form of Likert scale statements [11] with which top managers may agree or disagree to various degrees. The overall statement format allows for more substantive feedback, but the use of the Likert scale permits easier aggregation of judgments into an overall priority evaluation of the strategy elements. This latter approach also is conducive to assessing the "other" organizational strategy attributes. For instance, Likert scale items related to the "willingness of top management to accept change," and the "familiarity of management with the use of decision models" permit the assessment of these factors as they are perceived to be important by the managers who will ultimately be the users of the MIS [11].

Transforming the Organizational Strategy Set into the MIS Strategy Set

The heart of MIS strategic planning is the process through which the organizational strategy set is transformed into a set of system objectives, system constraints, and system design principles which comprise the MIS strategy set.

Figure 2 shows the overall process. The top of the figure shows various claimant groups which may have been identified. The upper wide rectangle is the "Organizational Strategy Set" which delineates organizational ob-

FIGURE 2   Overall MIS Strategic Planning Process

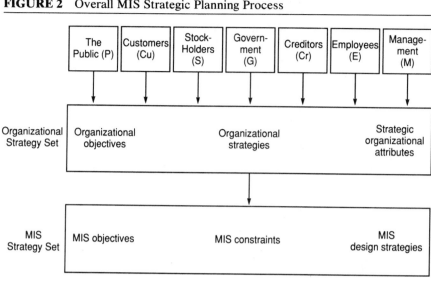

jectives, strategies, and other strategic attributes. The lower wide rectangle is the "MIS Strategy Set" entailing system objectives, constraints, and design strategies.

An Illustration of the Process.   Figures 3 and 4 illustrate in specific terms how the overall process of Figure 2 operates. Figure 3 is an illustrative explosion of the Organizational Strategy Set. The organizational objectives, strategies, and other attributes which are shown there are each related to those elements of the claimant structure from which it is primarily derived. For instance, the earnings objective (O_1) derives from the goals of stockholders (S), creditors (Cr), and management (M). The "recognition of the need for change" attribute (A_2) reflects both stockholder (S) and managerial (M) goals.

The organization's strategies are related to its objectives. This is also shown in Figure 3. For instance, the diversification strategy (S_1) is derived from two objectives (O_1 and O_6)—a desire for earnings and a need to eliminate vulnerability to the business cycle.

Figure 4 shows the MIS Strategy Set and how it is derived from the Organizational Strategy Set. It shows how system objectives, constraints, and design strategies are delineated and related to various elements of the Organizational Strategy Set as well as to other elements of the MIS Strategy Set. For instance, the MIS objective of improving the speed of billing (MO_1) is directly related to the organization's credit strategy (S_2). The constraints and environmental information (C_2 and C_3) are related

---

FIGURE 3   Organizational Strategy Set

Organizational Objectives	*Organizational Strategies*	*Strategic Organizational Attributes*
O_1: To increase earnings by 10 percent per year (S, Cr, M)	S_1: Diversification into new businesses (O_1, O_6)	A_1: Highly sophisticated management (M)
O_2: To improve cash flow (G, S, Cr)	S_2: Improvements in credit practices (O_1, O_2, O_3)	A_2: Poor recent performance has fostered a recognition of the need for change (S, M)
O_3: To maintain a high level of customer good will (Cu)	S_3: Product redesign (O_3, O_4, O_5)	A_3: Most managers are experienced users of computer services (M)
O_4: To be perceived as socially responsible (G, P)		A_4: High degree of decentralization of management authority
O_5: To produce high-quality, safe products (Cu, G)		A_5: Organization must be responsive to regulatory agencies
O_6: To eliminate vulnerability to the business cycle (S, Cr)		

---

respectively to various organizational attributes (A_1 and A_3) and specific MIS objectives (MO_2, MO_3, MO_4). The design strategy involving the systems inquiry capability (D_5) is derived from the *MIS objective* of providing quick response to customer inquiries (MO_7) which is, in turn, derived from the *organizational objective* of maintaining a high level of customer good will (O_3).

Figures 2, 3, and 4 also show how the "poor recent performance" strategic organizational attribute (A_2) leads to a system constraint that recognizes the possible future unavailability of necessary development funds (C_1), which in turn dictates both a modular design strategy (D_1) and a design strategy which recognizes that the system may never be finished

FIGURE 4   MIS Strategy Set

MIS Objectives	MIS Constraints	MIS Design Strategies
MO_1: To improve speed of billing (S_2)	C_1: Availability of funds for MIS development may be reduced (A_2)	D_1: Design on modular basis (C_1)
MO_2: To provide information on product failures (S_3)	C_2: System must incorporate best available decision models and management techniques (A_1, A_3)	D_2: Modular design must produce viable system at each stage of completion (C_1)
MO_3: To provide information on new business opportunities (S_1)	C_3: System must incorporate environmental information as well as internal information (MO_2, MO_3, MO_4)	D_3: System must be oriented to differential usage by various classes of managers (A_4, C_4)
MO_4: To provide information which will permit the assessment of the level of organizational objectives (O)	C_4: System must provide for different reports involving various levels of aggregation (A_4)	D_4: System should be responsive to the perceived needs of its user-managers (A_1, A_3, A_4)
MO_5: To provide timely and accurate information on recent performance (A_2)	C_5: System must be capable of producing information other than management information (MO_6)	D_5: System should have real-time inquiry capability (MO_7, O_3)—use COBOL (A_1, A_3)
MO_6: To produce reports desired by regulatory agencies (A_5)		
MO_7: To produce information which will permit quick response to customer inquiries (O_3)		

and may therefore be required to operate effectively at each stage of partial completion (D_2).

It is impractical to demonstrate all of the relationships which exist among the elements of the two strategy sets—one for the overall organization and one for the MIS. However, the figures show sufficient detail to illustrate the myriad of relationships as well as how they can be operationally developed from a claimant analysis.

The Methodology of the Process. The methodology which may be used for developing the MIS Strategy Set as shown in Figure 2 is one in which analysts make inferences, based on their experience and knowledge of information systems: the range of system objectives, characteristics, and design principles are shown to be consistent with the elements of the Organizational Strategy Set. For instance, a stated objective of one bank was ". . . to provide knowledgeable counseling on all of the customers' financial matters." This combined with a precise statement of the "businesses" that the bank is in allows the MIS analyst to define a range by interpreting "all" the work literally as well as in a more limited, but still reasonable, fashion. A range of system objectives is created in this way extending from:

> Provide basic data and reference information on stocks, bonds, options, real estate, etc.—a predefined range of financial alternatives that extends beyond those that form the "business" of the bank.

to:

> Provide data on all of those financial alternatives which are the "business" of the bank (e.g., savings accounts, treasury bills, trusts, certificates of deposit, etc.).

Ranges such as this can be derived from many different elements of the Organizational Strategy Set and used to construct alternative general designs for the MIS. In principle, this is a combinatorial problem. For instance, one MIS general design is represented by the combination of the most ambitious extremes in the range for each objective, constraint, and design principle: another one is made up of the least ambitious extreme for each element, etc. The analyst, in practice, will wish to construct only a *reasonable number* of alternative *reasonable designs* for presentation to management.

This process gives management the opportunity to select an MIS general design as well as provides the basis for understanding the alternative designs. This is because the designs have been generated from "business raw materials"—the elements of the Organizational Strategy Set—rather than on more typical, but less understandable, technical bases.

This process, therefore, provides both an intrinsic link between the organization's guiding influences and those which will guide the detailed design and implementation of the MIS. It also provides a basis for effective manager/analyst communication about the MIS—one of the most important, but least developed, aspects of MIS design.

CONCLUSIONS

The MIS Strategic Planning process involves the identification and assessment of an "Organizational Strategy Set"—an informational set which delineates the organization's mission, objectives, strategies, and other strategic attributes. This set can be transformed into another information set, an "MIS Strategy Set," which delineates system objectives, constraints, and design strategies.

The outputs of MIS strategic planning become the inputs to the subsequent systems development process. In many organizations these planning outputs have been arbitrary starting points for system development. The process described here *derives* these inputs to system development from the organization's most basic tenets. Such a process is much more likely to produce a system which is closely related to the organization, its strategy, and its capabilities.

The MIS strategic planning process described here cannot be delineated in algorithmic form because the relevant aspects of the Organizational Strategy Set will be vastly different in various organizations. However, the *process* of identifying and assessing the Organizational Strategy Set has been systematically outlined using the concepts of claimants and measurable claimant goals. Once organizational strategic elements have been identified, they can be validated through the structured queries of the organization's top management.

Once the Organizational Strategy Set has been delineated, its various elements can be transformed into MIS Strategy Set elements by analysts who are familiar with the available system alternatives, configurations, and attributes. This is a process which analysts perform in any case, but it is usually done with only the most vague reference to the elements of organizational purpose and strategy. The process described here necessitates an explicit and rational consideration of these relationships.

An important aspect of the MIS strategic planning process is that it ensures that the MIS is developed as an integral part of the organization and not merely appended to it. The process inherently requires manager/analyst interaction of the variety as specified by King and Cleland [7] and others [2, 4]; it would be foolhardy for the MIS analyst to attempt this process in isolation from management. This approach also provides for specific feedback from management, even in those cases where the Organization's Strategy Set is already well explicated. Such interaction has been identified as one of the primary requirements for successful MIS implementation.

This process further presents an operational framework within which the "information analyst"—a job title which resulted from an ACM educational study [3]—can operate in a system planning role. Previously, the role of the information analyst has been prescribed, but has been given no operational guidance that relates directly to the MIS field. The MIS strategic planning framework presented in this article provides such guidance.

The process does not explicitly deal with the assessment of priorities for a number of systems which might be a part of an overall MIS master plan. It does, however, provide a basis for explicating individual systems in a fashion which facilitates choice and priority setting. For instance, a system which is not closely related to many elements of the Organizational Strategy Set may inevitably be assigned a low priority since limited funds are best spent on those systems which most directly address those objectives that the organization as a whole is trying to achieve.

One objection to the described process can be raised in terms of its superficial circularity. The MIS design is to be based on organizational mission, objectives, and strategy which are themselves the product of management choice. Thus, a system which is meant to support management decision making is, in fact, designed on the basis of choices which have already been made. This difficulty is inherent in any systems design effort. Unfortunately many such systems are designed without knowledge of previous strategic organizational choices and are therefore obsolete before they are developed.

The relatively great longevity and enduring nature of organizational strategy, objective, and mission choices suggest that this planning approach is surely valid for the support of middle-level organizational decisions, a management level which Anthony has classified as the management control level [1]. Moreover, the approach is even valid for a MIS which is designed to support strategic choice, since there must be some starting point at which a system is developed to feed back information on the validity and degree of attainment of strategies already chosen. Such a system can directly support the selection of new future strategies, and it can be adapted to permit their assessment as well.

REFERENCES

1. ANTHONY, R. N. *Planning and Control Systems: A Framework for Analysis.* Harvard Business School, Division of Research, 1965.
2. ARGYRIS, C. "Management Information Systems: The Challenge to Rationality and Emotionality." *Management Science* 17, no. 6 (February 1971), pp. B275–B292.
3. ASHENHURST, R. L., ed. "Curriculum Recommendations for Graduate Professional Programs in Information Systems: A Report of the ACM Curriculum

Committee on Computer Education for Management." *Communications of the ACM* 15, no. 5 (May 1972), pp. 363–98.

4. CHURCHMAN, C. W., AND SCHAINBLATT, A. H. "The Researcher and the Manager: A Dialectic of Implementation." *Management Science* 11, no. 4 (February 1965), pp. B69–B87.

5. "Corporate Objectives." PPG Industries, Pittsburgh, Penn., undated, p. 13.

6. DEARDEN, JOHN, "MIS is a Mirage." *Harvard Business Review,* January–February 1972.

7. KING, WILLIAM R., AND CLELAND, D. I. "The Design of Management Information Systems: An Information Analysis Approach." *Management Science* 22, no. 3 (November 1975), pp. 286–97.

8. _____. "A New Approach to Strategic Systems Planning." *Business Horizons,* August 1975.

9. KING, W. R. "Methodological Optimality in OR," *OMEGA* 4, no. 1 (February 1976).

10. MURDICK, R. G., AND ROSS, J. E. *Information Systems for Modern Management.* 2nd ed. New Jersey: Prentice-Hall, 1975.

11. SCHULTZ, R. L., AND SLEVIN, D. P. "Implementation and Organizational Validity: An Empirical Investigation." *Implementing OR/MS.* New York: Elsevier, 1975, chapter 7.

12. "You Can Be Sure, If it's Industrial-Westinghouse." *Iron Age,* March 3, 1975, pp. 20–25.

17 The Line Takes the Leadership—IS Management in a Wired Society*

John F. Rockart

When George David conceptualized an approach to elevator maintenance based on a centralized computer communications network, he had no idea it would become a notable example of the use of information technology to gain competitive advantage. Yet the story of the major improvement in customer service made possible by OTISLINE, the Otis system, has been told and retold from the lectern and in the trade press. David, formerly head of Otis North America and now CEO of Otis Elevator Company, was something of a trailblazer: an executive outside the IS function proposing and implementing a major change in how the company used information systems.

The system itself is striking. Previously, loosely coordinated, decentralized maintenance efforts were carried out in more than 100 local offices; now Otis centrally coordinates the efforts of its nationwide repair force. Trouble calls are taken by highly trained, often multilingual operators who work from a computer screen to record all data concerning the problem elevator. Repair personnel are dispatched via a telephone/beeper system. Upon completion of the maintenance, all relevant information is once again recorded in the computer.

The advantages the system provides to Otis are manifold. Perhaps most

---

* Source: Reprinted from "The Line Takes the Leadership—IS Management in a Wired Society" by John F. Rockart, *Sloan Management Review*, Summer 1988, pp. 57–64, by permission of the publisher. Copyright 1988 by the Sloan Management Review Association. All rights reserved.

important is senior management's increased ability to view the status of maintenance efforts nationwide. A specialist can quickly be directed to a particular customer with a difficult problem. Frequent trouble from a specific type of elevator or a geographic locale can be observed as the pattern develops, and corrective action taken. The quality of telephone response to anxious customers can be closely monitored. And fault data, available both to management and the company's engineers and designers, is more precise, more copious, and more accessible than the information that previously worked its way up through the five-level chain of command.

Although many elements of this now rather well-known story are fascinating, one often overlooked factor is particularly significant. The system was conceptualized and its implementation driven not by information systems personnel but by George David himself. Ed Burke, Otis's director of MIS, asserts, "It was and is George's system. He saw the need. He saw the solution. I helped, but he made it happen."

Even a few years ago, executives like George David would have been almost unique. Today, however, there is a small but rapidly growing number of senior line and staff executives taking responsibility for significant strategic projects centered on computer and communication technology in their companies, divisions, or departments. A pattern of emerging line responsibility for such projects is now becoming clearer. This paper presents some conclusions derived from a study of line executives in 15 companies that have been proactive in their use of information technology. (The word *line* is used to encompass all managers—whether line or staff—having responsibility for a major segment of an organization.)

For the first three decades of the computer era, the key figures in information technology use were the information systems professionals. Today, for a number of reasons noted below, the shaping of information systems' direction is passing to line managers. No longer willing to delegate the strategic or tactical uses of this technology to the information systems department, these managers are taking the lead in applying information technology to the most important areas of their businesses. Many are using the technology as a core element in aggressive new approaches to the marketplace or to enhance control of internal operations, as Otis did.

Including information technology as a significant component in business planning and, thus, in the process of *conception* of new business strategies and tactics, is only one part of an emerging senior executive role. The other, and equally important, element of this role is the active direction of the *implementation* of new systems. I will examine the logic underlying the need for both parts of this role later in this paper. First, however, let us look at a few other examples of "the line taking the leadership."

- Three years ago Bob Campbell, president of the Refining and Marketing Division of the Sun Corporation, identified crude oil trading as perhaps the key business activity in his organization. He gave Woody Roe the job of improving Sun's efforts in this area. Roe quickly realized the trading process was dispersed to a large number of groups located worldwide, each acting relatively independently. Some reported to the management of other Sun divisions.

Although he had no information technology background, Roe envisioned a central trading room supported by information from Reuters and other trade data sources. He turned to Sun's information technology department for the technical design of the system, but then set out himself, with Campbell's support, to initiate the process and organizational changes needed to make the system effective. Today centralized, on-line trading is recognized by Campbell and other Sun executives as a major weapon in Sun's fight for increased revenue and profit in its very competitive industry.

- Dick Kennedy, while president of the Vitrified Products Division of the Norton Company, developed a strategic plan heavily based on the use of information technology. Realizing that his division (which manufactured grinding materials) was in a mature business, Kennedy focused on two critical success factors—low cost and excellent service. His business strategy was to make the division the international leader in both areas. To do so, he initiated a set of major information technology projects. These ranged from the "Norton Connection" (a computer-based telecommunications link between Norton and its distributors), to a more effective order-processing system, to a series of manufacturing technologies ultimately targeted at flexible manufacturing and automated materials control. Implementing several large, extremely complex systems at the same time is far from simple. But Kennedy had accomplished much of this, with considerable bottom-line impact, before Norton executive management combined his division with several others in a sweeping organizational realignment.
- In a similar manner, Jerome Grossman, president of the New England Medical Center (NEMC), took the initiative in using information technology to help him manage his 450-bed teaching hospital in Boston. Drawing upon his knowledge of the technology, he designed a "product-based" planning and control system of which any industrial manufacturing manager would be proud. The system, built with a relational database, now provides a wealth of information for future planning, day-to-day management, and retrospective analysis of operations.

The system is simple enough in concept. Each "product" the hospital delivers (e.g., a heart bypass operation) has a list of the resources (nursing hours, x-rays, etc.) that will be used to help the patient. This product/resource list (or bill of materials) is used in three major ways. First, for annual planning purposes, the expected number of patients in each category can be multiplied by the resource requirements for each, and the institution's total resource needs in x-ray, laboratories, and so on, can be roughly estimated. Second, as patients are treated, the institution can monitor the use of resources by resource category, by department, by product, or by physician. Third, comparisons can be made between expected and actual resource use by case type to help set prices in the future.

A sweeping change of this type, from simple year-to-year budgeting processes to much more specific, detailed resource management using state-of-the-art information technology, was conceptually innovative. But the real work had just begun. Implementing this new management system, which smacked of uncaring industrial practice, took significant education and persuasion on Dr. Grossman's part of the management team, the medical staff, and the trustees. Only a senior executive strongly committed to this strategy could possibly implement such a system. It is now in place at NEMC.

If war is too important to leave to the generals, the deployment of information technology is far too important, in 1988, to be left to information technologists. For many reasons, a growing number of line managers have realized this and are taking charge of information technology used in their organizations.

Line involvement with information technology is increasingly evident in the development of major new projects and systems, such as those described above. The new role of the line, however, has not diminished the influence of information systems executives. In fact, as the final section of this paper notes, their role has actually expanded.

THE FOURTH ERA OF INFORMATION
SYSTEMS MANAGEMENT

Each of the managers mentioned above has explicitly or implicitly realized that, in the past few years, information technology has gone through a radical change: both the applications and the effective management of information technology look very different than they did just a few years ago. In fact, this is the *fourth* major wave of information technology; each new type of technology has, in turn, led to a different era of applications and managerial processes. These eras can be called—after the applications each enabled—the accounting era, the operational era, the information era, and the "wired society."

- **The Accounting Era: IS Dominance.**   In the 1950s and early 1960s, with only batch-processing technology available, commercial computer use centered on the applications of the accountant who, conveniently, carried out payroll, accounts payable, and other operations in batches. In those early days, the information systems staff was in charge of all systems efforts. The computer professionals were responsible for conceptual design, programming, implementation, and operation of the system. In many cases the relevant manager (in charge of payroll or accounts receivable, for example) was more a "subject" of the new system than a contributor to it. The information systems staff swept into the department, interviewed the clerks, and designed the systems—most of which were barely understandable to anyone outside the computer hierarchy. Operating managers stood to the side; they provided some assistance and guidance, but the responsibility for system design and implementation rested clearly with the information systems people.

- **The Operational Era: Line Involvement.** As on-line systems and direct access files became available and computers grew faster and were made more reliable, it became feasible to computerize the firm's key logistical (operational) systems. Since these systems required continual real-time updates (e.g., withdrawals from and additions to inventory files) and direct access to their current status, they could be effectively implemented only in an on-line environment. IS dominance worked reasonably well for a few of the era's simpler systems; but more complex systems, such as manufacturing scheduling, proved very difficult to implement. It became clear that complex systems were not workable unless line managers helped to define their objectives and functionality. Thus began an era of line management involvement in the conceptualization, design, and implementation of systems. Despite good intentions, however, the degree to which line managers understood and were involved in these systems varied widely. In most instances, there was little doubt among the participants as to who was ultimately responsible for the system's success. It was still the information systems department.

- **The Information Era: Individual Decision Support.** The availability of improved, "fourth generation" user languages and relational databases, as well as the personal computer, ushered in a new era in the late 1970s and early 1980s. The focus changed from transaction processing, which epitomized the first two eras, to the use of information. Able at last to access and manipulate data and text, individual users reveled in the ability to "do their own thing." Many analytically oriented decision support systems were created. Staff worked hard to understand and exploit the new opportunities for information acquisition and manipulation. Information systems managers set up information centers and other end-user support organizations and turned much of the responsibility for end-user programming and information access over to the users. Yet information systems management retained its responsibility for developing and maintaining databases, setting computer and telecommunications standards, and other aspects of information technology. The seeds for line leadership in all aspects of computing were sown. What emerged from this era was a partnership between the users of information (who decided what they wanted to do and also did some programming) and the information technology organization (which provided networks, access to data, and so forth).

- **The Wired Society: Line Leadership in Strategic Systems.** Vastly improved communications capability has been the key technology change driving the most recent era. Combined with ever more cost-effective computer hardware and software, cheaper, higher band-width communications have led to the fourth era, perhaps appropriately characterized as the *wired society*. The label is relevant because a significant aspect of this era's applications is the wiring together of suborganizations within a single firm, and, more strikingly, of firms to each other. At Sun, crude trading information flows from around the world to one location. At Otis, the geographically distributed repair offices are no longer as independent; they are logically and physically wired to the corporate office. At Xerox and Hewlett-Packard, design, engineering, and manufacturing functions are now closely intertwined in the development of new products. Norton and a number of other companies are closely attached to their customers through terminal-based order entry systems.

It is this multiorganizational, multifunctional aspect of fourth era systems that makes line leadership imperative. Significant business understanding, which exists primarily at senior levels, must go into system conception. Equally important, implementation of these systems most often requires significant organizational change. Information technology management cannot effect these changes. Only line management can. The next sections develop this idea more fully.

LINE LEADERSHIP IN CONCEPTION AND IMPLEMENTATION

An entirely new level of opportunity, complexity, risk, and reward has been opened up by the new, communications-intensive information technology. Vastly greater managerial attention to the use of the technology is now demanded. The exact form of a system that, for instance, links a business to its customers is (or now should be) the result of a strategic managerial decision. Line managers must ensure that appropriate features within the system support the chosen strategy. The exact data to be gathered by salespeople with portable computers, for example, as well as the functionality of the system and the periodicity and rapidity with which data is gathered, is most appropriately dictated by line management.

As information technology becomes increasingly significant in business operations, its use should be shaped by the managers running the business. More significantly, if they are to be operated effectively, today's systems almost always require major, sometimes radical, alterations in an organization's structure, personnel, roles, and business processes—sometimes even in the culture of the corporation itself. Thus, the economic, behavioral, and political consequences of today's information technology applications should be well thought out *and* the requisite change processes effectively managed by those responsible for the management of the business itself. As Dudley Cooke, Sun's general manager of information systems, notes, "All the information technology people can do is provide the appropriate technology platform, program the system, and install the equipment. It is the task of line management to make the extremely difficult, but very necessary, changes in personnel, roles, allied systems, and even organization structure required to make today's uses of information technology pay off for the company.''

THE ORGANIZATION AS A DYNAMIC EQUILIBRIUM

The fact that major changes in information technology can profoundly affect the people, processes, structure, and strategy of an organization was documented in the pioneering theoretical work done by Harold Leavitt at Carnegie-Mellon University and by Alfred Chandler at M.I.T. Although they came from different academic backgrounds and were doing research in different fields, these two men independently developed compatible points of view.

Interested in comparative business history, Chandler investigated the changing strategy and structure of large industrial organizations in the United States.[1] He found that changes in an organization's structure followed changes in the firm's strategy and that organizational structure often had to be modified continually until it effectively supported the strategy. Chandler also focused on individuals and their roles in organizations and in organizational changes. He found that particular individuals played unique and crucial roles in developing the fit between the organization's evolving strategy and an appropriate structure. In addition, he noted that many structural changes and shifts in strategy were caused by changes in the technology. For example, Du Pont took advantage of new chemical processes to move from munitions supply into industrial chemicals by broadening its strategy and opening up that new field. (One can readily recast Chandler's ''structure follows strategy'' paradigm into four of the five interacting elements portrayed in Figure 1.)

Coming from an entirely different direction, Leavitt concluded that any organizational analysis should include four components: task, technology, people, and organizational structure.[2] He saw one of management's key functions as maintaining a ''dynamic equilibrium'' among these four elements. Although Leavitt's main interest was in the individual and that person's fit with the organization, he came up with the same four factors as Chandler did. The theoretical underpinnings of Leavitt's work came largely out of the social psychology field and drew on the work of Chapple and Sayles, Argyris, and others.[3]

In a paper that discussed the impact of information technology on corporate strategy, Michael Scott Morton and I modified Leavitt's approach.[4] First we changed his generic ''task'' into the broader concept of the organization's strategy (see Figure 1). This does not violate Leavitt's conceptual structure, since ''strategy'' represents a summing of an organi-

FIGURE 1   Leavitt's Balancing Act (Adjusted)

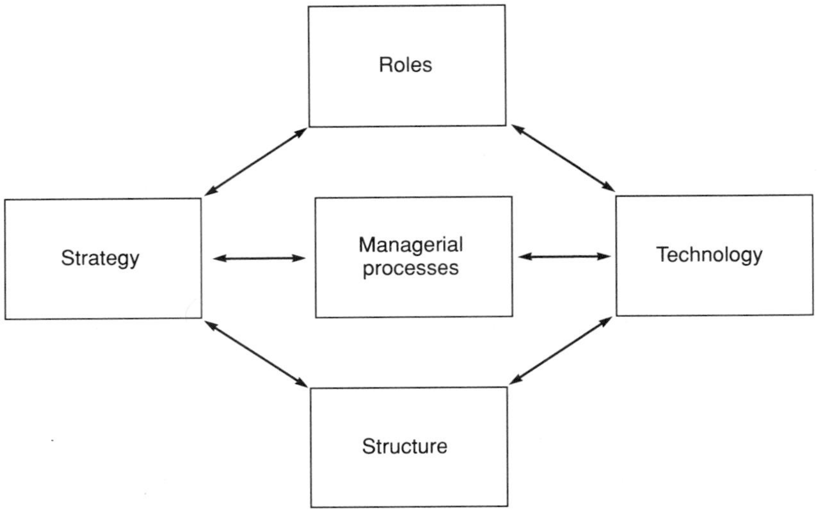

zation's tasks. Second, we included an additional box for "management processes." This is in the middle of the diagram, because we see management processes as part of the glue that holds the organization together. Here we include such processes as strategic planning; meetings, discussions, and evaluations that result in the annual or the capital budget; compensation; and personnel management. Every organization has such processes, and they represent a good deal of what is done in an organization.

IMPLEMENTATION AS TRANSFORMATION

Leavitt's conceptual structure, as modified in Figure 1, aids in understanding the necessity for line leadership in information technology's fourth era. Figure 2 notes four major stages of applications development. In era one, the accounting era, the data processing people carried out all of the functions—system conception, design and programming, implementation, and operation. Today, in era four, while the bulk of design, programming, and operation remains the domain of information technologists, conception and implementation need to be line dominated.

The logic behind the need for line management involvement in system conception is straightforward. The people who run the corporation, the

FIGURE 2 Four Major Stages of Applications Development: Leadership in
Stages of Project Management

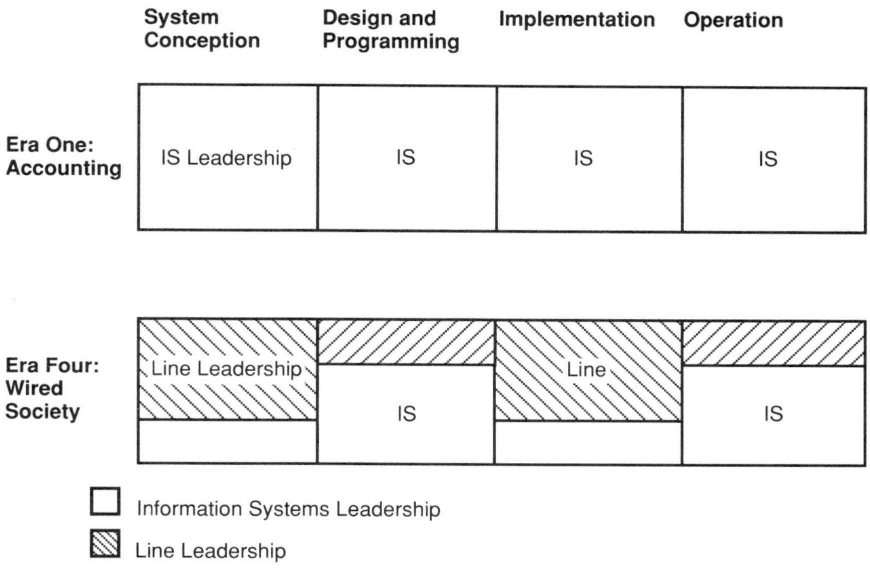

	System Conception	Design and Programming	Implementation	Operation
Era One: Accounting	IS Leadership	IS	IS	IS
Era Four: Wired Society	Line Leadership	IS	Line	IS

☐ Information Systems Leadership
▨ Line Leadership

division, or the department are the people who must envision the direction
in which they plan to drive their organization. Appropriate use of information technology can be a major factor in the accomplishment of that vision.
Just as effective leaders plan to deploy key people for significant tasks, so
too must they guide the most effective use of information technology.

The need for line involvement in implementation is more complex but
equally compelling. Figure 1 suggests why. Any change in the technology
will lead, as Leavitt notes, to changes in all or most of the other four
elements. In fact, the systems described earlier have all changed organizational roles, processes, and structures. The changes have not been minor.
At Otis, the roles of branch managers and district and corporate executives
were all affected. The number of organizational levels was questioned.
Several processes allied to maintenance, such as engineering data gathering, were also affected. Similarly, Sun's system caused more centralization of a major business process. Comparable proposed changes in the
major elements shown in Figure 1 can be traced in each of the other
companies discussed here and in almost all of the organizations we
studied.

These changes are so significant that the term *implementation* is too
weak a word to describe what takes place when systems such as these are
integrated into the organization's functioning. John Henderson at M.I.T.

prefers the word *transformation* for the third stage of project management noted in Figure 2, and he is right. When implementation is carried out with strong line direction (as it is at Otis, Norton, NEMC, and Sun), it becomes a transformation that cuts across previously independent divisions, functions, or other organizational subunits. It affects aspects of most (if not all) organizational elements noted in Figure 1. That is why this step of application development must now belong to the line. Only line management has the power to initiate and execute an organizational transformation of any magnitude. (See Levinson for an excellent description of the change process involved.)[5]

A MAJOR NEW RESPONSIBILITY

What results from this emerging pattern of line direction of fourth era information technology applications? Quite simply, the line managers we interviewed believe they have merely added another item to their list of significant responsibilities.

It can be argued that most managers have traditionally accepted three major responsibilities (see Table 1). First, they have always been responsible for the *operations* of their organization. For an accounts receivable supervisor, this means ensuring that the cash is collected. For a transportation manager, it means seeing that the trucks run on time and that deliveries are made. As one moves up from functions to divisions and from there to the organization as a whole, the "operations" job becomes one of managing lower-level managers.

In addition, line managers have always been responsible for control of two major resources, *money* and *people*. Although corporate staff groups may assist in these areas, the responsibility of a line manager to meet

---

TABLE 1 Significant Line Management
Responsibilities

Traditional
- Operations.
- Financial management.
- Personnel management.

Added in the 1960s
- Long-range and strategic planning.

Added in the 1980s
- Strategic use of information technology.

budget and revenue goals is clear, as is the responsibility to deploy, develop, and manage human resources.

About three decades ago, an additional major responsibility was added to each line manager's agenda. In the early 1960s, when it became increasingly evident that "planning" (beyond one-year budget projections) was vital, corporations attempted to meet that need using a central planning staff. Unfortunately, this did not work. When it was realized that the planning process needed to be integrally connected to each line manager's actual competitive environment, the primary responsibility for planning was shifted from staff planners to line managers. In most organizations today, line managers are responsible for annual, long-range, and strategic planning to ensure that their resources are used effectively to meet their goals.

In 1988, an increasing number of line managers are taking on an additional responsibility—that of actively exploiting information technology resources. For some, proactive management of information technology is as critical as the management of other resources, if not more so.

THE GROWING ROLE OF THE INFORMATION TECHNOLOGY MANAGER

Given the state of the technology and many line managers' lack of expertise about that technology, the line cannot develop strategic uses of information technology by itself. In every case we have seen, IS staff has been involved in system conception and implementation. This interaction ranges from simple education or consulting to serious involvement in translating ideas into systems or designing and assisting during implementation. For major new systems, a full partnership between the line and the IS group has most often been evident.

In fact, as the line role grows, the information systems group role is also expanding.[6] This is not a zero-sum game. While several traditional functions remain, the role of the senior information technology executive is a far more significant one today than ever in the past, along five major dimensions (see Table 2).

First, with regard to system development, even those systems in which the line is heavily involved require greater competence and skills on the part of the IS organization than ever before. To effectively play the helping role noted above, IS personnel need significant knowledge of the business. Equally important, the technical design, programming, and operation of these business-critical, often highly complex, systems present a far greater challenge than did earlier-era systems. Today's systems require database, project-management, telecommunications, and a host of other skills not previously demanded of IS personnel.

Second, today's systems require the development and implementation

---

TABLE 2   The Information Systems Leadership Role

Traditional Major IS Functions
- Technical (sometimes business) design and programming.
- Project management.
- Operations.
- Staff activities (consulting, planning, education, etc.).

Newly Critical Functions in the Late 1980s and 1990s
- Design and programming of increasingly complex "mission critical" systems.
- Infrastructure development and maintenance (computers, network, software, data).
- Education of line management to its responsibilities.
- Education of IS management concerning the business.
- Proactive use of business and technical knowledge to "seed" the line with innovative ideas concerning effective uses of information technology.

---

of a general, and eventually "seamless," information technology infrastructure. The challenge to IS management of providing leadership for this profoundly important set of "highways" in the "wired society" cannot be overstated.

Third, there is a need to educate line management about its new responsibility. The line executives noted above are an intentionally biased sample. Not many like them exist today. The need now is to get *all* line executives to take on this new role, and it can only be done through formal and informal education, sometimes over an extended period of time.

Fourth, IS executives must educate themselves and their staffs about the business itself. Otherwise they will not be able to help line managers create systems that facilitate strategy implementation. Nor will they be able to carry out their fifth newly critical function, that of "seeding" line managers with ideas about effective applications of each new technology.

In short, the role of the information systems executive has also expanded. He or she is now a business executive—increasingly responsible for providing the line with knowledge about applicable technology and with the tools and infrastructure that allow development and implementation of innovative business systems. The ingredients of this leadership role were clearly expressed by Ed Schefer, previously the senior information executive at General Foods. Before his promotion to a senior line position, Schefer noted that he spent one third of his time running the IS organization, one third communicating with General Foods executives (both learning about the business and educating them about the technology), and one third of his time outside of General Foods—learning about advances in the technology and business conditions in the industry.

Thus, in the "wired society" there is a need for a significant line leadership role, but there is also a need for growth and expansion of the IS leadership role. With the increasing importance of information technology in industry today, these developments are far from surprising.

NOTES

1. A. D. Chandler, Jr., *Strategy and Structure: Chapters in the History of the Industrial Enterprise* (Cambridge: MIT Press, 1962).
2. H. J. Leavitt, "Applied Organizational Change in Industry," in *Handbook of Organizations,* ed. J. G. March (Chicago: Rand McNally, 1965).
3. E. D. Chapple and L. R. Sayles, *The Measure of Management* (New York: Macmillan, 1961); C. Argyris, *Personality and Organization* (New York: Harper & Row, 1957).
4. J. F. Rockart and M. S. Scott Morton, "Implications of Changes in Information Technology for Corporate Strategy," *Interfaces,* January–February 1984, pp. 84–95.
5. E. Levinson, "The Line Manager and Systems-Induced Organizational Change" (Cambridge: Sloan School of Management, M.I.T., Management in the 1990s comment draft, August 1985).
6. J. F. Rockart and R. Benjamin, "The Unique Role of Information Technology Organization" (Cambridge: Sloan School of Management, M.I.T., draft working paper, April 1988).

18 *End-User Computing: Are You a Leader or a Laggard?**

Thomas P. Gerrity
John F. Rockart

We are witnessing dramatic growth in the direct use of information technology as personal support tools by executives, managers, and professionals. These end users, not the traditional systems development staff, are now the key forces driving the acquisition and use of computer resources. In fact, current research indicates that the growth rate in end-user computing is at least five times that of conventional systems: a 50 to 100 percent growth rate per year has been the norm [1].‡

The following examples illustrate how the focus of information technology is shifting rapidly in organizations.

- At Xerox over 40 percent of the corporation's total computer resources are now devoted to direct support of end users. Although traditional computer "paperwork processing" is continuing to grow, its proportional share of computer resources is steadily shrinking vis-à-vis the end user. It is estimated that end-user consumption at Xerox will grow 75 percent by 1990 [2].
- Major corporate investments in personal computers are growing exponentially. One automotive company recently ordered 25,000 personal computers. At least one insurance company, The Travellers, installed

---

* Source: Reprinted from "End-User Computing: Are You a Leader or a Laggard?" by Thomas P. Gerrity and John F. Rockart, *Sloan Management Review*, Summer 1986, pp. 25–34, by permission of the publisher. Copyright 1986 by The Sloan Management Review Association. All rights reserved.
‡ Bracketed numbers cite the references at the end of the chapter.

2,000 personal computers, and there are several thousand more on order.

- Even top executives are getting into the act. The CEO of a national restaurant chain, along with his staff, interrogated an on-line system to analyze trends in customer preferences, simulated changes in menu items, and did "what-if" analysis of potential price changes. The chairman of Procter & Gamble also uses a personal computer to perform his own analysis of key business situations.

This new period, often referred to as either the "Third Era" or the Information Era, is an outgrowth of the First and Second Eras [3]. From its early accounting and clerical applications in the First Era [circa 1955–1964), the use of information technology expanded in the Second Era (1965–1974) to include direct support of many operational functions in the firm (e.g., manufacturing control, order entry). In the Third Era, the relevant technology now supports key *staff* and *managerial* needs. In other words, while the technology of the earlier eras served the paperwork or data processing needs of accountants and operational supervisors in a firm, the Third Era's end-user capabilities focus on *information, problem-solving,* and *communication* needs of a corporation's decision makers and their staff.

Unfortunately, despite the critical importance of end-user computing, the appropriate approach for managing it has not been developed in most companies. Although its benefits have been widely publicized, end-user managers are often still mired in the management techniques and processes developed during the first quarter century of the computer age—that is, techniques designed to support and control a very different set of computer uses [4]. Therefore, in this article, we will examine those factors that relate specifically to end-user computing:

- The strategic value and business impact of end-user computing activities.
- The pros and cons of three managerial approaches currently used to cope with end-user computing.
- The five key elements that we believe underlie the development of a successful end-user computing strategy for the Third Era.

WHAT END-USER COMPUTING CAN DO

Increase Individual Performance

The benefits of end-user computing are not readily justified in terms of return on investment of traditional information systems. Instead, enhanced efficiency and effectiveness of an individual professional or manager are often the initial payoffs. This measurement is at least as great and full of qualitative judgment as is the performance appraisal process of that same individual.

Increase Learning

Beyond such individual payoffs, we also observed in company after company that the real long-term value of end-user computing lies in the accelerated *learning* on the part of the user about his or her job, about the discovery of innovative new approaches to tasks that actually can transform the nature of the job, and finally about the new opportunities and limits of the technology itself. The growing body of end-user computing experience is producing more sophisticated and effective "clients" of the central IS organization than has ever been witnessed. And despite some of the frictions associated with *any* major change, such a growing knowledge base will ultimately benefit all.

Moreover, it is through this expanded organizational learning via end-user computing that *real leverage* is brought to two other payoff areas for information technology: (1) a competitive advantage and (2) improved internal organizational effectiveness.

Competitive Advantage

New product/market opportunities that yield *real* competitive advantage are generally spotted by professionals and managers who are "on the firing line"—that is, close to the markets and products—*and* who have a practical, working knowledge of new, enabling technologies. With the widespread development of end-user computing, practical uses of information technology are being discovered at the same time that such technology offers the greatest opportunities—and threats—in today's volatile marketplace. Some firms have used information technology to distinguish themselves from their competitors by locking up a distribution channel. American Hospital Supply, for example, posed a serious threat when it installed terminals in hospitals and thus allowed its customers to order directly. Hence, we believe that those firms that seize the opportunity to effectively manage end-user computing are creating capabilities needed to gain the lead in tomorrow's marketplace.

On the other hand, as critical as they are to corporate leadership or even to survival, major strategic competitive moves come only now and then. More often than not, what leads to corporate excellence is the cumulative effectiveness of a vast number of minor organizational improvements made by many people, not just the "bold strategic stroke" [5]. Task-related learning and exploration of end-user computing provides a strong base for making small improvements.

Improve Internal Organizational Effectiveness

There is a final managerial benefit. Virtually every business is living in increasingly turbulent and volatile marketplaces, and, as the uncertainty increases, the value of manageable access to good information also increases. Those organizations that are further up the "learning curve" in end-user computing have cadres of managers of all levels who have greater expertise in getting, using, and disseminating good management information for improved organizational effectiveness. Also, to the extent that our national (and each firm's) workforce is composed of more and more "knowledge workers" and information handlers, the leverage is even greater.

We see the effective diffusion of end-user computing as a relatively low-risk endeavor, kept in balance by normal budgetary controls. Therefore, it is of immense potential value to develop more effective information technology clients, enhance the prospects for achieving real competitive advantage, and contribute directly to improved organizational effectiveness. However, we also believe that time is of the essence: the leaders and laggards are being sorted out. Now is the time to select and implement effective management approaches to Third Era computing.

Dispelling Fears

Given that end-user managers of most organizations hardly even *know* all of the ways in which these tools are being used, it is not surprising that both information systems (IS) and senior managers are at least concerned, if not quite suspicious, that resources are being wasted on frivolous activities. For one thing, end-user professionals and managers are busy people—they have full-time jobs to do. Practically speaking, they make use of this technology only when it provides a direct, quick, and pragmatic benefit to getting their jobs done, usually by just doing some things faster and better.

Furthermore, most end users operate under normal budgetary constraints and are motivated to expend resources wisely. It is, therefore, startling to find some cases where a manager who has discretionary spending control over hundreds of thousands of dollars is held suspect for a considered purchase of a $3,000 personal computer.

Finally, we observed that another senior management fear—that personal computers will be bought and then left sitting idle on a manager's desk—is, in general, unfounded. Those managers whose planned use of a personal computer does not work out are usually quite quick to transfer it to someone who *will* make use of it. This is not to argue that there are not cases of wasted resources, or that some degree of standards, policies, and guidelines are not valuable. We simply find that, for the most part, end users can be trusted to make sound individual use of personal computers and similar tools to a much higher degree than is usually suspected in top management circles.

Overcoming Myopia

To a great extent, the rapid growth in end-user demand for information resources has "blind sided" many IS executives. This myopia is understandable given that for the past two decades IS managers have been struggling just to install each new wave of increasingly productive (and complex) hardware and software of First and Second Era computing. Faced by project backlogs ranging from two to four years, IS staffs have been tied down by developing or improving these paperwork processing systems. Available managerial time has also been invested in creating better and more refined approaches to plan and control those applications, which are now a steadily shrinking portion of the total information systems "pie." Thus, despite their dramatic importance, the Third Era changes that are under way have not been given significant management time and attention because the demand for traditional systems has continued to grow.

As a result, many IS executives are entering the era of end-user dominance without having prepared for it. For the most part, managerial approaches to Third Era computer use have been superficial, diffuse, and reactive. Separate groups often have been set up to control the use of personal computers, time sharing, and office systems. Most, however, are merely *responsive* to user-initiated demand. What is more, many IS managers have discovered that most of their critical management tools and skills, developed so painstakingly over the past 25 years, are of little value in managing Third Era developments.

THREE COMMON MANAGERIAL APPROACHES

The prevailing question is, What are companies actually doing? Although the details may differ, management typically has taken one of three general approaches to end-user computing—monopolist, laissez-faire, or the information center.

Monopolist Approach

Often the initial approach in many firms is for the IS organization to attempt to maintain firm control over all end-user computing, usually by limiting it severely. One consumer products company, scarred by the painful and costly evolution of its traditional information systems over the past two decades, adopted a "go-slow" attitude toward the integration of computers into the management process. Not only did the firm choose as the company standard a complex programming language, which is inaccessible to all but the best-trained users, but it also created a set of policies that actively discourages managers from utilizing computer resources. Each personal computer, for example, must be fully and painstakingly justified. And personal computer users are denied any access to corporate databases.

There are several variations of the traditional monopolist view, but they all spring from a basic belief that the IS organization should control *all* information processing: systems should be developed by a professional data processing staff to ensure efficient use of computer resources, good documentation, good controls on privacy and security of data, and strong financial controls over the use of the data processing resource.

The monopolist approach, however, is breaking down in most of those companies that are using it. There are several key reasons for its failure.

- There is not sufficient IS staff available to develop all of the needed systems. Users, faced with a two- to four-year backlog, are bypassing the "monopoly" by going to external time sharing or "bootlegging" in their own small computers.
- With the declining cost of computer hardware, it is becoming apparent that the monopolist's focus on control to maximize hardware efficiency is increasingly irrelevant.
- The documentation and controls necessary for development of large paperwork processing systems are unnecessary for many Third Era applications, which may be used only by their authors on a one-time basis or for a very short time.
- An increasing number of computer-savvy managers and staff professionals feel, and rightly so, that they can directly develop many systems more quickly and cheaply, with less friction, and more specifically targeted at their needs than can the traditional monopoly. They refuse to place a system in the central development backlog, which they know they can develop by themselves and have available much sooner. "Why should I wait eight months and pay $50,000 when I can do this over a couple of weekends on my IBM PC?" is a typical user response.

Laissez-Faire Approach

The laissez-faire approach is almost the opposite of the monopolist's view. Here, user-managers, as long as they have their own budgets, are allowed to buy whatever resources they please—time sharing, microcomputers, and even minicomputers. This approach reflects beliefs similar to those stated by one IS manager: "No central organization can plan for end-user computing. Each user is an individual with differing needs. The sum of these needs is too big, too complex, and too diverse. No single central group can possibly understand or control them all.'' The key here is for each user to make creative, effective use of the tools. If the corporation allows ''free-market'' access to computation, users will spend their own budgets more wisely than a central authority could possibly do. Therefore, it is outside the role of the IS manager to worry about end-user computing.

As a result of this approach, almost half of the corporate computer resources at one of the world's largest electronics companies are now being consumed by management and staff who are developing and running Third Era systems. The corporation's posture of letting people ''do their own thing'' has led to a current forecasted requirement of acquiring an additional large mainframe computer every six months just to support end users. Not surprisingly, senior management recently demanded reassurances that comparable benefits are being received from the increased computer costs.

In addition to financial considerations, the total ''laissez-faire'' philosophy has several other major drawbacks. Some are subtle, some are obvious, but all are increasingly apparent.

- There are many diverse hardware and software tools available today. Much can be gained by having a corporate center or centers of expertise continually study the available tools and help users match their perceived needs with appropriate technology.
- The ''invisible hand'' in this case is often driven by immediate and tactical needs of operational managers. While such applications can be valuable and useful learning experiences, major opportunities may be missed if no one identifies end-user systems that may be strategically beneficial to the organization. In other words, a firm needs to work in both directions—top down and bottom up—toward productive and strategic uses of the technology. An example of a top-down application is American Airlines' Sabre system: the airline leases terminals to travel agents, who in turn, use them for making reservations and ticketing on-line. American Hospital Supply's order processing system is an example of a bottom-up application in that it resulted from user needs.
- Users value ongoing support. Having received advice and consulting concerning appropriate hardware and software, users need continual updates in the use of software and other aspects of end-user computing. It is also ineffective to let users slowly and arduously track down the location of data specifically valuable to them, manage the transfer of data to their own systems, worry about data security and privacy, or maintain their own databases if they are sizable. These are all matters best supported by information systems professionals.
- Efficient use of Information Era technology demands some corporatewide standardization. Discounts are available from vendors for

quantity purchases. Training programs, however, can be run for only a small set of machinery and software—not for each of the hundreds of personal computers and thousands of software packages now available. Transfer of software and know-how is easier among end users using the same underlying tools. Central leadership is necessary to create an appropriately effective and evolving efficient "network architecture" to meet changing needs.

- Finally, the laissez-faire approach makes no provisions for transforming *ad hoc* quickly developed support systems into formal, ongoing, often-used support systems. This is a task best performed by IS professionals and is increasingly seen as necessary for some Information Era systems as they gain widespread use throughout organizations.

Information Center Approach

Recognizing the difficulties of the monopolist approach and some of the obstacles of the laissez-faire one, some major computer vendors, most notably IBM, are focusing on an organizational approach most commonly known as the "Information Center" (IC). This initial attempt to provide a focused managerial approach to end-user computing has much to offer.

For one thing, the IC is a centrally located group of personnel, distinct from the rest of the IS staff, to whom users come for guidance and support concerning the selection and use of appropriate hardware, software, and data. Strong "product" expertise, education, and ongoing training on each supported software language and user-oriented "package" (e.g., electronic mail, word processing, graphics, and statistical analysis systems) are available from various specialist members of the IC. In some cases, the IC is also in charge of ensuring that each application is "justified."

One such information center has been established in a major pharmaceutical company. The IC, staffed with IS support personnel, was charted to provide assistance, upon request, for *all* of the 23 end-user software tools that the company owned. The center's manager, however, soon found that his small staff's attempts to support the multitude of diverse users and their applications interests were highly inadequate to meet the demand. Because it lacked sufficient resources, the center began to founder. Other centralized ICs, even with a more limited range of products, found it difficult to serve the vastly increasing number of users who desire help.

The IC is the newest of three approaches, and it is closer to providing more effective results than the others. Many are quite successful. As usually practiced, however, the IC is an incomplete management solution for the Information Era. The information center focuses on support and, to an extent, control, of users. Both support and control are important, but there are several shortcomings to the usual IC implementation.

- The IC, as usually structured, is a centralized organization. Yet, users desire and need localized support [6].
- Although strong on technological and software product knowledge, most IC personnel often do not have the functional and applications knowledge, which is the end user's primary concern.
- The IC is a creation of the central IS department. User influence on its design, procedures, and services can be minimal. In addition, it may not even have the full backing of IS management and, therefore, may be viewed as an experimental palliative to user demands.
- Often the IC will represent only one or two of the four major end-user computing technologies: time sharing, communications networking, personal computers, and office systems. For effective end-user support, all four must be managed in coordination.
- The IC is often only *reactive* to expressed user needs. Yet, Third Era technology presents many opportunities that may not be recognized by technologically unsophisticated users. *Proactive* managerial efforts to identify and rank high payoff opportunities have been extremely useful in the organizations with which we have worked.
- Finally and perhaps most important, the IC is a solution expressed in terms of organizational structure. And structure should reflect strategy. However, the majority of the firms we have observed have neglected the critical initial step, the development of a *strategic direction* for the exploitation of Third Era technology. In the absence of a clear strategic context, the IC "solution" produces less value.

A NEW APPROACH: MANAGED FREE ECONOMY

Given the potential strategic benefits to the firm, end-user computing has won "center stage" and, therefore, demands much more than either a laissez-faire, "take-what-you-get" approach or limited, reactive management. Both approaches are patently inadequate because in the next few years increased end-user computing needs will cause many major companies to spend hundreds of millions of dollars in equipment, systems development, and user time.

What is needed to manage Third Era computing is a proactive and strategic approach called a *managed free economy*. This approach must balance two opposing but equally essential needs. Users must be allowed to create, define, and develop their own applications of the technology to fulfill their information needs. Yet, at the same time, some central authority must take responsibility to consult with users concerning what is feasible, to support users where special IS expertise can add value, and to ensure that the appropriate technical policy structure is in place.

The parallel to a regulated economy is clear. At the national level, the

United States has such an economy. Fiscal and monetary policies, the legal systems, antimonopoly regulations, and many other government-imposed guidelines determine the "rules of the game." Working within this framework, private organizations and individuals strive to maximize their own gains. Yet, they are bounded by a set of constraints, which, while they inhibit individual actions, serve to ensure that the nation as a whole will prosper.

The same is true for end-user computing. There is a need for "regulations." For example, a central authority must develop policies to limit the number of types of personal computers that can be used. This ensures that the training courses, support systems, and network protocols that must be established for each different type of computer can be put in place. While it is impossible to develop these support services for 100 brands of personal computers, it can be done well for a few. In like manner, software standards must be established; otherwise, users, having learned a particular spread-sheet or word processing package might, when transferred to another department, have to repeat an extensive learning process. In addition, a single electronic mail system should be established to allow communication across the organization.

Working within these few (although very significant) guidelines, computer users (like private U.S. citizens) are free to act in their own interest. They may select and program their own applications, maintain personal files, and do and act as they see fit with regard to purchasing and using computer software and hardware: within bounds, the regulated individual is free. Like the national economy, the end-user environment should be regulated just enough to ensure that the optimum balance is maintained between government control and individual freedom.

FIVE CRITICAL ATTRIBUTES

The three managerial approaches, including many variations and hybrids of those described, vary significantly from company to company. Some are markedly successful from both user and IS management viewpoints. Many are not. Although the exact implementations differ, those approaches considered to be successfully by both users and IS exhibit all or most of the five critical attributes of the "managed free economy" approach?

1. A stated end-user strategy.
2. A user/IS working partnership.
3. An active targeting of critical end-user systems and applications.
4. An integrated end-user support organization.
5. An emphasis on education throughout the organization.

Stated Strategy

Users continually ask the questions: "What is IS going to do to support me?" "What is the end-user strategy?" "What is IS management's view of the general directions of Third Era computing?" "What end-user hardware and systems will be supported by IS?" "Will the specific support mechanisms (e.g., education, hardware discounts, ongoing assistance) be provided?" In short, users desire a statement of strategic direction and knowledge of the key elements of its implementation.

The development of a strategy, therefore, requires both an assessment of the technology and a determination of user application needs. As new products are continually being introduced, the shape of end-user product direction becomes increasingly clear. Future user needs can be determined in large part by an analysis of staff department computer needs. After all, staffs are the major manipulators of information in the firm; they are the focus of 80 to 90 percent of all end-user computing [7].

Working Partnership

Both the strategy and all programs growing out of the strategy must reflect user needs. In the past, the "rules of the game" in information systems were formulated by the IS organization to effect efficient implementaton of paperwork processing systems. Today, the "rules" regarding justification of systems, pricing of services, access to data, privacy, and security need to be reexamined. Because these rules so strongly affect end users, it is important that they be worked out in collaboration with end users and their IS management.

For example, at Gillette, a set of policies and guidelines very different from those previously governing the earlier eras have been developed to support end-user computing. The key to their development is a policy group including end-user departments and several senior managers from these departments. The policy committee is chaired by a user manager. While significant expertise is added to the committee's deliberations by IS, the policies that evolve are clearly seen to reflect the needs of users.

Targeting Critical Systems and Applications

Allowing ideas for uses of the new technology to merely "bubble up" from individual users is not enough. Individual managers are noticeably short range and "local" in their thinking. Systems with long-range benefits, which span multiple individuals or departments, or which require special technological expertise to envision and formulate, are not often generated from end users alone. Therefore, to ensure that limited IS resources are used well, leading companies are implementing broad strategic-minded scans of critical end-user applications now made possible by the new technology.

At Southwest Ohio Steel, the senior management team engaged in a Critical Success Factors-based study of corporate information needs [8]. What emerged from the study was the recognition that Third Era technology could be most effectively used to provide, among other things, an information marketing database. This database is now being accessed daily by officers and managers of the firm, including Jacques Huber, marketing vice president.

Integrated Support Organization

The skills necessary to assist end users are vastly different from the skills required to design and program systems in the IS organization. First, end-user support personnel must focus on end use, not on technology. Second, because support personnel provide expert advice, they must not only be knowledgeable of a wide spectrum of new tools and techniques, but they must also have the desire and the skills to *teach* and *help*, not to *do*. Working with users in this capacity requires patience and interpersonal skills not commonly found in traditional IS personnel.

Even more important than the skill requirements is the need for an organization to have a separate identity—that is, a central support organization. Much hard work is required to develop the elements of an end-user strategy. In addition, ongoing user support is essential. If user support is merely a secondary function of the regular IS organization, any crisis in conventional processing can steal significant resources away from the Third Era tasks. A focus on ongoing support must be maintained or users lose confidence. To maintain this focus, separate, dedicated organizations already have been formed in many leading companies. Although we expect that this organization will eventually evolve and merge with other parts of the information systems organization, its specialized role appears to demand organizational separation today.

At Gillette, for instance, all aspects of end-user computing are under the direction of one senior manager in IS. Policies, guidelines, and strategic directions are well thought out and advertised. Experts are available from this central staff to consult about time-sharing products, personal computers, and office systems.

Still, end users are busy people who require extensive support. Therefore, the support person must be local—physically close by—available, and able to speak the users' language about their business needs [9].

At Owens Corning Fiberglass, Paul Daverio, vice president for information systems, transferred special IS personnel to the staff departments that are responsible for finance, personnel, etc. This was done to provide on-site end-user consulting. Another case in point is Texas Instruments. Here, end users in each department or division can make use of three levels of support. First, and most effective, are the homegrown functional specialists in the department: finance, marketing, or other users who have become the local, available computing experts. They, in turn, are supported by IS computing consultants who have more overall computing knowledge and a set of guidelines on applications that should be executed by personal computers, time sharing, or office systems hardware and software. Referrals can be made, if necessary, to the appropriate specialty hardware or software experts. What is more, with a single IS person as a focal point for all the user specialists, knowledge about the entire end-user environment in each organization can be more effectively consolidated for shaping the evolving end-user computing strategy.

Education throughout the Organization

End-user technology is coming to market in extraordinary diversity. Yet, IS personnel are often uneducated. We find that less than 1 in 10 of the IS systems analysts today have more than a cursory acquaintance with the new technology. Senior management, in general, is not adequately informed. And middle management, deluged with an extraordinary number of claims by vendors and confused about what moves to make, needs an increased understanding of the ways in which the technology can best be applied to particular tasks. A well-thought-out educational program, adapted to the needs of each type of "student," is absolutely necessary to allow an organization to make effective use of the technology.

ARCO met this challenge head-on. A 10-day program has been devised and instituted to reeducate 1,000 of the company's top IS personnel. The course centers on the concepts, tools, and techniques of the Third Era. In addition, short seminars are being given to the top senior management. The seminars stress both basic concepts and current, effective uses of the new technology within ARCO. Courses for middle management are being developed as well.

CONCLUSION: SHIFT THE FOCUS

This is an era when astute leadership in exploiting information technology will create a competitive edge in the marketplace. Yet, many managers, fearing that they will lose control over computing costs, hesitate to pursue the substantial benefits offered by this technology. Before the end-user era, an analysis of the costs and benefits of each major proposed application system or hardware purchase was possible through careful scrutiny of the IS budget. Today, however, such single-point control is no longer possible: usage is scattered widely throughout the organization—and in much smaller increments.

Still, adequate control over computer utilization *is* feasible. Ensuring that the five attributes are in place will produce a working partnership between user management and IS staff, who together can implement two quite different but complementary forms of "control" over the computing environment.

A first and vital step is to develop a set of policies, standards, and guidelines. This will ensure a standard technical and management environment, which can yield significant benefits: volume hardware and software discounts from vendors and education programs and assistance for a limited set of standard products will be made available. In addition, such policies will enable users to move freely from one part of the organization to another without having to learn a new set of hardware and software systems. All users will be assured that their personal computers "connect" to the network, which will allow access to one another and to remotely stored data.

After the guidelines are established, individual end-user projects of size must be scrutinized to ensure they have business value. The responsibility for this control belongs to the local unit's line management. Therefore, line management must be increasingly knowledgeable of the potential value of technology—at least to the extent necessary to determine whether expenditures on computers or communications make good business sense. Such knowledge requires, as we have already noted, that these managers receive an education in technology. An IS staff can and should be consulted for advice in specific instances, but the basic control over what is being done—in an era when virtually everyone in the corporation will soon have a terminal—has shifted from the staff experts to the line organization.

REFERENCES

1. ROCKART, J. F., AND FLANNERY, L. "The Management of End-User Computing." *Communications of the ACM,* October 1983, pp. 777–84.
2. BENJAMIN, R. I. "Information Technology in the 1990s: A Long-Range Planning Scenario." *MIS Quarterly,* June 1982, pp. 11–31.
3. ROCKART, J. F., AND SCOTT MORTON, M. S. "Implications of Changes in Information Technology for Corporate Strategy." *INTERFACES,* January–February 1984, pp. 84–95; ROCKART, J. F. "The Role of the Executive in the New Computer Era." In *Global Technological Change: A Strategic Assessment.* Proceedings of a Symposium for Senior Executives, MIT Liaison Program, June 21–23, 1983.
4. ROCKART AND FLANNERY, October 1983; HENDERSON, J. C., AND TREACY, M. E. "Managing End-User Computing for Competitive Advantage," *Sloan Management Review,* Winter 1986, p. 3; ARKUSH, E. "Beyond End-User Computing: Managing in the Third Era." *The Journal of Information Systems*

Management, Spring 1986, p. 58; ROCKART, J. F. AND TREACY, M. E. "The CEO Goes On-Line." *Harvard Business Review,* January–February 1982, pp. 82–88.

5. PETERS, T. J., AND WATERMAN, R. H. JR. *In Search of Excellence.* New York: Harper & Row, 1982.
6. ROCKART AND FLANNERY, October 1983, p. 783.
7. Ibid., p. 779.
8. ROCKART, J. F. "Chief Executives Define Their Own Data Needs." *Harvard Business Review,* March–April 1979, pp. 81–93; ROCKART, J. F., AND CRESCENZI, A. D. "Engaging Top Management in Information Technology." *Sloan Management Review,* Summer 1984, pp. 3–16.
9. WITHINGTON, F. G. "Coping with Computer Proliferation." *Harvard Business Review,* May–June 1980, pp. 152–64.

19 Creating Competitive Weapons from Information Systems*

Charles Wiseman
Ian C. MacMillan

Metpath, a large clinical laboratory, competes in a tough commodity business where low differentiation of service has led to a lack of customer loyalty and frequent price discounting. Doctors send specimens to the labs for processing, and timely test results are often critical for diagnosis and treatment. Metpath has enhanced its customer service by installing computer terminals and linking them to its lab computers so that, for a small monthly fee, physicians can retrieve test results as soon as they are known.

From a purely technical point of view, this is an on-line database application. Strategically, however, Metpath is consciously using this information system as a competitive weapon in two ways: (1) to build barriers against new and existing competitors by raising the information system ante; (2) to gain advantage over other labs by differentiating an otherwise commodity service by keeping records of patient data on file and by offering financial processing services through billing and accounts payable applications. This differentiation is intended to secure the loyalty of physicians who normally have a tendency to switch from lab to lab in search of lower costs.

The Metpath system reflects a significant departure from the traditional purpose of information systems (IS): to automate an organization's basic

---

* Source: Reprinted with permission from *Journal of Business Strategy*, Fall 1984. Warren, Gorham & Lamont, Inc, 210 South St., Boston, MA 02111. Copyright © 1984. All rights reserved.

business processes like payroll, order entry, and accounts receivable or to satisfy the information needs of its managers and professionals for improved decision making.

Also far from traditional are the extended uses made by American Airlines and United Airlines of their computerized reservation systems, SABRE and Apollo, respectively. Developed in the mid-1970s at a cost of over $300 million, these information systems are no longer employed merely as neutral scheduling mechanisms to automate the seat reservation process. Rather, they are used as weapons in the struggle for a competitive edge.

SABRE and Apollo give priority listing to American and United flights when travel agents request information on their computer terminals. An agent who uses the SABRE system and requests a listing of flights from New York to Los Angeles with stops in between knows that the first few screens may not show the most direct way, nor the least expensive way, but for sure they'll show the American way. In the computerized travel agency market, American and United dominate, with shares of 41 percent and 39 percent, respectively. (Over 80 percent of the nation's 20,000 travel agencies, accounting for more than 60 percent of airline ticket sales, are computerized.) In regions where the airline with the reservation system has numerous flights, the prioritization procedure can lead to as much as 20 percent additional business.

The two cases above involve *strategic information systems*—computerized information systems used to support an organization's competitive strategy, its strategy for gaining advantage over its competitors.

Emerging from the convergence of technological innovations in information processing (including telecommunications) and competitive forces reshaping industry landscapes, strategic information systems form a new variety of information system, radically different in organizational use from traditional management information systems and from the more recent decision support systems. As competition increases, information systems will become critical to gaining a competitive edge.

This article provides an instrument, called an "option generator," for identifying opportunities to gain a competitive edge, via use of modern information systems technology and, generally, by adding value to the products and services currently offered to clients.

GENERATING STRATEGIC OPTIONS

The option generator helps vastly expand the search for strategic opportunities by asking planners to address the questions in Figure 1. Using this series of questions, a business unit can generate systematically more than

FIGURE 1 Major Options to Secure a Competitive Advantage

	Suppliers	Customers	Competitors
Differentiation			
Cost			
Innovation			

100 possibilities for using information systems to create a competitive edge. In the authors' experience, not one company that has seriously attempted to find such an edge has failed to do so. This does not mean, however, that the advantage that is identified can be implemented without commitment of resources, particularly software development. But the option generator helps create a large number of possible opportunities to get the edge on competitors.

WHAT IS THE STRATEGIC TARGET?

The first and broadest set of options comes from the selection of a strategic target on which to focus the information systems advantage. Here a planner can pick one of three possible choices—the target can be a supplier, a customer, or a competitor. *Suppliers* include those who provide raw materials, capital, labor, or services. *Customers* include those who retail, wholesale, warehouse, distribute, or use the products sold. *Competitors* include those currently in the industry, possible new entrants, firms in other industries offering substitute products, or other organizations competing for scarce resources. The following examples illustrate strategic information systems targeted at the supplier, customer, and competitor arenas.

Supplier as Target

Equitable Life Assurance, the nation's third largest insurer, developed an on-line system to tie the firm's field offices with its seven regional offices, four warehouses, and corporate headquarters in New York. The warehouses stock all inventory items required by the company.

In the past, warehouse purchasing agents often lacked information to analyze vendor bids and determine the best buy. With the new inventory control and purchasing system, Equitable corporate purchases most of the inventory supplies from a distributor in New York and then offers them at a marked-up price to the warehouses. The warehouses are free to buy supplies from corporate or to go outside if they find a better deal. The information system gives them leverage during vendor negotiations, since they have on-line access to the inventory database and can check the terms of all recent deals struck for items they want.

This is an example of a strategic information system targeted at a supplier group that has enabled Equitable to reduce the bargaining power of suppliers. The firm estimates that the system has saved it over $2 million a year, as well as increased the reliability and quality of deals it cuts with its suppliers.

Customer as Target

Wetterau, the fourth largest U.S. food wholesaler, has prospered by concentrating on small, independent supermarkets. Up to 1982, according to Ted Wetterau, the chairman, "the cornerstone of our whole business was that we would not service the chains."

But the slack economy of 1982 and a costly battle to defeat an unexpected takeover attempt in the fall of 1981 stalled the company's efforts to gain new business. Moreover, with the total number of independent grocers declining by 35 percent in 10 years (from 174,000 units in 1970 to 113,000 in 1980), Wetterau had to revise its strategy. For the first time, the St. Louis–based concern decided to offer its wide array of services and volume discounts to chains of 10 to 20 units.

The backbone of Wetterau's diversification move in its targeted retailer arena is its expertise with electronic check-out scanners (point-of-sale terminals) and computerized inventory systems. Wetterau has more than 100 scanner-equipped stores on-line with its host computer, which updates prices, tracks reordering information, generates shelf labels, and performs many other functions (which supermarket executives are hesitant to reveal here because a competitive edge might be lost). In any case, this is the bait that the technologically undernourished chains might find too appetizing to resist; at least that's what the top management of Wetterau's seems to be betting on.

Competitor as Target

According to E. F. Hutton, packaged investment products accounted for 30 percent of its commission revenues last year, up from 4 percent five years ago. Packaged investments are bundled, often unique products targeted directly at the competitive offerings and designed to build customer loyalty and increase fee revenue. Financial service firms like Hutton use information systems as a "manufacturing process" to create tailored products.

The development of a recent CD fund gives a glimpse of the manufacturing process used to produce these new products. At 6 A.M., traders at a brokerage house called London to order sheafs of CDs from foreign banks, which often pay higher rates than their U.S. counterparts. By 11 A.M. they had accumulated $50 million of the paper. The next step in the fund-creation process depended on an information system that took the prices and rates, juggled them according to the firm's objectives and constraints embodied in its computer program, and arrived at management fees and commissions: Thirty-six hours after the start of this production run (job-shop style, to be sure), brokers were ready to start selling the fund.

Behind all the promotional hoopla surrounding such new products in the financial services industry, there is generally an information system playing a critical role in product development, processing, or distribution. Shearson/American Express's managed commodity account, for example, has investments directed by a computerized portfolio management system. Merrill Lynch's Cash Management Account depends for its existence on database and laser technology.

Multiple Targets

Strategic information systems can be used to secure an edge with more than one target or to support activities in one arena so that advantage can be gained in another. The manager of General Electric's distribution center for large appliances in Kentucky uses an information system that helps GE keep down its substantial shipping costs so that its retailers can maintain competitive prices.

Xerox, Pratt & Whitney, General Motors, and others require their suppliers to provide computer-generated data on product quality, inventory levels, and the like for the items they supply. This is less an attempt to gain advantage over suppliers than a desire to produce more efficiently to meet competitive costs. But for the suppliers, the ability to respond to these new information systems-based demands from their customers might create a competitive advantage. As these large customers formulate supplier strategies in response to (especially international) competition, these strategies are often aimed at reducing the number of suppliers to a select few who can provide not only the desired components, but also valued-added services like quality-control reports. In this situation, a supplier's information system expertise can create a decisive edge in securing long-term contracts which would preempt the business from competitors.

WHAT STRATEGIC THRUST CAN BE USED AGAINST THE TARGET?

Once a target has been selected, the option generator suggests three strategic thrusts: differentiation, cost, and innovation. This results in nine possible major options to secure a competitive advantage: a differentiation, cost, or innovation thrust targeted at suppliers, customers, or competitors (Figure 1). The aim of a *differentiation* thrust is to either (1) reduce the differentiation advantages that suppliers, customers, or competitors enjoy vis-á-vis your organization or (2) increase the differentiation advantages you enjoy vis-á-vis your suppliers, customers, or competitors.

The aim of the *cost* thrust is to (1) reduce or avoid your costs vis-á-vis suppliers, customers, or competitors, (2) help your suppliers or customers reduce or avoid their costs so that you gain preferred treatment from these stakeholders, or (3) increase your competitors' costs.

The aim of the *innovation* thrust is to find new ways of doing business through the use of information systems. These new ways include, but certainly are not limited to, the use of information systems to transform steps on an existing industry (value-added) chain, diversify into new industries or markets, redefine the existing business, or create new businesses. Innovative strategic information system applications like the airline reservation systems developed by American and United, or the cash management account of Merrill Lynch, are preemptive strikes. They are major moves made ahead of the competitors, which allow the firms to secure advantageous positions from which they are difficult to dislodge because of advantages they have captured by being first movers [5].*

---

* Bracketed numbers cite the references at the end of this chapter.

The following examples illustrate uses of the three basic thrusts of differentiation, cost, and innovation.

Differentiation as the Thrust

The air traffic controller's strike illustrates the use of information systems to *reduce* the differentiation advantages of labor, in this case the controllers. Prior to striking, controllers were seen as highly trained specialists in short supply. The federal government's decision to dismiss the strikers was based in part on the availability of a new flow control information system.

According to labor relations expert Harley Shaiken of M.I.T., what doomed the strike was the "government's skillful use of a new weapon—information systems technology—to keep air traffic moving, gutting the strikers' leverage." Soon after the walkout, 75 percent of the commercial flights were operating while 75 percent of the controllers were marching on the picket line.

By performing many of the controllers' tasks, the information system dramatically reduced the controllers' bargaining power, making the skill they had less valuable. Though air traffic control is *still* a skilled occupation, the pool of new applicants has been widened because the required level of expertise and training has been reduced. With reduced supplier differentiation advantages come lower buyer costs, so the price of controller labor has fallen.

This next example shows how Pacific Intermountain Express (PIE) *increased* its advantage through differentiation. PIE, a 63-year-old trucking firm based in California, competes in the newly deregulated, commodity-like trucking industry. To attract customers, PIE has developed an information system that allows shippers to call the computer to track the status of a shipment. This is important for misplaced or delayed shipments, emergencies, etc. Strategically, it created a way for PIE to differentiate its service from its competitors' and to attract shippers, thus increasing its profit opportunities. As W. D. Beatenbough, president of PIE, put it, "In trucking today, we all use the same highways and the same freight terminals. Our only competitive advantage is to stand out technologically."

Cost as the Thrust

To support a cost reduction thrust in the customer arena (in contrast to Equitable's cost reduction thrust described above in the supplier arena), the Hartford Insurance Company provides customers who have complex exposures and multiple claims with a computer-generated loss control analysis. Breaking out losses by location, time of day, type of accident, and so on, this information system pinpoints accident causes and, after preventive measures are taken, can lead to substantially lower premium costs for customers and, therefore, more business for Hartford.

Innovation as the Thrust

Toys "R" Us, the number one toy chain in the United States, has captured an impressive 11 percent share in the toy market. With over 165 stores, the company relies on a sophisticated information system to keep track of what's selling so it can take quick markdowns to rid itself of slow movers. This information system is not the only reason for the chain's rapid rise to the top in this highly competitive industry: spacious parking lots, well-organized stores, and good management also count. But the information system is an essential ingredient.

Toys "R" Us selected the innovative thrust by using the information system's expertise and resources the company had developed in the toy market to support its diversification into the children's apparel market. When the spinoff Kids "R" Us was formed, response from the competition was immediate. "The new chain has upset everyone in the market," according to a spokesman from a group of 285 specialty and department stores nationwide. Clearly, Toys "R" Us is using the same information systems-based strategy it employed successfully in the toy market to enter the children's apparel sphere.

WHAT STRATEGIC MODE CAN BE USED?

Once a strategic target and thrust have been selected, the next set of options is generated by asking which opportunities can be created by selecting a strategic mode: Are there opportunities to employ information systems *offensively* to increase an edge or *defensively* to reduce an edge now held by one of the targets? The following examples illustrate the offensive and defensive modes.

Offensive as the Mode

The offensive use of information systems against competitors is illustrated by some of the extensions of the airline reservation systems mentioned above. For example, the new cut-rate airlines contend that American and United overcharge them just to be listed. Airlines without their own system complain that the intricacies of SABRE and Apollo often stymie attempts to create innovative packages. As one rival put it, "If you're out of sync with their reservation system, then whatever you're doing won't exist." Finally, Braniff and Continental have argued that their recent cash flow problems are due in part to these automated reservation systems: When multiple carriers are involved, the first carrier in the itinerary is considered the ticketing airline, so it collects all the revenues, but repays the others only when the flight is over.

Defensive as the Mode

The previously cited case of the flow control system developed by the U.S. Department of Transportation illustrates the defensive mode of the differentiation thrust targeted at suppliers. Targeting customers instead, a Chicago law firm used its telephone information system, which monitors calling activity, to discover that it was substantially underbilling clients because its lawyers were careless about recording time spent on the telephone with clients.

WHAT DIRECTION OF THRUST CAN BE USED?

The involvement of both line and information systems executives is critical for the development of strategic information systems. In the selection of the information system direction, this is paramount. The direction indicates whether the strategic information system will be used by the organization or be provided by it as the output, and high expertise in information systems technology and resources is required to identify *usage* and *provision* opportunities. Note again that none of the options produced by the options generator is mutually exclusive (e.g., a strategic information system may be used by the firm *and* provided to stakeholders). The aim is merely to trigger ideas about options available: In fact, the more ideas the merrier. The following examples illustrate the usage and provision directions of strategic information systems.

Usage as the Direction

Scholastic Magazine, a 60-year-old publisher of elementary and secondary school materials and a subsidiary of Xerox, faces mounting pressures due to decreasing school enrollments and budgets. New product development and marketing skills are two key factors of success for *Scholastic* in the 1980s.

To meet its new challenges, the company maintains a marketing database with information on its product sales, 16,000 school districts, teachers and students who have bought its products, millions of U.S. households (i.e., census-derived demographic data), and so on. This marketing information system produces sales penetration ratios (e.g., sales/teacher, sales/student, etc.), district profiles, and the like.

Scholastic uses this information system to fine-tune the efforts of its 100 sales representatives. But the most critical use of this system is in direct mail, the major method it uses to reach the school market. *Scholastic* mails over 50 million items a year, using its marketing information system as one would a telescopic lens on a rifle. Without it, like many of its competitors who lack such a system, *Scholastic* would be shooting in the dark. With it, *Scholastic* is able to define market segments exactly and to aim at the targets with a high degree of confidence.

Provision as the Direction

In 1977, Merrill Lynch announced its innovative Cash Management Account (CMA), an information system–based product that *provided* under one umbrella three appealing services to investors: credit through a standard margin account, cash withdrawal by check or Visa debit card, and automatic investment of cash, dividends, and the like, in a Merrill-managed money market fund. Without a 162-step (subsequently patented) computer program and the firm's resources in database and laser printing technology, the product would never have gotten off the ground.

Merrill sold the CMA through its brokers to investors with minimum balances of $20,000. The exponential growth of the CMA (180,000 accounts in 1980, 560,000 in 1981, and over 900,000 in 1982) was fueled by free-trip prizes to Hawaii and Puerto Rico that Merrill offered to the brokers who sold the most CMAs. These efforts brought in over 450,000 new accounts that had not been with Merrill previously. Merrill reaps over $60 million a year in fees for the more than $20 billion it manages in the three money market funds associated with the CMA product.

With this innovative information system–based product, Merrill preempted the market with a monopoly position for four years. Competition from other financial services organizations did not appear until 1981, and at the close of 1982. Merrill's closest rival, Dean Witter, had only 90,000 customers for its Active Asset Account. Only in 1983 did Merrill's premier position erode when banks and other financial service organizations finally entered the market with similar products and the information systems technology needed to develop them.

WHAT INFORMATION SYSTEM SKILLS CAN WE USE?

The last set of options by which to seek advantage lies in the choice of information system skills. Fundamentally, all information system applications require at least one of three generic skills: information processing, information storage, or information transmission. The competitive advantage must be created from an application of these skills. Note again, these options are not mutually exclusive. That is, a strategic information system can process *and* store, store *and* transmit, and so on. The following examples illustrate options that capitalize on processing, storage, or transmission skill.

Processing as the Skill Used

The information system–based product launched by National Decisions Systems is called "1980 U.S. Census." It consists of five volumes of statistical data derived from Census Bureau computer tapes that are sold at less than cost by the Bureau. National Decisions added value by developing programs to generate analyses and displays from the raw data. This new product is sold to those involved in market research, demographic analysis, and so on. In this marketplace, National Decisions enjoys first mover advantages.

Storage as the Skill Used

Ford Motor Company, working with AT&T's Information Systems division and its new digital network product, Net/1000, has developed an auto parts inventory system for its dealers. Data is stored on Net/1000 and made available to dealers who need auto parts for repairs. The system allows dealers who may have incompatible computers or terminals to search each other's inventories. The net effect is improvement in customer service and an increase in dealer loyalty, an important consideration for automobile manufacturers in this period of intense global competition.

Transmission as the Skill Used

Dun and Bradstreet, the information service and publishing conglomerate, has a new, value-added product aimed at the Fortune 1000 market. It is a delivery system for the firm's on-line databases.

The product allows users to access all D&B databases with one standard procedure through its packet-switched network, DunsNet. It includes IBM personal computers, bundled with fourth generation languages and graphics software, and is targeted for financial departments. Many of these departments are customers of D&B's software subsidiary, McCormack and Dodge Corporation, a supplier of general ledger, accounts receivable, and other financial software products.

SYSTEMATICALLY IDENTIFYING STRATEGIC
INFORMATION SYSTEMS

Developing an effective information system is not done without effort. To achieve maximum benefit requires a joint effort on the part of line management and information systems managers. The best way to do this systematically is to have them *jointly* develop a competitive strategy for the business unit. As most planners are well aware, this process involves (1) assessing the current competitive strategy and position, (2) assessing environmental factors affecting the business, and (3) developing a strategy to meet the anticipated challenges over the planning period. What is less obvious is that substantial strategic information system opportunities can be uncovered at all stages in the process.

The competitive strategy process begins by establishing a working definition of the unit's business, which captures the current scope of its activities and shows how it differentiates itself across segments and from its competitors. By analyzing the unit's products and markets, one can pin down current scope: customer groups served, customer needs satisfied, and technologies employed to meet customer needs [1]. However, in this stage many opportunities to create information system advantages can be uncovered, and opportunities to identify strategic targets, thrust, and modes can be identified.

In the next stage, similar opportunities arise. After a working definition of the business has been formulated, the existing and potential competitors are identified and comparisons made of the unit's performance to its principal competitors'. The purpose is to determine the extent of one's competitive advantages if they exist [2]. In this stage, opportunities to provide or use information systems, drawing on one's processing, storage, or transmission skill, can be identified—particularly if information system managers are participating in the process.

After an assessment of competitive strategy and position, a Porter-type [4] industry analysis of the competitive environment creates opportunities to identify possible innovative uses of information systems. Analysis of the $4 billion fragmented junkyard (i.e., automotive salvage) industry might reveal, for example, consolidation opportunities. The industry already uses computers to handle inventory, to aid in purchase decisions made at salvage auctions, and to prevent loss of sales because sales people don't know whether a part is in stock.

An entrepreneurial firm clearly has the opportunity to build a national service company to stock, locate, and deliver used parts to any U.S. city within 24 hours. Insurance adjusters who make 50 to 70 million requests a year for parts would certainly be eager customers for such a service, a service that could never become operational without an information systems–based service.

Attention paid to environmental variables (economic, social, demographic, and governmental) [3] should also stimulate the search for other strategic information system applications. A trend of increased governmental regulation might be the impetus for developing information systems to cut through the bureaucratic morass that slows down new product introductions.

In the stage of developing a competitive strategy for the business unit, after internal and external assessments have been made, an important step is to decide whether a redefinition of the business is called for. If so, an essential ingredient of this redefinition might be an information systems component, as it was for Reuters, the international news-gathering service based in London. Reuters redefined its business in the early 1970s by developing a computerized information and retrieval system targeted for banks, stock and commodity traders, and other businesses. The system provided the latest prices from stock, bond, money, oil, commodity, and other international markets. Additional economic services were added as the business evolved.

At the heart of the system is the Reuters' monitor, a video screen and keyboard that gives immediate access to financial and general news databases. Today, there are over 11,000 subscribers in over 60 countries. This information system–based service accounted in 1981 for over 85 percent of Reuters's sales ($254 million) and 100 percent of its profits ($30 million, pretax).

Alternatively, a firm could use its information systems capabilities for a corporate strategy of diversification-through-acquisition. The example of McKesson Corporation's entry into the embryonic distribution industry for personal computer software illustrates this opportunity. The current industry leader is Softsel Computer Products (1983 sales estimate: $75 million), followed by Micro D (1983 sales estimate: $28 million), and SKU Inc. (1983 sales estimate: $25 million). The market for personal computer software, now at $2.1 billion, is projected to reach $11.7 billion by 1988, with 25 percent handled by distributors. It is "the nation's fastest-growing distribution business," according to T. E. Drohan, president and chief executive officer of McKesson Corporation, a $4.08 billion distributor of drugs and health care products, alcoholic beverages, and industrial chemicals. McKesson has acquired SKU with the intent to expand the scope of its distribution business. This move is expected to transform the cottage industry of software distribution (with after-tax margins of at most 4 percent) into a larger, more profitable game. McKesson is using previously developed information systems as the synergistic fuel for its entry vehicle. The computerized order entry systems and other proprietary products it provides to over 16,000 mass merchandisers, supermarkets, and other outlets, will be tailored to this new marketplace. These information systems will not be used merely as aids to improve efficiency but as weapons to shape competitive strategy.

McKesson has proved to be an innovative user of information systems.

Through the use of information systems, it has differentiated itself from its rivals and diversified successfully into adjacent industries. "The name of the game," says CEO Drohan, "has become adding value to distribution. Our primary goal is to set ourselves apart from the competition in dramatic enough ways that we become the first distributor a supplier thinks of. At the other end, by tying your customers to you as tightly as possible, you get more and more of his business as he grows."

If the past is prologue to the future, current and new participants in the software distribution industry can expect McKesson to use its information systems to increase its competitive advantage by:

- Establishing on-line links with software suppliers and retailers.
- Providing information to suppliers and retailers to help them better manage inventories, collect and analyze market data, and sales campaigns.
- Providing retailers with shelf management plans, price labels, inventory systems, and the like.
- Conducting computer-related technical seminars for suppliers and retailers.
- Joining with software suppliers to develop new products.
- Marketing associated services through its network.

In the process of developing a competitive strategy for one's business unit, one can equally well identify similar opportunities by systematic use of the key questions in Figure 2.

IMPLICATIONS

In developing information system opportunities, there are several points to remember. First, the systematic search for strategic information systems opportunities should be conducted within the context of competitive

---

FIGURE 2 Option Generator

1. What is our strategic target?
   Suppliers   Customers   Competitors
2. What strategic thrust can be used against the target?
   Differentiation   Cost   Innovation
3. What strategic mode can be used?
   Offensive   Defensive
4. What direction of thrust can be used?
   Usage   Provision
5. What information system skills can we use?
   Processing   Storage   Transmission

---

strategy development. Only then can the business unit be sure that it has systematically and comprehensively explored all options.

Second, the active participation of information system professionals is necessary if the business unit is to identify all strategic information systems opportunities and to defend against strategic information systems' threats from its competitors. Creating information system advantages consumes resources, so it is best to actively involve the specialists as early and as intensively as possible—the rewards tend to exceed the costs.

Third, the role of the unit's information systems group, important as it is for identifying strategic information system opportunities, is critical for implementing any competitive strategy that must be supported by all but the most primitive information systems. Unless information systems planning is synchronized with the business unit's strategy, the unit will face misalignments of resource allocation, incorrect priority setting, and delays in system delivery that might well put its strategy in jeopardy. To ensure alignment of information systems development and the execution of the competitive strategy, full communication between line business managers and information systems managers must be ensured [6].

Finally, like the experimental physicists who discovered a new class of atomic particles with the aid of a formal framework for their search (in this case Dirac's theory of matter) and instruments designed from the theory, business and information systems managers now have a framework (competitive strategy) and an instrument (the options generator) to uncover new options for competitive advantage. Just as the physicists who scanned bubble-chamber photographs in search of the particles Dirac's theory had predicted knew what they were looking for and could search systematically for it, so too can a business unit search for information systems opportunities to gain a decisive edge. With more than 100 options to search for, it would be very surprising if a business unit did not find at least one.

REFERENCES

1. ABELL, D. *Defining the Business: The Starting Point of Strategic Planning.* Englewood Cliffs, N.J.: Prentice Hall, 1980.
2. HAX, A., AND N. MAJLUF. "The Use of the Industry Attractiveness-Business Strength Matrix in Strategic Planning." Cambridge, Mass.: MIT, Sloan School of Management, 1982.
3. HOFER, C., AND D. SCHENDEL. *Strategic Formulation: Analytical Concepts.* St. Paul, Minn.: West Publishing, 1978.
4. MACMILLAN, I. "Preemptive Strategies." *Journal of Business Strategy,* Fall 1983, pp. 16–26.
5. PORTER, M. *Competitive Strategy: Techniques for Analyzing Industries & Competitors.* New York: Free Press, 1980.
6. WISEMAN, C. *Strategy and Computers: Information Systems as Competitive Weapons.* Homewood, Ill.: Dow Jones-Irwin, 1985.

20 *Rattling SABRE—New Ways to Compete on Information**

Max D. Hopper

I have built my career, and American Airlines has built much of its business, around massive, centralized, proprietary computer systems. Developing these systems consumed millions of man-hours and billions of dollars, but their marketplace advantages were huge. As a result, our experience underscored the competitive and organizational potential of information technology. At the risk of sounding immodest, we helped define an era.

That era is over. We are entering a new era, one in which the thinking that guided "best practice" as recently as five years ago is actually counterproductive. In this new era, information technology will be at once more pervasive and less potent—table stakes for competition, but no trump card for competitive success. As astute managers maneuver against rivals, they will focus less on being the first to build proprietary electronic tools than on being the best at using and improving generally available tools to enhance what their organizations already do well. Within their companies, they will focus less on developing stand-alone applications than on building electronic platforms that can transform their organizational structures and support new ways of making decisions.

Who, by now, cannot recite the computer-based success stories of the 1970s and 1980s?

- SABRE, American Airlines's reservation system, which eventually became a computerized reservation system (CRS), and Apollo, the other

* Source: Reprinted by permission of *Harvard Business Review*. "Rattling SABRE—New Ways to Compete on Information" by Max D. Hopper (May/June 1990). Copyright © 1990 by the President and Fellows of Harvard College; all rights reserved.

leading CRS, transformed marketing and distribution in the airline industry.

- American Hospital Supply's ASAP order-entry and inventory-control system generated huge sales increases for the company's medical products and turned it into an industry leader.
- United Service Automobile Association used its Automated Insurance Environment—a collection of telecommunication systems, databases, expert systems, and image-processing technologies—to consistently outperform its insurance industry rivals in service quality, premium growth, and profitability.
- Mrs. Fields Cookies relied on its Retail Operations Intelligence system, an automated store management network, to build and operate a nationwide chain of 400 retail outlets without a costly and stifling headquarters bureaucracy.

These and a handful of other well-known computer systems (the Information Technology Hall of Fame, if you will) represent an important chapter in the application of electronic technologies to build competitive advantage and enhance organizational effectiveness. But it is time to turn the page. In 1984, F. Warren McFarlan published an influential article in *HBR* on the competitive potential of information technology.[1] He asked managers to consider how information systems might benefit their companies. Could the technology build barriers to competitive entry? Could it increase switching costs for customers? Could it change the balance of power in supplier relationships? He went on to argue that for many companies the answer was yes. By being the first to develop proprietary systems, pioneers could revolutionize their industries.

Increasingly, however, the answer is no. While it is more dangerous than ever to ignore the power of information technology, it is more dangerous still to believe that on its own, an information system can provide an enduring business advantage. The old models no longer apply.

THE INFORMATION UTILITY

The new era is driven by the greatest upheaval in computer technology since the first wave of modern computer development 30 years ago. We are finally (and just barely) beginning to tap the real potential of computer functionality. As we change what computers can do, we must change what we do with computers.

Think of it as the emergence of an "information utility." Using superfast RISC architectures, hardware suppliers are delivering enormous processing power at remarkably low costs. UNIX and other software and communications standards are bringing unprecedented portability among different vendors' products and among different classes of products. Software tools like relational databases, expert systems, and computer-aided software engineering are helping create powerful applications that meet specialized needs at reasonable costs. The ultimate impact of these and other technical developments is to give end users greater power to shape their computer systems and manage their information needs. Increasingly, technology is allowing groups and individuals within companies to perform many of the functions once reserved for data processing professionals.

It is hardly news to most managers that technology is changing faster than ever. Yet I wonder how many appreciate just how radical and rapid the changes are. Over the past two decades, price/performance ratios for computer technology improved at an annual compound rate of roughly 10 percent. In recent years, those ratios improved at a compound rate closer to 40 percent. This massive acceleration in performance will have profound implications for how computers are used and how useful computers are. Three features of the new environment will be particularly important.

Powerful workstations will be a ubiquitous presence in offices and factories, and organizations will use them far more intensively and creatively than they do today. One of the paradoxes of the information age is that computers become easier to use as they become more powerful and complex. That's what is so important about dramatic hardware advances like microprocessors with a million transistors on a chip. Personal workstations running at near supercomputer speeds will finally be powerful enough to be simple and thus truly useful. Meanwhile, new graphical user interfaces are creating screen environments (electronic desktops) that make it quicker for employees to become skilled with their workstations, to move between systems without extensive retraining, and to develop the confidence to push the functionality of their machines.

In the not-so-distant future, computers will be as familiar a part of the business environment as telephones are today. They will also be as simple to use as telephones, or at least nearly so. As a result, companies will find it harder to differentiate themselves simply by automating faster than the competition. It will be easier for every organization to automate and to capture the efficiency benefits of information technology. This leaves plenty of room for competitive differentiation, but differentiation of a new and more difficult sort.

Companies will be technology architects, rather than systems builders, even for their most critical applications. The widespread adoption of standards and protocols in hardware, software, and telecommunications will dramatically recast the technology-management function. At American Airlines, for example, we have spent 30 years handcrafting computer systems. We like to think we're better at this than most and that our skills in hardware evaluation, project management for software development, and systems integration have given us an important leg up on the competition. But we look forward to the day when we can buy more and more of our hardware and software from third-party vendors capable of tailoring their systems to our needs—and that day is rapidly approaching.

InterAAct, our major new initiative for organizational computing, is a good example. Unlike SABRE, which incorporates a vast amount of AMR-developed technology, InterAAct is built around hardware and software provided by third-party vendors: workstations from AT&T, IBM, and Tandy; minicomputers from Hewlett-Packard; HP's NewWave presentation software and Microsoft Windows; local area networks from Novell. We play a role in systems integration (in particular, merging the networks), but outside suppliers are capable of delivering more value than ever before.

Of course, if we can buy critical hardware and software from outside vendors, so can our competitors. Our skills as electronic-tool builders, honed over decades, will become less and less decisive to our information technology strategy. This may sound like bad news, but we welcome it. We're not in business to build computer systems; our job is to lead in applying technology to core business objectives. We don't much worry if the competition also has access to the technology; we think we can be smarter in how we use it.

Economies of scale will be more important than ever. We have entered the age of distributed computing, an age in which a young company like MIPS Computer Systems delivers a $5,000 workstation with processing speeds comparable to those of a $3 million IBM 3090 mainframe. Yet the amount of information required to solve important business problems also keeps growing, as does the capacity of telecommunications systems to transmit data quickly and reliably between distant locations. More than ever, then, the benefits of distributed computing will rely on access to vast amounts of data whose collection and storage will be managed on a centralized basis. The proliferation of desktop workstations will not erode the importance of scale economies in information processing.

Consider the airline industry. American Airlines began working on a computerized reservation system in the late 1950s as the volume of reservations began to outrun our capacity to handle them with index cards and blackboards. In 1963, the year SABRE debuted, it processed data related to 85,000 phone calls, 40,000 confirmed reservations, and 20,000 ticket sales. Today there are 45 *million* fares in the database, with up to 40 million changes entered every *month*. During peak usage, SABRE handles nearly 2,000 messages per *second* and creates more than 500,000 passenger name records every day. As we enhance SABRE, we are aggressively replacing ''dumb terminals'' in travel agents' offices, airline reservation offices, and airports with workstations capable of intensive local processing. But as a system, SABRE still works only in a centralized environment. The level of data collection and management it must perform dwarfs the demands of the 1960s just as thoroughly as the performance of today's computers dwarfs the performance of their ancestors.

The continued importance of scale economies has at least two major implications for information technology. First, truly useful computer systems are becoming too big and too expensive for any one company to build and own; joint ventures will become the rule, rather than the exception. Second, organizations (like AMR) that have developed centralized systems will eagerly share access to, and sometimes control of, their systems. For companies to remain low-cost providers of information, they must tap the enormous capacities of their systems. Tapping that capacity requires opening the system to as many information suppliers as possible and offering it to as many information consumers as possible.

FROM SYSTEMS TO INFORMATION

I do not mean to diminish the pivotal role of information technology in the future or to suggest that technology leadership will be less relevant to competitive success. Precisely because changes in information technology are becoming so rapid and unforgiving and the consequences of falling behind so irreversible, companies will either master and remaster the technology or die. Think of it as a technology treadmill: Companies will have to run harder and harder just to stay in place.

But that's the point. Organizations that stay on the treadmill will be competing against others that have done the same thing. In this sense, the information utility will have a leveling effect. Developing an innovative new computer system will offer less decisive business advantages than before, and these advantages will be more fleeting and more expensive to maintain.

The role of information technology has always been to help organizations solve critical business problems or deliver new services by collecting data, turning data into information, and turning information into knowledge quickly enough to reflect the time value of knowledge. For 30 years, much of our money and energy has focused on the first stage of the process—building hardware, software, and networks powerful enough to generate useful data. That challenge is close to being solved; we have gotten our arms around the data gathering conundrum.

The next stage, and the next arena for competitive differentiation, revolves around the intensification of analysis. Astute managers will shift their attention from *systems* to *information*. Think of the new challenge this way: In a competitive world where companies have access to the same data, who will excel at turning data into information and then analyzing the information quickly and intelligently enough to generate superior knowledge?

On Wall Street, there are stock traders who wear special glasses that allow for three-dimensional representations of data on their screens. They need three dimensions to evaluate previously unimaginable quantities of information and elaborate computer models of stock patterns. Manufacturers Hanover has developed an expert system to help its foreign-currency traders navigate through volatile markets.

In our industry, powerful new tools are helping us answer faster and more precisely questions we have struggled with for years. What is the best price to charge for each perishable commodity known as an airline seat? How do you reroute aircraft after a storm disrupts airport operations? How do you distribute your aircraft between airports? How do you meet the special needs of each passenger without pricing your basic service out of reach? As the process of analysis intensifies, decisions we once made monthly, we'll make weekly. Those we made weekly, we'll make daily. Those we made daily, we'll make hourly.

Consider yield management, the process of establishing different prices for seats on a flight and allocating seats to maximize revenues—that is, calculating the optimal revenue yield per seat, flight by flight. Yield management is certainly one of the most data-intensive aspects of the airline business. Computers review historical booking patterns to forecast demand for flights up to a year in advance of their departure, monitor bookings at regular intervals, compare our fares with competitors' fares, and otherwise assist dozens of pricing analysts and operations researchers. During routine periods, the system loads 200,000 new industry fares a day. In a "fare war" environment, that figure is closer to 1.5 million fares per day.

The initial challenge in yield management was to build software powerful enough to handle such demanding analyses. We spent millions of dollars developing SABRE's yield-management software, and we consider it the best in the world. Indeed, we believe our pricing and seat-allocation decisions generate hundreds of millions of dollars of incremental annual revenue. For years, we guarded that software jealously. Since 1986, however, we have sold SABRE's revenue-management expertise to any company that wanted to buy it. One of our subsidiaries—called AA Decision Technologies, many of whose members built our original yield-management applications—is knocking on the doors of airlines, railroads, and other potential customers. Why? Because we believe our analysts are better at using the software than anyone else in the world. Whatever "market power" we might enjoy by keeping our software and expertise to ourselves is not as great as the revenue we can generate by selling it.

Similarly, Mrs. Fields has begun marketing to other retail chains the sophisticated networking and automation system with which it runs its cookie operations. Price Waterhouse is helping companies like Fox Photo evaluate and install the Retail Operations Intelligence system, the backbone of Mrs. Fields's nationwide expansion.

This is the competitive philosophy with which American Airlines is entering the new era: We want to compete on the use of electronic tools, not on their exclusive ownership.

COMPUTERS AND COMPETITION: SABRE RECONSIDERED

Perhaps no case study better illustrates the changing competitive role of computer technology than the evolution of the system that helped define the old era—SABRE. According to conventional wisdom on SABRE, the fact that American Airlines developed the world's leading computerized reservation system generated substantial increases in traffic for us by creating market-power advantages over the competition. This has always been a difficult proposition to document. Analysts once pointed to so-called screen bias as a source of marketing advantage, even though the government-mandated elimination of such biases in 1984 produced no appreciable decline in bookings for American Airlines. Others argued that American's access to CRS data regarding the booking patterns of travel agents gave us an incalculable information and marketing edge over our rivals—an argument that has proven groundless. Now the experts speak of a halo effect that by its very nature is impossible to identify or document.[2]

We are proud of what SABRE has achieved, and we recognize that it represents a billion-dollar asset to the corporation. But I have always felt the folklore surrounding SABRE far exceeded its actual business impact. SABRE's real importance to American Airlines was that it prevented an erosion of market share. American began marketing SABRE to travel agents only after United pulled out of an industry consortium established to explore developing a shared reservation system to be financed and used by carriers and travel retailers. The way American was positioned as an airline—we had no hubs, our routes were regulated, and we were essentially a long-haul carrier—meant that we would have lost market share in a biased reservation system controlled by a competitor. SABRE was less important to us as a biased distribution channel than as a vehicle to force neutral and comprehensive displays into the travel agency market.

My concerns about the conventional wisdom surrounding SABRE, however, go beyond the issue of market power. SABRE has evolved through four distinct stages over the past 30 years. In each stage, it has played different roles within American Airlines, and each role has had a different impact on the industry as a whole. Unfortunately, most analysts mistake the CRS distribution stage for the entire story. To do so is to invariably draw the wrong lessons.

SABRE took shape in response to American's inability to monitor our inventory of available seats manually and to attach passenger names to booked seats. So SABRE began as a relatively simple inventory-management tool, although by the standards of the early 1960s, it was a major technical achievement.

Over the years, the system's reach and functionality expanded greatly. By the mid-1970s, SABRE was much more than an inventory-control system. Its technology provided the base for generating flight plans for our aircraft, tracking spare parts, scheduling crews, and developing a range of decision-support systems for management. SABRE and its associated systems became the control center through which American Airlines functioned.

American installed its first SABRE terminal in a travel agency in 1976, inaugurating its now familiar role as a travel-industry distribution mechanism. Over the decade that followed, we added new services to the database (hotels, rail, rental cars), built powerful new features to help travel agents offer better service, increased the installed base of SABRE terminals, and created a training and support infrastructure. SABRE now operates in more than 14,500 subscriber locations in 45 countries. Largely as a result of the proliferation of such systems, travel agents now account for more than 80 percent of all passenger tickets as compared with less than 40 percent in 1976. SABRE and its CRS rivals truly did transform the marketing and distribution of airline services.

Today, however, SABRE is neither a proprietary competitive weapon for American Airlines nor a general distribution system for the airline industry. It is an *electronic travel supermarket,* a computerized middleman linking suppliers of travel and related services (including Broadway shows, packaged tours, currency rates) to retailers like travel agents and directly to customers like corporate travel departments. Speak with any of the 1,800 employees of the SABRE Travel Information Network, the system's marketing arm, and you will hear that their division doesn't treat American Airlines materially differently from the other 650 airlines whose schedules and fares are in the system. American pays SABRE the same booking fees as other airlines do. SABRE's capacity to write tickets and issue boarding passes works similarly on other large carriers as it does on American flights. Although limited performance differences remain (largely as a result of SABRE's technical heritage as an in-house reservation system), SABRE programmers are working to overcome these limitations and put all carriers on an equal footing in the long term.

I don't deny that there is some halo effect from SABRE that benefits American Airlines in the marketplace, although we have never been able to determine the magnitude or causation. But the core identifiable benefit American Airlines now receives from SABRE is the revenue it generates. This is not an inconsequential advantage, to be sure, but it is difficult to argue that the SABRE system tilts the competitive playing field in ways that uniquely benefit American Airlines. This is not necessarily how we would prefer it, but it is what the technology, the market, and the U.S. government demand. There is no compelling reason for a travel agency to accept a CRS that does not provide the most comprehensive and unbiased system for sorting through thousands of potential schedules and fares. If SABRE doesn't do the job, another system will. SABRE's industry-leading U.S. market share of 40 percent means that rival systems account for three out of every five airline bookings.

I receive weekly reports on our "conversion wars" with Covia, whose

Apollo reservation system remains our chief competitor, and the other U.S.-based CRS systems. Subject to contract-term limitations that are established by the U.S. government, it takes only 30 days for a travel agent who is unhappy with SABRE to pull the system out and install a competing system. If a CRS can be replaced within a month by a rival system, can it really be considered a source of enduring competitive advantage? The old interpretations of SABRE simply no longer apply.

As a group of HBR authors argued, "Early developers of single-source or biased sales channels should plan for the transition to unbiased electronic markets. That way, they can continue to derive revenues from the market-making activity."[3] The alternative, they might have added, is for the biased channel to disappear altogether in favor of unbiased markets offered by other suppliers.

This is the future of electronic distribution. It is increasingly difficult, if not downright impossible, for computerized distribution systems to bind customers to products. Smart customers simply refuse to fall into commodity traps. (Indeed, American Hospital Supply has opened ASAP to products from rival companies.) It is increasingly difficult to design information systems that locked-out competitors or coalitions of locked-out competitors can't eventually imitate or surpass. It is increasingly difficult for one company to marshal the financial resources to build new information systems on the necessary scale.

We are applying these new rules outside the airline realm. AMRIS, a subsidiary of AMR, is developing a computerized-reservation and yield-management system for the hotel and rental car industries. Its power and sophistication will exceed anything currently available. We expect that the introduction of the Confirm system, scheduled for 1991, will affect pricing strategies and marketing techniques in the hotel and rental car industries in much the way Apollo and SABRE transformed the airline business. But we are not approaching the system itself in the same way we approached SABRE—at least three major differences stand out.

For one, we are not going it alone. AMRIS has formed a joint venture with Marriott, Hilton, and Budget Rent-A-Car to develop and market the Confirm system. Moreover, there will be nothing biased about Confirm's reservation functions—no tilted screen displays, no special features for the sponsors. Finally, the management aspects of the system, such as the yield-management software, will be generally available to any hotel or rental car company that wants to buy them. Confirm's sponsors are participating in the creation of the most sophisticated software in the world for their industries; but the moment the system is operational, they will offer its tools to their competitors around the world.

Not all companies will benefit equally from this new system. As is true with marketing or finance or employee development, some organizations will excel in manipulating, analyzing, and responding to the data Confirm generates. But no company will be locked out of access to the data or the opportunity to use it to compete. As in airlines and so many other industries, competition shifts from building tools that collect data to using generally available tools to turning data into information and information into knowledge.

BUILDING THE ORGANIZATIONAL PLATFORM

As with competition between companies, technological change will have profound consequences for the role of computers within companies. Until recently, I was not a champion of office automation. Workstations were simply not powerful enough nor affordable enough nor easy enough to use nor capable enough of being integrated into networks to justify large investments in organizational computing. Indeed, a visitor to my office would be hard-pressed to find more than a handful of personal computers on the desks of the information technology professionals.

In the last few years, though, as a result of the technology changes I have outlined here, my caution has given way to genuine enthusiasm. But in this area, too, it is time for new thinking. Understandably, given the earlier limitations of the technology, most companies approached office automation with an "applications" mind-set. They developed discrete systems to make administration more efficient, to improve planning and control, or to deliver particular services more effectively.

We are taking a different approach. AMR has embarked on a multiyear, $150 million initiative to build an information technology platform modeled directly on the utility concept. This platform, called "InterAAct," provides for the convergence of four critical technologies: data processing, office automation, personal computing, and networking. InterAAct will provide an intelligent workstation for every knowledge worker at AMR and will guarantee that every employee, no matter the rank or function, has easy access to a workstation. These workstations will be part of local area networks connecting work groups and a corporatewide network linking every location in the company, from departure gates in Boston to the underground SABRE facility in Tulsa, Oklahoma, to the CEO's office in Dallas/Fort Worth.

The goal of InterAAct is *not* to develop stand-alone applications but to create a technology platform—an electronic nervous system—capable of supporting a vast array of applications, most of which we have not foreseen. InterAAct is an organizational resource that individuals and groups can use to build new systems and procedures to do their jobs smarter, better, and more creatively. It should eliminate bureaucratic obstacles and let people spend more time on real work—devising new ways to outmarket the competition, serve the customer better, and allocate resources more intelligently.

InterAAct began to take shape in 1987, and rollout started last June. It will take at least three years to extend the platform throughout the AMR organization. We are approaching the project with four guiding principles.

1. The platform must give each employee access to the entire system through a single workstation that is exceptionally easy to use and that operates with a standard user interface throughout the company.

2. The platform must be comprehensive, connecting all managerial levels and computing centers within the company, and be connectable to other companies' platforms.

3. The project must generate hard-dollar savings through productivity gains that are quantifiable in advance, and it should be rolled out in stages to ensure that it is delivering those hard-dollar savings.

4. The project must be managed as much as an *organizational* initiative as a technology initiative. Installing a powerful electronic platform without redesigning how work is performed and how decisions are made will not tap its true potential.

Installing InterAAct is partly a matter of faith. But $150 million projects cannot be justified on faith alone. After extensive study (including in-depth analyses of how 300 AMR employees from different parts of the company actually spend their time), we estimated that extensive automation could produce enough hard-dollar savings to generate a 10 percent return on the InterAAct investment. AMR's standard hurdle rate is 15 percent, so corporate directors with a pure financial mind-set would not have approved this project. That's where faith comes in. We are confident that the "soft-dollar" benefits—better decisions, faster procedures, more effective customer service—will boost returns on InterAAct well above the hurdle rate. Still we are rolling out the project in stages and testing its impact along the way to be sure the hard-dollar savings materialize first.

I don't know how InterAAct will change our company's organizational structure and work practices over the next five years. But I guarantee there will be major changes. Most large companies are organized to reflect how information flows inside them. As electronic technologies create new possibilities for extending and sharing access to information, they make possible new kinds of organizations. Big companies will enjoy the benefits of scale without the burdens of bureaucracy. Information technology will drive the transition from corporate hierarchies to networks. Companies will become collections of experts who form teams to solve specific business problems and then disband. Information technology will blur distinctions between centralization and decentralization; senior managers will be able to contribute expertise without exercising authority.[4]

We are currently at work on a series of InterAAct applications to reduce common sources of frustration and delay within AMR. Why should employees remain in the dark about the status of resource requests? On-line forms and electronic signature control, to be introduced later this year, will help speed such approval processes. Why should an employee's personnel file remain locked away and inaccessible? A pilot project at the Dallas/

Fort Worth airport allows baggage handlers to use a workstation to check how much overtime they have accrued. Eventually, employees should be able to file their own insurance claims or check on their reimbursement status. With respect to bureaucratic procedures, the potential of an electronic platform is obvious: eliminate paper, slash layers, speed decisions, simplify the information flows.

Other organizational possibilities are even more far-reaching. InterAAct standardizes spreadsheets and databases, provides direct access to the corporate mainframes, and will eventually support automatic report generation. The new ease and speed with which analysts will be able to accumulate and disaggregate data, conduct "what-if" scenarios, and share information should accelerate the planning and budgeting process. It's not our job to design a new planning process. InterAAct gives our analysts the potential to redesign systems to best suit their needs.

Finally, and perhaps of greatest importance, InterAAct will allow senior executives to make their presence felt more deeply without requiring more day-to-day control. Eventually, executives should be able to practice selective intervention. The information system, by virtue of its comprehensiveness, will alert senior managers to pockets of excellence or trouble and allow them to take appropriate action more quickly. Over time, the role of management will change from overseeing and control to resolving important problems and transferring best practices throughout the organization.

WHO NEEDS THE CIO?

The ultimate impact of the hardware, software, and organizational developments I have described is to proliferate and decentralize technology throughout the organization. Piece by piece and brick by brick, we and others are building a corporate information infrastructure that will touch every job and change relationships between jobs. Much work remains to be done. We need better tools, more connectivity, and richer data that reflect the real business needs of our companies. But in all these areas, momentum is moving in the right direction.

As technology reshapes the nature of work and redefines organizational structures, technology itself will recede into the strategic background. Eventually—and we are far from this time—information systems will be thought of more like electricity or the telephone network than as a decisive source of organizational advantage. In this world, a company trumpeting the appointment of a new chief information officer will seem as anachronistic as a company today naming a new vice president for water and gas. People like me will have succeeded when we have worked ourselves out of our jobs. Only then will our organizations be capable of embracing the true promise of information technology.

NOTES

1. F. Warren McFarlan, "Information Technology Changes the Way You Compete," *Harvard Business Review,* May-June 1984, p. 98.
2. For a comprehensive review of CRS technology in the airline industry, see Duncan G. Copeland and James L. McKenney, "Airline Reservation Systems: Lessons From History," *MIS Quarterly,* June 1988.
3. Thomas W. Malone, JoAnne Yates, and Robert I. Benjamin, "The Logic of Electronic Markets," *Harvard Business Review,* May-June 1989, p. 168.
4. For a good overview of the organizational possibilities, see Lynda M. Applegate, James I. Cash, Jr., and D. Quinn Mills, "Information Technology and Tomorrow's Manager," *Harvard Business Review,* November-December 1988, p. 128.

21 Managing the Introduction of Information Systems Technology in Strategically Dependent Companies*

James I. Cash, Jr.
Poppy L. McLeod

ABSTRACT

The primary focus of computer and communication technology application in some companies has shifted from efficiency/process improvement to strategic/competitive uses. Companies that have become strategically dependent on computer and communications technology have found that the requisite processes of technology forecasting, tracking, research and development, introduction, and management of new technology are unwieldy and almost impossible to operationalize, given traditional administrative and organizational approaches. This paper proposes that a contemporary organization, strategically dependent on computer and communications technology, should: (1) establish an organizational unit with specific responsibility for these processes and (2) use a contingency framework for the design of ongoing administrative infrastructure to effectively manage new technology. The organizational unit is called the *Emerging Technology group,* and an example description from Air Products and

* Source: J. I. Cash, Jr. and P. L. McLeod, "Managing the Introduction of Information Systems Technology in Strategically Dependent Companies," *Journal of Management Information Systems,* vol. 1, no. 4 (Spring 1985), pp. 5–23.

Chemicals, Inc., is provided. The contingency framework proposed is based on the phases model developed by McKenney and McFarlan.

INTRODUCTION

The evolution of computer and communications technology, used in information processing systems (abbreviated hereafter as IS), and its impact on organizations have sparked significant general research interest. Two recent articles [11, 17]* have focused attention on how developments in information systems technology have made feasible many new applications that have strategic importance. Further, some companies are almost totally dependent on this technology to operationalize and implement their competitive business strategy. For this set of companies it is critical to identify and exploit relevant new technology as quickly as possible. However, the rate of new product announcements, new vendors, and technology options has evolved and will continue to evolve much faster than most companies can effectively assimilate and exploit them.

In this paper we propose two steps managers of these companies can take to address this problem. First, we suggest they adopt a contingency framework for the design of administrative systems to manage technology assimilation. Inherent in this proposal is a shift to managing new technology from an organizational learning perspective, rather than a cost or technology delivery and efficiency perspective. Using insights obtained from selected literature on technology assimilation, organizational behavior, and our empirical observations, we attempt to prescribe guidelines for effectively managing a wide variety of technology options in a manner that ensures the most time-effective introduction and assimilation of appropriate technology. In particular, we will draw heavily from work by McFarlan and McKenney on technology assimilation [12].

Second, against the backdrop of a contingent technology assimilation framework, we define and illustrate one example of an organization that should be established with specific responsibility to manage the identification and introduction of new technology with high pay-off potential. We call this organization the "Emerging Technology" group and rely heavily on Burns and Stalker's study of the entry of British and Scottish firms into the electronics industry during the post-World War II era to anticipate key management issues [3]. Although their study did not focus specifically on IS technology, the management concerns that faced those companies are identical to concerns which face a number of companies today that have grown strategically dependent on IS technology.

We have also found it helpful to use the model of organizational learning

---

* Bracketed numbers cite the references at end of this reading.

presented by Chris Argyris and Donald Schon to describe the way organizations successfully exploit new technologies [1]. According to this model organizational learning can be divided into two types—single-loop and double-loop. We will argue later that successful exploitation of a new IS technology involves double-loop learning.

In the sections following we first define what we mean by "strategic dependence" on information systems technology and "successful exploitation" of new technology. Next is an overview of McKenney and McFarlan's phases framework, followed by a detailed examination of each phase and the key management issues that must be resolved. Finally we describe the "Emerging Technology" (ET) group that should be established in companies strategically dependent on IS technology.

STRATEGIC DEPENDENCE ON INFORMATION SYSTEMS TECHNOLOGY

A popular contemporary approach to determining a corporation's competitive strengths and weaknesses is analyzing the firm's *value-added stream* [2, 7, 13, 20]. This term refers to the "value" added to a product or service as it moves through the functional areas of a business, through distribution channels, and is finally acquired by the end consumer. Figure 1 presents this idea in graphic form. Analyzing the value-added stream of a given company, and comparing it to the current and projected stream for the industry and/or competitors, provides a basis for developing corporate strategy. This framework has also proven very useful in tracing the use of IS technology in business organizations by determining the penetration of IS technology into parts of the value-added stream. Further, an assessment of strategic dependency on IS technology is provided by determining the most critical parts of the value-added stream and assessing the

FIGURE 1

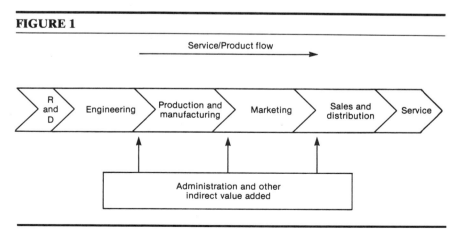

current and future dependence of these parts on IS technology. Our research indicates a significant increase in the percentage of total value-added, directly dependent on IS technology for a wide range of companies.

Several trends have contributed to the penetration of IS technology into a firm's value-added stream. First, the dramatic reduction in cost of IS technology (the cost of executing 1,000 instructions has declined from $15.00 to $0.07), accompanied by increased functionality, has permitted its use in ever-increasing application areas over time. (See Figure 2.) Numerous applications that were not feasible in 1965 were feasible by 1975, and so forth. Second, penetration of technology into wider ranges of applications has been aided by the desire of many managers to exploit the decreasing cost of technology to offset increasing personnel, material, and energy costs (Figure 3). Finally, the technology has been embedded into some products (appliances, cars, etc.) and services (home banking). Invisible to many senior managers, information systems technology has become so pervasive in the business value-added stream of many organizations that some firms rely almost exclusively on this technology to support their competitive thrust (e.g., banks and insurance companies).

A question one senior manager interviewed asked was, "How dependent on IS technology is my firm to (*a*) improve market access; (*b*) provide product and company differentiation; (*c*) facilitate new product and service introductions; or (*d*) introduce operational efficiencies which comprise our major competitive thrusts for the 1980s?"

FIGURE 2

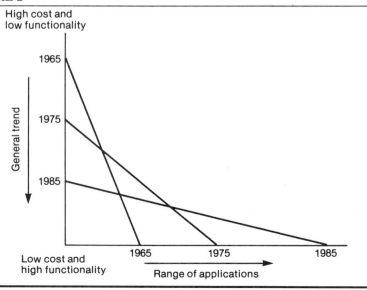

FIGURE 3

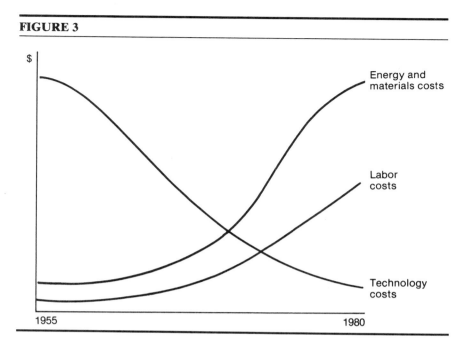

We think these are the key questions which define how "strategically dependent" a given company may be on information systems technology. Clearly the answer to these questions will vary across industries (see Figure 4), across firms in a given industry, and across strategic business units within a firm. Likewise the importance of a given competitive thrust (e.g., improved market access versus differentiation) will vary across these same contexts. However, in a given company or industry, value-added analysis permits ordering of alternative competitive thrusts and explicitly determines the degree of strategic dependence on IS technology.

Further, "successful exploitation" of new IS technology can be defined by the extent or number of high value-added applications implemented in a given company. An example schematic of a framework for determining successful exploitation is shown in Figure 5 [7]. The vertical axis represents alternative competitive thrusts in a specific organization we studied. These thrusts are ordered by the overall value added to the company. The higher up the axis, the higher the overall value to the firm and vice versa. The horizontal axis represents the evolution in functionality of IS technology over time. Companies have moved from crude batch systems that limited use of IS technology almost exclusively to back-office systems to interactive, transaction processing systems which use database management software and improved communications capability, which made feasible a much broader range of applications. Further, distributed com-

FIGURE 4

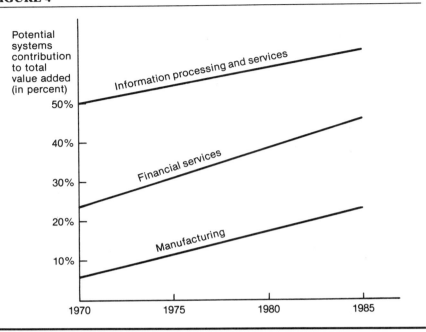

puting, including networks, personal computing, office workstations, etc., have been introduced on a broad scale and continue to increase the number of feasible applications (Figure 2). The key question senior managers must ask in this context is:

> Are we retrofitting newer IS technology functionality to low value-added applications (losers); or are we using the new functionality to exploit opportunities further up the value-added axis (winners)?

The optimal approach for firms that are strategically dependent on IS technology is illustrated by the "winners" vector in the chart.

Organizations that have successfully implemented and exploited IS technology (the winners vector in Figure 5) seem to exhibit what Argyris and Schon [1] have described as double-loop learning. Double-loop learning involves making changes in the norms and standard operating procedures of an organization. In the most general sense the organization not only "learns" to identify and adapt to new requirements but also to anticipate them. Organizations exhibiting double-loop learning with regard to assimilating new IS technologies will allow the technology to lead them into entirely new functions while simultaneously using the technology to improve current practices. For example, a major distributor of periodicals and newspapers to retailers competed in an industry in which success was

---

FIGURE 5

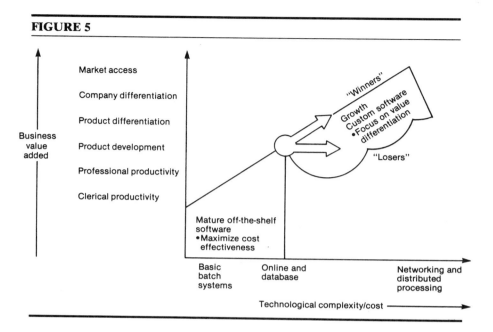

highly correlated with being the low-cost competitor [11]. Most of the competitors in this industry used IS technology exclusively to reduce the cost of their current operating procedures. Many of their customers were unable to track profitability of individual periodicals.

The distributor developed a laser-scanning application that facilitated the development of a model that calculated profitability for periodicals at the retailer's location(s) and compared it to similar data from other customers. Demographic data about the neighborhood surrounding the retailer was added later. The distributor developed a series of recommendations which helped the retailer make better product and product-mix decisions, improving the retailers' cash flow. Concurrently, the distributor increased the price of its service to customers and over time changed the primary basis for competition in the industry from exclusively *cost* to *service*. The distributor used IS technology as the enabling vehicle to change its competitive strategy, but in so doing had made dramatic changes to its own organizational infrastructure and business processes.

In contrast, organizations that fall along the "losers" vector in Figure 5 generally exhibit single-loop learning. Argyris and Schon defined single-loop learning as simplistic problem detection and solving. This approach maintains the organization's equilibrium (i.e., no attempt is made to understand or make changes to basic structural problems that precipitate the need for change or adaptation).

ASSIMILATING NEW IS TECHNOLOGY

Researchers interested primarily in describing the impact of new technology on organizations for general managers have found it useful to describe the assimilation of the technology as occurring in stages. Best known among these researchers are Cyrus Gibson and Richard Nolan [15, 16] and Warren McFarlan and James McKenney [12]. Gibson and Nolan focused on large-scale computer technology and the development of centralized data processing departments during the late 60s and early 70s. They described four key growth processes which defined stages of an assimilation process. More recently, McFarlan and McKenney observed that organizations are concurrently experiencing multiple technology assimilation patterns associated with new IS technology uses in the office, such as word processing, electronic mail, and filing; individual uses such as microcomputers; and organizational uses such as CAD/CAM, distributed DP, highly integrated databases, and MRP. In their view an organization should manage the assimilation of these technologies in *phases,* since the assimilation pattern is different for each technology despite their coexistence. Although numerous other works have been focused on the assimilation of technology in organizations, for the purposes of this paper we wanted to focus on work that was oriented toward general management and had been effectively communicated to a wide audience. We have thus chosen the McFarlan and McKenney work to communicate our management guidelines for effective management of new IS technology introduction because of its contemporary relevance.

The original phases model as proposed by McFarlan and McKenney is listed below.

Phase 1: Technology Identification and Investment

This phase involves identifying technologies of potential interest to the company and funding a pilot project. In this phase the pilot project may be thought of as akin to advanced R&D. The key outputs of the project should be seen as expertise on technical problems involved in the use of the technology, plus a first guess at the types of applications where it might be most useful. Although a metric for deciding to continue or discontinue exploring may be required, it is generally inappropriate to demand any hard ROI payoff identification either before or after the implementation of this project.

Phase 2: Organizational Learning and Adaptation to the Technology

The objective during this phase is to take the newly identified technology of interest to an organization where a first level of technical expertise has been developed and encourage user-oriented experimentation. This is generally accomplished through a series of pilot projects. The primary purpose of these pilot projects is to develop user-oriented insights as to the potential profitable applications of this technology and to stimulate user awareness of the existence of the technology. Repeatedly it has happened that what the IS department thought during Phase 1 was going to be the major implication of a new technology turned out to be quite different by the end of Phase 2. As is true of Phase 1, effectiveness is the keyword for Phase 2.

Phase 3: Rationalization and Management Control

Phase 3 technologies are those which are reasonably understood by both IS personnel and key user personnel as to their end applications. The basic challenge in this phase is the development of appropriate tools and controls to ensure that the technology is being utilized efficiently. In the earlier phases the basic concerns revolve around stimulating awareness and experimentation. In this phase the primary attention turns to development of appropriate administrative infrastructure to ensure that cost-effective applications are developed as efficiently as possible and that they can be maintained over a long time. Formal standards, cost-benefit studies, and chargeout mechanisms may all be appropriate for technologies in this phase as their delivery and use is rationalized.

Phase 4: Maturity and Widespread Transfer of the Technology

Technologies in this phase have essentially passed through the gauntlet of organizational learning with technological skills, user awareness, and management controls in place. Often the initiating organization will move on to new technologies and spend no energy on transferring the expertise. A major danger focuses on the fact that new technologies may obsolesce this expertise, and that organizational ridigity could slow the process of adaptation to the new technology.

We propose that these four phases can be grouped together into two broader categories for organizational planning. Phases 1 and 2 belong in one category (PHASE I), and Phases 3 and 4 belong in the other (PHASE II). The difference between them can be described as *forecasting, tracking, assessing, learning, creating, and testing versus general usage, acceptance, and support.* More simply, we refer to the grouping as *innovation versus control.* Our initial empirical work and the work of others in this area support the view that different parts of the organization will (or should) be responsible for these different functions. McFarlan and McKenney explicitly recommend that PHASE I activities be kept separate from PHASE II activities, ''so the efficiency goals of II do not blunt the effectiveness [goals] of the other (I).'' Support for this idea comes from the organizational behavior literature. For example, James March and Herbert Simon [10], in their classic book on organizations, referred to the innovation versus control functions as unprogrammed versus programmed activity. To enable and encourage unprogrammed or innovative activity, they recommend that organizations make special and separate provisions for it. Frequently this involves the creation of special units for the innovative purpose.

Burns and Stalker [3] also discuss separating the innovative and creative functions from the implementation and control functions in organizations. They conducted a study of 20 manufacturing firms in Scotland and England during the post-World War II era which were in diverse businesses ranging from textiles to television and radio. What these companies had in common was their interest in exploring the fledgling electronics industry. The movement of the new technology from testing and piloting stages to distribution, implementation, and control stages was discussed by Burns and Stalker in the late 50s; the concerns they raised are similar to those facing many IS and general managers today. For firms strategically dependent on IS, the challenge involves requisite innovation based on new IS technology versus maintenance of more established, production-oriented applications of IS technology.

Burns and Stalker found there were cultural differences between the electronics research and development laboratories and the production workshops of the companies they studied. We believe that comparable cultural differences exist within today's organizations between the units responsible for PHASE I of IS technology assimilation and PHASE II (e.g., information center versus traditional applications development). According to Burns and Stalker, linguistic differences accounted for much of the cultural incompatibility between the two types of organizational departments. They reported that the engineers and scientists of the development laboratories spoke a different language and had different norms of interaction from the personnel in the production divisions. The management of these companies had to find ways of translating the language of the laboratory into the language of production. Ironically, the problem was aggravated by the fact that most companies separated the R&D labs as much as possible (physically in most cases) from the rest of the organization in order to avoid cultural clashes. We found similar linguistic differences between effective managers of PHASE I and PHASE II IS technology.

Burns and Stalker observed that the most successful companies in exploiting the electronics technology were those companies that adopted an organic organizational structure for innovation. An organic structure roughly means that supervisor-subordinate relationships are informal, and there is considerable flexibility of functioning. On the other hand, they observed that organizations that were more established in the electronics industry sustained their competitive advantage by effective use of mechanistic organizational structure—roughly the polar opposite of an organic structure. Burns and Stalker conceived of these two types of structure as the endpoints on a continuum. In their view organizations that fell somewhere on the continuum between these two endpoints delivered conflicting messages to employees and were less effective.

We argue that the organic-mechanistic distinction applies to the PHASE I and PHASE II IS technology. PHASE I activities require an organic structure, and PHASE II activities require a mechanistic structure. Most contemporary IS organizations have achieved effective mechanistic structure. We propose a new organizational unit be established to address PHASE I technology exploitation and management—the Emerging Technology (ET) group. It should reside in the information systems organization, on an equal level with application development and operations departments. We discuss the ET group in more detail in the following section.

Key Management Issues

We have identified three key issues that require the attention of general management when designing an organization to effectively introduce new technology: organization, management control, and leadership (Figure 6). The IS technology strategy of the firm is a key input to constrain choices in the three areas.

Each specific issue must be explicitly monitored and managed during each phase of the technology assimilation. First is the question of *proper organizational structure* for conducting the innovative versus control functions of the assimilation process. Management must decide on the appropriate location and personnel for each function. Second, managers must consider the appropriate *management control systems* to have in

---

FIGURE 6 Overview of Key Issues

	Phase	
Issues	*I* *Innovation* *Effectiveness*	*II* *Control* *Efficiency*
Organization	Organic (ET)	Mechanistic (traditional/IS)
Management control	Loose/Informal	Tight
Leadership	Participating	Directive (telling to delegating)

place during each phase. The reward systems, communication systems, development systems, and resource allocation systems are all components of management control systems. Next, management must be concerned with *leadership*. In what ways should it differ during each phase? Hersey, Blanchard, and Hambleton [9] have described a model of situational leadership that we think is useful for describing leadership during the two phases of technology assimilation. They identify four leadership styles based on a leader's level of attention to the task and to interpersonal relationships. We will describe each style as we discuss leadership within each of the phases. Finally, the IS technology strategy must be clearly articulated and well understood. "IS technology strategy" refers to the firm's overall commitment to the exploitation of IS technology for competitive business positioning following one of three styles: (*a*) innovators— first to introduce new competitive uses of IS technology, (*b*) early adopters, (*c*) effective/efficient followers. In what follows we will address the three issues as they apply to each of the phases, but are primarily concerned about PHASE I.

Management Issues: PHASE I

Typically, a separate group emerges that is primarily responsible for introducing a new technology into the organization. We argue a permanent organization should be established with this responsibility. The atmosphere within this group, which we call the Emerging Technology (ET) group, during Phase I is exploratory and experimental. Examples of current technologies that such a group would explore would be laser disks and local area networks. The organizational structures and management controls are loose and informal. Cost accounting and reporting are flexible (though accuracy is essential), and little or no requirement exists for pro forma project cost-benefit analysis. The leadership style resembles what Hersey, Blanchard, and Hambleton refer to as "participating." That is, the distinctions between leaders and subordinates are somewhat clouded, and the lines of communication are shortened. The level of attention to relationships is high relative to the task orientation. Several researchers have noted the importance of informality for innovation and organizational learning. Burns and Stalker, for example, placed great emphasis on the informality of the R&D departments of the companies they studied.

This description of the ET group that we have just given is similar to Burns and Stalker's description of an organic structure. Further, Robert Miles [14], in an extensive study of the tobacco industry, referred to the informality as organizational slack and stated that "the creation or utilization of slack normally requires the temporary relaxation of performance standards." In the companies we studied, standards of efficiency were greatly reduced during the early testing phases of a new IS innovation.

Organizations strategically dependent on IS technology should view Phase I activities as an integral part of their ongoing response to pressures to adapt to their changing environments. We argue that the ET group be established to specifically address this issue and serve as a key part of the company's effort to exhibit what Argyris and Schon call "double-loop" learning.

Illustrative of the pressure and responses that lead to establishment of a separate department is the dramatic growth of "information centers" in response to end-user computing. These facilities were generally staffed with nontraditional data processing professionals and had very different accounting, justification, and cost-benefit systems associated with them. Firms strategically dependent on IS technology cannot afford to reactively establish such mechanisms. They must proactively forecast, assess, and test appropriate technology to maintain or gain competitive advantage. These activities will not occur without specific responsibility assigned to a person or an organizational unit. The role of this unit is similar to the role of a corporate R&D department.

Two key assumptions contained in the position analysis for ET are noteworthy because of their variation from the general corporate R&D model. The first is that the manager of ET and the organization are charged with the role of a facilitator, rather than a guru. This implies use of professionals outside the ET organization to forecast, track, and assess technology evolutions. For example, a person in the database administrator's organization might be partially funded by ET to forecast, track, and test new DBMS products. The second assumption is that ET is responsible for what we call intraorganizational technology transfer. This refers to the role of designing and managing the Phase 2 introduction and diffusion of the targeted technology in the company. This is the key role of an ET group when contributing to double-loop learning in a company. ET must facilitate the development of user-oriented, creative applications of the new technology. Then participate in discussions about: how the new applications could best be developed and implemented, education and training of appropriate users and IS professionals using the new technology, and changes in strategy or structure that may result from implementing the new technology and associated applications.

After the personnel directly involved with the new technology (e.g., the Emerging Technology group) develop the ability to support it, management makes a decision whether or not to provide additional resources to continue the diffusion of the technology throughout the organization (Phase 2). With requisite support of senior management, the emerging technology group begins to teach others throughout the organization how to utilize it and to encourage experimentation. One of the chief concerns of the ET manager at this point is effectively marketing it to the rest of the organization. (In some organizations the job of selling IS will be easy because the organizational culture encourages innovation and experimentation. According to March and Simon, innovation in such companies is *institutionalized*. They also state that the aspiration levels of organizations tend to rise automatically, thus creating natural pressures toward innovation. The skillful salesperson of IS technology will take advantage of those pressures.)

Again the cultural differences between laboratory and workshop are important here. Part of the task of selling this technology to other parts of the organization is finding a way to translate the unique language associated with the technology to a language compatible with the larger organizational culture. Burns and Stalker discussed this problem at great length as it existed in the organizations they studied. According to them, these cultural differences existed more in the minds of the organizational participants than in any objective reality. They said these "artifacts" resulted from the natural tendency for people, "when faced with problems in human organizations of an intractable nature, to find relief in attributing the difficulties to the wrong-headedness, stupidity, or delinquency of the others with whom they had to deal" [3].

The issue here, however, is not to determine whether the cultural differences exist only in the mind of the beholder but rather, given that they do exist somewhere, what can be done about them. They reported two solutions that were used by their sampled companies which merit consideration by companies faced with assimilating IS technology. One of these solutions was to have members of the design department supervise the production of the new design and vice versa. Translating this to the IS context, the solution would mean taking persons from the ET group and putting them in charge of the portion of the user community experimenting with the new technology, or taking users and putting them in charge of projects in the ET group. The trouble with this solution, as documented by Burns and Stalker, is that frequently there are wide gaps between the level of technical (distinct from technology) expertise of the subordinates and their manager. Usually the subordinates will know more about the technology or business process than the manager does. We think, if chosen carefully, this is a viable approach, if managerial skills are specifically identified as a type of technical expertise. Charles Perrow [18], in his critical analysis of complex organizations, reflects this attitude and suggests that managerial skills should be considered as a type of technical expertise. We think this is especially true of those companies strategically dependent on IS technology.

The other solution Burns and Stalker reported finding in the companies they studied was the creation of special intermediaries whose job it was to serve as the liaison between the design and production shops in the organizations. McFarlan and McKenney advocate a similar strategy, suggesting the development of integrating devices, "such as steering committees, user department analysts, etc." This strategy increases bureaucracy of the organization structure, but for many organizations it may be the most effective solution to the translation problem.

It is also important for ET managers to analyze manifested or potential resistance from the organizational members to the change brought about by the new technology. Burns and Stalker point out that a high percentage of resistance to change stems from the reluctance of organizational members to disturb delicately balanced power and status structures. ET managers should be prepared to adopt what Hersey and Blanchard refer to as a "selling" leadership style. This style is characterized by high task orientation and high levels of interpersonal interaction. Major organizational changes threaten long-established positions and open up opportunities for new ones. The advocate of a new IS technology who is not aware of the political ramifications of the new system will be faced with unpleasant unanticipated consequences.

Once the range of potential uses of the new technology has been generated and appropriate users have become acquainted with the new technology, management must make a decision about putting the technology permanently into place. At this juncture the assimilation project moves away from the innovative stages of PHASE I to the control stages of PHASE II via Phase 3.

Management Issues: PHASE II

The focus of PHASE II is rationalization and control of the new technology. While the main concern during PHASE I was the effectiveness of the technology, in PHASE II management is concerned with efficiency. In attempting to install the necessary controls over the technology, management's task is to define the goals and criteria for technology utilization. The leadership style here resembles what Hersey and Blanchard refer to as "telling." There is low interpersonal involvement relative to task orientation. During this phase the organizational members are better able to judge the appropriateness and feasibility of their goals for the new technology than they were during PHASE I. We see the traditional IS organization and associated administrative systems as appropriate for this phase. Listed below are some special concerns the IS manager must address.

The issue of appropriate management control systems is answered while addressing the organization question of efficient boundaries. Which functions should be confined to the IS division? Which should be decentralized? And further, which should be contracted outside the organization altogether? Oliver Williamson [21], whose writings discuss efficiency of organizational structure, says the location of organizational boundaries will be determined by what he refers to as the transaction costs of dealing with markets outside the organization. Closely related to the consideration of efficient boundaries is the consideration of resource dependence. According to Jeffrey Pfeffer and Gerald Salancik [19], organizations are dependent on their environments for certain resources, and they seek ways to manage that dependence by changing either themselves or their environments. Thus, a key task of the IS manager during Phase 3 is to assess the dependencies created by this new technology and to seek ways of managing it.

We think the "responsibility spectra" of Buchanan and Linowes [4] is an effective framework for translating the work of the aforementioned organizational designers (Williamson, Pfeffer, Salancik) to the IS context. Although their work was focused on distributed data processing, it provides an effective way of determining appropriate responsibility for operation, support, development, training, documentation, analysis, budgeting and funding, evaluation, priorities, security, standardization, etc. We believe decisions along these dimensions must be made as you enter PHASE II. More important, individual and separate decisions should be made for each major new technology (i.e., chargeout policy for micros is very different from mainframes or minis). Simplistic standardized approaches to efficient management of new technology are inappropriate in this decade.

The activities during this phase determine whether the company will exhibit single-loop or double-loop learning. As the organization moves through PHASE II, it learns not only to correct the problems accompanying the new technology but also to anticipate and avoid them altogether. More important, management should begin to change some of the organization's standard operating procedures (if appropriate) to take advantage of the new technology. The growing familiarity with the technology causes management to be more comfortable with taking full advantage of its capabilities even when basic structural changes are required. Those organizations strategically dependent on the technology should begin to apply it in ways that will move them up their value-added scale (Figure 5). This may involve changes in company strategy, distribution channels, market access techniques, or product or service definition, which implies double-loop learning would be occurring.

IS managers during Phase 4 typically exhibit a leadership style resembling Hersey and Blanchard's "delegating" style. Here interpersonal involvement and task orientation are low. Because operating procedures are well understood and awareness is high, the managers let subordinates run the show. The activities of Phase 4 include supporting the Phase 1, Phase 2, and Phase 3 activities that may be occurring throughout the organization and transferring the technology to a wider spectrum of systems applications.

The organization at this point will be operating within explicitly and implicitly agreed on parameters with respect to the new technology. Pfeffer refers to these parameters as an organization's world view. The task of sensitive management will be to manage the changes in that world view caused by new technologies and to seek out those technologies that will be compatible.

SUMMARY

Firms strategically dependent on information systems technology must continually search for opportunities to gain competitive advantage by innovative and creative use of new technology. However, because of the number of vendors and products in combination with the frequency of their new introductions, it is becoming increasingly difficult to address this requirement. We have argued managers should take two steps to enhance their ability to successfully exploit IS technology:

a. Adapt a contingent framework for concurrently managing IS technology at different points of organizational assimilation.
b. Establish an organizational unit (ET) with specific responsibility.

The ET group is best suited for organizations that have high strategic dependence on IS technology. It will be most effective in organizations that have strong commitments to research and development in non-IS areas, but that understand the role and management of such activities. Further, we used the value-added stream and ordered value-added axis to facilitate choosing the most appropriate technology investment and evaluating how successful exploitation of technology has been.

REFERENCES

1. ARGYRIS, C., AND D. A. SCHON. *Organizational Learning: A Theory of Action Perspective.* Reading, Mass.: Addison-Wesley Publishing, 1978.
2. BLAKE, J., AND J. GOODRICH. "Capitalizing on Opportunities Created by Deregulation of the Banking Industry." McKinsey and Co., Inc., September 1981.
3. BURNS, T., AND G. M. STALKER. *The Management of Innovation.* London: Tavistock Publications Limited, 1979.
4. BUCHANAN, J., AND R. LINOWES. "Understanding Distributed Data Processing." *Harvard Business Review,* July–August 1980.
5. CASH, J. I. "McGraw Hill Book Company: Microcomputer Resource Center." Harvard Business School Case Services #9-182-017, 1982.
6. _____. "AIR PRODUCTS AND CHEMICALS, INC.: MIS EVALUATION OF END-USER SYSTEMS." HARVARD BUSINESS SCHOOL CASE SERVICES #9-182-005.
7. CASH, J. I.; M. MCLAUGHLIN; AND R. HOWE. "Changing Competitive Groundrules: The Role of Computer and Communication Technology in the 1980s." Harvard Business School Research and Course Development Profile, 1983.

8. CASH, J. I.; F. W. McFARLAN; AND J. L. McKENNEY. *Corporate Information Systems Management: Text and Cases.* Homewood, Ill.: Richard D. Irwin, 1983.

9. HERSEY, P.; K. H. BLANCHARD; AND R. K. HAMBLETON. "Contracting for Leadership Style: A Process and Instrumentation for Building Effective Work Relationships." *Perspective in Leader Effectiveness.* Ohio University Center for Leadership Studies, 1980.

10. MARCH, J. S., AND H. A. SIMON. *Organizations.* New York: John Wiley & Sons, 1958.

11. McFARLAN, F. W. "Information Technology Changes the Way You Compete." *Harvard Business Review,* May–June 1984.

12. McFARLAN, F. W., AND J. L. McKENNEY. "The Information Archipelago—Maps and Bridges." *Harvard Business Review,* September–October 1982, pp. 109–19.

13. McLAUGHLIN, M., AND R. HOWE. "Formulating Information Resource Strategies for the 1980s." Booz Allen & Hamilton, 1981.

14. MILES, R. *Coffin Nails and Corporate Strategies.* Englewood Cliffs, N.J.: Prentice-Hall, 1982.

15. NOLAN, R. L. "Managing the Crisis in Data Processing." *Harvard Business Review,* March–April 1979, pp. 115–26.

16. NOLAN, R. L., AND C. F. GIBSON. "Managing the Four Stages of EDP Growth." *Harvard Business Review,* January–February 1974, pp. 76–88.

17. PARSONS, G. L. "Information Technology: A New Competitive Weapon." *Sloan Management Review,* Winter 1983.

18. PERROW, C. *Complex Organizations: A Critical Analysis.* Glenview, Ill.: Scott-Foresman, 1979.

19. PFEFFER, J., AND G. R. SALANCIK. *The External Control of Organization: A Resource Dependence Perspective.* New York: Harper & Row, 1978.

20. PORTER, M. E. *Competitive Advantage: Creating and Sustaining Superior Performance.* New York: Free Press, 1984, chap. 2.

21. WILLIAMSON, O. *Markets and Hierarchies: Analysis and Antitrust Implications.* New York: Free Press, 1975.

22 *The Shape of IS to Come**

Robert F. Morison

Today the trend toward dispersing information systems, systems people, and systems management skills into business units is more pronounced than ever. This trend reaches far beyond personal computers on desk tops. Many IS people have moved out of central IS shops into business organizations—even in companies with a long-standing tradition of centralization.

At the same time, many business units are developing their own semi-professional systems organizations—business people who spend much of their time working with IT on behalf of other business people.

As businesses rely more and more heavily on information technology (IT) for their strategic initiatives and end-user computing is absorbed into standard business practices, a perennial question arises: What will the future shape of the information systems (IS) organization be?

And as the dispersed resources succeed, what roles remain for the central IS organization?

These questions arise not from the physical distribution of hardware, software, and people to remote sites. Rather, it is *the transfer of control* and the fact that the systems being dispersed are *shared business-critical systems* that, in the end, will have organizational impact.

ORGANIZATIONAL CHOICES

Today, most corporations still need a sizeable central IS organization to perform some corporate-level activities and other tasks that business units are unwilling or unable to cooperate in accomplishing. If anything, compa-

* Source: "The Shape of IS to Come," Robert F. Morison, *Indications,* a publication of Index Group, Inc., vol. 7, no. 4 (July/August 1990), pp. 1–7.

nies are decentralizing and dispersing IS functions too fast, often in a frenzied effort to cut corporate staff and lower overhead.

Without question, dispersed systems and decentralization are good for business. What is not so clear is exactly how to balance centralized and decentralized computing, and how to get the most out of each.

If decentralization occurs in absence of a coherent coordinating body, then dispersed computing will tend toward chaos. The technological infrastructure will fragment, and human resource development will suffer. Building cross-functional applications will be next to impossible. And the corporation will forfeit the ability to behave consistently in the marketplace.

The coordinating influence that will smooth the way for effective decentralization can be embodied in a model described below, a useful melange of centralization and decentralization, called "virtual centralization," that for most companies is still a few years away.

DECENTRALIZATION IS HERE

For now, despite the frenzied pace, the atmosphere in which dispersed systems are being implemented is much healthier than it was several years ago. Dispersed systems no longer represent a renegade effort by a user organization dissatisfied with its IS department. According to research done by PRISM (Partnership for Research in Information Systems Management, a joint offering of Index Group and Hammer and Company), most dispersed systems are now being developed jointly, one way or another, even if the mix of responsibilities is not always clear.[1]

The applications running on dispersed systems have an increasing impact on the business, having by and large reached beyond basic automation to more creative functions. Nationwide, PRISM research turned up an emphasis on marketing, sales support and customer service applications—areas traditionally underserved by a corporate-oriented IS function. The applications studied proved to be feature-rich, robust and widely interfaced with related local and corporate systems. Some qualified as cross-functional in scope or cross-organizational in impact.

Some of the techniques for dispersing systems have matured since the mid-1980s as well. Early efforts to establish, within IS, "account managers" and technical support groups who were aligned with specific business units have given way to other mechanisms. IS is lending its people to business units as business analysts, data managers, and even surrogate managers of a business unit's local IS activities. The technical support groups may report directly to or be located with the business units.

FORM FOLLOWS FUNCTION

While this dispersal is generally good for the business and its effective use of IT, neither decentralized nor centralized organizational structures offer solutions in and of themselves.

The basic structure of IS will typically follow that of the business at large. Decentralization of IS occurs most quickly and readily in companies with autonomous, entrepreneurial business units and a decentralized approach to management. In more tightly integrated business structures with more control-oriented management styles, dispersal will be slower and most IS resources will remain centralized.

However, the best shape for IS may not be an exact mirror of the business structure. In fact, given the potential roles of IT and the IS function as agents of business change, we can expect that, in some organizations, the shape of IS will *anticipate* the shape of the business in one direction or the other. In highly centralized companies trying to foster

---

FIGURE 1   Survey Data: What to Centralize

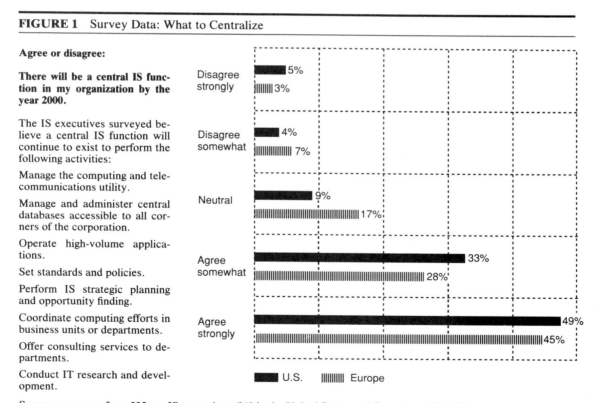

Agree or disagree:

There will be a central IS function in my organization by the year 2000.

The IS executives surveyed believe a central IS function will continue to exist to perform the following activities:

Manage the computing and telecommunications utility.

Manage and administer central databases accessible to all corners of the corporation.

Operate high-volume applications.

Set standards and policies.

Perform IS strategic planning and opportunity finding.

Coordinate computing efforts in business units or departments.

Offer consulting services to departments.

Conduct IT research and development.

Survey responses from 335 top IS executives (243 in the United States and Canada, and 92 in Europe).

entrepreneurism and push management control down into the organization, IS may decentralize more rapidly than other functions and work to implant the management information systems needed for local autonomy. In a highly decentralized company that relies on cross-functional coordination, IS may be more centralized than the rest of the organization and focus its efforts on a common infrastructure and cross-functional systems.

Also note that the natural locus for "central" IS is typically corporate staff; but if the corporation consists of highly autonomous companies that communicate little more than to report their financial results, the logical "center" can vary.

BOTH DIRECTIONS AT ONCE

There are few cases where the trend toward dispersal is pure, where the migration of IS is unidirectional. At the same time that companies are moving user-oriented workstations and networks into local business units, many are centralizing (or recentralizing) their large data centers.

Similarly, although dispersal may be the rule, individual business units or functions may seek to put some of their IT resources under the stewardship of central IS. This typically happens with business functions that moved into dispersed computing early (e.g., engineering), but that now seek operational efficiencies, economies of scale, and professional management of the systems already in place. So, at the same time that some users are asserting their independence of IS, others may be "coming home."

Nor are there examples of pure centralization of IS. Even in the most monolithic and centralized businesses, the personal computing revolution has put an end to the monopoly position of IS.

The focus of the dispersed systems debate in 1990, then, can rest on which activities to centralize or decentralize, not on choosing a credo and adhering to it.

ACTIVITIES DEMANDING CENTRAL COORDINATION

The range of IS activities and services demanding central coordination is wider than many IS managers predicted five years ago.[2] The activities and services best handled centrally fall into three broad, interrelated domains:

1. Corporate resources.
2. Quality assurance.
3. Economies of expertise.

Corporate resources include not only databases and applications of corporatewide interest, but also all facets of the computing infrastructure that help tie the corporation together:

Architecture, including technology infrastructure, applications, data and organization. The architecture establishes the guidelines for decisions about the deployment of computing resources and the computing standards (and the relative flexibility of those standards) that are in effect at any given time.

Planning. Although most applications planning and budgeting may take place within business units, these plans must be centrally assembled, evaluated, and rationalized in terms of overall corporate strategy. It is also necessary to coordinate a long-term strategic plan for IS: a well-developed vision not only of how the corporation will use IT in the future but also of how the IS function will be shaped within the corporation.

Managing shared resources. The obvious candidates here are telecommunications resources and key databases. Also in this category are mainframe data centers; these should be managed centrally whenever the economies of scale from consolidation outweigh the diseconomies (and telecommunications costs) of distancing these facilities from the business units they serve.

Cross-functional systems design and development. These systems bridge functions and thus demand cross-organizational participation and compromise on behalf of the overall corporate good. The most dramatic business process improvements through cross-functional systems involve the redrawing of organizational boundaries and the streamlining of business functions. The designers of these new processes, organizations, and systems must be able to assume a corporatewide perspective.

QUALITY ASSURANCE

The second area of centralized activities, "quality assurance" (QA), is meant here in a broad sense. Clearly, it is in the corporation's interests to have the best possible computing practices followed everywhere. But best practice means more than effective management of local business unit systems.

Both dispersed and central systems must be properly positioned within the corporate computing context: adhering to architecture and standards, and participating in appropriate corporate information flows. Systems and systems management techniques should also be shared across the company. For these reasons, corporatewide QA remains a function of the central IS group.

Quality assurance activities typically include:

Review services. Even when certain user units have grown highly sophisticated and capable in their use of IT, outside reviews help to promote system quality. IS might provide services to review applications design, applications interfaces, compliance with architecture guidelines, data validity and integrity, systems documentation, systems security, and overall system performance. Distinct from a traditional EDP audit, this type of review is concerned primarily with the business and technical functionality of the system. Similar to these review services are consulting services (whereby central IS provides expertise not available in the business unit), and services specifically aimed at empowering users and promoting good computing practice, such as development centers.

Clearinghouse. Keeping track of technologies, applications, and practices across the company. The purpose of the clearinghouse is to monitor computing activities, help dispersed units avoid bad practice, and propagate the best practices across business units. The role of "monitor" does not in this case connote a conservative posture; in fact, the clearinghouse should be particularly attuned to recognizing and valuing innovative computing practices discovered in the business units.

Education. Organizing and promoting user and user-management education in information systems. The goal is to impart the hard-won experience of IS to user units in an efficient and accelerated way. Educational activities range from the fairly formal (e.g., vendor-provided training on new products) to the informal (e.g., companywide user groups). They may also include an education/consulting hybrid embodied in a "business manager's IS advisor." This person provides critical skills in the area of managing technology and systems people, a skill set most likely missing from the experience and/or inclination of line managers. The IS advisor is someone senior line managers can turn to for help in planning and budgeting systems projects, overseeing systems people, aligning systems with corporate direction, identifying opportunities and priorities, working with vendors, and resolving other systems-related problems.

ECONOMIES OF EXPERTISE

The third area in which it is also appropriate to take a centralized approach is in achieving "economies of expertise" wherever valuable knowledge and skills are scarce.

Regardless of whether people with rare expertise reside in central or dispersed IS units, they should be available to serve corporate needs. Thus, such expertise must be centrally inventoried and coordinated.

These experts are of several types:

They may have technical specialties (e.g., in advanced telecommunications) that no business unit needs full-time and no business unit can afford.

They may have broad experience that makes them most valuable to the corporation as general consultants and designers of cross-functional systems.

They may be involved in activities that amount to knowledge acquisition on behalf of the corporation (e.g., technology research and development). Such knowledge acquisition must be coordinated corporatewide to avoid reinventing the wheel and to ensure rapid propagation of knowledge gained.

Maintaining economies of expertise also demands corporate-level management of the corporatewide IS human resource. The career development of key individuals must be actively promoted; IS people need both management-development and succession-planning programs.

In central and dispersed IS organizations alike, this involves careful rotation of people among business functions, and between systems-oriented and functionally-oriented roles. Only then do we develop the versatile, hybrid people able to apply IT as a catalyst for productive business change.

In heavily dispersed organizations, there is a danger of valued employees losing the chance to build seniority and status in the organization simply because their group is so small. If a critical mass of staff cannot be maintained, then ample opportunities for networking with colleagues in other units must be provided so that the IS professionals can get the peer support, technical skills advancement, career paths and professional identity they need.

Central IS should also review and advise business units on their local practices for managing the IS human resource.

These three major areas represent the wide range of activities that must be coordinated and performed as consistently as possible corporatewide— and that demand the watchful eye of a central IS presence. Treating them centrally allows companies to move many computing activities closer to the users while retaining just the efforts that benefit most from central coordination.

VIRTUAL CENTRALIZATION

The recommendation for central coordination of key activities and the outline of roles for a central IS function do not necessarily imply the need for a central IS organization of any great size. The activities described

---

FIGURE 2   Virtual Centralization: A Theoretical Model

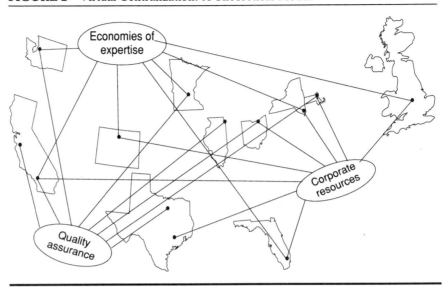

---

above can all be accomplished by decentralized organizational structures.

Theoretically, all these "central IS" functions can be performed by representatives of decentralized IS and business units working part-time or on a project basis. Instead of relying on a central IS organization, corporations can rely on communications capabilities (e.g., electronic mail and computer conferencing) to link people dispersed across business units, and on management systems that encourage people to work together in the corporate interest at appropriate times. In particular, performance-measurement and reward systems must value the work done in corporate roles as highly as they value contribution to local business units.

This type of "virtual centralization"—coordination without a large central organization—is at work in many functions:

Corporatewide IS plans and architectures are often developed by a council of representatives of all major business units, perhaps with the facilitation of one or several corporate IS planners.

Cross-functional systems are best built by cross-organizational teams whose loyalty lies with the corporation (as opposed to their home business units) for the duration of the project.

Most of the systems information clearinghouse function can be performed electronically (by computer conferencing and groupware), as long as business unit representatives are motivated to contribute to and draw upon the information base. An individual or cross-organizational council can manage the content and monitor the use of the clearinghouse.

FIGURE 3   Survey Data: How Much to Decentralize

Agree or disagree:

An increasing number of systems are being conceived and coded by end users.

In the U.S., 48% of the IS directors surveyed said an increasing number of information systems are being conceived and coded by end users. They also estimated that end users in their organizations currently account for an average 12% of all corporate information systems. They projected that by 1995, end users would be developing an average 34% of all systems.

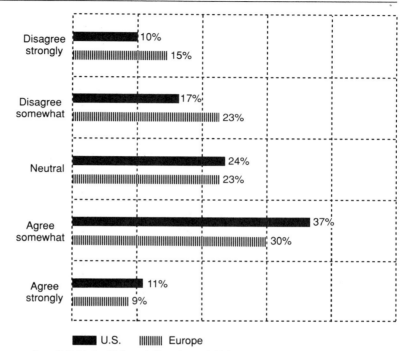

Survey responses from 335 top IS executives (243 in the U.S. and Canada, and 92 in Europe).

- Technology R&D can be highly distributed, as long as experts can communicate with one another, work on loan to other business units, plan and manage the introduction of new technology, and come together on a project basis.
- IS review services can be provided by teams from peer business units, rather than from corporate IS.
- IS management functions in the areas of education and human resources can be performed by councils of business unit IS leaders.
- Similar councils of IS and business managers can jointly manage shared resources, such as data centers.

Given when a function must be physically centralized (e.g., the corporate telecommunications control room), it can be managed or overseen by a cross-organizational team. Alternately, a single business unit may perform a function (e.g., technology R&D, development center) on behalf of the corporation as a whole—a form of internal "outsourcing." A business unit may also be designated as a "competency center"—home for a critical mass of skilled specialists available to all business units.

Thus, "central IS" will, in a decentralized business environment, become less a specific staff group and more a virtual organization.

This virtual staff is composed of individuals drawn (again, by appropriate management systems and performance incentives) from across the corporation. People come together as needed, on either a periodic or a project basis, to perform corporate-level activities. They are literally "networked"—by electronic and voice mail, computer conferencing, groupware, and shared applications and databases.

REAL-LIFE GLIMPSES OF VIRTUAL CENTRALIZATION

A few large corporations are experimenting with various forms of virtual centralization today, although they do not necessarily call it that within their own organizations.

Aetna Life and Casualty Company took the opportunity presented by a veteran vice president's retirement to change its organizational structure in information systems. First, the company loosed IS from its mooring under the corporate administration, creating a senior vice president-level IS chief. John Loewenberg took the job more than a year ago.

Next, Aetna began to reverse the almost complete decentralization of IS to the business units that was in place when Loewenberg came on board. The company felt needs were for a more coherent computing architecture, better leveraged IT investments, and a stronger training program.

Since then, the company has made moves to recentralize the activities that would address those needs: chiefly a corporatewide office computing platform and a centralized IS operations function. The next target is the computing and telecommunications infrastructure, with the goal of reintroducing some level of common systems and delivering mission-critical applications faster. There is currently no plan to move applications development away from the business units.

Armco Advanced Materials Corporation, a $550 million steel manufacturer based in Butler, Pennsylvania, relied on almost entirely dispersed IS functions as recently as two years ago. Different business areas ran their own systems, which in this case had led to redundancies in data and processing power, and some instances of conflicting information. There was no effective mechanism for addressing overall corporate IS goals.

A new chief information officer, Tom Lutz, set out to bring more coordination to the information systems at the same time he replaced obsolete applications. (The average age was 17 years.) The approach was an unusual one: leave the variety of heterogeneous hardware in place in the units and provide integration through third-party software packages and a customized network.

What Armco gained was widespread access to consistent corporate data. The data was also much more timely than it had been—a critical issue for a steel company that must provide detailed information about the forging processes for each steel order to its largest customers. Armco is now able to offer that information on-line and is working to expand that EDI service to other customers and suppliers.

In this case, what the company recentralized was its own highest-priority IS item: the data itself. But Armco in no way lost the close involvement of its line managers in the information systems that serve them; in fact, unit and department managers continue to devote substantial time to working regularly with the IS staff on business processes and information flows. And it is the line managers who must justify IT expenditures to top management and who are accountable for results.

THE CONTEMPORARY MIX

The organizational model described above combines almost complete decentralization of IS people with virtual centralization of key activities. However, the pure model has practical drawbacks; it will not and, indeed, should not be implemented very soon in most cases.

The ability to manage such virtual centralization is three to five years away in most companies. Immediate implementation is impeded by:

Lack of systems management sophisticiation within business units.

Lack of the management systems and motivators that enable people to divide their attention between local and corporate requirements.

Lack of the technical infrastructure to link dispersed teams electronically.

Lack of executive management understanding of the need to balance dispersed and corporate computing.

Another barrier may exist in some organizations stemming from a perception at the executive level that such a streamlined central IS function has lost all its ability to add value. In such an atmosphere, central IS may find itself the target for budget cuts and may need to be able to demonstrate its value at all times.

Over the next few years, both IS's and line managements' experience with dispersed systems will broaden and deepen, filling some of the gaps. Management education will help, as will further progress in cohesive architectures and robust network facilities.

The organizational shape of IS, now and in the near future, will be a mix of decentralized groups, a (probably shrinking) central group, and functions performed through virtual centralization. The shape will change continually, and the trend will not be unidirectional: At the same time that some formerly central activities disperse, the central IS organization may grow temporarily in order to perform a corporate-level function (e.g., dispersed systems reviews) previously missing.

Above all, the shape of IS must not be determined based on a philosophical belief in the goodness of centralization or decentralization. Rather, the ideal shape is that mix which best serves the simultaneous demands for corporatewide coordination and productive dispersed computing.

NOTES

1. *See* the PRISM report, "Dispersed Systems Management," April 1990.
2. *See* the PRISM report, "Managing Dispersed Systems," 1985.

23 Measuring Information Systems Performance: Experience with the Management by Results System at Security Pacific Bank*

John P. Singleton
Ephraim R. McLean
Edward N. Altman

INTRODUCTION

The question "How well does your information systems department perform?" has been a difficult one for both IS professionals and top management to answer. When pressed, senior management will frequently respond, "Okay, I guess," leaving IS management unsure as to what exactly to do next to improve this vague response. Even if the answer is more positive, it is still difficult to know on what basis this judgment is being made. Conversely, if it is negative, the IS department is often the last to know. As was pointed out in Nolan's "The Plight of the EDP Manager"

* Source: Reprinted by special permission from the *MIS Quarterly* vol. 12, no. 2 June 1988. Copyright 1988 by the Society for Information Management and the Management Information Systems Research Center at the University of Minnesota.

[6],‡ more than one IS director has found that the first indication of trouble has been the announcement that he is being fired!

For many organizations, the need to answer this question in a more precise manner has become particularly important in recent years. As information systems assume a more strategic role in companies, the ad hoc estimates of the past must be replaced by more systematic measures in the future. But the pervasive character of many of the new information systems now being installed, and the rapidly changing technologies which underlie these systems, both serve to make this measurement task a more difficult one than that faced by many other parts of the business.

Of course, this question of "How well are you doing?" really has two parts. The first is the fundamental issue of the *actual* quality of the information services being provided and the extent to which they are supporting and contributing to the objectives of the business. The second is how this quality of service is *measured* over time. In other words, one, How good are you? and two, How do you *know* how good you are?

The first question will naturally vary from organization to organization, depending upon such things as the talent, experience, and motivation of the people in the IS function, as well as on the openness and receptivity of the business as a whole to the potential contributions of IS. Over the years, many articles and books have been written about how to improve the management of IS. More recently, McFarlan [4], Porter [9], Wiseman [11], and others have focused on how the IS function can even affect the overall competitive posture of the enterprise. Consultants abound in their advice on how to do a better job in developing systems, running the data center, reducing costs, supporting end-users, and/or providing strategic advantage.

These efforts are all worthwhile and more is needed. However, in most cases they do not address the fundamental measurement questions: How do you know if these actions have been successful? Are we better this year than we were last year—or worse? Are these measures agreed upon and readily understandable? Are they shared with, and used by, top management?

If such IS measurements are not in place, ongoing evaluation becomes exceedingly difficult. This article, therefore, focuses on *measurement;* specifically, the manner in which the Security Pacific Automation Company (SPAC), tracks the performance of the information services it provides to Security Pacific National Bank and to Security Pacific Corporation, its holding company.

---

‡ Bracketed numbers cite the references at the end of the chapter.

THE PROBLEM OF MEASUREMENT

As Peter Drucker has said, "If you can't measure it, you can't manage it." Without systematic measurements, managers have little to guide their actions other than their own experience and judgment. Of course, these will always be important; but as businesses become more complex and global in their scope, it becomes increasingly more difficult to rely on intuition alone.

Over the years, different systems of measures have been developed in each of the areas of the business. First came accounting and the various financial and economic measures of performance. In manufacturing and operations, the fields of engineering and science contributed measures of efficiency, quality, and the like. In marketing and advertising, other measures like market share and penetration emerged. Each field has its own "numbers" which convey its success in meeting its objectives. Information systems is not—or at least should not be—any different. As McLean [5] has pointed out, it must be measured like any other part of the business.

Of course, there is no one measure that covers all aspects of IS activity, just as there is no single measure that captures the complete picture of a firm's economic health. What is needed is a *set* of measures, appropriate for the activity of objectives being measured. In Anthony's classic work on *Planning and Control Systems* [1], he identified three levels or aspects of management that occur in all organizations: operational, managerial, and strategic. At each level, different measures are appropriate. At the operational level, *efficiency* and productivity are key. At the managerial level, the *effectiveness* of the organization and the management becomes essential. Finally, at the strategic level, the *competitiveness* of the enterprise itself is of central concern.

Initially, computers and information systems were focused almost exclusively on operational and transactional systems; and it was here that nearly all of the measures that are in use today evolved. Measures of uptime, throughput, network availability, jobs processed, mean-time to failure, and reruns are but a few of the many production statistics that are maintained by most data center managers. Correspondingly, detailed data on project budgets and schedules serve as indicators to IS management of system development performance. However, these measures are frequently for internal use only and are either meaningless or irrelevant to the users for whom the systems being measured were designed.

If measures are to be truly creditable, they must be jointly determined. It does little good if the "actual" performance, as measured internally, is at wide variance with the users' perception of this same service. If "actual" and "perceived" differ significantly, it is a clear indication that the measurement system is not working properly. As will be described below, one of the key features of the Service Level Agreements in SPAC's Management by Results system is the central role played by the Bank's users in determining the SLA standards of performance. This joint determination of acceptable levels of IS service goes a long way towards making information systems a meaningful and valued part of the way users function at the bank.

While a "shared vision" of information systems' contribution to the entire business is important, it becomes even more so as the focus moves from operational to managerial to strategic concerns. The evaluation process must, of necessity, become more qualitative and less quantitative. Thus, agreement between IS and top management about what information systems *should* accomplish—and what it *has* accomplished—are at the core of this evaluation process. Furthermore, it must be formal and ongoing; ad hoc or after-the-fact judgments always run the risk of being "too little and too late."

However, as firms search for ways in which this can be accomplished, there is little to guide them in this endeavor. In a recent comprehensive review of articles on enterprise-level performance, Crowston and Treacy [3] state:

> Implicit in most of what we do in MIS is the belief that information technology has an impact on the bottom line of the business. Surprisingly, we rarely know if this is true. It is very difficult to trace and measure the effects of information technology through a web of intermediate impacts upon enterprise level performance.

They go on to describe the current primitive state of the art of IS measurement and conclude by calling for better theoretical models and tests of these models in real world settings.

Certainly such criticisms are well deserved and much work needs to be done to improve this state of affairs. However, in the meantime, companies must do something; and, in fact, some are making substantial progress in developing these measures and in using them to evaluate their IS organization. The Security Pacific Automation Company is one such company.

In the following sections, some background on the bank and on SPAC will be provided. This will be followed by descriptions of the four main parts of the Management by Results system: Strategic Planning, Service Level Agreements, Commitment Planning, and Performance Appraisal and Compensation. Next will be a discussion of how this multipart system was implemented and what benefits have resulted from its use so far. Finally, some of the broader implications of the use of such measures will be discussed in the concluding section.

SECURITY PACIFIC CORPORATION

Headquartered in Los Angeles, Security Pacific Corporation (SPC), a diversified financial services firm with assets of over $64 billion, is the nation's sixth largest bank holding company. SPC's three primary business units are the California Banking and Real Estate Industries System (providing both consumer and commercial banking services in California), the Capital Markets System (providing services worldwide in the areas of wholesale banking and capital markets), and the Financial Services System (providing many of the Corporation's nonbank financial products). SPC operates over 1,200 offices throughout the United States (over 600 in California alone) and in 27 foreign countries, with a total of 35,000 employees. SPC has recently acquired a number of major banks throughout the West: in Arizona, The Arizona Bank; in Oregon, Orbanco; and, pending approvals, in Nevada, The Nevada Bank, and, in Washington State, Rainier Bancorporation. While today each of these first three business units contribute equally to the Corporation's earnings, SPC's goal is to have its interstate banking activities become an equal contributor to the Corporation's earnings by the 1990s.

Security Pacific Automation Company (SPAC), the data processing arm of the Corporation, was created in 1984 as a separate division of Security Pacific National Bank (SPNB) to serve the bank, the corporation, and external markets. More recently, SPAC has become a subsidiary of the bank's holding company to facilitate the integration of SPC's recent interstate banking acquisitions. SPAC is responsible for the development of advanced technology systems for the corporation's worldwide activities and for the administration of internal data processing and bank operations functions. Activities include transaction processing, telecommunications (both voice and data), advisory services, and software development. SPAC has approximately 3,600 employees and a 1987 budget of nearly $300 million.

SPAC's management is committed to operating a professional IS organization that will serve as a key strategic contributor to SPC. To accomplish this goal, SPAC has developed a system of six interdependent functions—human resources, finance, operations, commitment planning, strategic and tactical planning, and entrepreneurship—that are illustrated in Figure 1. To achieve success, all these functions must be properly managed—and thus measured.

The first steps in the development of the Management by Results (MBR) system began at SPAC in 1982. It was evolutionary in character and components were added as the process became better understood. In its present form, it now comprises four linked parts: Strategic Planning, Service Level Agreements, Commitment Planning, and Performance Appraisal and Compensation. Each will be described in turn.

Strategic Planning

SPAC currently employs the Delphi Method of Strategic Planning as developed by the Hendrix Information Group of Rolling Hills Estates, California. This method uses a consensus, team-building approach to

---

FIGURE 1   The Management by Results System

SPAC Ways to Excellence

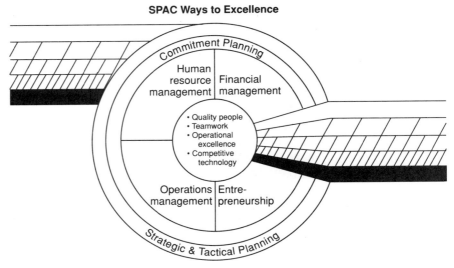

Copyright 1986, 1987 Security Pacific National Bank.

---

establish strategies, goals, and implementation plans for SPAC. An important aspect of this approach is the manner in which it deals with the attitudes, perceptions, and emotions of those involved in the planning process. Considerable effort is spent on building agreement and ownership of the plan among those who are involved with its development.

The IS Strategic Plan, which is prepared annually, serves to establish the linkage between the users' business plans and the IS plan; and it provides the foundation for the subsequent Service Level Agreements and Commitment Planning programs. The deliverables include a mission statement, an overview of the overall values and goals for IS, a statement of strategy and of the objectives that must link to this strategy, a detailed list of the important tasks and projects that must be undertaken, the milestones that must be met, an identification of the critical issues, and, lastly, procedures for Plan revisions. In addition, contingency plans are established to deal with unforeseen developments.

Service-Level Agreements

Service Level Agreements (SLAs) are user-driven definitions of the products and services provided by SPAC, or, more specifically, "A SLA is a formal written agreement developed jointly between SPAC and its customers defining a specific product or service to be provided."

This negotiation process between SPAC and the user defines four levels of performance—"excellent," "above average," "average," and "unsatisfactory"—as well as how this performance will be measured. Also, it is important to note that these definitions are in terms that are understandable to the user. The resultant SLAs, typically one page long, define the standards of performance, the methods of calculating performance, the reporting procedures for unsatisfactory performance, and the names and signatures of the user and SPAC representatives who are responsible for the agreements. All agreements are dated and, unless renewed, expire in 12 months. (See Figure 2 for a sample SLA format.)

Generally, a SLA between SPAC and a user will require several additional agreements, called Resource Service Agreements (RSAs), within SPAC itself. "A RSA is a formal written agreement developed jointly by the manager of a product or service (the person within SPAC who signed the SLA with the user) and the manager of the SPAC resources needed to support this product or service" (see Figure 3). For example, the SLA required to support Security Pacific's 660 ATM (automatic teller machine) network will need to have RSAs with the SPAC managers of hardware, systems software, applications software, networking, and the unit that balances the machines and refills the ATMs with cash. By clearly identifying the responsibilities of each manager, the finger-pointing which sometimes occurs when things go wrong can thereby be minimized.

The process of establishing these RSAs is very important, for not only does it serve to identify the various dependencies throughout the IS organization—and obtain management's commitment to provide these resources—but occasionally it identifies a resource that is controlled by a user, thus requiring the definition of a RSA outside IS. For example, the ability to distribute reports to the bank's branches by the scheduled time each morning is highly dependent on when the input arrives from the

---

FIGURE 2 Service-Level Agreement Format

DESCRIPTION
% ON-LINE SYSTEM IS AVAILABLE
SERVICE GOALS

EXCELLENT	ABOVE AVERAGE	SATISFACTORY	UNSATISFACTORY
99%	98%	97%	LT 97%

PROCEDURES FOR UNSATISFACTORY _____

CALCULATION METHOD _____

EFFECTIVE DATE _____   EXPIRATION DATE _____

USER SIGNATURE _____

SERVICER'S SIGNATURE _____

FIGURE 3 Example of a Resource Service Agreement

Product and Resource Matrix	Resource Areas			
	Electronic Services	Operations	Computer Services	Telecomm. Network
PRODUCT: Automated Teller Machine (ATM)				Owner
SLA: ATM 24-hour availability (ATM24)				Owner
RSAs:				
Central site hardware avail.—24 hr.			X	
System software avail.—24 hr.			X	
Application software avail.—24 hr.	X			
Internal response time—24 hr.	X			
Telco availability—24 hr.				X
Tapes loaded			X	
SLA: ATM prime time availability (ATMPR)				Owner
RSAs:				
Central site hardware avail.—prime			X	
System software availability—prime			X	
Application software avail.—prime	X			
Internal response time—prime	X			
Telco availability—prime				X
Tapes loaded			X	
SLA: ATM customer info. services (ATMCS)				Owner
RSAs:				
Average overall queue time		X		
Average length of call		X		
Percent calls resolved		X		
System loads completed			X	
ATM information system availability	X			
System software availability			X	
Central site hardware availability			X	
Telco availability				X

Copyright 1986, 1987 Security Pacific National Bank.

branches the previous night. RSAs have therefore been established defining these responsibilities.

SLAs and RSAs are used not only with the major on-line and batch systems within SPAC, but also on many other IS activities, as well as on defining the relations with outside vendors and suppliers. These latter agreements are not binding in a legal sense; but accurate records of vendors' commitments—and their subsequent performance against these commitments—are valuable in the contract negotiation and vendor selection processes that occur at regular intervals.

Once the SLAs are in place, performance monitoring begins and status is reported back to the user on a monthly basis. Typical reports show, by month and by year-to-date, the total number of SLAs in effect and the number that are rated excellent, above average, average, and unsatisfactory (see Figure 4). In this way senior management has a key report of SPAC's overall operational performance, provided on a consistent and timely basis.

One of the major reasons that the use of SLAs has been so successful within the bank is the requirement that both SPAC *and* user signatures are needed for the SLA under negotiation to become official. And these individuals must be the responsible line managers, not staff managers or assistants.

At first, many user departments were not certain about whom this person should be; and it forced them to think through the services they were offering to the public and to identify the responsible manager. Now, these managers, and their SPAC counterparts, are the focal points for any questions that arise around these major bank products. This has improved communications not only between these two key individuals but also among those who work with them. They no longer work at cross purposes, not knowing who to call when something goes wrong or where to go to get needed resources.

This enhanced communication has enabled SPAC to become proactive,

FIGURE 4   Service-Level Agreements User Management Report

	Jan.	*Feb.*	*Mar.*	*April*
SLAs in effect	42	42	39	39
Excellent	33	36	29	32
Above average	4	3	2	4
Satisfactory	4	2	4	2
Unsatisfactory	1	1	4	1*

April below satisfactory performance

* See explanation of (1) unsatisfactory SLA in April.
Copyright 1986, 1987 Security Pacific National Bank.

rather than reactive, in helping SPC solve its business problems. The SLAs help to establish common goals and provide for better visibility of trends and performance. Also, the users have been impressed that the IS organization would have enough confidence in itself to be willing to be measured by the user—on the user's terms. More than anything else, this has led to the establishment of better business relationships between the user and SPAC.

Commitment Planning

Commitment Planning works in conjunction with the Strategic Planning and Service-Level Agreement programs by helping to ensure that SPAC personnel are motivated and rewarded to accomplish the results they have committed to in their Strategic Plan and SLAs. As will be discussed in the following section, a manager's score on his or her Commitment Plan is directly linked to the level of compensation he or she receives.

The Commitment Plan is negotiated between the employee and the manager and defines what the employee will accomplish during the measurement period, the different levels of performance, and how this performance will be measured. The standard categories of accountability are Service-Level Management (i.e., the SLAs); Financial Management; Personnel Management; Major Projects; and New Business, Marketing, and Sales. The Commitment Planning process thereby guarantees that specific SLAs (and RSAs) and action items from the Strategic Plan are included in the individual Commitment Plans for the managers in SPAC.

Key to the success of the Commitment Planning process is that the commitments are defined and measured in objective terms. A typical commitment in a Commitment Plan under Service-Level Management would be to ensure that all SLAs are met and at a performance level of "above average" or better. Under Financial Management, a commitment might be for a budget spending reduction, with "excellent" being 5 percent under budget; "above average," 3 percent under budget; "average," on budget; and "unsatisfactory," over budget (see Figure 5).

Ways have been devised to include in an individual's Commitment Plan items that do not lend themselves readily to objective criteria. For instance, several years ago it was felt that SPAC was not promoting enough employees from within. Therefore, a new item was added under Personnel Management. Managers were to be measured on the percentage of openings filled by internal candidates. One manager's Plan was "excellent," if 90 percent of the promotions were filled by internal candidates; "above average," if 85 percent, and so on. To encourage entrepreneurship within SPAC, an item under New Business read: "Obtain approval and funding for new projects or business ventures this year." The measurement of this was "excellent," three projects; "above average," two projects; "average," one project; and "unsatisfactory," no projects.

FIGURE 5 Commitment Plan Example

Item	Due Date	Satisfactory	Above Average	Excellent
Achieve SLA	Ongoing	97%	98%	99%
Manage budget	12/87	On plan	3% below (1.4 M)	5% below (2.3 M)
Implement image system	10/87	10/87	9/87	8/87
Internal promotions	12/87	75%	85%	90%
Develop marketing policies	12/87	12/87	10/87	8/87

The Commitment Planning program works because it is based on direct negotiations between the employee and his or her manager. This helps to ensure that what the employee is expected to do is clearly defined and mutually understood. In addition, success is defined; and the measurement tool used to determine the performances rating is discussed and documented. Finally, the plan provides a key input to the employee's performance appraisal. However, the Commitment Plan can be updated if major changes occur in the environment. Employees quickly realize that management is serious about its various programs when they know that their pay is going to depend upon their meeting their commitments to these programs!

These individual Commitment Plans, when linked with the Service-Level Agreements, help ensure that no aspect of SPAC's overall Strategic Plan is overlooked. A chain is formed: services are described, performance standards are established; measurements are defined; responsible individuals are identified; commitments are obtained; and performance is measured. In this way, inconsistent or conflicting behavior can be avoided. Managers are not pursuing objectives that are, in reality, of only minor importance to the bank; and, conversely, important projects and services are not neglected because no one is committed to ensuring their success.

Performance Appraisal and Compensation

The fourth, and final, component of MBR is the Performance Appraisal and Compensation program. It does little good to develop plans, create SLAs, and gain commitments without having a way to translate this commitment into action and to reward the individual when this action is successful.

Of course, many companies try to do this with periodic performance reviews and merit increases or bonuses linked to superior performance. Unfortunately, most of these systems are highly subjective in nature and rely on the opinion of the employee's manager on whether a raise or bonus should be awarded. This can lead to resentment and misunderstanding when the employee does not feel that he or she has been fairly treated or has been measured against an unclear standard.

The Commitment Planning process introduces a measure of objectivity that helps to avoid many of these problems. It uses the commitments that have been mutually agreed upon as a basis for determining the size of the raise that the employee will receive. In this way, there are few surprises at review time, for both the employee and his or her manager have been tracking the same data throughout the year.

Of course, there is still a need for subjective judgment in the appraisal process. Any set of numbers must be tempered with the other factors and circumstances that bear on an individual's performance and contribution to the business. But with MBR, the subjective component—with its potential for bias or favoritism—is much smaller than it might otherwise be. Employees now feel that the process is much fairer, even though it is much harder to hide poor performance than it was previously.

A second part of the Performance Appraisal and Compensation program is a special bonus plan. The objective of this bonus program is to provide a vehicle that enables senior management to reward individual performance that is above and beyond normal levels. Recognition is also given to individuals who are especially effective at developing and providing management talent to the organization. The bonus program enables some of the eligible SPAC managers to earn up to an additional 50 percent of their annual salaries. Approximately 160 of SPAC's top executives (out of a total of 3,600 employees) currently participate in this program. The awards are intended to be highly flexible and very competitive. For any given year, a significant number of the executives in the program will probably not earn any bonus at all.

Bonuses are awarded only if both the corporation and SPAC meet their financial plans. The size of the bonus pool is determined by taking a percentage of the salaries of the executives who are eligible to participate. Funding for the pool comes from both corporate earnings and SPAC chargeback fees. Awards are determined by ranking each individual's contribution to the business and then calculating what percentage—if any—he or she should receive. And as with the salary increases, the Commitment Plans play an important role in this determination.

In addition to this program, there is another special incentive program for which all SPAC employees are eligible. It awards bonuses to any employee or group of employees within SPAC who achieve outstanding performance. These awards are to recognize special contributions that occur anywhere in the company and at any time during the year.

IMPLEMENTATION CONSIDERATIONS

There are several key factors that prompted SPAC to undertake the MBR program described above. In the early 1980s, SPAC was a department without a clear definition of the products and services that it was providing to the bank. Its budget was growing at a rate of nearly 30 percent per year and many users were unhappy with the department's performance. Several development projects were significantly over budget and had to be cancelled. It was difficult to hold IS accountable and its credibility was low with both user and executive management.

In 1982, a commitment was made by executive management to address these problems. Out of this came the Management by Results system, which heralded a number of changes. But with these changes came resistance at all levels. The new procedures being introduced challenged the established ways of doing things and upset many ingrained habits. As with any cultural change, some managers could not—or would not—adapt. A fair amount of turnover occurred, both voluntary and involuntary. Morale suffered. But senior management persisted, feeling that, if SPAC was to become a valued business partner, it was crucial for MBR to succeed.

The measurement system that was a part of MBR was particularly troublesome for some managers. They felt that it was alright to establish standards and track performance for their subordinates, but *their* responsibilities were much too unstructured to be the subject of such measurement. The first measures, therefore, attacked the more structured aspects of SPAC; and, as these became accepted, they were expanded to other areas. Now most IS managers accept this as the way things are done. Indeed, they even take a measure of pride in the fact that they can now talk with their users in concrete terms and have agreed-upon measures to describe their performance and contribution to the bank.

For other organizations which are considering adopting such measurements, they should be approached with some caution. Without the strong commitment of senior management in both the IS and host organizations, it is unlikely that the natural resistance that will be encountered can be overcome. Also, the organization needs time to adjust. The MBR system took nearly three years to develop and install at the bank. However, now that many of the concepts and processes have been refined, it should take considerably less time for other organizations; they should be able to take advantage of this experience.

EXPERIENCE WITH MBR

Since the introduction of the Management by Results system five years ago, a number of benefits have been realized within the SPC environment. These are discernible at the operational, managerial, and strategic levels.

Naturally, it would be foolish to claim that these were all due simply to the installation of a measurement system. MBR is a tool and only that. As was pointed out at the beginning of this article, many things contribute to the success of information systems within organizations, and a good measurement system is just one of them. But in the case of SPAC, it made a particularly important contribution, for it allowed user and IS management alike to see how well IS was serving the organization; and, when the results were less than satisfactory, it could point out what areas needed attention and which managers were responsible.

Operational Measures

Because most of the SLAs had their origins in the operational aspects of the business, the benefits are correspondingly most visible in this area. In 1984, 86 percent of all of the SLAs achieved a rating of "above average" or "excellent." By 1986, this had grown to 98 percent, even though some of the performance standards had been increased due to experience and rising expectations (i.e., the performance levels required to achieve an "above average" or "excellent" rating were made tougher). Also, over the same two years, the number of SLAs was expanded significantly, covering many activities that were previously thought to be unsuitable for measurement.

In the matter of costs, a turnaround in budget growth for SPAC was accomplished during this same period. Whereas the total budget for IS had grown by 32 percent in 1984 and 10 percent in 1985, by 1986 this trend was reversed with an actual decrease in budget of 1 percent in spite of a growth in the volume of paper transactions by 3 percent and in electronic transactions by 20 percent. This was coupled with a 10 percent reduction in staff for the most recent year (from 3,933 to 3,576). In fact, SPAC has just 62 more employees today than it had in 1983 (3,576 vs. 3,514).

These results led a leading bank market research firm to report in a confidential survey that "in the last four years, Security Pacific's performance has improved 200 to 300 percent. In operating service volume, they moved from 19th out of 20 to eighth place nationally and are the top rated wholesale bank in California" [2].

Managerial Measures

Although more difficult to quantify, the results achieved at the managerial level are nevertheless still quite real. First of all, users within the bank are not bound to use only those services that are provided by SPAC. Unlike the operational area, where there is little choice as to who will do the demand deposit accounting or operate the ATMs, at the managerial level there is a wide variety of options available to the user. If bank managers find that their decision support or other less-structured information processing needs are not being met by SPAC, they can go elsewhere for service. Because there is a full-cost internal chargeback scheme, SPAC must be competitive with these alternative sources of computing. The willingness of bank users to pay for these services, where these funds are not captive and could be spent for other purposes if the alternative uses are perceived to have a higher return, is a strong indication of the value accorded them. And the measurement itself has a "face validity" because it is similar in kind to other unconstrained resource allocation decisions made by bank managers.

Another formal mechanism used at both the operational and managerial levels is a series of oversight or steering committees for each of the major areas of the bank. These groups of senior users and IS managers meet monthly to review SLA performance and progress in their respective areas, in addition to making judgments about future priorities. Their informal assessment of the effectiveness of the information services being provided for their areas serves as a valuable adjunct to the more formal SLAs. In addition, there is a Data Processing and Telecommunications Committee of the board of directors of the corporation that provides oversight for these individual groups as well as addressing the broader policy issues relating to IS and the corporation.

In a recent review by this committee, SPAC was rated so highly that the board began to question why certain areas of the corporation were not using SPAC more actively than they were. It is through mechanisms such as these that a shared vision of the role of IS within Security Pacific is forged, one that views SPAC as a full-fledged business partner, not merely as a purveyor of technology.

Strategic Measures

As was pointed out earlier, measuring the value of information systems at the enterprisewide level is the hardest of all. As Napoleon once said, "Victory has a hundred fathers; defeat is an orphan." If a business is successful, there are many claimants to this success; and it is extremely hard to isolate the extent of each contribution. Moreover, it may be organizationally dysfunctional even to attempt to do so.

Occasionally, of course, a single system can be identified whose benefits are so clear and whose impact is so substantial that there can be little question about its value to the organization's overall competitive posture. Systems like American Airlines' SABRE and American Hospital Supply Corporation's ASAP [7] are two such examples, but it is difficult to find many others that are as strategic in their impact as these are. In most cases the effect is more cumulative. No one system by itself can be identified as *the* cause of a company's increased success; but all systems, taken together, can have a measurable impact. Such is the case of SPAC.

In analyzing SPAC's contribution at the strategic level, Porter's three generic strategies [8] provide a useful framework; they are (1) be a low cost producer, (2) provide product differentiation, and (3) use niche or scope marketing. In each of them SPAC has played a role.

In a 1984 Salomon Brothers report [10], they predicted, "We believe that Security Pacific will become one of the *low cost producers* [emphasis added] in the commercial banking industry. . . . Its electronic banking developments will enhance the company's future profitability by extending the range of products and services available to its customers, by lowering breakeven thresholds, and by improving the timeline and accuracy of transaction functions." Being a low cost producer is a central part of the bank's—and thus SPAC's—strategy and considerable progress has been made toward meeting this goal. To measure their progress, they track business, not IS, variables. A key measure of this is the overall profit per employee, a frequently used measure of corporate productivity. In the two-year period, 1984 to 1986, it has increased by 17 percent ($10,175 to $11,877).

On the dimension of *product differentiation,* a number of new financial products or improved ways of marketing existing products have been made possible through the use of information technology. For instance, 43 Security Pacific Business Banking Centers have been created, offering PC-based automated banking services for the corporate "middle market." This is a product, using IS technology in a central way, that is substantially different from other banking products currently being offered in California. Other IS-based products are also being developed, but it is beyond the scope of this article to attempt to describe them; and besides, some of them are still under development and thus confidential.

Finally, SPAC has helped enlarge the *scope* of the bank's activities throughout the West. The recent acquisition by the corporation of the several major banks mentioned earlier was supported in a very material way by SPAC. A key component of the holding company's interstate banking strategy is the confidence top management has in SPAC's ability to contribute significantly to these acquisitions. The success in managing—and measuring—these SPAC activities has provided the bank with a new competitive weapon.

CONCLUSION

Lord Kelvin is reported to have said, "Without measurement, we have no science, only art." In Security Pacific Automation Company's Management by Results system, there is probably both art and science. Clearly, many of the IS measures currently in use within the bank need refinement and enhancement. But with each additional year of experience, more confidence is gained in the accuracy of the measures and more insight gleaned as to where further improvements can be made. Other parts of the bank, unrelated to IS, are now beginning to experiment with SLAs to measure their own activities. SPAC has even begun to offer its measurement experience to outside organizations (on a fee basis) to help them implement similar management processes.

However, in closing, one word of caution is in order. It was pointed out earlier that MBR is just a tool. And like any tool, it is only as good as the person—or the organization—using it. In the hands of an unskilled individual, a fine tool can produce only average results. Conversely, a highly skilled professional is often handicapped when forced to work with relatively primitive tools. The significant payoffs occur when skilled individuals are provided with quality tools. Such has been the experience at Security Pacific with its Management by Results system. In a very tangible way, they have advanced the state of the art in IS measurement.

REFERENCES

1. ANTHONY, ROBERT N. *Planning and Control Systems: A Framework for Analysis.* Graduate School of Business Administration, Harvard University, 1965.
2. Confidential report. The name of the market research firm cannot be released.
3. CROWSTON, KEVIN, AND MICHAEL E. TREACY. "Assessing the Impact of Information Technology on Enterprise Level Performance." *Processing of the Seventh International Conference on Information Systems,* 1986.
4. McFARLAN, F. WARREN. "Information Technology Changes the Way You Compete." *Harvard Business Review,* May–June 1984.
5. McLEAN, EPHRAIM R. "Assessing Returns from the Data Processing Investment." In *Effective vs. Efficient Computing,* ed. F. Gruenberger. New York: Prentice-Hall, 1973.
6. NOLAN, RICHARD L. "The Plight of the EDP Manager." *Harvard Business Review,* May–June 1973.
7. PETRE, P. "How to Keep Customers Happy Captives." *Fortune,* September 2, 1985.
8. PORTER, MICHAEL E. *Competitive Strategy.* New York: Free Press, 1980.
9. PORTER, MICHAEL E., AND VICTOR E. MILLAR. "How Information Gives You Competitive Advantage." *Harvard Business Review,* July–August 1985.
10. SALOMON BROTHERS, INC. *Investment Opinion—Security Pacific Corporation,* September 28, 1984.
11. WISEMAN, CHARLES. *Strategy and Computers: Information Systems as Competitive Weapons.* Homewood, Ill.: Dow Jones-Irwin, 1985.

V Computer Impact on Personnel, Organizations, and Society

In addition to knowledge on computer hardware and software, information systems and their applications, and the management of information systems, an awareness of the impact information technology has both within and outside the organization is important, too. Within the organization, the impact is felt primarily in the ways in which the organization's processes, structure, and ethics are affected and in the impact on both nonmanagerial and managerial human resources. Outside the organization, in the societal environment, impacts are felt in such areas as privacy invasion, loss of individuality, and computer-assisted crime.

The lead article, Reading 24, is "The Coming of the New Organization" by the esteemed management writer Peter F. Drucker. Drucker's overall theme is that we are evolving from a period wherein organizations have been structured around departments and divisions to an era in which the information-based organization and the organization of knowledge specialists dominate. Unlike organizational prototypes of the past, Drucker's "new organization" will be knowledge-based and composed of specialists who direct and discipline their own performance through organized feedback from colleagues, customers, and headquarters. The information-based organization of the next two decades will have its own special management problems, and Drucker discusses what these challenges are likely to be.

A broad perspective on information technology (IT) and its characteristics and challenges are presented by Peter G. W. Keen in Reading 25, "Computers and Managerial Choice." Keen identifies and describes the major dimensions of IT to include: (1) time, (2) software, (3) interdependence with other components of the technology base, (4) interdependence with organizational change and learning, and (5) requirements for new skills in applying technology. He concludes that many of the failures that occur while introducing new systems into the workplace reflect the fact that the importance of these dimensions are overlooked. Keen thinks these five dimensions are often hidden, but that they all demand senior-level management's awareness and policy decisions. Failure to see and manage these dimensions of IT may result in managers having to take them by default from the more unidimensional frame of reference of vendors and technical specialists.

In Reading 26, "IT in the 1990s: Managing Organizational Interdependence," John F. Rockhart and James E. Short continue to address the impact of information technology (IT) on organizations and their practices. Their central focus is on the idea that IT provides a new approach to one of management's oldest problems—that of managing interdependence, a dimension introduced in Reading 25. They go on to suggest that a firm's ability to continuously improve the effectiveness of managing interdependence is the critical element in responding to new and pressing competitive forces. The authors discuss four approaches to managing technology that have been used in the past. Then they present five examples of managing interdependence, which they think are models for the future.

Reading 27, "Four Ethical Issues of the Information Age," introduces us to a significant issue in today's organizations and society—the ethical dimension of what managers do. In this reading, Richard Mason suggests that we face many challenges in this age of information and that a central question before us is whether the kind of society being created is the one we want. Of particular importance are four major issues that have been made paramount by information technology: privacy, accuracy, property, and accessibility. Major questions posed relative to these issues include: What information about one's self must a person reveal to others? Who is responsible for the authenticity, fidelity, and accuracy of information? Who owns information and the channels through which it is transmitted? What information does a person or organization have a right or privilege to obtain? Mason clearly sees that what organizations and managers do about these and other ethical issues not only shapes the nature of organizations but also significantly dictates the kind of world in which we will live.

"Ethics in the Information Age" by Bruce E. Spiro is Reading 28, and it continues the ethics theme begun in the previous selection. Whereas Reading 27 addressed specific ethical issues, this reading focuses on the challenge of developing standards of conduct and codes that would be helpful for information managers. Spiro presents in his reading the code of ethics and standards of conduct that have been developed by the Data Processing Management Association (DPMA). The standards presented provide specific statements of behavior in support of each elements of the code. The standards represent what the professional information manager and specialist should abide by, in addition to the appropriate laws of their country and community. The tenets that comprise the standards include: obligations to management, employer, fellow members of the profession, and society. Spiro goes on to advance the idea that information professionals must take actions to ensure that information ethics are taught at all levels in our schools and are accepted in business as an essential part of operations.

Reading 29 is "Jesse James at the Terminal" by William Atkins. This reading introduces us to the characteristics and events in a typical computer crime. This interesting tale of computer derring-do illustrates for us the intricacies involved in a criminal's plot to defraud a fictitious company that had installed state-of-the-art security measures. As happens in so many computer capers, the story's ending turns almost on a quirk of fate. The article is extremely useful to us here because it illustrates what organizations are really up against in developing a secure computer environment.

The theme of computer crime and security continues in Reading 30, "Deterring Computer Crime," by Kenneth Rosenblatt. Rosenblatt starts by describing the magnitude of computer crime as being in the $3 billion to $5 billion a year range. He observes that it is a growing problem and yet very little is being done to deter it. He discusses why traditional approaches do not work and then goes on to argue that two elements are needed: (1) potential criminals must be convinced that they will be apprehended and (2) they must be convinced that their punishment will be harsh. He says that neither of these elements are now present. He goes on to suggest that local police departments cannot catch computer offenders, and that the states or the federal government need to fund regional task forces that are highly specialized and trained. Finally, offenders must be punished with a consequence that is fitting to the crime. This sanction would include a prohibition against computer offenders working with computers for a certain period after conviction. Rosenblatt sees computer crime as a growing threat to our economy and one that must be addressed in new and novel ways—immediately.

The impact of information technology on where people do their work is described in Reading 31, "The Growth of the Home Office," by Roberta Furger. Telecommuting, the practice of employees doing computer-based work from their homes, is discussed in this reading. Telecommuting proponents assert that the practice is on the increase and will hit its peak by the mid-1990s. This trend promises to have far-reaching effects for both employers and employees. The author describes how all the elements are in place for more extensive use of telecommuting, including attractive incentives for both organizations and employees alike. One major barrier at this point is that it represents such a radical change in the way people view work that it will probably be an evolutionary process as organizations move toward it. One thing is clear: As more and more jobs revolve around computers, it becomes increasingly evident that *where* the job is performed is no longer limited to the traditional office setting.

Reading 32, "The Terrors of Technostress," by John P. McPartlin, closes out this part of the book with coverage of a special kind of impact information technology has on people. This condition is known as "technostress." The more we work with machines, the more our minds try to think and act like machines—that is, we are adapting to computers, rather than having computers adapt to us. This unnatural adaptation creates technostress, a sign that we are having to fight to keep our emotional and creative selves intact. The author describes the frequency and kinds of technostress that are faced by the people who work with information technology. The social costs of technostress can be enormous in the form of psychological burn-out and employee turnover and the resulting need to rehire and retrain. Managers need to be aware of the human costs of the computer revolution and what strategies and actions need to be employed to deal with these costs.

24 *The Coming of the New Organization**

Peter F. Drucker

The typical large business 20 years hence will have fewer than half the levels of management of its counterpart today, and no more than a third the managers. In its structure, and in its management problems and concerns, it will bear little resemblance to the typical manufacturing company, circa 1950, which our textbooks still consider the norm. Instead it is far more likely to resemble organizations that neither the practicing manager nor the management scholar pays much attention to today: the hospital, the university, the symphony orchestra. For like them, the typical business will be knowledge-based, an organization composed largely of specialists who direct and discipline their own performance through organized feedback from colleagues, customers, and headquarters. For this reason, it will be what I call an information-based organization.

Businesses, especially large ones, have little choice but to become information-based. Demographics, for one, demands the shift. The center of gravity in employment is moving fast from manual and clerical workers to knowledge workers who resist the command-and-control model that business took from the military 100 years ago. Economics also dictates change, especially the need for large businesses to innovate and to be entrepreneurs. But above all, information technology demands the shift.

Advanced data processing technology isn't necessary to create an information-based organization, of course. As we shall see, the British built just such an organization in India when ''information technology'' meant the

---

quill pen, and barefoot runners were the "telecommunications" systems. But as advanced technology becomes more and more prevalent, we have to engage in analysis and diagnosis—that is, in "information"—even more intensively or risk being swamped by the data we generate.

So far most computer users still use the new technology only to do faster what they have always done before, crunch conventional numbers. But as soon as a company takes the first tentative steps from data to information, its decision processes, management structure, and even the way its work gets done begin to be transformed. In fact, this is already happening, quite fast, in a number of companies throughout the world.

We can readily see the first step in this transformation process when we consider the impact of computer technology on capital-investment decisions. We have known for a long time that there is no one right way to analyze a proposed capital investment. To understand it we need at least six analyses: the expected rate of return; the payout period and the investment's expected productive life; the discounted present value of all returns through the productive lifetime of the investment; the risk in not making the investment or deferring it; the cost and risk in case of failure; and finally, the opportunity cost. Every accounting student is taught these concepts. But before the advent of data processing capacity, the actual analyses would have taken man-years of clerical toil to complete. Now anyone with a spreadsheet should be able to do them in a few hours.

The availability of this information transforms the capital-investment analysis from opinion into diagnosis—that is, into the rational weighing of alternative assumptions. Then the information transforms the capital-investment decision from an opportunistic, financial decision governed by the numbers into a business decision based on the probability of alternative strategic assumptions. So the decision both presupposes a business strategy and challenges that strategy and its assumptions. What was once a budget exercise becomes an analysis of policy.

The second area that is affected when a company focuses its data processing capacity on producing information is its organization structure. Almost immediately, it becomes clear that both the number of management levels and the number of managers can be sharply cut. The reason is straightforward: It turns out that whole layers of management neither make decisions nor lead. Instead, their main, if not their only, function is to serve as "relays"—human boosters for the faint, unfocused signals that pass for communication in the traditional pre-information organization.

One of America's largest defense contractors made this discovery when it asked what information its top corporate and operating managers needed to do their jobs. Where did it come from? What form was it in? How did it flow? The search for answers soon revealed that whole layers of management—perhaps as many as 6 out of a total of 14—existed only because these questions had not been asked before. The company had had data galore. But it had always used its copius data for control, rather than for information.

Information is data endowed with relevance and purpose. Converting data into information thus requires knowledge. And knowledge, by definition, is specialized. (In fact, truly knowledgeable people tend toward overspecialization, whatever their field, precisely because there is always so much more to know.)

The information-based organization requires far more specialists overall than the command-and-control companies we are accustomed to. Moreover, the specialists are found in operations, not at corporate headquarters. Indeed, the operating organization tends to become an organization of specialists of all kinds.

Information-based organizations need central operating work, such as legal counsel, public relations, and labor relations, as much as ever. But the need for service staffs—that is, for people without operating responsibilities who only advise, counsel, or coordinate—shrinks drastically. In its *central* management, the information-based organization needs few, if any, specialists.

Because of its flatter structure, the large, information-based organization will more closely resemble the businesses of a century ago than today's big companies. Back then, however, all the knowledge, such as it was, lay with the very top people. The rest were helpers or hands, who mostly did the same work and did as they were told. In the information-based organization, the knowledge will be primarily at the bottom, in the minds of the specialists who do different work and direct themselves. So today's typical organization in which knowledge tends to be concentrated in service staffs, perched rather insecurely between top management and the operating people, will likely be labeled a phase, an attempt to infuse knowledge from the top, rather than obtain information from below.

Finally, a good deal of work will be done differently in the information-based organization. Traditional departments will serve as guardians of standards, as centers for training and the assignment of specialists; they won't be where the work gets done. That will happen largely in task-focused teams.

This change is already under way in what used to be the most clearly defined of all departments—research. In pharmaceuticals, in telecommunications, in papermaking, the traditional *sequence* of research, development, manufacturing, and marketing is being replaced by *synchrony*: specialists from all these functions work together as a team, from the inception of research to a product's establishment in the market.

How task forces will develop to tackle other business opportunities and problems remains to be seen. I suspect, however, that the need for a task force, its assignment, its composition, and its leadership will have to be decided case by case. So the organization that will be developed will go beyond the matrix and may indeed be quite different from it. One thing is clear, though: It will require greater self-discipline and even greater emphasis on individual responsibility for relationships and for communications.

To say that information technology is transforming business enterprises is simple. What this transformation will require of companies and top managements is much harder to decipher. That is why I find it helpful to look for clues in other kinds of information-based organizations, such as the hospital, the symphony orchestra, and the British administration in India.

A fair-sized hospital of about 400 beds will have a staff of several hundred physicians and 1,200 to 1,500 paramedics divided among some 60 medical and paramedical specialties. Each specialty has its own knowledge, its own training, its own language. In each specialty, especially the paramedical ones like the clinical lab and physical therapy, there is a head person who is a working specialist, rather than a full-time manager. The head of each specialty reports directly to the top, and there is little middle management. A good deal of the work is done in ad hoc teams as required by an individual patient's diagnosis and condition.

A large symphony orchestra is even more instructive, since for some works there may be a few hundred musicians on stage playing together. According to organization theory then, there should be several group vice president conductors and perhaps a half-dozen division VP conductors. But that's not how it works. There is only the conductor-CEO—and every one of the musicians plays directly to that person without an intermediary. And each is a high-grade specialist, indeed an artist.

But the best example of a large and successful information-based organization, and one without any middle management at all, is the British civil administration in India.

The British ran the Indian subcontinent for 200 years, from the middle of the 18th century through World War II, without making any fundamental changes in organization structure or administrative policy. The Indian civil service never had more than 1,000 members to administer the vast and densely populated subcontinent—a tiny fraction (at most 1 percent) of the legions of Confucian mandarins and palace eunuchs employed next door to administer a not-much-more populous China. Most of the Britishers were quite young; a 30-year-old was a survivor, especially in the early years. Most lived alone in isolated outposts with the nearest countryman a day or two of travel away, and for the first 100 years there was no telegraph or railroad.

The organization structure was totally flat. Each district officer reported directly to the "Coo," the provincial political secretary. And since there were nine provinces, each political secretary had at least 100 people reporting directly to him, many times what the doctrine of the span of control would allow. Nevertheless, the system worked remarkably well, in large part because it was designed to ensure that each of its members had the information he needed to do his job.

Each month the district officer spent a whole day writing a full report to the political secretary in the provincial capital. He discussed each of his principal tasks—there were only four, each clearly delineated. He put down in detail what he had expected would happen with respect to each of them, what actually did happen, and why, if there was a discrepancy, the two differed. Then he wrote down what he expected would happen in the ensuing month with respect to each key task and what he was going to do about it, asked questions about policy, and commented on long-term opportunities, threats, and needs. In turn, the political secretary "minuted" every one of those reports—that is, he wrote back a full comment.

On the basis of these examples, what can we say about the requirements of the information-based organization? And what are its management problems likely to be? Let's look first at the requirements. Several hundred musicians and their CEO, the conductor, can play together because they all have the same score. It tells both flutist and timpanist what to play and when. And it tells the conductor what to expect from each and when. Similarly, all the specialists in the hospital share a common mission: the care and cure of the sick. The diagnosis is their "score"; it dictates specific action for the x-ray lab, the dietitian, the physical therapist, and the rest of the medical team.

Information-based organizations, in other words, require clear, simple, common objectives that translate into particular actions. At the same time, however, as these examples indicate, information-based organizations also need concentration on one objective or, at most, on a few.

Because the "players" in an information-based organization are specialists, they cannot be told how to do their work. There are probably few orchestra conductors who could coax even one note out of a French horn, let alone show the horn player how to do it. But the conductor can focus the horn player's skill and knowledge on the musicians' joint performance. And this focus is what the leaders of an information-based business must be able to achieve.

Yet a business has no "score" to play by except the score it writes as it plays. And whereas neither a first-rate performance of a symphony nor a miserable one will change what the composer wrote, the performance of a business continually creates new and different scores against which its performance is assessed. So an information-based business must be structured around goals that clearly state management's performance expectations for the enterprise and for each part and specialist and around organized feedback that compares results with these performance expectations so that every member can exercise self-control.

The other requirement of an information-based organization is that everyone take information responsibility. The bassoonist in the orchestra does so every time she plays a note. Doctors and paramedics work with an elaborate system of reports and an information center, the nurses's station on the patient's floor. The district officer in India acted on this responsibility every time he filed a report.

The key to such a system is that everyone asks: Who in this organization depends on me for what information? And on whom, in turn, do I depend? Each person's list will always include superiors and subordinates. But the most important names on it will be those of colleagues, people with whom one's primary relationship is coordination. The relationship of the internist, the surgeon, and the anesthesiologist, is one example. But the relationship of a biochemist, a pharmacologist, the medical director in charge of clinical testing, and a marketing specialist in a pharmaceutical company is no different. It, too, requires each party to take the fullest information responsibility.

Information responsibility to others is increasingly understood, especially in middle-sized companies. But information responsibility to oneself is still largely neglected—that is, everyone in an organization should constantly be thinking through what information he or she needs to do the job and to make a contribution.

This may well be the most radical break with the way even the most highly computerized businesses are still being run today. There, people either assume the more data, the more information—which was a perfectly valid assumption yesterday when data were scarce, but leads to data overload and information blackout now that they are plentiful. Or they believe that information specialists know what data executives and professionals need in order to have information. But information specialists are tool makers. They can tell us what tool to use to hammer upholstery nails into a chair. We need to decide whether we should be upholstering a chair at all.

Executives and professional specialists need to think through what information is for them, what data they need: first, to know what they are doing; then, to be able to decide what they should be doing; and finally, to appraise how well they are doing. Until this happens MIS departments are likely to remain cost centers, rather than become the result centers they could be.

Most large businesses have little in common with the examples we have been looking at. Yet to remain competitive—maybe even to survive—they will have to convert themselves into information-based organizations, and fairly quickly. They will have to change old habits and acquire new ones. And the more successful a company has been, the more difficult and painful this process is apt to be. It will threaten the jobs, status, and opportunities of a good many people in the organization, especially the long-serving, middle-aged people in middle management who tend to be the least mobile and to feel most secure in their work, their positions, their relationships, and their behavior.

The information-based organization will also pose its own special management problems. I see as particularly critical:

1. Developing rewards, recognition, and career opportunities for specialists.

2. Creating unified vision in an organization of specialists.
3. Devising the management structure for an organization of task forces.
4. Ensuring the supply, preparation, and testing of top management people.

Bassoonists presumably neither want nor expect to be anything but bassoonists. Their career opportunities consist of moving from second bassoon to first bassoon and perhaps of moving from a second-rank orchestra to a better, more prestigious one. Similarly, many medical technologists neither expect nor want to be anything but medical technologists. Their career opportunities consist of a fairly good chance of moving up to senior technician, and a very slim chance of becoming lab director. For those who make it to lab director, about 1 out of every 25 or 30 technicians, there is also the opportunity to move to a bigger, richer hospital. The district officer in India had practically no chance for professional growth except possibly to be relocated, after a three-year stint, to a bigger district.

Opportunities for specialists in an information-based business organization should be more plentiful than they are in an orchestra or hospital, let alone in the Indian civil service. But as in these organizations, they will primarily be opportunities for advancement within the specialty, and for limited advancement at that. Advancement into "management" will be the exception, for the simple reason that there will be far fewer middle-management positions to move into. This contrasts sharply with the traditional organization where, except in the research lab, the main line of advancement in rank is out of the specialty and into general management.

More than 30 years ago General Electric tackled this problem by creating "parallel opportunities" for "individual professional contributors." Many companies have followed this example. But professional specialists themselves have largely rejected it as a solution. To them—and to their management colleagues—the only meaningful opportunities are promotions into management. And the prevailing compensation structure in practically all businesses reinforces this attitude because it is heavily biased towards managerial positions and titles.

There are no easy answers to this problem. Some help may come from looking at large law and consulting firms, where even the most senior partners tend to be specialists, and associates who will not make partner are outplaced fairly early on. But whatever scheme is eventually developed will work only if the values and compensation structure of business are drastically changed.

The second challenge that management faces is giving its organization of specialists a common vision, a view of the whole.

In the Indian civil service, the district officer was expected to see the "whole" of his district. But to enable him to concentrate on it, the government services that arose one after the other in the 19th century (forestry, irrigation, the archaeological survey, public health and sanitation, roads) were organized outside the administrative structure, and had virtually no contact with the district officer. This meant that the district officer became increasingly isolated from the activities that often had the greatest impact on—and the greatest importance for—his district. In the end, only the provincial government or the central government in Delhi had a view of the "whole," and it was an increasingly abstract one at that.

A business simply cannot function this way. It needs a view of the whole and a focus on the whole to be shared among a great many of its professional specialists, certainly among the senior ones. And yet it will have to accept, indeed will have to foster, the pride and professionalism of its specialists—if only because, in the absence of opportunities to move into middle management, their motivation must come from that pride and professionalism.

One way to foster professionalism, of course, is through assignments to task forces. And the information-based business will use more and more smaller self-governing units, assigning them tasks tidy enough for "a good man to get his arms around," as the old phrase has it. But to what extent should information-based businesses rotate performing specialists out of their specialties and into new ones? And to what extent will top management have to accept as its top priority making and maintaining a common vision across professional specialties?

Heavy reliance on task-force teams assuages one problem. But it aggravates another: the management structure of the information-based organization. Who will the business's managers be? Will they be task-force leaders? Or will there be a two-headed monster—a specialist structure, comparable, perhaps, to the way attending physicians function in a hospital, and an administrative structure of task-force leaders?

The decisions we face on the role and function of the task-force leaders are risky and controversial. Is theirs a permanent assignment, analogous to the job of the supervisory nurse in the hospital? Or is it a function of the task that changes as the task does? Is it an assignment or a position? Does it carry any rank at all? And if it does, will the task-force leaders become in time what the product managers have been at Procter & Gamble: the basic units of management and the company's field officers? Might the task-force leaders eventually replace department heads and vice presidents?

Signs of every one of these developments exist, but there is neither a clear trend nor much understanding as to what each entails. Yet each would give rise to a different organizational structure from any we are familiar with.

Finally, the toughest problem will probably be to ensure the supply, preparation, and testing of top management people. This is, of course, an old and central dilemma as well as a major reason for the general acceptance of decentralization in large businesses in the last 40 years. But the existing business organization has a great many middle-management positions that are supposed to prepare and test a person. As a result, there are usually a good many people to choose from when filling a senior management slot. With the number of middle-management positions sharply cut, where will the information-based organization's top executives come from? What will be their preparation? How will they have been tested?

Decentralization into autonomous units will surely be even more critical than it is now. Perhaps we will even copy the German *Gruppe* in which the decentralized units are set up as separate companies with their own top managements. The Germans use this model precisely because of their tradition of promoting people in their specialties, especially in research and engineering; if they did not have available commands in near-independent subsidiaries to put people in, they would have little opportunity to train and test their most promising professionals. These subsidiaries are thus somewhat like the farm teams of a major-league baseball club.

We may also find that more and more top management jobs in big companies are filled by hiring people away from smaller companies. This is the way that major orchestras get their conductors—a young conductor earns his or her spurs in a small orchestra or opera house, only to be hired away by a larger one. And the heads of a good many large hospitals have had similar careers.

Can business follow the example of the orchestra and hospital where top management has become a separate career? Conductors and hospital administrators come out of courses in conducting or schools of hospital administration, respectively. We see something of this sort in France, where large companies are often run by men who have spent their entire previous careers in government service. But in most countries this would be unacceptable to the organization (only France has the *mystique* of the *grandes écoles*). And even in France, businesses, especially large ones, are becoming too demanding to be run by people without firsthand experience and a proven success record.

Thus the entire top management process—preparation, testing, succession—will become even more problematic than it already is. There will be a growing need for experienced business people to go back to school. And business schools will surely need to work out what successful professional specialists must know to prepare themselves for high-level positions as *business* executives and *business* leaders.

Since modern business enterprise first arose, after the Civil War in the United States and the Franco-Prussian War in Europe, there have been two major evolutions in the concept and structure of organizations. The first took place in the 10 years between 1895 and 1905. It distinguished management from ownership and established management as work and task in its own right. This happened first in Germany, when George Siemens, the founder and head of Germany's premier bank, *Deutsche Bank,* saved the electrical apparatus company his cousin Werner had founded after Werner's sons and heirs had mismanaged it into near collapse. By threatening to cut off the bank's loans, he forced his cousins to turn the company's management over to professionals. A little later, J. P. Morgan, Andrew Carnegie, and John D. Rockefeller, Sr., followed suit in their massive restructurings of U.S. railroads and industries.

The second evolutionary change took place 20 years later. The development of what we still see as the modern corporation began with Pierre S. du Pont's restructuring of his family company in the early 1920s and continued with Alfred P. Sloan's redesign of General Motors a few years later. This introduced the command-and-control organization of today, with its emphasis on decentralization, central service staffs, personnel management, the whole apparatus of budgets and controls, and the important distinction between policy and operations. This stage culminated in the massive reorganization of General Electric in the early 1950s, an action that perfected the model most big businesses around the world (including Japanese organizations) still follow.

Now we are entering a third period of change: the shift from the command-and-control organization, the organization of departments and divisions, to the information-based organization, the organization of knowledge specialists. We can perceive, though perhaps only dimly, what this organization will look like. We can identify some of its main characteristics and requirements. We can point to central problems of values, structure, and behavior. But the job of actually building the information-based organization is still ahead of us—it is the managerial challenge of the future.

25   *Computers and Managerial Choice**

Peter G. W. Keen

Managers don't know much about computers. The field of information technology (IT) is now too broad for anyone to really be able to master it. IT—computers, communications, data, workstations, and the analytical and technical disciplines that shape software and its applications—is like the word *transportation,* which runs the gamut from bicycles to airplanes and involves many hidden economic and social issues. But someone who can ride a bike is not qualified to be a transportation planner. And car dealers and mechanics are not the most reliable sources of judgment on policy priorities for public transportation. By the same token, knowing how to use a personal computer will not help managers take charge of the IT planning process in large firms, and the opinions of technicians and vendors should not be the basis for spreading IT across the firm into more and more aspects of work. There has to be a set of policies based on a broader understanding of options and impacts.

Policy is not the same as planning. Every large firm has already made, and continues to make, massive commitments to office technology, dealer order-entry systems, computer-aided design and manufacturing, electronic banking, and the like. None of these are casually undertaken. A variety of planning methodologies, as well as people, are used to carry out plans. But policy should drive plans. Policy is the set of explicit, top-level mandates and directives that provide criteria for planning and selecting specific applications of IT. Policy should be simple, but not simplistic. It is management's statement about the ways things will be done. Most firms

---

* Source: Reprinted, by permission of the publisher, from *Organizational Dynamics,* Autumn 1985. © 1985 American Management Association, New York. All rights reserved.

have not been resolving IT policy questions at the top. The management process has been marked by delegation to a technical cadre that, in the past, was largely isolated from the mainstream of the organization and had a focused, but narrow, style of thinking that left out "behavioral" issues.

Delegation is still the norm in many companies, especially at middle levels (e.g., for data processing and telecommunications functions) but, on the whole, technical people are more sensitive to the broader business and organizational implications of IT than most of their senior managers. Technical people may at times have a simplistic perspective on problems, but they are at least—and at last—making a real effort to place the technology in a wider context. Their most common question is becoming, "How do we get senior management to understand this?"

This question becomes more and more important as IT pushes out from its traditional domain of automating clerical processes into just about every level of work and every function of the business. Telecommunications have become the information highway system for customer service, internal communication and coordination, and business innovation. Personal computers, word processors, order-entry systems, engineers' workstations, and so forth, are the bicycles, cars, and trucks using that highway. IT intentionally and radically changes the office landscape, the nature of work, the dynamics of competition, and the economics of doing business.

Because delegation has for so long been used in implementing IT, top managers are now sanctioning radical organizational change without recognizing that they are doing so. Office technology is just one example of investments being made in the name of productivity with no clear picture of how the organization might, would, or should be different as a result. There is a vast amount of literature on the unintended consequences—not always negative ones—of office technology and on the naive views of work, people, and productivity that too often lead to the transformation of technical successes into organizational failures.

Just as IT managers need to build a more sophisticated understanding of the business, so must executives and decision makers gain a more sophisticated sense of the technology—and the actual and potential organizational consequences and opportunities it produces—if they truly are to be people who manage, execute, and decide. *Sophisticated* is not the same as *detailed*. The real issue is how little, not how much, managers must understand about IT. It has become fashionable to talk about the need for "computer literacy" in schools and in business. It is really too late for that. Managers need *computer fluency*. Literacy usually adds up to little more than confidence building through a crash course on personal computers. It narrows the issues to the visible aspects of the technology: hardware, software, and individual uses. Computer fluency relates to understanding choices and consequences.

Managers need a vocabulary for reviewing choices. Most of the words, claims, and ideas now in use come either from vendors or from people who have a deterministic perspective on IT. Its advocates see it as a causal force toward the Office of the Future, the Information Age, productivity, competitive advantage, and the like. Dissenters also see IT as a causal force, but toward dehumanization of work, loss of autonomy, and a new form of scientific management—as sterile as Taylorism, though couched in less purely economic terms. Each of these extremes obscures the issue of choice. If IT is a directly causal force—whether on society, organizations, or individuals—then choices are irrelevant. For the proponents, the message is, "You have no choice but to get on the bandwagon"; for the dissenters it is, "It's going to happen anyway and you won't like it." If, however, the same technology has different impacts depending on how, where, and when it is applied, then obviously choices do matter.

The issue of managerial choices for IT is a key one. Even though it is hard to predict the degree of causality and the specific consequences of options, computer fluency does address two major questions that will substantially determine large organizations' state of health in the future: What are the economic costs and benefits of IT? What are the organizational and individual costs and benefits of IT? The answers that managers reach should be the basis for their policies and should reflect computer fluency, which includes (1) an understanding of the choices and their potential or likely consequences, (2) an understanding of one's own values and those of the organization, and (3) a recognition of one's responsibility to make sure that IT supports those values.

Although technical innovation and design are still important, information technology has moved out of that domain and now is part of the structure of everyday life and of organizational and social innovation and design. It has moved into the domain of values: What sort of an organization is desired, and what will the result be if particular choices about IT are made? Yet no established tradition exists for helping managers set policies for IT. The starting point is to build a vocabulary that allows managers to understand the key aspects of the technology, to highlight what is known about choices and impacts and, above all, to put the question of values in the foreground.

THE DIMENSIONS OF IT

IT is both physical and abstract. The planning process and vocabulary, not surprisingly, are built around the visible and physical parts: lines of code in software development, hardware capacity in annual planning, numbers of terminals, and so forth. Yet the same physical technologies can have very different impacts, depending on these implicit, abstract dimensions of IT:

• Time.

- Software (its intellectual assumptions and analytical techniques).
- Interdependence with other components of the technology base.
- Interdependence with organizational change and learning.
- Requirements for new skills in applying technology.

Many of the failures that occur while introducing new systems into the workplace reflect the fact that the importance of these dimensions are overlooked. Different impacts of the same physical technologies in particular contexts are easily explained by studying these dimensions of IT. For example, managers and professionals are generally receptive to using personal computers and decision-support systems. Secretarial, clerical, and administrative workers often have mixed responses. The physical technology is the same in both instances: a workstation with a screen at which the person manipulates text and numbers. In many instances, the activity is also the same—managers do budgets on spreadsheets plus a little word processing, and secretaries do lots of word processing plus some spreadsheet work.

The difference in reactions within and across these groups relates mainly to the interdependence betweeen IT and organizational change, and particularly to IT's impact on autonomy. An implicit value held by builders of decision-support systems is that these systems will be used by managers on an optional basis. They will not be required to use them. The intention is not to impose procedures or sanctions on managers. Often, the same respect is not held for the autonomy of secretaries or administrative staff. They are given no choices. The technology is the same, but the application is defined with an implicit, and probably unrecognized or unintentional, choice about the trade-off between productivity and autonomy.

In an instance like this, overlooking the relationship between the physical system and the abstract issue of autonomy obscures a choice and a consequence: How should we design and introduce the system? Who gains and who loses? Must gains in productivity mean losses in autonomy? In some cases, the technology itself directly implies a change in autonomy; this is especially true when the system paces the worker, instead of the other way around. In this instance, values also come into play: Should we introduce the system at all?

When these questions are not asked, systems people are surprised when managers, who can act to preserve their autonomy, choose not to use a new tool that intrudes on that autonomy. Secretaries and customer-service personnel, who may not have a choice, surprise systems staff by finding ways to bypass this new constraint on how they work or by exhibiting negative reactions. Both kinds of behavior are called "resistance," as if the person is intentionally responding to the new technology. In fact, the behavior is an unintentional reaction to some intrinsic aspect of the technical system.

Until a very few years ago, the physical dimensions of technology dominated the planning process. It was difficult to make the hardware work, harder to design and deliver software, and even harder to make hardware, software, data, and communications work together. Now technology has been tamed. While it is still a challenge to manage large-scale projects and solve specific problems that arise in integrating technical components and applying technology in particular areas, standard technologies on the whole have become fairly easy to install. However, these technologies are not always easy to implement. Installation—making systems work technically—largely depends on the physical dimensions of IT. But making them work organizationally, and then getting real benefits from them, increasingly relate to the hidden, nonphysical aspects of IT.

The Time Dimension

Clearly, implementing information technology takes time—and generally lots of it. No one expects an office complex to be built in a few months, just because its components are commonplace and easy to assemble, or a new highway to be planned, designed, and delivered simply and quickly. In each instance, the lead time may be from 2 to 10 years, and that is true for IT projects as well. A large software system is comparable in scope to building an office. Putting in place a new high-capacity telecommunications facility involves the same type of planning, nuts-and-bolts engineering, and dealing with regulations, ordinances, and contractors as does a highway. It is rare that any innovation using IT, even one that is rushed, can be completed in less than 18 months. It can be installed quickly—the microcomputers unpacked and a short training course provided—but, in general, it will take still another year before the system is really implemented. It takes time to mesh a new system into the context of jobs, people, and organizational processes.

In addition, every major project requires either very precise design specifications, pilots, or prototypes to help shape them, feasibility studies, or proposal requests. It takes three times as long to test a piece of software as it does to write it. Training should take up about 20 percent of the time and budget. It may be from two to five years before a new system is fully self-sustaining and institutionalized.

The lead times are often not anticipated. The history of data processing has been marked by the "mythical man month"—the programmer's optimistic estimate of the time required to complete a system. This estimate is often wrong by a factor of between 2 and 10, because the estimate covers only program design and coding. Time is the dimension the vendor's ads omit; they imply that, since the word processor, software package, or personal computer is ready and available, installation alone will bring the company benefits.

One of the worst consequences of inattention to the lead times is the artificial selection of delivery dates by managers, often with the acquiescence of technical staff. Managers may decide that a new system has to be in place by, say, January 1, for business reasons or because they simply want to move as fast as possible. They assume that, if people work harder and management is willing to throw resources at the project, lead time can be reduced. Frederick P. Brooks' comment about the "tar pit" of software engineering explains why this does not work: "When a task cannot be partitioned because of [its sequential steps], the application of more effort has no effect on the schedule. The bearing of a child takes nine months, no matter how many women are assigned."

When unrealistic delivery dates are set, rarely does the manager pay the price but, rather, the supervisors of the work unit affected by the new system and the junior technical staff working on the project do. IT becomes a force for disruption and demoralization instead of innovation when systems are parachuted into the workplace with unrealistic deadlines, unrealistic expectations, and impossible demands on subordinates.

When delegation is the strategy, the manager often takes no responsibility for problems. The blame generally falls on technical staff. This allows some managers to play what Eugene Bardach calls the "reputation game": Managers aggressively encourage IT projects, set deadlines that cannot be met, and then take credit for being innovators without having to pick up the pieces when projects get into trouble, as they almost inevitably do.

As IT becomes a force for competitive innovation, it is natural for managers to sponsor new projects and to be in a hurry to get results. It is also tempting for them and for technical staff to be optimistic about lead times. It is morally wrong to play the reputation game, but several of the most publicized IT "successes" described in the business press one year turn out to be failures the next. These failures are almost predetermined from the start by the sign-off on the project-delivery schedule. One of the easiest ways to disrupt a work unit is to parachute an IT innovation into it—to drop in the technical vehicle with minimal preparation and without sufficient resources and a timetable that will allow it to be implemented and assimilated smoothly.

One of the main resources needed for projects with a long lead time is education. This is not the same as training. Firms generally provide too much training too late. Training focuses on the basics of the new system—how to operate the terminal and implement procedures. Education should precede, not follow, implementation and should give people a vocabulary to help them participate in design and development, influence attitudes, build awareness, and explain the rationale for the new system and the work changes it implies. In the firms that have taken advantage of the business opportunities IT creates and have provided support for the difficult process of change, education is one of the fastest-growing components of the IT budget, especially education for senior managers.

Senior managers must make sure that the issue of lead time is both brought out and understood and that *they* do not cause problems by insisting on unrealistic schedules. The responsibility here is partly economic and partly ethical. When lead time is ignored, the real costs are not budgeted for and the likelihood of failure increases rapidly. Most managers associated with major software development projects in the 1970s saw this happen. In addition, resources had to be added to fight the fires created by falling behind schedule, so that the investment did not have to be written off. Obviously, managers have an economic responsibility to fulfill and must not let this happen.

Managers' ethical responsibility is to not allow disruption of a work unit because either the technical staff has been overly optimistic in its estimates or the sponsoring business manager has demanded adherence to an impossible schedule. Parachuted projects usually do not work as intended or expected. The middle manager or supervisor usually has to pick up the pieces, often struggling to get the new system in place while keeping the old procedures, even though there are resources available for only one of the systems. It is very easy for these managers to become the victims of IT, because a top-level manager is in a hurry and the data processing specialist agrees to an impossible schedule.

Software (Intellectual Assumptions and Analytical Techniques)

Until recently, the whole planning process for IT focused on hardware. Gradually managers have learned that it is software, not hardware, that is the premium item and the costly element in most information systems. But, more and more, software and hardware are sold as a single system (word processors, for example, or integrated personal computers) *and,* as a result, the distinction becomes blurred. The package gets the attention, so that software, like hardware, is seen as being a physical aspect of the system. Rather than viewing software as the embodiment of intellectual assumptions and analytical techniques, managers are looking at software in terms of screen layouts, menus, graphs, spreadsheets, and so forth.

Software itself is a means, not an end. Every piece of software and the workstation or personal computer by which it is accessed contain an implicit assumption about the end, which is a "better" or "more productive" something. However, technology should not define ahead of time what is better or more productive. For instance, every aspect of office technology should first examine what it means for a secretary to be more productive or a manager to be more effective. The early term *office automation* reflects a view of the office as a factory in which the same principles of work rationalization and structuring used in Taylorism can be applied to automating clerical functions. The tools of office automation were often applied without recognizing that they embodied a theory of how they should be used. The definitions and assumptions about the abstraction *productivity* were only implicit. Managerial responsibility depends far more on making them explicit and checking that they are acceptable than on probing into the details of the physical technology. Too often, reviews of software packages compare features and functions, but not assumptions.

In several emerging application areas, the physical technology is only as valid as the intellectual base underneath it. "Expert systems," for instance, will be paced by developments in cognitive science and psychology, rather than by chips and software. The usefulness of much database management software will depend on new concepts and methods for data administration, which include handling the complex issues of politics and authority in standardizing information and procedures. The effectiveness of teleconferencing has been hampered by a lack of a clear understanding of how to handle social factors in these settings: for example, moderating an electronic meeting, interrupting, and setting up suitable agendas.

Any definition of productivity is partly one of values. Software tools often contain their designers' hidden (and perhaps unconscious) values. Office automation reflects engineers' ideas about how word processing should be "improved"—ideas built on the economist's ethos of efficiency. More recently, there has been a shift toward stressing such "value-added" benefits of office technology as improved communication, better decision making, faster reaction to ad hoc situations, better presentations through graphics, and so forth. Here the focus is on support of people, not automation of functions. The choice of tools, at least in part, is an acceptance or reinforcement of values. Yet many commentators on office technology are concerned about the degree to which values are ignored by organizations. They point out that management does not have to accept the ethos of automation to derive benefits. Shoshana Zuboff explains that IT has the capacity to both automate and "informate" the process to which it is applied. Her term *informate* refers to technology's capacity to augment and support work, to give people a broader sense of understanding of—and control over—their activities, and to help them make a greater contribution to their organization as a result. Zuboff's distinction between automating and informating highlights the fact that there are choices: Managers do not have to automate to increase productivity.

In practice, though, the tendency is to informate managers and automate the lower levels of the organization. Judith Gregory's "Race against Time," which summarizes research findings on the impact of office technology on female workers, is a compelling contrast to the glowing promises about "knowledge workers" in the office of the future. On the other hand, the literature on decision-support systems emphasizes the importance of managerial autonomy and judgment in the use of interactive computer systems. The difference in the two visions is not one of technology.

The automating of one telephone company's directory-assistance service is an example of the extent to which the dominant value choice is used in wide-scale application of IT. When a customer phones, the service agent uses a CRT to search for the requested name and to look for variants of spelling or synonyms. When the match is made, the agent hits a key that activates a recording of the phone number. Management monitors the number of enquiries per agent, the amount of idle time, the agent's politeness, the response time, and so forth. There are "worker of the week" awards, with the best agents' performances displayed on notice boards. Work quotas are used as the basis for almost every aspect of reward and evaluation. The entire process is explicitly managed like an assembly plant, and personal links between the customers and the agent (conversation, reading the number, and so forth) are kept to a minimum.

The benefits to the company and the customer have been significant. Costs have dropped and service has improved. Workers seem fairly happy with the system. It may well be that this extreme example of automating, rather than informating, work is, in this context, a more effective choice. Or it may not be; it is not clear whether the phone company's management considered any other options.

Automation is also being used in many banks, where the pieces of paper and "hand-offs" involved in letters of credit or mortgage applications are streamlined; all the steps are handled by a single person at a workstation. Some of the banks stress the extent to which the job is now informated: The service professional has a better sense of the customer's relationship with the bank and has more direct contact with customers and, instead of being a fragmented and routinized set of procedures, the task is now a whole and, more meaningful one.

While such claims may partly be management's justification for introducing radical change into the workplace, they nevertheless acknowledge that automating the worker the way the telephone company has may not be viewed entirely as progress and, more importantly, that the technology does allow choices. Zuboff's distinction between *informate* and *automate* has to become part of the vocabulary for thinking about the options in technology. The manager's workstation informates. Must workstations of the secretary, order-entry clerk, and service agent necessarily automate? That question does not get asked when the focus in planning is on the physical aspects of an information system.

Interdependence with Other Components of the Technology Base

It is outside the scope of this article to present a detailed discussion of the technology itself, but managers need to have a sense of the issues IT groups are now dealing with that are very different from their traditional concerns of systems development and operations. The problem now is to fit the individual technical components together, rather than to make each one work by itself. The goal is to create an integrated capability in which the multiservice workstation accesses a range of services via a communications link.

Conceptually, integration is fairly simple. In practice, the technical problems are immense. The word *incompatible,* which is the opposite of *integrated,* means: "This device cannot access this service even if common sense says it should be able to do so." Incompatibility has been the norm, rather than the exception, partly because individual vendors' equipment and software use special conventions, techniques, and "protocols." (An analogy to protocols is Morse code and semaphore; the same information is sent in very different forms.) Until very recently, every major type of application or media—videotex, transaction processing, word processing, database management, and so forth—was independent of the others.

Integration is now the goal, to save money, to avoid proliferation and duplication of facilities, and to create the computer equivalent of the telephone—a single-access point to a wide range of locations and applications. "Stand-alone systems" like word processors and personal computers can be used effectively for small-scale applications, but the main payoffs with IT come from linkage to remote data resources and access to a telecommunications highway system.

While the payoffs from the move toward integration increase, so does the complexity of the technical and managerial issues that need to be resolved. Many of these issues become political and change the criteria for investment, by shifting attention away from specific applications and equipment and redirecting it toward funding the long-term IT infrastructure. In particular, policies and standards are needed to avoid incompatibility. For example, only if all personal computers in the firm use the *XYZ* operating system can they access the central computer's data resources. The main problem is not so much what the technical standards should be but who should enforce them.

The management process for IT increasingly has to resolve this issue of authority: Who decides? The more a particular component of IT depends on other components for its long-term value and use, the more salient this question becomes. Moreover, the issue of authority has become more pressing because, over the past few years, the old monopoly of data processing, which used to have full control over the technical base and most decisions concerning it, has been broken. Microcomputers, office technology, and end-user software have created a free market for IT and encouraged local autonomy in decision making. Within data processing, the trend is toward distributed development among local technical units whose priorities may be very different from those of the central group—which has to focus on corporate needs for information and communication. The local units are looking for the most cost-effective solutions to their own needs, which may conflict with the central group's concern with integration and standards.

Regulating the free market for IT is a top-management policy issue. Are standards just guidelines that business units and local data processing units can choose to ignore, or are they standards with teeth, in that the central unit has veto power? What is the basis for choosing which aspects of the IT plan require standards? When there is no explicit policy and corresponding match between the authority and responsibility of the central and local units, issues are resolved mainly through political infighting.

Since the technology itself is changing mostly in the areas most relevant to integration (especially telecommunications), the central IT group is facing a stressful situation. It has total responsibility for creating a new customer-delivery base, building new data resources, helping business units to exploit office technology and personal computers, and rationalizing the existing incompatible facilities. It may have little of the formal authority needed to match the responsibility and may have to rely on informal influence and on building credibility with business units. The major barrier the IT group faces in trying to influence organization members is the past history of data processing departments and their reputation for bureaucracy and poor understanding of, and interest in, the wider organization. The IT group now has to learn how to market, negotiate, and present its case in business terms. The key term in the IT manager and planner's vocabulary should now be *architecture*—the long-term blueprint for defining the infrastructure and moving toward integration. In most businesses, the architecture is becoming the strategy; it is the transportation plan that makes possible specific types and volumes of traffic and constrains other ones. IT managers' most commonly expressed concern is how to get senior managers to understand the opportunities, problems, and trade-offs involved.

The interdependence of more and more aspects of the building blocks of IT is putting new pressures on technical people and general managers alike. Once again, the technology itself and its intended use contain this largely hidden dimension of interdependence. While this nonphysical dimension relates mainly to the potential impacts on the users of systems— productivity, autonomy, and so forth—interdependence is far more relevant to the management process for IT as a whole. At one level, it is easy for general managers to view interdependence as the responsibility of the technical planners and not as something that needs their attention.

Many of the issues relevant to architecture and integration are essentially technical, especially in the area of standards. But more and more of them relate to policy and to the responsibility of top managers who already have authority and established influence. Too much is being left to the IT community, including, in many instances, guessing at business priorities and defining the long-term highway system within the constraints of short-term cost recovery. Many IT managers are more sensitive than top management to the relationships between integrated technologies and organizational change. In a sense, their role has changed from running a railroad to designing a transportation plan, but without clear policy guidance. Clearly, this will not work. The interdependence of IT technology requires policy, which in turn requires computer fluency. A general imbalance in authority and responsibility currently exists, and businesspeople either have to accept more responsibility or give clearer mandates and directives to IT managers so that they can handle the long-term issues through a less ambiguous and conflicted political process. Delegation impedes integration and architecture.

Interdependence with Organizational Change and Learning

Not all interdependencies are technical. Many applications of IT presuppose significant changes in how work is done and in the attitudes, skills, expectations, and understanding of the people who do it. Currently, there is one computer workstation for roughly every 20 workers in the United States. The projected ratio in most industries is one for every two or three workers well before 1990. That figure has already been reached in many companies in financial services and engineering and in information-intensive departments in manufacturing firms, such as customer service and administration.

Thus, parts of IT are directly associated with radical, not incremental, organizational change. In fact, it is more meaningful to think of the Information Age, Office of the Future, Factory of the Future, and the like as being part of a major change in the nature of work—and, hence, of workers—than as part of the computer revolution. Whenever a terminal is used to "mediate work," or telecommunication links are put in place to redistribute access to information or to reshape coordination and management control, or capital is invested to substitute technology for labor, then the work place is altered, and major adaptations are required in structures, procedures, skills, and relationships.

The whole planning process for IT should thus be viewed from the start in terms of organizational change, and resources should be committed on that basis. That rarely happens. Instead, the plans are based on installing the technology itself. The data processing "Fiasco Hall of Fame" is full of instances of how inattention to organizational, political, and behavioral issues lead to technically sound projects failing badly. There is rich literature on effective implementation that shows how to anticipate and resolve most of the causes of such failures by diagnosing organizational issues early on, piloting and phasing of change, making education and support available, creating liaison roles to bridge the cultural gap between users and builders of systems, and providing meaningful participation.

Many of these principles are now practiced by IT groups. The need for involvement and management's commitment have become part of conventional wisdom in the systems field. Building a new cadre of "hybrids" has become a priority; these are people who are fluent about technology and at least literate about the business and organizational context, or vice versa. While many technical staffs may never be fully comfortable with the less-structured context of the technology, there are very few IT managers who do not now accept that implementation must be a joint venture between technicians and "users." Many now reject the term *user* and substitute *client* or *customer*.

Even so, systems still fail for largely nontechnical reasons. Discussions of organizational change in the context of IT usually focus on "resistance." There has been an underlying assumption that workers passively or actively oppose new technology. The term *resistance* assigns responsibility to the user community. It is they who must adapt to the technology, and not to do so is to undermine it. However, implementation research puts the responsibility back on the technical staff; they have to learn how to manage the process of change and recognize the legitimacy of resistance in many instances. The implementation literature suggests that the problem is more the lack of mutual understanding and that resistance is a symptom, not a pathology; the costs of change are seen as greater than the benefits.

A deeper problem concerns the content of change, and that cannot be handled either by users or by systems developers. Both groups can learn to work together and, if most of the problems of adaptation are attitudinal or relate to a need for mutual understanding, then education, use of phases during implementation, and open channels of communication with technical staff will resolve difficulties. But managers have to ask which people will have reason to continue to resist, which ones will not be able to adapt, and which ones should be viewed as supernumaries, to be replaced or carried out of corporate charity. Answering these questions forces managers to face up to an issue that is, if not value-laden, then at least value-expressive: the intended and expected impacts of IT and the consequent trade-offs behind corporate gains and individual costs. The truism within the IT field is that technology enhances existing jobs—when management so chooses to direct its application to do so—and creates new ones. The implicit equation is:

$$\text{Technical change} + \text{Resources and time for implementation}$$
$$= \text{Learning} + \text{Economic benefits to the firm} + \text{Benefits to the worker}$$

This equation is suspect. It may be true in the aggregate for many firms, but individuals will not always gain—not even with resources for smoothing implementation and careful attention to facilitating change. The following are examples of what seem to be, if not trends, then at least more than straws in the wind:

- Every large U.S. and European organization seems to be able to reduce corporate head-office staff by 20 percent or more when IT is used as a driving element in improving productivity.

- In many craft-based industries, workers displaced by IT do not get back into the labor force. One U.S. study tracked 100 newspaper compositors over several years; close to half were unable to find work. In West Germany, 150,000 jobs have disappeared in publishing because of IT.
- In manufacturing, IT is helping reduce labor costs per unit faster than production is rising: This means a net loss of jobs.
- Study after study shows that the introduction of new systems substantially changes the power, influence, and centrality of managers and staff. The direction of change is hard to predict. The roles of some managers are reduced because they are little more than information coordinators and message switchers; now they are bypassed. Others' positions are enhanced as the technology strengthens their roles as monitors or overseers. In general, though, it is clear that middle-level staff are under pressure from the diffusion of IT, and it is a little hard to see where, why, and how they should get involved, learn, and adapt.

These changes create stress and personal loss for some people. That does not mean changes must be avoided. Head-count reduction, improved information flows, and elimination of unnecessary bureaucracy are attractive economic benefits and part of the increasing contribution IT makes to business. The cost-benefit equation is complex and certainly, in some instances, the firm's benefits are complemented by gains for most of its staff. Whatever the consequences, though, management has to take direct responsibility for both deciding on the content of change implicit in IT and for making sure the process of change is as smooth as is reasonably possible.

Requirements for New Skills in Applying Technology

Just as technology presupposes changes in the work units affected by its introduction, it also requires new skills on the part of those who bring about change. The world of data processing remained fairly stable between the early 1960s and early 1980s, in terms of knowledge, techniques, and career paths. The key roles were technical, and the main promotion path led from computer programmer/analyst to project leader to manager. Little cross-fertilization occurred between technical and business units.

That lack of intercommunication is changing at a pace that no IT unit can keep up with. Differentiated technologies and applications require highly differentiated skills, many of which involve an unusual mix of up-to-date technical knowledge and organizational experience; the first implies relative youth and a strong technical background and the other implies technical obsolescence and some level of maturation. Managing IT now means far more than just project administration and supervision of technical work.

A shortage of good IT staff in the traditional skills of applications development, systems programming, and such technical specialties as database management and telecommunications has always existed. However, the problem of finding new specialists for emerging (or rather exploding) technical fields and people who can operate effectively at the boundaries between the technical and business world are exponentially more difficult. It is no exaggeration to say that in any large firm one needs to remove only five key people from the IT unit to bring its strategic developments to a halt.

At the same time, the blockage to the introduction of IT is no longer the "user" community but the middle-level ranks of data processing. These are, on the whole (but obviously with exceptions), the people who were at first locked into a narrow view of IT and its applications and now are confronted with a set of technical skills and a knowledge base that is rapidly becoming obsolete. The longer-term planning issues for IT center on architecture and integration. The most immediate ones concern human resources development: forecasting people's needs; recruiting and retaining key staff members; identifying new roles, jobs, and skills; and cultivating real managers, rather than just senior technicians.

For now these issues are mainly a problem for managers of the IT function. But a new issue has now been added to the broader agenda: What type of organization and people should direct the deployment of IT, since it affects more and more aspects of the business and determines organizational climate and management style? IT managers have to work within the constraints of head counts, budgets, existing job descriptions, and supply of and demand for particular skills. They are not experts on either organizational change and development or human resources planning—in fact, their distinctive analytic skills generally mean that they have difficulty handling "people" issues.

Therefore, IT managers will need help from senior management. One consequence of delegation as a strategy has been isolation, psychologically and organizationally, of just about every aspect of the units responsible for IT. Isolation can be ended only when senior managers take a much more active role in choices about IT application, and when managers help to break down the barriers between technicians and business people. One urgent need is systematic cross-fertilization. Many IT units are encouraging the transfer of their own people into other departments. There has to be movement in the other direction, too.

The cost of retaining the existing management process for IT is that old mistakes will be repeated. Technical factors will drive planning and delivery. Well-intentioned technicians will make elementary mistakes about business and organizational factors that will create business and organizational consequences. Senior managers will try other forms of delegation. IT will remain a force as much for disruption as for positive economic and organizational change.

IT AND MANAGERIAL VALUES

Clemenceau's statement that war is too important to leave to generals can be applied to IT. Organizational change is too important to leave to technical specialists. Just as Lincoln's or Roosevelt's strategies for war needed first-rate field commanders, the deployment of IT has to rely on first-rate technical staff, but managers have to take over at the policy and planning level. The hidden dimensions of IT—time, intellectual assumptions and analytical techniques, technical interdependencies, interdependence with change and learning, and the new skill base for applying IT—all demand senior-level management's awareness and then senior-management's policy decisions.

Recognizing the hidden dimensions of IT forces managers to acknowledge the value-expressive, rather than value-free, nature of their decisions. The dimensions are a reminder of just how much lies under the visible iceberg, and how the technical product and the vendor's advertisements are only part of the issue. The human element is not peripheral but central to the choices about and impacts of IT. The full calculus of benefits and costs is distorted when the hidden dimensions are overlooked, but managerial responsibility and self-interest alike require that they be considered from the start. Ignoring them increases the likelihood that an application will not bring the expected payoffs or that the organizational costs will be painful and inequitable.

As long as managers are not fluent about IT, the technical factors will drive decision making and, in many instances, technical people will control the management debate. They will tend to understate the importance of the nontechnical dimensions, either for professional reasons or because of their specialized perspective and generally rationalist conception of organizational needs and processes. They have no reason to act otherwise. Their skills are unusual and come from an intense and highly focused training. Their role is to direct the deployment of the technology, not to worry about highly ambiguous and contentious business and organizational problems. It is not up to them to make business decisions and relieve managers of responsibility.

As long as computers were seen as strange and incomprehensible and managers were largely uninformed and lacked confidence in this area, delegation was the only practical strategy. The organizational impacts of IT over the past decade have been fairly limited, and managers have had little direct contact with computers. They could proceed in their careers without having to get involved in decisions about IT. Even now, they can evade involvement. But they must not be allowed to remain on the sidelines. Information technology has the potential to reshape office and factory landscapes and to alter the entire climate and culture of firms. In some industries, it is close to impossible to define a business strategy that does not rest on, or at least lean against, IT. Managerial choices about IT matter, and they will either reflect explicit values or take them by default from vendors' and technical specialists' more unidimensional frame of reference. The stakes involved in making choices are high—no less than the economic and organizational health of the firm.

26 *IT in the 1990s: Managing Organizational Interdependence**

John F. Rockart
James E. Short

For the past two decades, the question of what impact information technology (IT) will have on business organizations has continued to puzzle academics and practitioners alike. Indeed, in an era when the business press has widely disseminated the idea that IT is changing the way businesses operate and the way they relate to customers and suppliers, the question of technology's impact on the organization itself has gained renewed urgency.

The literature suggests four major classes of impact. First, there is the view that technology changes many facets of the organization's *internal structure,* affecting roles, power, and hierarchy. A second body of literature focuses on the emergence of *team-based,* problem-focused, often-changing work groups, supported by electronic communications, as the primary organizational form.

Third, there is the view that organizations today are "*disintegrating*"— their borders punctured by the steadily decreasing costs of electronic interconnection among firms, suppliers, and customers. Companies, it is believed, will gradually shift to more market-based organizational forms, with specialized firms taking over many functions formerly performed within the hierarchical firm.

---

* Source: Reprinted from "IT in the 1990s: Managing Organizational Interdependence" by John F. Rockart and James E. Short, *Sloan Management Review,* Winter 1989, pp. 7–16, by permission of the publisher. Copyright 1989 by the Sloan Management Review Association. All rights reserved.

Finally, a fourth view of organizational change arises from a technical perspective. Here, it is argued that today's improved communications capability and data accessibility will lead to *systems integration* within the business. This, in turn, will lead to vastly improved group communications and, more important, the integration of business processes across traditional functional, product, or geographic lines.

While each of these four "IT impact" perspectives offers important insights, there are significant and unresolved questions about each. To shed additional light on this issue, the Center for Information Systems Research (CISR) at the MIT Sloan School of Management recently conducted a 14-month study of 16 major companies. Emerging from this study is the strong belief that the current "IT impacts" picture is incomplete. There is clear evidence for a fifth viewpoint that draws on and expands these perspectives, providing a more integrated, managerial view with important implications for today's executives.

We will argue here that information technology provides a new approach to one of management's oldest organizational problems: that of effectively *managing interdependence*. Our fundamental thesis is that a firm's ability to continuously improve the effectiveness of managing interdependence is the critical element in responding to new and pressing competitive forces. Unlike in previous eras, managerial strategies based on optimizing operations *within* functional departments, product lines, or geographical organizations simply will not be adequate in the future.

By "effective management of interdependence," we mean a firm's ability to achieve concurrence of effort along multiple dimensions of the organization.[1] Companies have historically been divided into subunits along several dimensions, such as functional departments, product lines, and geographic units. It has long been understood that the activities in each of these dimensions, and in each of the subunits *within* these dimensions (e.g., branch offices, manufacturing locations), are far from independent. Many approaches have been devised to manage this evident interdependence. Each approach has the goal of producing the concurrence of effort necessary to allow the organization to compete effectively in the marketplace. Information technology has now been added to these approaches—and it is in this role that it will have its major impact on the firm.

COMPETITIVE FORCES DRIVING THE NEED TO MANAGE INTERDEPENDENCE

The need to effectively coordinate the activities of individual organizational subunits is vastly greater in 1989 than it was even a few years ago. Competitive pressures are now forcing almost all major firms to become global in scope, to decrease time to market, and to redouble their efforts to manage risk, service, and cost on a truly international scale (see Figure 1).

FIGURE 1   What Is Pushing the Need to Manage Interdependence?

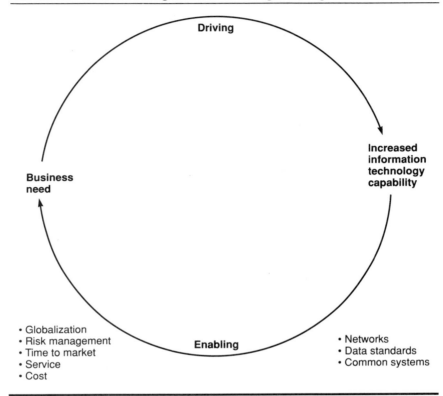

- *Globalization.* In a world linked by international communication networks and television, global competition stresses the firm's ability to innovate, to capture global levels of manufacturing efficiency, and to understand international marketing and the diversity of the world's markets. All require increasing knowledge and coordination of the firm's operations throughout geographically dispersed subunits.
- *Time to market.* Black & Decker now brings new products to market in half the time it took before 1985. Xerox and Ford have claimed similar improvements in key product lines. "Time to market" refers to the firm's ability to develop new products quickly and to deliver existing products effectively. In either case, compressing time to market requires increased integration of effort among functional departments, such as design, engineering, manufacturing, purchasing, distribution, and service.
- *Risk management.* Market volatility and competitive pressures can easily overwhelm a firm's ability to track and manage its risk. In one highly publicized incident, Merrill Lynch lost more than $250 million when it

failed to adequately oversee an employee trading a complex form of mortgage-backed securities.[2] Whatever the industry, the globalization of markets and global market volatility increase the need for effective risk management across once independently managed operations.

- *Service.* "The excellent companies really are close to their customers," Peters and Waterman wrote in *The Search for Excellence.* "Other companies talk about it; the excellent companies do it."[3] Of course, service is based not only on the effectiveness of a single repairperson, but also on management's ability to have organizationwide knowledge of customer's and equipment's status and problems.

- *Cost.* For nearly all organizations, cost reduction is always a concern. In industries where foreign competitors are becoming dominant, reductions in workforce are an increasing reality.

In sum, global competition, risk, service, and cost today require firms to tightly couple their core internal and external business processes. As firms begin to draw these processes together, slack resources (e.g., inventory, redundant personnel) are being reduced.

It is here that information technology plays a major role. Vastly improved communications capability and more cost-effective computer hardware and software enable the "wiring" together of individuals and suborganizations within the single firm, and of firms to each other. It is this multifunctional, multilevel, multiorganizational, coordinative aspect of current technology that provides managers with a new approach to managing interdependence effectively.

TECHNOLOGY'S MAJOR IMPACTS ON THE ORGANIZATION

Several decades of work have produced conflicting perspectives on technology's impacts on the organization. Here we briefly review the four approaches noted above.

Major Changes in Managerial Structure, Roles, and Processes

In an early, celebrated article, Leavitt and Whisler argued that information technology would lead to a general restructuring of the organization, ultimately eliminating middle management.[4] In their view, IT moved middle managers out of traditional roles, and allowed top managers to take on an even larger portion of the innovating, planning, and other "creative" functions required to run the business.

Others were quick to comment on these predictions. Some speculated that IT would lead to greater organizational centralization, greater decentralization, reduced layers of middle or upper management, greater centralization of managerial power, or, alternatively, decentralization of managerial power.[5] Others developed contingency-based models of organizational impact.[6] While it is clear that IT has affected organizations in many ways, it is also clear that this often conflicting literature has produced very little insight into how managers should plan for IT-enabled role or structural changes within their firms. Three newer perspectives begin to address this issue.

"The Team as Hero"

According to this second view, teams and other ad hoc decision-making structures will provide the basis for a permanent organizational form. Reich, for example, argues that a "collective entrepreneurship," with few middle-level managers and only modest differences between senior managers and junior employees, is developing.[7] Drucker speculates that the symphony orchestra or hospital may be models of future team-based organizations.[8]

The relationship between teams and technology in much of this work appears based on a technical dimension. On the one hand, this view stresses technology's role in enabling geographically dispersed groups to better coordinate their activities through enhanced electronic communications.[9] On the other hand, some authors stress the importance of "groupware" in facilitating teamwork through better decision-making aids and project and problem management.[10]

Unfortunately, the team-based literature to date is highly speculative. As a general model of organizational structure, it leaves many questions unanswered. Primary among these are the long-term implications of organizing in a manner that moves primary reporting relationships away from the more usual hierarchical functional, geographic, or product structures. These structures work to immerse employees in pools of "front line," continually renewed expertise. Team members separated too long from these bases tend to lose their expertise.[11]

Corporate "Disintegration": More Markets and Less Hierarchy

A third perspective argues that today's hierarchical organizations are steadily disintegrating—their borders punctured by the combined effects of electronic communication (greatly increased flows of information), electronic brokerage (technology's ability to connect many different buyers and suppliers instantaneously through a central database), and electronic integration (tighter coupling between interorganizational processes). In this view, the main effect of technology on organizations is not in how tasks are performed (faster, better, cheaper, etc.), but rather in how firms organize the flow of goods and services through value-added chains.

There are two major threads to this argument. Malone, Yates, and Benjamin state that new information technologies will allow closer integration of adjacent steps in the value-added chain through the development of electronic markets and electronic hierarchies.[12] Johnston and Lawrence argue that IT-enabled value-adding partnerships (VAPs) are rapidly emerging.[13] Typified by McKesson Corporation's "Economist" drug distribution service, VAPs are groups of small companies that share information freely and view the whole value-added chain—not just part of it—as one competitive unit.

These proposals, however, are very recent and have only small amounts of sample data to support them. And the opposite case—the case for increased, vertical integration of firms—is also being strongly propounded.[14]

Systems Integration: Common Systems and Data Architecture

A fourth, more technically oriented view is that business integration is supported by systems and data integration. Here the concept of IT-enabled organizational integration is presented as a natural outgrowth of two IT properties: improved interconnection and improved shared data accessibility.[15] In this view, "integration" refers to integration of data, of organizational communications (with emphasis on groups), and of business processes across functional, geographic, or product lines.

THE NEED TO MANAGE INTERDEPENDENCE

While each of these four approaches offers important insights, there is a need for a fifth perspective that expands these views into a more active managerial framework. Our research suggests that the concept of "managing interdependence" most clearly reflects what managers *actually do* in today's business organizations.

Managers, of course, oversee innumerable large and small interdependencies. What happens in one function affects another. Although companies maintain "independent" product lines, success or failure in one product line casts a long shadow on the others. Individual specialists are also highly interdependent. Surgeons, for example, cannot operate without nurses, technicians, and anesthetists. And even the simplest of manufacturing processes requires the precise interconnection of hundreds of steps. Other examples:

- Production engineers rely on product designers to design parts that can be easily and quickly fabricated. Conversely, designers depend on product engineers to implement design concepts faithfully.
- Sales representatives for a nationwide or a worldwide company are also

interdependent. The same large customer may be served by many sales offices throughout the world. Common discounts, contract terms, and service procedures must be maintained. Feedback can be important.
• Companies themselves rely on other companies to supply parts or services. The current shortage of memory chips, and the resulting shortage of some types of computer hardware, is a good example of intra-company interdependence.

In sum, interdependence is a fact of organizational life. What is different today, however, is the increasing need to manage interdependence, as well as technology's role in providing tools to help meet this need.

How do companies today manage interdependence? Several approaches have been proposed. Mintzberg, for example, argued that firms coordinate work through five basic mechanisms: mutual adjustment, direct supervision, standardization of work process, standardization of work output, and standardization of worker skills.[16] Lawrence and Lorsch found that successful companies differentiated themselves into suborganizations to allow accumulation of expertise and simpler management processes driven by shared goals and objectives.[17] Conversely, these same successful firms adopted integrating mechanisms to coordinate work activity across suborganizations. Lawrence and Lorsch postulated five mechanisms to manage the needed integration: integrative departments, whose primary activity was to coordinate effort among *functional* departments; permanent and/or temporary cross-functional teams; reliance on direct management contact at all levels of the firm; integration through the formal hierarchy; and integration via a "paper-based system" of information exchange.

Galbraith later expanded the intellectual understanding of managing integration through people-oriented mechanisms.[18] He noted that direct contact, liaison roles, task forces, and teams were used primarily for lateral relations, permitting companies to make more decisions and process more information without overloading hierarchical communication channels. He also introduced the concept of computer-based information systems as a vertical integrator within the firm.

FIVE EXAMPLES OF MANAGING INTERDEPENDENCE

Today, Galbraith's vision of computer-based information systems as a *vertical* integrator appears prescient, if incomplete. Given pressures from the "drivers" noted earlier, major aspects of information technology (networks, for example; see Figure 1) serve increasingly as mechanisms for both horizontal and vertical integration. In particular, our work has uncovered six organizational contexts where IT-enabled integration efforts strikingly improved a company's ability to manage its functional, product, or geographic subunits. We focus here on five of the six contexts, as illustrated in Figure 2. (A sixth area of interest, interorganizational integration, is well documented in the literature, and can be viewed as carrying intra-organizational integration into the multifirm context.[19])

Value-Chain Integration

Lawrence and Lorsch noted the use of ''human integrators'' to manage concurrence of effort between adjacent functions in the value-added chain (e.g., between manufacturing, distribution, and sales) more than 20 years ago. Today this integration is performed increasingly by using electronic networks, computers, and databases. Firms attempt between-function integration for at least one of three reasons: to increase their capacity to respond quickly and effectively to market forces; to improve the quality of conformance to customer requirements; or to reduce costs.[20]

We have found that successful between-function integration collapses the multistage value-added chain into three major segments: developing new products, delivering products to customers, and managing customer

---

FIGURE 2 Managing Interdependence in Five Organizational Contexts

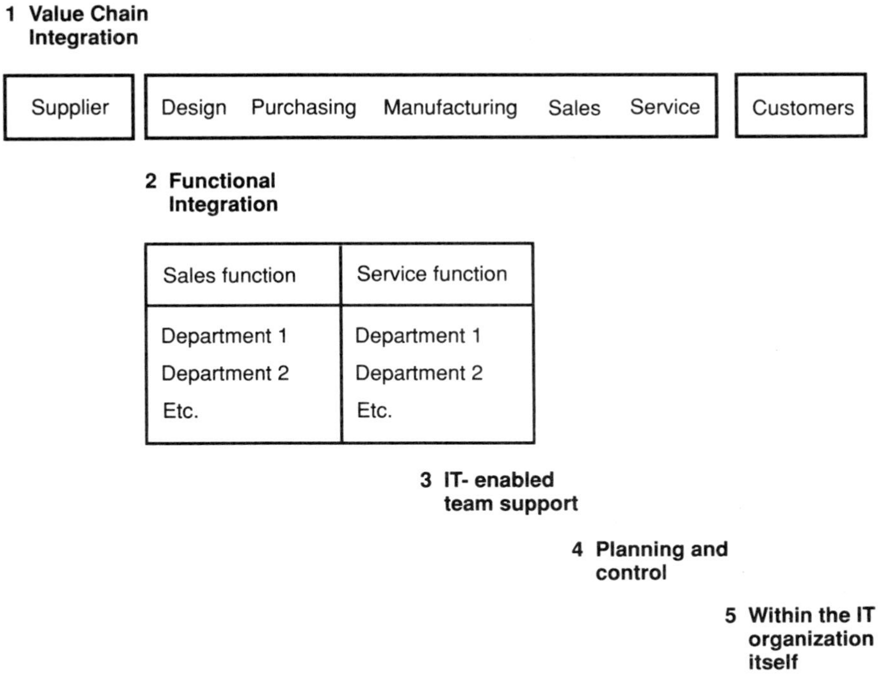

1 Value Chain Integration

Supplier	Design Purchasing Manufacturing Sales Service	Customers

2 Functional Integration

Sales function	Service function
Department 1	Department 1
Department 2	Department 2
Etc.	Etc.

3 IT- enabled team support

4 Planning and control

5 Within the IT organization itself

relationships (see Figure 3).[21] In manufacturing companies, for example, it is clear that interdependence revolves around these three macro-organizational activities. In the insurance industry, discussions with five major companies revealed that the same three segments were targets for functional integration.

Turning to the two "ends" of the modified value-added chain—the product design segment on the one end, and the customer service segment on the other—the effects of technology-enabled integration are clear. To speed *product development,* companies such as Xerox, Lockheed, and Digital are introducing CAD/CAM and other design aids that provide integrated support to product designers, product engineers, materials purchasing, and manufacturing personnel involved in the design-to-production process. This compression has resulted in joint "buy-in" on new product designs, eliminating a lengthy iterative development process (which occurred because designers did not take the needs and capabilities of other departments into account). Dramatically shortened product development time has been the consequence of this buy-in.

At the *customer service* end of the chain, Otis Elevator, Digital, and Xerox have developed service strategies and new service markets based on electronic networks, an integrated database of customer and service history, and fault signaling that goes directly from the damaged equipment to the supplier's maintenance-monitoring computer. The advantages of Otis's centrally coordinated electronic service system have been well publicized.[22] Perhaps the most important advantage is senior managment's ability to view the status of maintenance efforts nationwide and to direct sales and service attention where needed. In addition, it is now feasible to

FIGURE 3   Product Development, Product Delivery, and Customer Service and Management: Collapsing the Value-Added Chain

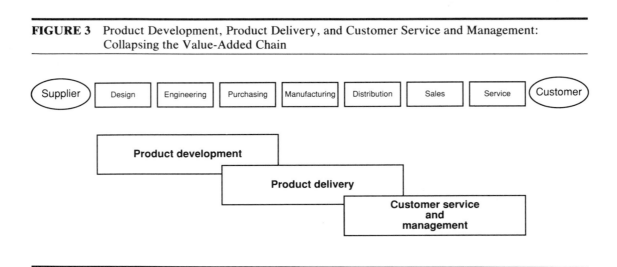

provide the company's design, engineering, and manufacturing personnel with direct access to fault data.

In many ways the most interesting stage of the collapsed value chain is *product delivery,* which requires integrating several different information systems: order entry, purchasing, materials resources planning, and distribution management. The critical business issues are to provide customers with information about when orders will be completed, and to forecast and manage outside supplier, product manufacturer, and product distribution processes.

No company has yet accomplished the large-scale integration of functions and systems required to fully manage product delivery. A division of the Norton Company, however, pioneered efforts in this direction in the mid-1980s. Norton initiated a set of major IT projects, ranging from the "Norton Connection" (a computer-based telecommunications link between the company and its distributors), to a more effective order processing system, to a series of manufacturing technologies targeted at flexible manufacturing and automated materials control.[23] More recently, Westinghouse initiated a product delivery integration process in several segments of the company. And at General Foods a series of task forces has been charged with developing a similar approach.

Most efforts, however, are more limited in scope. British Petroleum Company's chemical business has developed an integrated order management process spanning 13 divisions. Baxter Healthcare Corporation is working to enhance its well-known ASAP order entry system to provide customers with full product line visibility to their 125,000-plus products. And a host of manufacturing integration projects have been initiated at Digital Equipment Corporation, Ford Motor, IBM, General Motors, Hewlett-Packard, and Texas Instruments, to name just a few.

Functional Integration

Many companies are also recognizing the interdependence of multiple units *within* the same function. This recognition has led to several actions designed to improve coordination across subunits—for example, centralization of functions, central management of geographically separate units, and (in some firms) the development of common systems and/or standard data definitions to facilitate coordinating organizational units.

At Sun Refining and Marketing Company, for example, senior management identified crude oil trading as one of the most critical business activities in the firm three years ago. At that point, Sun's traders were dispersed worldwide, each acting relatively autonomously. Sun began developing a centralized, on-line trading function supported by integrated market information from Reuters and other trade data sources. Today, Sun recognizes the importance of its integrated trading function in managing risk exposure and in developing effective pricing strategies for the volatile crude market.

At Chemical Bank in New York, foreign exchange trading has become the largest profit generator. To improve management of its worldwide trading operations, Chemical's information technology efforts have ranged from advanced trader work stations to more effective integration of the "front end" (booking a transaction) with the back office (transaction clearance and settlement). The bank has also improved capital markets auditing through the use of expert systems support.

And finally, while OTISLINE can be viewed as an application enabling integration across stages of the value-added chain, it is also an integrating mechanism within the field maintenance organization itself. Customers with difficult problems can immediately be directed to a specialist, not left to the limited resources of a remote branch office. Frequent trouble from a specific type of elevator can be observed as the pattern develops, and corrective action taken on a nationwide basis. In addition, the quality of telephone responsiveness to anxious customers can be closely monitored.

Similarly, a number of other companies are working aggressively to coordinate the efforts of subunits within a single function, whether it be manufacturing, maintenance, purchasing, sales and marketing, or others. Kodak has developed an executive support system to assist in the worldwide scheduling of manufacturing plants. Digital is installing common MRP systems throughout all of its manufacturing plants. And so it goes. The business drivers underscoring each of these efforts range from service to cost to time-to-market to global responsiveness—but they all recognize that no single unit in a major function is truly independent.

IT-Enabled Team Support

Ken Olsen, chairman of Digital Equipment Corporation, believes that the ability to bring teams together electronically is one of the most important features of the company's IT capability. Ford Motor has claimed that the "Team Taurus" approach, much of it IT-enabled, shaved more than a year off the time needed to develop, build, and bring to market the new Taurus/ Sable model line. In the future, as Drucker points out, many tasks will be done primarily by teams.[24]

Teamwork, of course, is not a new way to coordinate interdependent activities among separate units in an organization. What *is* new is that electronic mail, computer conferencing, and videoconferencing now facilitate this process. Today, it is feasible for team members to coordinate asynchronously (across time zones) and geographically (across remote locations) more easily than ever before.

The development and use of computer software to support teams is also moving into an explosive phase. There is a growing body of software labeled *groupware,* a generic name for specialized computer aids designed to support collaborative work groups. As Bullen and Johansen point out, "Groupware is not a thing. Rather, it is a perspective on computing that emphasizes collaboration—rather than individual use."[25] Several companies, including Xerox, General Motors, Digital, Eastman Kodak, IBM, and AT&T, are experimenting with state-of-the-art meeting and conferencing aids in addition to more "routine" communications systems such as electronic mail or voice mail systems.

Planning and Control

For the past two or three decades, the managerial control process has looked much the same across major companies.[26] Before a new fiscal year begins, an intense planning process culminates with an extended presentation to senior management of each small business unit's (SBU's) proposed activities. Agreed-upon plans are then monitored on a monthly basis. Parallel to this formal control process is an informal system of "keeping in touch," by which senior management assures itself that "all is going well" in key areas of the business in the interim between formal reports.

Volatility in the business environment, coupled with technology's ability to provide management with efficient communication and information, is radically changing this traditional planning and control scenario. The major issue is how best to use IT for coordination and control of the firm's activities.

At Xerox, chairman David Kearns and president Paul Allaire have implemented an executive support system that now makes the annual planning and control process a more on-line, team-based, communication- and coordination-based process. The system requires all of Xerox's 34 business units to submit their plans over an electronic network in a particular format. Doing this allows the staff to critique the plans more effectively and to reintegrate these plans when looking for such factors as competitive threats across all SBUs, penetration into particular industries by all SBUs, and so forth.

More important, each SBU's plans can be reviewed not only by senior executives and corporate staff but also by other top officers in the firm. Each officer receiving an SBU's plans is encouraged to send corporate headquarters an electronic message raising the issues he or she sees in the plan. The officer may also be asked to attend the review meeting. There is no "upfront" presentation at this meeting. Only the issues raised by the executives, the staff, or the other officers are discussed.

In short, Allaire's planning and control process is a computer-age process. Through the network, it draws on the entire executive team for input. Understanding of the important issues facing each SBU is deeper and its activities are, therefore, sometimes subtly, sometimes more precisely, coordinated with those of the other SBUs.

A team-based, network-linked approach to the senior executive job of managing the business is also in evidence at Phillips Petroleum Company's Products and Chemicals Group. There, executive vice president Robert Wallace is linked to his other top nine executives through an executive support system that provides on-line access not only to one another but also to varying levels of daily sales, refinery, and financial data. External news summaries relevant to the business are entered into the system three times a day. Unlike Allaire, who limits his input to planning and review meetings, Wallace has used the system to take operating command of a few critical decisions for the business. In the volatile petroleum pricing arena, Wallace believes that he and his top executive team can confer with the advantage of data access and can make better pricing decisions than those further down the line. He cites increased profits in the tens of millions as a result of the system.

By far the majority of senior executives today do not use their systems in nearly as dramatic a manner as Allaire and Wallace do.[27] Yet the technology provides the capability for better coordination at the senior management level. It also provides opportunities to move decisions either up or down in the organization. Team decision making is a growing reality, as geographically separated executives can concurrently access and assess data and communicate in "real time." Vertical on-line access to lower levels of data and text, however, violates some established management practices. Yet informal telephone-based systems have always provided some of this information. In an era where management is seen more as a cooperative, coaching activity than as an iron-fisted one, vertical as well as horizontal networking may come of age.

Within the IT Organization Itself

Line managers and information technology managers are also finding themselves more mutually dependent than ever before. Today, there is a small but rapidly growing number of senior line and staff executives who are taking responsibility for significant strategic projects centered on computer and communication technologies in their companies, divisions, or departments. We have described elsewhere the full extent and importance of "the line taking the leadership."[28]

As the line role is growing with regard to innovative systems, the role of the information systems group is becoming more complex, more demanding, and more integrated into the business. Our sample of companies included several firms whose IT planning efforts involved significant degrees of partnership between the line businesses and their IT organizations in designing and implementing new systems.[29] This necessary degree of partnership places four major demands on the IT organization.

First, with regard to systems development, even those systems in which the line is heavily involved require greater competence and skills on the part of the IT organization. The technical design, programming, and operation of business-critical, complex systems present a far greater challenge than do systems of previous eras. Today's integrated, cross-functional product delivery systems require database, project management, telecommunications, and other skills not previously demanded of IT personnel.

Second, today's new systems require the development and implementation of a general, and eventually "seamless," information technology infrastructure (computers, telecommunications, software, and data). The challenge to IT management is to provide leadership for this vital set of "roads and highways" in a volatile competitive environment.

Third, there is a need for IT management to help educate line management to its new responsibilities. And fourth, IT executives must educate themselves and their staffs in all significant aspects of the business. Only if this happens will IT personnel be able to knowledgeably assist line management in creating effective, strategy-enhancing systems.

The concomitant demand on line management is twofold: the need to learn enough about the technology to incorporate its capabilities into business plans, and the need to select effective information technology personnel and to work closely with them.

THE NEW MANAGERIAL AGENDA: THINK INTERDEPENDENCE

Tomorrow's successful corporations will require increasingly effective management of interdependence. IT-enabled changes in cross-functional integration, in the use of teams, or in within-function integration will force individual managers' agendas to change as well. In short, what managers do now and what they will do in the future is in the process of important change.

Dimensions of Change

What areas of emphasis for senior managers stem from the increasing interdependence of organizations? In our view, there are five.

- *Increased role complexity.* The typical manager's job is getting harder. One dimension of this difficulty is in the increased pace of organizational change. As companies seek new business opportunities by aggressively defining and executing "new ways of doing things"—for example, new strategies, new products and services, new customers—managers must adjust more rapidly and frequently to new situations. Similarly, companies must also respond to heightened competitive pressures by improving internal processes. Again, managers must respond quickly to these new situations.

A second dimension of increased role complexity is the manager's need to cope with unclear lines of authority and decision making. As interdependence increases, sharing of tasks, roles, and decision making increases. Managers will be faced with making the difficult calls between what is local to their function and what is global to the business. Moreover, as planning and control sytems change, line managers must work more effectively with a wider range of people in the firm.

- *Teamwork.* Teams are real. A vastly increased number of space- and time-spanning, problem-focused, task-oriented teams are becoming the norm. This growth in peer-to-peer (as opposed to hierarchical) activities requires new managerial skills and role definitions.

- *A changing measurement process.* Measurement sytems are also changing. Measuring individual, team, or suborganizational success is difficult in an environment where cooperative work is increasingly necessary. New measurement approaches will have to be devised. A transitional period, during which people will need to adjust both to a changing work mode and to a changing measurement process, will result. As new measurement systems evolve, they will almost surely lag behind the changed organizational reality.

- *A changing planning process.* Information technology is enabling the new planning approaches required to meet new competitive conditions. Our research underscores two major new capabilities. First, better information access and information management allow firms to target what is most critical to the organization. Second, organizations now have the ability to conduct "real-time," stimulus-driven planning at all levels—in short, to bring key issues to the surface and react to them quickly. The technology provides both the conduit for moving critical data to all relevant decision makers and more important, the capability to disseminate changes in direction to all parts of the firm.

- *Creating an effective information technology infrastructure.* People-intensive, integrative mechanisms are limited in what they can accomplish. Accessible, well-defined data and a transparent network are, therefore, the keys to effective integration in the coming years. Developing these resources, however, is not easy. Justifying organization-spanning networks whose benefits are uncertain and will occur in the future, and whose costs cannot be attributed clearly to any specific suborganization, is in part an act of faith. Developing common coding systems and data definitions is a herculean job. This task increases short-term costs for long-term gain—a practice not encouraged by most of today's measurement systems.

NOTES

The authors wish to acknowledge the contributions of colleagues Christine V. Bullen, J. Debra Hofman, and John C. Henderson, Center for Information Systems Research, MIT Sloan School of Management, to the research on which this article is based.

1. A precise definition of "interdependence" has generated considerable disagreement among students of organizational behavior. An early and influential view is contained in J. D. Thompson, *Organizations in Action: Social Science Bases of Administrative Theory* (New York: McGraw-Hill, 1967).

   Also see critiques of Thompson's work by: J. E. McCann and D. L. Ferry, "An Approach for Assessing and Managing Inter-Unit Interdependence—Note," *Academy of Management Journal* 4 (1979), pp. 113–19; and B. Victor and R. S. Blackburn, "Interdependence: An Alternative Conceptualization," *Academy of Management Journal* 12 (1987), pp. 486–98.

2. "The Big Loss at Merrill Lynch: Why It Was Blindsided," *Business Week,* 18 May 1987, pp. 112–13.

   See also "Bankers Trust Restatement Tied to Trading Style," *New York Times,* 22 July 1988, p. D2.

3. T. J. Peters and R. H. Waterman, Jr., *In Search of Excellence* (New York: Harper & Row, 1982), p. 156.

4. H. J. Leavitt and T. L. Whisler, "Management in the 1980s," *Harvard Business Review,* November–December 1958, pp. 41–48.

5. For more on organizational centralization, see: M. Anshen, "The Manager and the Black Box," *Harvard Business Review,* November–December 1960, pp. 85–92; T. L. Whisler, *The Impact of Computers on Organizations* (New York: Praeger, 1970); I. Russakoff Hoos, "When the Computer Takes over the Office," *Harvard Business Review,* July–August 1960, pp. 102–12.

   Also see D. Robey, "Systems and Organizational Structure," *Communications of the ACM* 24 (1981), pp. 679–87.

   On organizational decentralization, *see* J. F. Burlingame, "Information Technology and Decentralization," *Harvard Business Review,* November–December 1961, pp. 121–26; *also see* J. L. King, "Centralized versus Decentralized Computing: Organizational Considerations and Management Options," *Computing Surveys* 15 (1983), pp. 319–49.

   On reduced layers of middle or upper management, *see* C. A. Myers, ed., *The Impact of Computers on Management* (Cambridge, Mass.: MIT Press, 1967), pp. 1–15.

   On greater centralization of managerial power, *see* A. M. Pettigrew, "Information Control as a Power Resource," *Sociology* 6

(1972), pp. 187–204; J. Pfeffer, *Power in Organizations* (Marshfield, Mass.: Pitman, 1981); and M. L. Markus and J. Pfeffer, "Power and the Design and Implementation of Accounting and Control Systems," *Accounting, Organizations and Society* 8 (1983), pp. 205–18.

On decentralization of managerial power, *see* S. R. Klatsky, "Automation, Size and the Locus of Decision Making: The Cascade Effect," *Journal of Business* 43 (1970), pp. 141–51.

6. Carroll and Perin argue that what managers and employees *expect* from technology is an important predictor of the consequences observed.

    See J. S. Carroll and C. Perin, "How Expectations about Microcomputers Influence Their Organizational Consequences" (Cambridge, Mass.: MIT Sloan School of Management, Management in the 1990s, working paper 90s:88–044, April 1988).

    Similarly, Invernizzi found that the effectiveness of the process used to introduce technology into the organization strongly influenced its ultimate impact. *See* E. Invernizzi, "Information Technology: From Impact on to Support for Organizational Design" (Cambridge, Mass.: MIT Sloan School of Management, Management in the 1990s, working paper 90s:88–057, September 1988).

7. R. B. Reich, "Entrepreneurship Reconsidered: The Team as Hero," *Harvard Business Review,* May–June 1987, pp. 77–83.

8. P. F. Drucker, "The Coming of the New Organization," *Harvard Business Review,* January–February 1988, pp. 45–53.

9. M. Hammer and G. E. Mangurian, "The Changing Value of Communications Technology," *Sloan Management Review,* Winter 1987, pp. 65–72.

10. C. V. Bullen and R. R. Johansen, "Groupware: A Key to Managing Business Teams?" (Cambridge, Mass.: MIT Sloan School of Management, Center for Information Systems Research, working paper No. 169, May 1988).

11. O. Hauptman and T. J. Allen, "The Influence of Communication Technologies on Organizational Structure: A Conceptual Model for Future Research" (Cambridge, Mass.: MIT Sloan School of Management, Management in the 1990s, working paper 90s:87–038, May 1987).

12. T. W. Malone, J. Yates, and R. I. Benjamin, "Electronic Markets and Electronic Hierarchies," *Communications of the ACM* 30 (1987), pp. 484–97.

13. R. Johnston and P. R. Lawrence, "Beyond Vertical Integration—The Rise of the Value-Adding Partnership," *Harvard Business Review,* July–August 1988, pp. 94–104.

14. T. Kumpe and P. T. Bolwijn, "Manufacturing: The New Case for Vertical Integration," *Harvard Business Review,* March–April 1988, pp. 75–81.

15. R. I. Benjamin and M. S. Scott Morton, "Information Technology, Integration, and Organizational Change" (Cambridge, Mass.: MIT Sloan School of Management, Center for Information Systems Research, working paper No. 138, April 1986).

    Also see S. Kiesler, "The Hidden Message in Computer Networks," *Harvard Business Review,* January–February 1986, pp. 46–60.

16. H. Mintzberg, *The Structuring of Organizations* (Englewood Cliffs, N.J.: Prentice-Hall, 1979).

17. P. R. Lawrence and J. W. Lorsch, *Organization and Environment: Managing Differentiation and Integration* (Homewood, Ill.: Richard D. Irwin, 1967).

18. J. Galbraith, *Organization Design* (Reading, Mass.: Addison-Wesley, 1977). Galbraith also introduced the concept of the organization as information processor in this work. He distinguished computer-based, vertical information systems from lateral relations and emphasized the division of organizations into suborganizations because of the need to minimize the cost of communications.

19. S. Barrett and B. R. Konsynski, "Inter-Organization Information Sharing Systems," *MIS Quarterly* 4 (1982), pp. 93–105; R. I. Benjamin, D. W. DeLong, and M. S. Scott Morton, "The Realities of Electronic Data Interchange: How Much Competitive Advantage?" (Cambridge, Mass.: MIT Sloan School of Management, Management in the 1990s, working paper 90s:87–038, February 1988).

    See also N. Venkatraman, "Changing Patterns of Interfirm Competition and Collaboration" (Cambridge, Mass.: MIT Sloan School of Management, Management in the 1990s, working paper, forthcoming).

20. On quality process management, *see* G. A. Pall, "Quality Process Management" (Thornwood, N.Y.: The Quality Improvement Education Center, IBM, 16 February 1988).

21. Although our three collapsed segments in the value chain are integral units, data does flow from one to another. The three segments are also interdependent, but less strongly so than the functions within each segment.

22. "Otis MIS: Going Up," *InformationWEEK,* 18 May 1987, pp. 32–37; J. F. Rockart, "The Line Takes the Leadership—IS Management in a Wired Society," *Sloan Management Review,* Summer 1988, pp. 57–64; W. F. McFarlan, "How Information Technology Is Changing Management Control Systems" (Boston: Harvard Business School, Case Note No. 9–187–139, 1987).

23. Rockart (1988).

24. Drucker (1988).

25. Bullen and Johansen (1988).

26. R. N. Anthony, *Planning and Control Systems: A Framework for Analysis* (Boston: Harvard University Press, 1965).

27. J. F. Rockart and D. W. DeLong, *Executive Support Systems: The Emergence of Top Mangement Computer Use* (Homewood, Ill.: Dow Jones-Irwin, 1988).

28. Rockart (1988).

29. T. J. Main and J. E. Short, "Managing the Merger: Strategic IS Planning for the New Baxter" (Cambridge, Mass.: MIT Sloan School of Management, Center for Information Systems Research, working paper No. 178, September 1988).

27 *Four Ethical Issues of the Information Age**

Richard O. Mason

Today in Western societies more people are employed collecting, handling, and distributing information than in any other occupation. Millions of computers inhabit the earth and many millions of miles of optical fiber, wire, and air waves link people, their computers, and the vast array of information-handling devices together. Our society is truly an information society, our time an information age. The question before us now is whether the kind of society being created is the one we want. It is a question that should especially concern those of us in the MIS community, for we are in the forefront of creating this new society.

There are many unique challenges we face in this age of information. They stem from the nature of information itself. Information is the means through which the mind expands and increases its capacity to achieve its goals, often as the result of an input from another mind. Thus, information forms the intellectual capital from which human beings craft their lives and secure dignity.

However, the building of intellectual capital is vulnerable in many ways. For example, people's intellectual capital is impaired whenever they lose their personal information without being compensated for it, when they are precluded access to information which is of value to them, when they have revealed information they hold intimate, or when they find out that the information upon which their living depends is in error. The social contract among people in the information age must deal with these threats

* Source: Reprinted by special permission of the *MIS Quarterly* vol. 10, no. 1, January 1986. Copyright 1986 by the Society for Information Management and the Management Information Systems Research Center at the University of Minnesota.

to human dignity. The ethical issues involved are many and varied; however, it is helpful to focus on just four. These may be summarized by means of an acronym—**PAPA.**

Privacy: What information about one's self or one's associations must a person reveal to others, under what conditions, and with what safeguards? What things can people keep to themselves and not be forced to reveal to others?

Accuracy: Who is responsible for the authenticity, fidelity, and accuracy of information? Similarly, who is to be held accountable for errors in information, and how is the injured party to be made whole?

Property: Who owns information? What are the just and fair prices for its exchange?
Who owns the channels, especially the airways, through which information is transmitted? How should access to this scarce resource be allocated?

Accessibility: What information does a person or organization have a right or a privilege to obtain, under what conditions, and with what safeguards?

PRIVACY

What information should one be required to divulge about one's self to others? Under what conditions? What information should one be able to keep strictly to one's self? These are among the questions that a concern for privacy raises. Today, more than ever, cautious citizens must be asking these questions.

Two forces threaten our privacy. One is the growth of information technology, with its enhanced capacity for surveillance, communication, computation, storage, and retrieval. A second, and more insidious threat, is the increased value of information in decision making. Information is increasingly valuable to policy makers; they covet it even if acquiring it invades another's privacy.

A case in point is the situation that occurred a few years ago in Florida. The Florida legislature believed that the state's building codes might be too stringent and that, as a result, the taxpayers were burdened by paying for buildings which were underutilized. Several studies were commissioned. In one study at the Tallahassee Community College, monitors were stationed at least one day a week in every bathroom.

Every 15 seconds, the monitor observed the usage of the toilets, mirrors, sinks, and other facilities and recorded them on a form. This data was subsequently entered into a database for further analyses. Of course, the students, faculty, and staff complained bitterly, feeling that this was an invasion of their privacy and a violation of their rights. State officials responded, however, that the study would provide valuable information for policy making. In effect the state argued that the value of the information to the administrators was greater than any possible indignities suffered by the students and others. Soon the ACLU joined the fray. At their insistence the study was stopped, but only after the state got the information it wanted.

Most invasions of privacy are not this dramatic or this visible. Rather, they creep up on us slowly as, for example, when a group of diverse files relating to a person and his or her activities are integrated into a single large database. Collections of information reveal intimate details about a person and can thereby deprive the person of the opportunity to form certain professional and personal relationships. This is the ultimate cost of an invasion of privacy. So why do we integrate databases in the first place? It is because the bringing together of disparate data makes the development of new informational relationships possible. These new relationships may be formed, however, without the affected parties' permission. You or I may have contributed information about ourselves freely to each of the separate databases, but that by itself does not amount to giving consent to someone to merge the data, especially if that merger might reveal something else about us.

Consider the study that was circulating during the early 1970s. It's probably been embellished in the retellings, but it goes something like this. It seems that a couple of programmers at the city of Chicago's computer center began matching tape files from many of the city's different data processing applications on name and I.D. They discovered, for example, that several highly paid city employers had unpaid parking fines. Bolstered by this revelation, they pressed on. Soon they uncovered the names of several employees who were still listed on the register but who had not paid a variety of fees, a few of whom appeared in the files of the alcoholic and drug abuse program. When this finding was leaked to the public, the city employees, of course, were furious. They demanded to know who had authorized the investigation. The answer was that no one knew. Later, city officials established rules for the computer center to prevent this form of invasion of privacy from happening again. In light of recent proposals to develop a central federal databank consisting of files from most U.S. government agencies, this story takes on new meaning. It shows what can happen when a group of eager computer operators or unscrupulous administrators start playing around with data.

The threat to privacy here is one that many of us don't fully appreciate. I call it the threat of exposure by *minute description*. It stems from the collection of attributes about ourselves and use of the logical connector "and." For example, I may authorize one institution to collect information "A" about me, and another institution to collect information "B" about me; but I might not want anyone to possess "A and B" about me at the same time. When "C" is added to the list of conjunctions, the possessor of the new information will know even more about me. And then "D" is added and so forth. Each additional weaving together of my attributes reveals more and more about me. In the process, the fabric that is created poses a threat to my privacy.

The threads which emanate from this foreboding fabric usually converge in personnel files and in dossiers, as Aleksandr Solzhenitsyn describes in *The Cancer Ward:*

> Every person fills out quite a few forms in his life, and each form contains an uncounted number of questions. The answer of just one person to one question in one form is already a thread linking that person forever with the local center of the dossier department. Each person thus radiates hundreds of such threads, which all together, run into the millions. If these threads were visible, the heavens would be webbed with them, and if they had substance and resilience, the buses, streetcars, and the people themselves would no longer be able to move. . . . They are neither visible, but material, but they were constantly felt by man. . . .
>
> Constant awareness of these invisible threads naturally bred respect for the people in charge of that most intricate dossier department. It bolstered their authority. [1, p. 221]*

The threads leading to Americans are many. The United States Congress's Privacy Protection Commission, chaired by David F. Linowes, estimated that there are over 8,000 different record systems in the files of the federal government that contain individually identifiable data on citizens. Each citizen, on average, has 17 files in federal agencies and administrations. Using these files, for example, Social Security data has been matched with Selective Service data to reveal draft resisters. IRS data has been matched with other administrative records to tease out possible tax evaders. Federal employment records have been matched with delinquent student loan records to identify some 46,860 federal and military employees and retirees whose paychecks might be garnished. In Massachusetts welfare officials sent tapes bearing welfare recipients' Social Security numbers to some 117 banks to find out whether the recipients had bank accounts in excess of the allowable amount. During the first pass, some 1,600 potential violators were discovered.

Computer matching and the integration of data files into a central databank have enormous ethical implications. On the one hand, the new information can be used to uncover criminals and to identify service requirements for the needy. On the other hand, it provides powerful political knowledge for those few who have access to it and control over it. It is ripe for privacy invasion and other abuses. For this reason many politicians have spoken out against centralized governmental databanks.

---

* Bracketed numbers cite the references at the end of this chapter.

As early as 1966, Representative Frank Horton of New York described the threat as follows:

> The argument is made that a central databank would use only the type of information that now exists, and since no new principle is involved, existing types of safeguards will be adequate. This is fallacious. Good computermen know that one of the most practical of our present safeguards of privacy is the fragmented nature of present information. It is scattered in little bits and pieces across the geography and years of our life. Retrieval is impractical and often impossible. A central databank removes completely this safeguard. I have every confidence that ways will be found for all of us to benefit from the great advances of the computermen, but those benefits must never be purchased at the price of our freedom to live as individuals with private lives. [2, p. 6]

There is another threat inherent in merging data files. Some of the data may be in error. More than 60,000 state and local agencies, for example, provide information to the National Crime Information Center, and it is accessed by law officers nearly 400,000 times a day. Yet studies show that over 4 percent of the stolen vehicle entries, 6 percent of the warrant entries, and perhaps as much as one half of the local law enforcement criminal history records are in error. At risk is the safety of the law enforcement officers who access it, the effectiveness of the police in controlling crime, and the freedom of the citizens whose names appear in the files. This leads to a concern for accuracy.

ACCURACY

Misinformation has a way of fouling up people's lives, especially when the party with the inaccurate information has an advantage in power and authority. Consider the plight of one Louis Marches. Marches, an immigrant, was a hardworking man who, with his wife, Eileen, finally saved enough money to purchase a home in Los Angeles during the 1950s. They took out a long-term loan from Crocker National Bank. Every month Louis Marches would walk to his neighborhood bank, loan coupon book in hand, to make his payment of $195.53. He always checked with care to insure that the teller had stamped "paid" in his book on the proper line just opposite the month for which the payment was due. And he continued to do this long after the bank had converted to its automated loan processing system.

One September a few years ago, Marches was notified by the bank that he had failed to make his current house payment. Marches grabbed his coupon book, marched to the bank, and, in broken English that showed traces of his old country heritage, tried to explain to the teller that this dunning notice was wrong. He had made his payment, he claimed. The stamp on his coupon book proved that he had paid. The teller punched Marches' loan number on the keyboard and reviewed the resulting screen.

Unfortunately, she couldn't confirm Marches' claim, nor subsequently could the head teller, nor the branch manager. When faced with a computer-generated screen that clearly showed that his account was delinquent, this hierarchy of bankers simply ignored the entries recorded in his coupon book and also his attendant raving. Confused, Marches left the bank in disgust.

In October, however, Marches dutifully went to the bank to make his next payment. He was told that he could not make his October payment because he was one month in arrears. He again showed the teller his stamped coupon book. She refused to accept it, and he stormed out of the bank. In November, he returned on schedule as he had done for over 20 years and tried to make his payment again, only to be told that he was now two months in arrears. And so it went until inevitably the bank foreclosed. Eileen learned of the foreclosure from an overzealous bank debt collector while she was in bed recovering from a heart attack. She collapsed upon hearing the news and suffered a near fatal stroke, which paralyzed her right side. Sometime during this melee Marches, who until this time had done his own legal work, was introduced to an attorney who agreed to defend him. They sued the bank. Ultimately, after months of anguish, the Marches received a settlement for $268,000. All that the bank officials who testified could say was, "Computers make mistakes. Banks make mistakes, too."

A special burden is placed on the accuracy of information when people rely on it for matters of life and death, as we increasingly do. This came to light in a recent $3.2 million lawsuit charging the National Weather Service for failing to predict accurately a storm that raged on the southeast slope of Georges Bank in 1980. As Peter Brown steered his ship—the *Sea Fever*—from Hyannis Harbor toward his lobster traps near Nova Scotia, he monitored weather conditions using a long-range, single sideband radio capable of receiving weather forecasts at least 100 miles out to sea. The forecasts assured him that his destination area near Georges Bank, although it might get showers, was safe from the hurricane-like storm that the weather bureau had predicted would go far to the east of his course. So he kept to his course. Soon, however, his ship was engulfed in howling winds of 80 knots and waves cresting at 60 feet. In the turbulence Gary Brown, a crew member, was washed overboard.

The source of the fatal error was failure of a large-scale information system which collects data from high-atmosphere balloons, satellites, ships, and a series of buoys. These data are then transmitted to a National Oceanographic and Atmospheric Administration computer, which analyzes them and produces forecasts. The forecasts, in turn, are broadcast widely.

The forecast Peter Brown relied on when he decided to proceed into the North Atlantic was in error because just one buoy—station 44003 Georges Bank—was out of service. As a result, the wind speed and direction data it normally provided were lost to the computer model. This caused the forecasted trajectory of the storm to be canted by several miles, deceiving skipper Peter Brown and consequently sending Gary Brown to his death.

Among the questions this raises for us in the information age are these: "How many Louis Marcheses and Gary Browns are there out there?" "How many are we creating everyday?" The Marches received a large financial settlement; but can they ever be repaid for the irreparable harm done to them and to their dignity? Honour Brown, Gary's widow, received a judgment in her case; but has she been repaid for the loss of Gary? The point is this: We run the risk of creating Gary Browns and Louis Marcheses every time we design information systems and place information in databases which might be used to make decisions. So it is our responsibility to be vigilant in the pursuit of accuracy in information. Today we are producing so much information about so many people and their activities that our exposure to problems of inaccuracy is enormous. And this growth in information also raises another issue: Who owns it?

PROPERTY

One of the most complex issues we face as a society is the question of intellectual property rights. There are substantial economic and ethical concerns surrounding these rights—concerns revolving around the special attributes of information itself and the means by which it is transmitted. Any individual item of information can be extremely costly to produce in the first instance. Yet, once it is produced, that information has the illusive quality of being easy to reproduce and to share with others. Moreover, this replication can take place without destroying the original. This makes information hard to safeguard since, unlike tangible property, it becomes communicable and hard to keep it to one's self. It is even difficult to secure appropriate reimbursements when somebody else uses your information.

We currently have several imperfect institutions that try to protect intellectual property rights. Copyrights, patents, encryption, oaths of confidentiality, and such old-fashioned values as trustworthiness and loyalty are the most commonly used protectors of our intellectual property. Problem issues, however, still abound in this area. Let us focus on just one aspect: artificial intelligence and its expanding subfield, expert systems.

To fully appreciate our moral plight regarding expert systems, it is necessary to run back the clock a bit, about 200 years, to the beginnings of another society: the steam energy–industrial society. From this vantage point we may anticipate some of the problems of the information society.

As the Industrial Age unfolded in England and Western Europe a significant change took place in the relationship between people and their work. The steam engine replaced manpower by reducing the level of personal physical energy required to do a job. The factory system, as Adam Smith described in his essay on the pin factory, effectively replaced the laborer's contribution of his energy and of his skills. This was done by means of new machines and new organizational forms. The process was carried even further in the French community of Lyon. There, Joseph Marie Jacquard created a weaving loom in which a system of rectangular, punched holes captured the weaver's skill for directing the loom's mechanical fingers and for controlling the warp and weft of the threads. These Jacquard looms created a new kind of capital, which was produced by disembodying energy and skill from the craftsmen and then reembodying it into the machines. In effect, an exchange of property took place. Weaving skills were transferred from the craftsman to the owner of the machines. With this technological innovation, Lyon eventually regained its position as one of the leading silk producers in the world. The weavers themselves, however, suffered unemployment and degradation because their craft was no longer economically viable. A weaver's value as a person and a craftsman was taken away by the new machines.

There is undoubtedly a harbinger of things to come in these 18th-century events. As they unfolded, civilization witnessed one of the greatest outpourings of moral philosophy it has ever seen: Adam Smith's *Theory of Moral Sentiments* and his *Wealth of Nations,* the American Revolution and its classic documents on liberty and freedom, the French Revolution and its concern for fraternity and equality, John Stuart Mill and Jeremy Bentham and their ethical call for the greatest good for the greatest number, and Immanuel Kant and his categorical imperative, which leads to an ethical utopia called the "kingdom of ends." All of this ethical initiative took place within the historically short span of time of about 50 years. Common to these ideas was a spirit which sought a new meaning in human life and which demanded that a just allocation be made of social resources.

Today that moral spirit may be welling up within us again. Only this time it has a different provocator. Nowhere is the potential threat to human dignity so severe as it is in the age of information technology, especially in the field of artificial intelligence. Practitioners of artificial intelligence proceed by extracting knowledge from experts, workers, and the knowledgeable, and then implanting it into computer software where it becomes capital in the economic sense. This process of "disemminding" knowledge from an individual and subsequently "emminding" it into machines transfers control of the property to those who own the hardware and software. Is this exchange of property warranted? Consider some of the most successful commercial artificial intelligence systems of the day. Who owns, for example, the chemical knowledge contained in DYNDREL, the medical knowledge contained in MYCIN, or the geological knowledge contained in PROSPECTOR. How is the contributor of his knowledge to be compensated? These are among the issues we must resolve as more intelligent information systems are created.

Concern over intellectual property rights relates to the content of information. There are some equally pressing property rights issues surrounding the conduits through which information passes. Bandwidth, the measure of capacity to carry information, is a scarce and ultimately fixed commodity. It is a "commons." A commons is like an empty vessel into which drops of water can be placed freely and easily until it fills and overflows. Then its capacity is gone. As a resource it is finite.

In an age in which people benefit by the communication of information, there is a tendency for us to treat bandwidth and transmission capacity as a commons in the same way as did the herdsmen in Garrett Hardin's poignant essay, "The Tragedy of the Commons," (subtitled: "The population problem has no technical solution; it requires a fundamental extension in morality"). Each herdsman received direct benefits from adding an animal to a pasture shared in common. As long as there was plenty of grazing capacity the losses due to the animal's consumption were spread among them and felt only indirectly and proportionally much less. So each herdsman was motivated to increase his flock. In the end, however, the commons was destroyed and everybody lost.

Today our airways are becoming clogged with a plethora of data, voice, video, and message transmission. Organizations and individuals are expanding their use of communications because it is profitable for them to do so. But if the social checks on the expanded use of bandwidth are inadequate, and a certain degree of temperance isn't followed, we may find that jamming and noise will destroy the flow of clear information through the air. How will the limited resource of bandwidth be allocated? Who will have access? This leads us to the fourth issue.

ACCESS

Our main avenue to information is through literacy. Literacy, since about A.D. 1500 when the Syrians first conceived of a consonant alphabet, has been a requirement for full participation in the fabric of society. Each innovation in information handling, from the invention of paper to the modern computer, has placed new demands on achieving literacy. In an information society a citizen must possess at least three things to be literate:

One must have the intellectual skills to deal with information. These are such skills as reading, writing, reasoning, and calculating. This is a task for education.

One must have access to the information technologies which store, convey, and process information. This includes libraries, radios, televisions, telephones, and, increasingly, personal computers or terminals linked via networks to mainframes. This is a problem in social economics.

Finally, one must have access to the information itself. This requirement returns to the issue of property and is also a problem in social economics.

These requirements for literacy are a function of both the knowledge level and the economic level of the individual. Unfortunately, for many people in the world today both of these levels are currently deteriorating.

There are powerful factors working both for and against contemporary literacy in our organizations and in our society. For example, the cost of computation, as measured in, say dollars per MIPS (millions of instructions per second), has gone down exponentially since the introduction of computers. This trend has made technology more accessible and economically attainable to more people. However, corporations and other public and private organizations have benefited the most from these economies. As a result, cost economies in computation are primarily available to middle and upper income people. At the same time computer usage flourishes among some, we are creating a large group of information-poor people who have no direct access to the more efficient computational technology and who have little training in its use.

Reflect for a moment on the social effects of electronically stored databases. Prior to their invention, vast quantities of data about publications, news events, economic and social statistics, and scientific findings had been available in printed, microfilm, or microfiche form at a relatively low cost. For most of us access to this data had been substantially free. We merely went to our public or school library. The library, in turn, paid a few hundred dollars for the service and made it available to whomever asked for it. Today, however, much of this information is being converted to computerized databases and the cost to access these databases can run in the thousands of dollars.

Frequently, access to databases is gained only by means of acquiring a terminal or personal computer. For example, if you want access to the *New York Times Index* through the Mead Corporation service you must first have access to a terminal and communication line and then pay additional hookup and access fees in order to obtain the data. This means that the people who wish to use this service possess several things. First, they know that the database exists and how to use it. Second, they have acquired the requisite technology to access it. And third, they are able to pay the fees for the data. Thus, the educational and economic ante is really quite high for playing the modern information game. Many people cannot or choose not to pay it and, hence, are excluded from participating fully in our society. In effect, they become information "dropouts" and in the long run will become the source of many social problems.

PAPA

Privacy, accuracy, property, and accessibility—these are the four major issues of information ethics for the information age. Max Plank's 1900 conception that energy was released in small discrete packets called "quanta" not only gave rise to atomic theory but also permitted the development of information technology as well. Semiconductors, transistors, integrated circuits, photoelectric cells, vacuum tubes, and ferrite cores are among the technological yield of this scientific theory. In a curious way, quantum theory underlies the four issues as well. Plank's theory and all that followed it have led us to a point where the stakes surrounding society's policy agenda are incredibly high. At stake with the use of nuclear energy is the very survival of mankind itself. If we are unwise we will either blow ourselves up or contaminate our world forever with nuclear waste. At stake with the increased use of information technology is the quality of our lives should we, or our children, survive. If we are unwise, many people will suffer information bankruptcy or desolation.

Our moral imperative is clear. We must insure that information technology, and the information it handles, are used to enhance the dignity of mankind. To achieve these goals we must formulate a new social contract, one that insures everyone the right to fulfill his or her own human potential.

In the new social contract, information systems should not unduly invade a person's privacy to avoid the indignities that the students in Tallahassee suffered.

Information systems must be accurate to avoid the indignities the Marcheses and the Browns suffered.

Information systems should protect the viability of the fixed-conduit resource through which it is transmitted to avoid noise and jamming pollution and the indignities of "The Tragedy of the Commons."

Information systems should protect the sanctity of intellectual property to avoid the indignities of unwitting "disemmindment" of knowledge from individuals.

And information systems should be accessible to avoid the indignities of information illiteracy and deprivation.

This is a tall order; but it is one that we in the MIS community should address. We must assume some responsibility for the social contract that emerges from the systems that we design and implement. In summary, we must insure that the flow of those little packets of energy and information called quanta that Max Plank bequeathed to us some 85 years ago are used to create the kind of world in which we wish to live.

REFERENCES

1. SOLZHENITSYN, ALEKSANDR I. *The Cancer Ward*. New York: Dial Press, 1968.
2. U.S. HOUSE OF REPRESENTATIVES. *The Computer and Invasion of Privacy*. Washington, D.C.: U.S. Government Printing Office, 1966.

28   *Ethics in the Information Age**

Bruce E. Spiro

We hear a lot about ethics in the media these days. Lately, it seems that on a daily basis some government official is being charged with a violation of ethical practices. Business and industry leaders are in the news for unsavory actions. Even educational and religious institutions aren't escaping the public's more watchful eye.

Is it a change in our moral fiber or is it just more publicity? No doubt, the present investigative nature of the media accounts for some of the current interest, but I think there is more. In short, ethical issues are not as simple as they once were.

In addition to greater opportunities and challenges, the changing times have made our lives much more complicated. What was once well understood, if not universally maintained, is now cloaked in mystery and misinformation and has somehow escaped traditional controls.

To be sure, the information age has brought society new ideas and situations along with a tremendous potential for increased productivity and the ability to explore new fields and technologies.

Data Processing Management Association (DPMA) and other professional societies have sought to address ethical problems within the IS profession through specific codes and standards of conduct. DPMA took the process one step further by establishing enforcement procedures that provide a legal base for enforcement and due process for anyone accused of a violation.

WHY ARE CODES NECESSARY?

All of these codes and standards are designed to instruct and guide the IS professional in the performance of his or her job. These guidelines explain the responsibilities of an IS professional to an employer and community.

These tools are essential in establishing an ethical and moral environment. Most of the time, they do the job for which they were intended—to define what the ethical conduct of an information professional should be. They were not developed easily or without controversy, and, as change continues, hopefully they will be modified to reflect new situations and technologies.

Why bother? We all know right from wrong and, even if we didn't, what's the problem? Take, for example, the concept of trust. Without ethics there is no way to trust your neighbors, supervisors, or peers.

It would be terrible to live in a world without trust. Possessions would be yours only as long as you could defend them. The concept of personal property, as we know it, would cease to exist.

Mankind has recognized this fundamental truth, and much of our society's rule of law is built upon an understanding of the rights of others. Much more importantly, it isn't clear that people actually recognize right from wrong. It has become very common to hear someone charged with a violation of ethics complain that "I didn't break any rules." One would think that specific rules would be unnecessary in order for intelligent people to recognize a dishonest practice. Yet, without "rules," there are many who claim that they didn't know what they did was wrong or that they made a "mistake in judgment."

But can property be "stolen" if it isn't gone? Even more crucial, aren't ideas just as tangible as personal property, reports, or computer programs? For that matter, what is different about information ethics? Do the same rules apply?

ADVANCEMENT

Two aspects are clear: Rapid technological change, and the lack of constant reinforcement hinder the advancement of ethics in the information age.

This age came upon us too quickly for the development of thoughtful and orderly standards of ethics. In one generation, the industry went from start-up to full speed. Conversely, in agriculture, this progress took thousands of years, and, in industry, centuries.

Change has been the one constant in IS over the past three decades. Technology has advanced so rapidly that we have trouble keeping up, much less pondering its social impact or moral significance.

We were still contemplating the difference between the tedious and error-prone manual updating of financial records and almost instantaneous revisions of computer-based, record-keeping systems when we were faced with such things as universal identification codes. Now, the standardization of communications, document production, and operating systems present us with a new set of privacy and confidentiality concerns.

Information technology has moved from a closely held, kind of "magical" pursuit, to a very common practice that is employed by just about everyone. Back in the 1960s and even the 70s (so long ago in the information sciences), there were relatively few who could use the computer at all. And, looking back, perhaps none who used the power very well.

Because of the small number of people involved, information ethics had importance to a limited audience and was discussed only by professional societies. Codes of ethics, standards of conduct, and enforcement procedures were established for the information professional by all of the major professional societies associated with IS. These pertain, however, only to the "professional information processor." But what about the development of information skills and knowledge among a constantly growing group of end-users?

Elementary school children understand how to use computers. But "whiz kids" in the nation's junior high schools know more about IS than some of our leading experts did a decade ago.

The bottom line: moral and ethical perceptions haven't caught up with the rapid growth of the IS industry, its end users, and developers. Furthermore, laws on the books are uneven and have not been subject to revisions by the courts. And, there is no commonly understood foundation to current laws.

FUNDAMENTAL STANDARDS

In the past, we have relied upon the home and the church to provide the fundamental underpinnings of our moral practices. The Ten Commandments and their counterparts in other religions establish the broad framework on which morals and ethics are built.

"Thou shalt not kill" and "Thou shalt not steal" are clear and definitive and pertain to aspects of everyday life. These ideas are understood by all, whether they choose to live by them or not. There is no excuse to say, "I didn't understand," or, "I thought it was all right."

From childhood, people are taught what is right and wrong. From parents ("Don't do that, you wouldn't want someone to do it to you.") to the churches ("the wages of sin"), these fundamental ethical concepts are reinforced daily.

Even with this powerful foundation, these standards don't "reach" everyone. From Wall Street executives to holdup men, there are those who believe that these rules were meant for someone else. Simply, these standards govern the rest of the world—at least the civilized parts of it.

When the rights of others are balanced against the good of the individual, however, a great insight and strong appreciation of moral and ethical concepts is necessary to counteract the instinct for professional "survival."

PROMOTION OF ETHICS

Promoting IS ethics is even more difficult. When was the last time we heard our mother say, "You shouldn't copy that disk. It is the intellectual property of someone else." Of all the sermons we hear each week, how many deal with unauthorized use of data or a computer?

The idea that something can be stolen when it is still in possession of its rightful owner is not an easy one to understand or appreciate. Today, few can make the distinction between the concept of proprietary or personal information and casual gossip. These are concepts not familiar in the church or home. One day that may be the case, but for now it is necessary to look elsewhere for the foundation of information ethics.

Who better than the information executive who has grappled with these ethical concepts for a very long time? IS professionals may not have all the answers, but certainly they have more experience with ethical issues than others.

Moreover, information executives understand the structure of their companies better than most of their peers. Once the majority of people understand that foundation, information ethics will fall into place. Clearly, the question is, How do we get people to understand?

If the clergy and parents aren't equipped to teach ethics, I suggest that our schools, with assistance from information executives, can. The concepts of information value, intellectual property, and the rights of privacy, to name a few, must be taught and continually reinforced.

This process must start at an early age and continue throughout a student's educational process to ensure that ethics are a part of the workplace. As we move keyboarding earlier in the educational process, the teaching of information ethics must follow.

There is no reason that intellectual property rights cannot be understood by a first-grader. In some situations, these concepts are already being taught to first- and second-graders and being understood.

Information professionals also must ensure that the teaching of ethics is not an isolated instance, but the standard for all of the nation's schools. We must also identify and publicize successful ethics programs at all levels of education as well as of business and industry.

Most importantly, professionals from other disciplines must become involved in this ethics movement. And where legislative action is needed, information executives should make it happen. Only then will information ethics become more than a piece of paper that receives only lip service.

Effective ethical standards will be developed sooner or later no matter what information professionals do. If we do nothing, the cycles of technological development—and national regulatory agencies—will assume those responsibilities.

As the value of information ethics grows, the pressures required to induce change will be brought to bear on a continuing basis. But this process will take a long time and, meanwhile, many will be severely hurt, and we will hear some familiar excuses: "I thought it was all right," and "I didn't know."

The courts will decide issues based on old and sometimes irrelevant concepts until a new "morality" is developed. It will be difficult, but it doesn't need to be that way.

Information professionals must take the actions necessary to have information ethics taught in our schools at all levels and accepted in business and industry as an essential part of every operation. The challenge is great but we can do it. We must do it.

FOCUS 1

The DPMA (Data Processing Management Association) has developed its Code of Ethics and Standards of Conduct to deal with ethical issues in the information systems industry. DPMA's membership represents a cross section of industry professionals with a foundation of experience that dates back to the mid-50s. DPMA's focus on ethics is reflected in its membership, legislative and educational endeavors. At DPMA, ethics will always be a major focus of the association's activities.

Code of Ethics

I acknowledge:

That I have an obligation to management; therefore, I shall promote the understanding of information processing methods and procedures to management using every resource at my command.

That I have an obligation to my fellow members; therefore, I shall uphold the high ideals of DPMA as outlined in its Association Bylaws. Further, I shall cooperate with my fellow members and shall treat them with honesty and respect at all times.

That I have an obligation to society and will participate to the best of my ability in the dissemination of knowledge pertaining to the general development and understanding of information processing. Further, I shall not use knowledge of a confidential nature to further my personal interest, nor shall I violate the privacy and confidentiality of information entrusted to me or to which I may gain access.

That I have an obligation to my employer whose trust I hold; therefore, I shall endeavor to discharge this obligation to the best of my ability, to guard my employer's interests, and to advise him or her wisely and honestly.

That I have an obligation to my country. I shall uphold my nation and shall honor the chosen way of life of my fellow citizens.

I accept these obligations as a personal responsibility and as a member of this association. I shall actively discharge these obligations and I dedicate myself to that end.

FOCUS 2

These standards expand on the Code of Ethics by providing specific statements of behavior in support of each element of the Code. They are not objectives to be strived for; they are rules that no true professional will violate. It is first of all expected that information processing professionals will abide by the appropriate laws of their country and community. The following standards address tenets that apply to the profession.

Standards of Conduct

In recognition of my obligation to management I shall:

- Keep my personal knowledge up to date and insure that proper expertise is available when needed.
- Share my knowledge with others and present factual and objective information to management to the best of my ability.
- Accept full responsibility for work that I perform.
- Not misuse the authority entrusted to me.
- Not misrepresent or withhold information concerning the capabilities of equipment, software or systems.
- Not take advantage of the lack of knowledge or inexperience on the part of others.

In recognition of my obligation to my fellow members and the profession I shall:

- Be honest in all my professional relationships.
- Take appropriate action in regard to any illegal or unethical practices that come to my attention. However, I will bring charges against any

person only when I have reasonable basis for believing in the truth of the allegations and without regard to personal interest.

- Endeavor to share my special knowledge.
- Cooperate with others in achieving understanding and in identifying problems.
- Not use or take credit for the work of others without specific acknowledgement and authorization.
- Not take advantage of the lack of knowledge or inexperience on the part of others for personal gain.

In recognition of my obligation to society I shall:

- Protect the privacy and confidentiality of all information entrusted to me.
- Use my skill and knowledge to inform the public in all areas of my expertise.
- To the best of my ability, insure that the products of my work are used in a socially responsible way.
- Support, respect, and abide by the appropriate local, state, provincial, and federal laws.
- Never misrepresent or withhold information that is germane to a problem or situation of public concern, nor will I allow any such known information to remain unchallenged.
- Not use knowledge of a confidential or personal nature in any unauthorized manner or to achieve personal gain.

In recognition of my obligation to my employer I shall:

- Make every effort to ensure that I have the most current knowledge and that the proper expertise is available when needed.
- Avoid conflict of interest and insure that my employer is aware of any potential conflicts.
- Present a fair, honest, and objective viewpoint.
- Protect the proper interests of my employer at all times.
- Protect the privacy and confidentiality of all information entrusted to me.
- Not misrepresent or withhold information that is germane to the situation.
- Not attempt to use the resources of my employer for personal gain or for any purpose without proper approval.
- Not exploit the weakness of a computer system for personal gain or personal satisfaction.

29 *Jesse James at the Terminal**

William Atkins

This cautionary tale of computer derring-do shows how a present-day miscreant almost gets away with a $2 million heist before his company knows something is missing. Embedded in this scenario are the outlines of the typical computer crime. Though the fictional TechneeCorp had installed some state-of-the-art security measures, it had failed to implement several vital personnel procedures. At almost every stage of his plot to defraud Technee, the criminal could have—and should have—been caught. As happens in many computer capers today, the story's ending turns almost on a quirk of fate.

Jesse James was angry. Seething. How could they pass him over for promotion again? Jesse had been sure that the company would long ago have recognized and rewarded his ingenuity. But it hadn't, and he was mad. If they weren't going to give him what he deserved, he'd get it himself.

If one could trust appearances, Jesse was the very model of a modern systems analyst. At 29, he had put in six years with TechneeCorp. He came in early and stayed late. He even took his personal computer home so he could work nights and weekends. He had learned the company's computer system quickly, and just as quickly he had devised ways to bypass the controls and make it work better.

Though Jesse fit the picture of the up and coming computer professional, he prided himself on his connections to his dashing and courageous predecessor, the intrepid robber of banks and trains. He had the name, of course, although his name, Jesse James Wheeler, came from his two grandfathers, so the conjunction happened entirely by chance. He also had the cleverness. His knowledge of TechneeCorp's computer system would bring him more money than a gun ever could.

Jesse's daring namesake had always sought to justify his banditry on grounds of persecution. Moreover, the original James gang used to brag that it had never robbed a friend, a preacher, a Southerner, or a widow. Jesse decided that he would be as considerate. He would not steal from anyone but the faceless corporation.

He decided to set up a fictitious vendor-payable account in the computer, then transfer payments directly to his bank account.

Maxim:
When information systems are involved,
beware of disgruntled employees.

Like many large companies, TechneeCorp maintained extensive EDP operations with centralized and distributed computer systems as well as a flock of microcomputers wired into both. Management understood the value of its electronic treasure trove and had taken steps to protect it.

Special access-control software allowed terminal users—identified by user codes and passwords—to access only records for which they were authorized and to perform only specific, authorized functions, such as reading files or adding or deleting information. The software could also limit the amount of information available to each authorized user, restrict the central computer to private, secured phone lines, or allow access to certain terminals only. Perhaps most important, the software kept records of who accessed what, from which terminal, and when.

Jesse had known for some time that the specialized audit software existed, but its secrets were closely guarded by the auditors themselves. They caused his biggest worry: Since he didn't know where the system's traps lay, he couldn't be certain of avoiding them. He decided to minimize the risk of being caught. During the robbery he would leave a little "present"—a special program that would cover his tracks by eliminating any record of the payment transactions.

While working on his microcomputer, Jesse had noticed an inordinately long wait after he signed on with his user code and password before the central computer responded that he was logged on and could proceed. He decided to ask his supervisor about this. "Not to worry," said Matt, "it's just security. The system cuts you off. It drops the line, so to speak, and dials you back. Or, I should say, it dials back the phone number you should be using. That's how it knows every terminal tapping into it is right where it ought to be." Matt also told Jesse that every supervisor had a frequently changed password that allowed access to the "secured" systems. He had designed many of these features himself and was justly proud of them.

Maxim:
All employees must be sensitive to
security.

TechneeCorp's security managers had done all they and the insurance
company had deemed necessary. They knew about even more sophisticated and exotic access-control devices—there were gadgets that scanned
potential users' fingerprints, voiceprints, even the blood vessels in their
retinas—but they came at a price TechneeCorp wasn't willing to pay.

Jesse needed a password that would give him access to supervisory
functions because, to divert funds to a fictitious account, he first had to be
able to create that account. He needed a partner and he found Frank—a
computer operator with a bit of a gambling problem. Nothing serious, just
a few hundred each week. Frank had no love for Technee, either. But he
did have a way of getting the master password list.

Maxim:
Investigate your computer personnel
before hiring, and be alert to evidence of
such personal problems as compulsive
gambling and alcoholism.

Frank used to work at Technee's world headquarters; in fact, somewhat
against his wishes, he'd been transferred to Jesse's eastern region office in
Newark only a few weeks before. So nobody thought much about it when
Frank showed up at WHQs' impressive office complex in Stamford, Connecticut. The sensitive nature of TechneeCorp's business necessitated its
state-of-the-art physical security system. Both outside and inside the modern structure, surveillance cameras silently scanned every movement, day
and night.

Frank knew the cameras had picked him up the minute he pulled into the
employee lot. But he didn't care. His parking pass was still on his wind-
shield. And his ID badge hanging from his lapel cleared him to enter both
the building and the computer installation.

Maxim:
Keep all personnel records and
privileges up to date.

"Hi, Frank," said Butch, smiling from ear to ear. Butch was Technee's
oldest security guard. Even though he knew Frank had been transferred,
he didn't bother to check whether he should be there. After all, he'd
known him for three years.

To get the password list, Frank needed to enter the computer installation. He could do that the same way he always had—by punching a
four-digit code into a key pad on the door panel. True, they had changed
the code since Frank left, but getting the new code wouldn't be that
difficult.

Frank simply wandered into the programming section. "Hey!" he yelled at no one in particular. "What's the code this week?" "It's 313," came the reply from a frosted glass cubicle. Like all the codes, this was simply a telephone area code. Following standard procedure, Frank prefixed a "1," punched 1-313, and entered the installation.

The main computer was, as befitted its delicate eyes, ears, and sinuses, enclosed in a scrubbed-clean room to the right, sealed off from the printers with their nasty dust, confetti and vibrations. Frank turned left into the print room, and, after a few minutes of ruffling through the output reports that awaited pickup, found what he wanted—the list of supervisor password codes and the special terminal passwords.

"I've got the passwords," thought Frank in silent triumph. "But I couldn't have done it if those people hadn't helped me. In the end, people are what's important."

Maxim:
Keep all security codes strictly secret.

During his six years with Technee, Jesse had learned about many of the complete operation's security features. Quite early on, he had noticed that, whereas each vendor account number had only six digits, the order entry group keyed seven numbers into the system.

He knew that the seventh digit was a check digit—part of the security system—and to create a new account he would have to devise a correct check digit of his own. Since he knew many of the accounts' full numbers, Jesse could use his own computer and a simple program to arrive at the numerical process that unlocked all the account numbers. Having the check digit process and the passwords, he could construct new account numbers that the system would readily accept.

Jesse's first assault on TechneeCorp was a failure. The kind of failure, in fact, that would have bloodied, if not killed, his train-robbing namesake. As he had often done before, Jesse brought home his personal computer. Remembering what Matt had told him about the callback security feature, he first took the precaution of forwarding his office phone calls automatically to his home phone. "No control device exists," he thought smugly, "that can tell when a call's being forwarded." Using the password list Frank had given him, he logged on and entered Matt's supervisor code.

He headed straight for the program for creating new accounts—and directly into a very expensive, very subtle, and very clever trap. For though the system seemed to be following his instructions obediently, in reality it was doing nothing he asked and was all the while recording his every move. Jesse had been snared by a state-of-the-art audit software package that gave him access to a set of false files and freedom to do as he wanted.

To give due credit to his thespian talents, it must be noted that Jesse showed no trace of panic when the chief security officer of WHQ called him into Matt's office the next afternoon. There on the desk was the evidence—a printout declaring:

```
OPERATOR IDENTIFIED AS
SUPERVISOR 31688
ON INVALID SUPERVISOR
TERMINAL 5479,
TELEPHONE NUMBER 555-2564,
ACCESSED THIS PROGRAM
FROM 1954:50 TO 2003:25,
6.19.85.
```

Matt, of course, denied using Jesse's terminal—as did Jesse himself. The building guards could not say for sure that Jesse had taken a terminal home the previous night. He was off the hook; there was no way they could prove he—and not someone else—had used his terminal.

The experience, though almost fatal, proved immensely valuable to Jesse, for now he possessed a piece of vital knowledge—namely, that there was another level of security to be breached. The company had installed a security system on the terminals themselves, so that not all terminals could do all things.

Jesse needed a supervisor's terminal. And he needed it on a Thursday so that Friday morning the accounts payable program would make a payment to "his" account.

Maxim:
Sophisticated security software systems
are only as reliable as
the people who guard them.

Another long day at the office. Time to scoop up the micro and lug it off to do some homework. At the employee exit, Danny, the security guard, was just getting ready for a restful evening, "Hey, Danny! My computer's on the fritz and I've got a boatload of work tonight. How's about letting me into Matt's office so I can use his? He said I could use it anytime."

Danny had never paid much attention to those typewriter-TV screen things; seen one, seen 'em all. Jesse, of course, knew better. He needed Matt's five-star Supervisor I with circuit boards that would make that audit software program roll out the red carpet. While picking up the machine, he set the call-forward to his home phone. With unusual good cheer, he wished Danny a good evening. He himself intended to have one.

It is 11:30 P.M. Jesse is seated comfortably in his bedroom. His elaborate preparations are behind him. It had all come down to this: the silent predator with his elemental weapons—Jesse James with a terminal and a modem.

It had all been rather simple. Using everything he had learned at Technee, Jesse tapped into its central computer and created an account in his name. He had noted carefully all the necessary numbers: account, check digit, vendor, bank, ABA transit, and bank account. Carefully, he read from his notes. By simply inputting the appropriate purchase order and balances, he initiated next-cycle payment transactions totaling $2 million. He then applied a finishing touch of criminal acumen: a little time bomb—a program that would remove all evidence.

Jesse didn't sleep a wink that night. He alternated between imagining how he would spend such an enormous amount of money—villas, yachts, wining and dining, gambling—and gloating over how he had beaten the billion-dollar TechneeCorp with all its policies, procedures, and precautions.

In the morning, Jesse panicked. The long night had taken its toll. When the alarm had sounded he had turned it off automatically and fallen asleep. Now it was 7:15 A.M. He got dressed quickly, grabbed the computer, and dashed for his car. Usually at work no later than 7 A.M., Jesse knew that Matt came in about 8.

Practically knocking someone over, he rushed breathless up to Bob at the guard desk. "Is Matt in yet?" he asked. Jesse's mind was racing as he tried to figure out what he could say if Matt was already there. The monitoring system would show that there was no problem with Jesse's terminal. How would he be able to explain taking Matt's?

"Haven't seen him," replied Bob. The answer seemed to take an eternity to sink in. He just stood there. "Thank goodness," he said finally. He didn't even notice the stares Bob and the other person gave him.

Jesse, explaining to Bob that he had used Matt's computer because his was broken, got him to unlock Matt's door. He set the machine down on the desk, connected it to the electrical outlet, plugged in the telephone jack, and cancelled the call-forwarding instruction. "What presence of mind!" he thought. "Switzerland, here I come."

Jane Clades, a waitress in TechneeCorp's executive dining room, hadn't missed a day since the doors opened at this branch just over nine years ago. She was proud to be part of TechneeCorp and its success; she felt she belonged.

She read the monthly employee bulletin regularly and had been interested recently in the article entitled "Security: Everyone's Responsibility." She liked the fact that TechneeCorp believed its first line of security was its people. The article emphasized a family image: everyone pulling together and all keeping alert. Jane also liked the friendly chief security officer from WHQ who wrote the article; he'd visit at least once every few months and always stopped in the restaurant for a cup of coffee.

Jane didn't like Jesse James's bumping into her that morning without one word of apology. He hadn't hurt her, but his bad manners annoyed her. She also kept thinking about how nervous he looked when he asked the guard to let him into a supervisor's office. Why did he need to get into that office in such a hurry? Why couldn't he just wait?

Jane told the short-order chef what had happened. As they talked, the more she thought Jesse James had behaved suspiciously, and the more the chef encouraged her to do something.

Telling herself she had nothing to lose and encouraged by the article she had read, Jane called TechneeCorp's chief security officer and told him her story.

Even with considerable assistance, security personnel took more than 36 hours of work around the clock to uncover enough evidence to indicate embezzlement. (If Jesse hadn't applied his time bomb program, they could have reconstructed events in a few hours.) Because they had no way to prove the crime, the rest was up to the chief security officer.

Waiting for his taxi to the airport, Jesse checked his luggage. It looked like everything was in order. In just 90 minutes, he would be on the plane; in a few hours, he would be skiing and beginning to enjoy the $2 million. He heard the door bell and, with a smile of anticipation, picked up his skis, boots, and the suitcase, and opened the door. Jesse's face turned white, his mouth went dry, and his legs began to shake. The last person he expected to see on his doorstep at high noon on a Sunday was the chief security officer of TechneeCorp.

"Do you know how you're going to spend it all yet?" asked the officer. Jesse couldn't believe he had made a mistake. He had to know where he had gone wrong. "I don't understand," he blurted out without thinking. "How did you work it out?"

The officer's bluff had worked.

And Frank had been right. In the final analysis, people make the difference.

30 *Deterring Computer Crime**

Kenneth Rosenblatt

Item: *A Silicon Valley software company discovered in 1988 that a recently fired employee was using her telephone to enter its computer system. Before she was apprehended, she had copied several million dollars' worth of the company's products. It is suspected that she had intended to send the software to the Far East.*

Item: *A Florida news editor who had moved from one television station to another was arrested in the spring of 1989 for allegedly entering his former employer's computer and copying confidential news stories.*

Item: *A group of young "hackers" were recently arrested in West Germany on charges that they had been paid by the Soviet Union to break into NATO computers.*

Though not as celebrated as the case of Robert Morris, the Cornell University graduate student charged with unleashing a "virus" over a nationwide data network, each of these instances reflects the same growing problem: computer crime. Offenses such as altering computer records to obtain money, stealing proprietary information stored on computers, destroying valuable data, and illegally copying commercial software exact a heavy cost for U.S. business. Ultimately, the cost is borne by consumers through higher prices. Although companies' reluctance to report breaches of security makes the losses hard to measure, a rough estimate by the accounting firm of Ernst & Young puts the cost of computer crime at between $3 billion and $5 billion a year.

And that may be just the beginning. Our society is about to feel the impact of the first generation of children who have grown up using com-

---

* Source: Reprinted with permission from *Technology Review*, February/March 1990, pp. 35–40, copyright 1990.

puters. The increasing sophistication of hackers suggests that computer crime will soar, as members of this new generation are tempted to commit more serious offenses. Besides raising prices, computer crime endangers our country's telecommunications systems, since phone-company switching computers are vulnerable to sabotage. The spread of scientific knowledge is also at risk; to prevent "viral" infections, research institutions may have to tighten access to their computer networks.

That computers have become tools for antisocial behavior is hardly surprising. What is surprising about computer crime is how little is being done to deter it: Industry will not beef up security, the police are not equipped to catch electronic thieves, and judges do not hand down the kind of sentences that will impress would-be computer criminals.

New strategies are urgently needed. The first step is to abandon the idea that local police departments can fight computer crime effectively. Instead, high-technology regions need special task forces whose sole purpose is to apprehend computer criminals. The second step is to fit the punishment to the crime. Although the most severe offenders should be sent to prison, there are more innovative and less costly ways to give typical computer abusers their due. Together, these steps will deter serious criminals and, more important, discourage similarly inclined teenagers from joining their ranks.

WHY TRADITIONAL APPROACHES DO NOT WORK

The first line of defense against computer crime—system security—is also the weakest. Computers are inherently vulnerable. Universities and large businesses must provide students and employees with access to computers by telephone. Such access allows others to invade those computers over the same phone lines. In industry, employees need to be able to use the company's mainframe computer to create a product. Thieves can easily transfer information from the mainframe to a small computer disk, which they then carry out or mail home. Because workers may need access to their colleagues' computer files, they often know several passwords besides their own. The theft then occurs without the "audit trail" needed to identify the culprit.

The obvious solution is to restrict access to the company computer. But tighter security makes developing a product more cumbersome, directly affecting the bottom line. Worse yet, it takes a toll on employee morale and productivity. One industry giant refuses to increase security because it would interfere with the firm's "atmosphere of trust"—even though the company has suffered at least a million dollars in theft losses over the last five years. The priorities of most Silicon Valley executives I have spoken to are similar.

Competition is an enemy of security. Unless every company is willing to accept the consequences of tighter restrictions, careful companies will lose money. Managers are unwilling to risk wholesale employee defections and lower sales for the largely invisible and long-term benefits of preventing theft.

Even if a computer crime is reported, the odds of arrest and conviction greatly favor the criminal. Although a few cases come under federal jurisdiction—especially if they involve telephone fraud or export-control violations—most computer crimes are the responsibility of the local police department and district attorney. Police departments are simply unsuited to the task.

Most police officers are not computer experts. They are unable to evaluate claims that a suspect has stolen trade secrets, and do not know how to trace unauthorized computer access. Many cases have been lost because an officer serving a search warrant did not know how to preserve evidence discovered on a computer. Horror stories abound of floppy disks being left in overheated evidence lockers or on the seats of police cars in the sun. More than once, a police officer who was not computer-literate has allowed a suspect to log onto a computer and destroy vital evidence without interference.

The only way police departments can investigate computer crimes effectively is to develop and maintain expertise. Special investigative units have been set up within a handful of police departments, including those of Los Angeles, Philadelphia, and Baltimore, as well as the Illinois State Police, the Tarrant County, Texas, District Attorney's Office, and the Arizona State Attorney General's Office. The Santa Clara County District Attorney's Office, where I work, maintains a high-technology unit in association with various Silicon Valley police agencies. Unfortunately, such units typically consist of one or two overworked investigators, and prospects for expansion appear dim.

One reason police departments hesitate to commit officers to investigating computer crime is that industry's problems are not a high priority. Because they are locally funded, police departments must concentrate on the problems that affect their community most visibly, such as drugs and street crime. The immediate victims of computer crime are seen as a small, wealthy group.

Industry further loses support by its reluctance to report computer crime. Although no statistics are available specifically for offenses involving computers, a study by Lois Mock, of the National Institute of Justice, and Dennis Rosenbaum, of the University of Illinois at Chicago, has found that only about 18 percent of trade-secret thefts are referred to law enforcement for prosecution. Industry security managers say companies fail to report crimes partly because they fear that publicity will alarm stockholders and advertise their vulnerability to attack, and partly because they lack confidence in the ability of law enforcement to respond.

Police departments also shy away from computer crime because the investigations are unusually complex. For example, it is sometimes necessary to infiltrate computer-based "pirate" bulletin boards run by hackers. These boards frequently offer stolen information to a select group willing to reciprocate. They can be treasure troves of stolen passwords, telephone access cards, credit card numbers, and illegally copied software. Although these pirate boards are usually open to the public, the illegal information is accessible only with special passwords.

With patience, skilled police officers using their own computers can gain the confidence of a board's operator and be allowed to enter those "secret levels." Police then obtain search warrants for telephone records, find the operator's home address, and seize the computer containing the stolen information. Recently, after infiltrating a bulletin board that pandered to pedophiles, police in San Jose discovered a plot to kidnap a child and kill him as part of a "snuff" film. The FBI arrested the conspirators in Virginia.

Not surprisingly, such investigations consume a lot more time than the average fraud case. Many, if not most, require coordination with other agencies. In tracing a hacker through several states, investigators must weave their way through the procedures of different telecommunications companies and computer networks, and through the restrictions imposed by federal privacy laws. Overlapping state and federal jurisdictions create their own problems.

Because the investigations are so demanding, cops on the computer-crime beat need a much lower caseload than other officers. A typical fraud investigator can handle 25 or 30 bad-check cases at a time. A computer-crime investigator may be overwhelmed with 5 cases, and be lucky to investigate 30 in a year.

To make matters worse, department policies often discourage qualified officers from volunteering to investigate computer crime. Promotions through the lower ranks are based upon skills learned on patrol, not at a computer terminal. Thus, officers requesting to stay on a computer assignment risk not being promoted, and those who wish to pursue their interest in computers leave law enforcement for more lucrative positions in private industry. What's more, police departments generally rotate officers through different assignments every two to three years. The learning curve for a computer-crime investigator is so steep that most officers are just becoming valuable when they are transferred.

Many of the same problems plague prosecutors. Most are not computer-literate, and the skills required to prosecute ordinary crimes are not readily transferable. Lacking skilled police backup, prosecutors must often investigate cases without assistance. Because of these tasks—and the time it takes to prepare for trial—a pair of prosecutors handling computer crime might file 25 cases in a good year. This conflicts with the emphasis many counties place on heavy caseloads.

Because computer crime is too much for traditional law enforcement to handle, the bulk of computer offenses go unpunished. Probably fewer than 250 cases have been prosecuted in the United States during the past decade. At this rate, prosecutions are too rare to deter computer crime.

If an offender is convicted, the usual penalties are also not much of a deterrent. Prisons are already overcrowded with violent criminals. So in sentencing a white-collar computer offender, a judge usually imposes a fine or community service, or sometimes a short stay in the county jail—but rarely a prison term. In some cases, offenders are even rewarded for their crimes, getting hired by computer companies as "security consultants." Recently, a 14-year-old offender said he had committed the crime so that the victim or some other company would offer him a job. Clearly, society can do a better job of discouraging people from becoming computer offenders.

TAKING A BYTE OUT OF CRIME

There are two elements to deterrence. First, potential criminals must be convinced that they will be apprehended. Second, they must be convinced that their punishment will be unacceptably harsh. Current methods for dealing with computer crime include neither element.

The only realistic way to improve the chances of catching computer offenders is to take the problem out of the hands of local police departments. A promising solution is for states or the federal government to fund regional task forces staffed by officers and prosecutors from local agencies. Those task forces would enjoy statewide jurisdiction, but be placed in high-technology regions. California, for example, might need three task forces of varying size—one in San Jose to cover Silicon Valley, one in Los Angeles, and one in San Diego. Police departments in the region, and possibly federal agencies as well, could lend officers to the task force for a period of, say, three to five years.

In addition to investigating such crimes as telecommunications fraud, theft of proprietary information, alteration of data, and software piracy, the task forces could assist local agencies in preserving and analyzing computer evidence seized in other cases. This function is becoming increasingly important as criminal enterprises (particularly narcotics and prostitution rings) rely more heavily upon computers for recordkeeping. One computer-crime unit recently helped authorities sift through floppy disks containing records of 40,000 customers of a large prostitution ring.

The task-force approach has several advantages. A stint of several years would give officers time to build proficiency. The prestige conferred by government funding would attract qualified investigators, particularly if salaries were set slightly higher than the norm for law enforcement. And industry would be more willing to report problems if it perceived that law enforcement had become organized, funded, and committed to fighting computer crime. Moreover, many company officials to whom I have spoken believe industry would gladly assume some of the cost of maintaining task forces. In fact, the terms of state or federal grants for task forces could require that trade associations contribute matching funds.

A regional task force of six full-time police officers and two prosecutors (plus equipment and periodic training) would probably cost about $750,000 a year. But the return on this investment could be swift. Even if the average computer crime caused losses of only $75,000—and some surveys put that figure much higher—a task force would be a success if it deterred 10 crimes each year.

TAILORING THE PUNISHMENT

The other element of deterrence—the certainty of harsh punishment—must reflect the fact that our penal system is already strained to its limit. Certainly, the worst offenders ought to do time; states should require that computer crimes resulting in damages of over $500,000 carry a mandatory four-year prison sentence. But it is possible to devise penalties that deter crime without burdening either the prisons or the taxpayers.

Many offenders depend psychologically and economically upon computers. They spend all their time with computers, and they work, or expect to work, in the computer industry. Thus, punishments that impinge upon this obsession will do more to curb abuses than fines or community service ever could. I suggest three such sanctions: confiscating equipment used to commit a computer crime, limiting the offender's use of computers, and restricting the offender's freedom to accept jobs involving computers. These penalties would be supplemented by a few days or weeks in a county jail—longer in serious cases.

In my experience, one of the best ways to hurt computer offenders, especially young hackers, is to take away their toys. First of all, the loss of the computer is worse than a few weekends picking up trash. Second, computers are too expensive for many young offenders to replace; nor are parents as likely to buy the juvenile another computer as they are to pay a fine on his or her behalf. Third, juvenile offenders are not happy about losing all the software—and possibly illicit information—on their disks. Finally, the sight of police swooping down and seizing an offender's computer brings home the consequences of computer crime in a way that later judicial proceedings cannot match. In California, legislation that I coauthored, and that becomes effective in 1990, mandates forfeiture of equipment used in a computer crime.

Of course, this sanction alone does not prevent a determined offender from buying another computer. Thus, in many cases, the offender's use of computers should be restricted as a condition of probation. California's new law allows courts to consider barring a serious offender from any access to computers whatever. Although this remedy is too harsh for any but extraordinary cases, offenders could at least be forbidden to possess or use modems. Without a modem, the hacker is out of the game.

The most powerful sanction against computer offenders is to restrict their livelihood by preventing them from working with computers for a certain period after conviction. Because many offenders cannot imagine doing anything else for a living, the foreclosure of a career in computing is a disaster to be avoided at all costs.

There are precedents for such punishment. In California, for example, a judge may prohibit an offender from engaging in employment related to past criminal behavior. And doctors and lawyers found guilty of misconduct are routinely barred from practicing their profession. The only problem with extending such a prohibition to computer professionals is finding reasonable limits.

Since computers pervade the workplace, an outright ban on working with them could rule out almost any employment, and could pose constitutional problems. Thus, while California courts may consider barring offenders from computer-related work by forbidding them to use computers, period, this power will probably be exercised only in extraordinary cases. For most offenders, a less drastic measure will be sufficient: allowing them to work with computers only after they have notified prospective employers of their convictions. Under the new California law, an offender may be subject to this restriction for three to five years. After applying for a job, the offender must attend a hearing along with the prospective employer to determine whether the computers he or she would use on the job are linked to others, and whether allowing the offender access to those computers would pose an unacceptable risk to society.

Although disclosing an offender's criminal history to employers is unusual, it is not without precedent. Government agencies may check the criminal records of candidates for a variety of jobs, both public and private, such as reading gas meters or working with minors. The records of applicants for various licenses—prospective security guards, alarm agents, and lawyers, for example—may also be checked. Nor will it be difficult to ensure that offenders are complying with the notification requirement. They already have to provide their probation officers with the name and address of their employer at all times.

Another measure that states should consider is setting up a "computer offender registry" for repeat or serious criminals. Bonding companies would have access to those records, and industries would decide which positions were sensitive enough to require bonded employees.

Regardless of the method, barring offenders from sensitive positions in computing will protect society by preventing *and* deterring computer crime. Offenders will not be able to obtain jobs where they pose a threat, and potential offenders will realize that they risk losing the most interesting work in computing.

As a growing threat to our economy, the problem of computer crime needs to be addressed immediately. Unlike drugs and street crime, it cannot be deterred by putting a cop on every corner. But we can put teams of smart, well-trained cops into every high-technology region in the country. We cannot afford to build prisons to hold all the computer offenders. But we can impose sentences that exploit their unique vulnerabilities.

31 *The Growth of the Home Office**

Roberta Furger

May 14, 1993, at 2 P.M.

That's when telecommuting will cease to be an aberration and start becoming a mainstream practice, according to Jack Nilles, a Southern California–based consultant on the subject. Nilles, who coined the term *telecommuting* in 1973, was joking about the date and time, but he couldn't be more serious when he talks about the future of this alternative way of working.

Nilles and other telecommuting proponents say the practice is on the increase and will hit its peak in the mid-1990s. If they're right, it's a change that's been a long time coming and one that could have far-reaching effects for both employers and employees.

For 10 years after introducing the concept of telecommuting, Nilles said he watched and waited to see how the market would react. "And the market sat there and said, 'Huh?'" Corporate America's response to telecommuting was lukewarm at best—a far cry from what the early prophets were predicting.

"In the early days, the vision was that, by 1990, 5 percent of the work force would be telecommuting," said Tom Miller, vice president of Link Resources, in New York. That type of ground swell, of course, hasn't occurred. What we have seen over the past few years, though, is a gradual but steady increase in the number of companies and government agencies that are either adopting formal telecommuting programs or are informally offering it as an alternative to the more traditional work week.

An idea that was once considered appropriate for only a few select jobs—such as writing and programming, for example—is gradually becoming something of a mainstream practice. Employers as diverse as American Express Bank, Ltd., in New York; Pacific Bell, in California; and the state of California have sanctioned telecommuting as a legitimate way to work. And they're not alone. Watchers of this phenomenon estimate that between 500 and 1,000 companies throughout the United States have some type of telecommuting program in place.

Proponents of telecommuting programs offer a variety of reasons for the increased interest in the home-office concept. These include a desire to cut down on rush-hour traffic; a need to offer alternative work hours to attract and retain highly skilled employees; a way to reduce office space; and a greater understanding and use of computer and telecommunications technology in business.

The state of California, for example, started a pilot project in telecommuting in 1983 as part of a larger effort to reduce the state's office-space requirements, said David Flemming, manager of the program.

But while it was office-space concerns that opened the door, "other factors have kept the program going, including transportation, traffic, air quality, and energy conservation," Flemming said.

Other employers, such as Travelers Insurance, in Hartford, Connecticut, have used telecommuting as a way of holding on to highly valued employees in a competitive job market. Travelers began a pilot project two years ago for the data processing staff after the company "began looking ahead [and recognized] we were in for a labor shortage," said Diane Bengston, assistant director, data processing human resources. "There were people who were leaving [their jobs] because of lifestyle changes. We saw this as an option to help retain employees, and it has worked that way."

Travelers Insurance isn't alone in using telecommuting to attract new employees and entice longtime employees to stay. The shortage of skilled workers, Nilles said, is prompting many in the private sector to rethink their position on telecommuting.

"The demand for skilled people is rapidly growing faster than supply. And it's only going to get worse," Nilles said. As a result, "companies need some way to differentiate themselves from the competition." Telecommuting provides one such distinction.

Other employers have turned to telecommuting as one way of reducing employees' commute time every day. In Southern California, for example, several employers are using telecommuting programs as part of a larger effort to comply with a recent government regulation requiring them to reduce the number of employees on the road each day.

Societal and job-related issues may be what's driving many telecommuting programs, but many believe it's the growing use of personal computers and related technology in business that is making the change possible.

"If there wasn't a need to open up a few more alternative work styles, we wouldn't [have started the program]," said Travelers' Bengston. "But it's the technology that lets us do it." Flemming takes a similar approach. "We rely on the technology, but the technology isn't the driving force. There was a time when the technology was driving us to find ways to use it. Now work options can drive the [use of] technology."

Gil Gordon, who publishes the *Telecommuting Review,* a monthly newsletter for employers with telecommuting programs, referred to what he calls "the technology triangle," consisting of the PC, fax machine, and answering machine. "As long as you have any two of these items," Gordon said, "there's no reason why you can't work at home as effectively as in the office."

Gordon believes the growth in telecommuting programs is tied to the growing influence of PCs in corporate America. "Today, if you go into any major corporation you take it for granted that you'll see PCs. But back in 1978, if the accounting department bought one Apple II computer it was considered a revolutionary step. People were skeptical at first, but once they found out what it could do, they bought more."

"We're seeing the same type of growth curve with telecommuting," Gordon said. "It had a slow beginning, but we're seeing a rapid increase [because we've overcome] a lot of the early skepticism."

Additionally, since a growing number of today's managers have been weaned on computer use, there's a greater understanding of "how portions of many jobs revolve around that box," Gordon said. And there's no reason why someone has to be in the office to perform those activities, he added.

Not all telecommuters, though, are sitting at a keyboard eight hours a day. Computer use varies considerably, depending on the nature of the job. In the state of California, for example, a recent study showed that roughly one half of the telecommuters used personal computers while working at home. At Travelers, on the other hand, the number of personal computer users is significantly higher, since the majority of telecommuters are programmers or programmer analysts.

Technology will become even more important in the growth of what Link Resources' Miller calls "the second wave of telecommuting." He believes the continued increase in telecommuting "depends on the growth of the digital infrastructure."

With the technology in place and business conditions ripe for alternative work arrangements, employers of all sizes and in a variety of industries are adopting telecommuting programs. Some examples illustrate the variety of approaches employers have taken to telecommuting.

FIGURE 1   The Telecommuter Profile

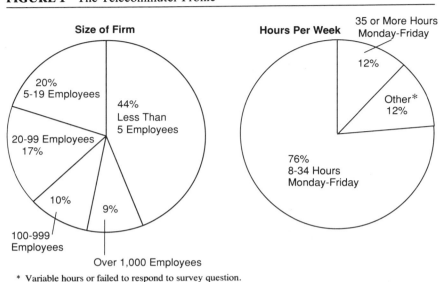

* Variable hours or failed to respond to survey question.

Source: Link Resources

- What started as a pilot project in the state of California has now become a full-fledged program with approximately 150 participants, most of whom are mid-level professionals such as architects, engineers, managers, auditors, and programmers, according to Flemming. On average, telecommuters spend 1.6 days at home. This figure varies among participants, but Flemming recommends that employees spend at least one day each week in the office to avoid isolation and provide face-to-face contact with coworkers.
- Los Angeles County is one of several Southern California employers who started a telecommuting program as a way of cutting down on the number of commuters each day. Regulation 15, enacted last year by the Southern California Air Quality Management District, requires employers to adopt traffic mitigation measures. Although the program only officially began last month, there are already 45 participants working one to three days at home, according to Margery Gould, a management analyst for the county. She expects the number of participants to increase to "a few hundred in a year or so."
- Pacific Bell adopted a pilot program in 1985 in response to the traffic congestion faced by Southern California workers when the Olympic games were held in Los Angeles. Although the company does not have a formal program in place, telecommuting is a sanctioned work practice. Roughly 500 employees now telecommute on a regular basis, according

to Dori Bailey, manager of media relations for Pacific Bell, in San Francisco. Any employee is eligible to participate, "as long as their work doesn't require face-to-face interaction," Bailey said.

- At Travelers, what started two years ago as a pilot project for the data-processing department has since evolved into a companywide program, Bengston said. She added, though, that the majority of participants are still from data processing. "Response has been slow in other departments."

Although the number and type of employees vary from one program to the next, most programs share some common features and have some basic guidelines that participants must follow.

Training—for both employees and their managers—is considered by many participants to be vital to a program's success. The state of California, for example, has an orientation program for participants and their managers "to help dispel some of the myths about telecommuting," Flemming said. Los Angeles County also has a mandatory training program for telecommuters and their managers. "It's not just a matter of picking up your work and going home," Gould said. At Travelers, there's even a support group for telecommuters that meets every two months "to discuss technical and personnel issues, help people come on board, and reduce isolation problems," Bengston said.

All employers emphasized the importance of managerial support for telecommuting programs and require manager approval before allowing an employee to take work home on a regular basis. "We stress that this is a management option; not an employee benefit," Gould said. "Employees don't have the right to telecommute."

Lissa Zanville, director of media relations for Pacific Bell, in Los Angeles, and a regular telecommuter herself, agreed that telecommuting isn't for everyone. "You have to be motivated, it has to be the right kind of job, and you have to have a boss who's understanding of the process." Without all three factors, she believed programs won't work out for either the employer or employee.

With the proper guidelines and training, however, early adopters of telecommuting programs point to a variety of benefits of the practice—

FIGURE 2   Equipment Owned by Telecommuters

Telephone answering machine	51%
Personal computer	46%
Modem	20%
Copier	9%
Fax	5%

Source: Link Resources

FIGURE 3   Leading Job Titles of Telecommuters

Position	Number	Percent of total
Executives and managers	360,000	14%
Salesworkers	310,000	12%
Construction trades	290,000	11%
Engineers and specialists	160,000	6%
Technicians and computer programmers	160,000	6%
Professional specialists	130,000	5%
Lawyers and accountants	130,000	5%
Artists	130,000	5%
Government sector	130,000	5%
Clerical support	50,000	2%
Other	750,000	29%
Total	2.6 million	100%

* Above jobs account for 75 percent of work force. Other jobs aren't easily classified in standard government categories.

Source: Link Resources.

---

among them, reduced absenteeism, higher employee morale, higher productivity, and lower turnover. While such testimonials are winning more and more companies over, the converts are still relatively few in number. The total number of telecommuters is still less than 1 percent of the work force, according to Gordon.

What's holding things back, many say, is that telecommuting involves a fairly radical change in the way people view work. "It's a social change," Nilles said. "And that's an evolutionary process."

Middle managers have been slow to embrace the concept of telecommuting because it represents a radical change in how they deal with employees. "It forces managers to focus on the work product; to look at the results, rather than surveying activities," Gould said.

"Managers were hesitant at first," Bengston said, "because they weren't used to managing people they couldn't see on a daily basis. But the people who were asking to telecommute were strong enough employees that the managers felt it was worth giving this thing a try."

And that's usually how it works; managers are hesitant at first, but the potential benefits are compelling enough for them to try it, despite their reservations.

Other companies have hesitated to adopt telecommuting programs because, unlike flextime or other modified work schedules, it's not something that can be applied evenly to all employees. "You can only do it with people who are self-starters and whose jobs lend themselves to measurements of results," Miller said. "Managers have to make decisions based on trust and their knowledge of their staff; ultimately, that's why many shied away.''

With the potential benefits pulling companies in one direction and long-time tradition pulling them in another, what's the future of telecommuting?

Miller and others who have been tracking the growth of telecommuting over the years see a continued increase in the practice. Freeways will only get more congested; lifestyle changes continue to prompt people to look for alternative work arrangements, and increased business competition forces companies to offer them.

As more and more jobs revolve around computers, it becomes increasingly evident that *where* the job is performed is no longer limited to the traditional office setting. The bottom line, Gordon said, is that ''more and more people are realizing you don't have to commute to compute.''

DISABLED TAKE ADVANTAGE OF HOME-OFFICE CONCEPT

For years, Carol D'Agostino went into the office five days a week. Then, several years ago, she came down with chronic viral fatigue syndrome, an illness that prevented her from continuing in the traditional 9-to-5 workaday mode. What could have been the end of a career, though, turned out to be the beginning of a new one.

Five years ago, through an internship with Queensborough Community College in New York, D'Agostino was placed in a program where she was able to work out of her home. She's now a senior research associate and managing editor for Link Resources, a research firm in New York. Unable to go into the office, she continues to work full-time out of her home.

''This has allowed me to work on a professional level, to develop talents, grow in my job, all those good things that you associate with being on site,'' D'Agostino said. ''Instead of sitting here like a bump on a log counting pennies, I'm able to make a decent living and contribute to my company.''

D'Agostino and others are part of a small but growing population of the disabled community who are riding the telecommuting wave. They're taking advantage of the technology and of corporate America's interest in the home-office concept. Some, like D'Agostino, have established on an individual basis home-office work arrangements with an employer. Others are part of a corporate program, such as that offered by American Express Bank, specially designed to provide alternative work arrangements for the disabled. In either case, they've established home offices, have access to up-to-date technology, and are regular full-time employees.

The technology, in fact, has been key to alternative work arrangements like D'Agostino's taking off. Her office is equipped with a facsimile machine, a Macintosh Plus and an AT-compatible system, several modems, and three printers—all of which was purchased by Link Resources. "People walk into the office and just gasp," D'Agostino said.

Employees participating in American Express's Off Site Processing Program (formerly called Project Homebound) are also set up with equipment purchased by their employer. In the case of these word processing employees, the equipment includes a fax machine, a Wang word processor, and a modem to transmit files back to corporate headquarters.

For people such as D'Agostino and Inez Crisa, who's been working in American Express's program for the past seven years, working at home is the only way they can maintain a full-time job. And it's an option that isn't widely available.

"It can be real tough to find meaningful work inside the home," D'Agostino said.

The American Express Program was established as a pilot project in 1981. At that time, 10 individuals were hired as independent contractors—having already been trained in word processing through a program jointly sponsored by Brooklyn College and the Private Industry Council. After one year, they were hired as full-time employees. The American Express employees—like D'Agostino at Link—receive all the benefits of other full-time employees at their firms.

Crisa, who suffers from a serious arthritic condition, said she had tried other work arrangements prior to joining the American Express program, but none of them worked out.

What makes the American Express program different, she explained, is the fact that "all work comes into the house via electronics." She doesn't have to go out and pick up or drop off work as she did in other jobs.

Lee Middleton, assistant vice president of American Express Bank, Ltd., described participants in the program as "bright, capable people who just happen to be unable to work full-time in the office. We've been able to unlock the potential of a lot of talented people who, because of the transportation barrier, haven't been able to contribute."

While employers and employees agree that these types of programs represent an important offering and provide excellent opportunities for those participating, they also note that such opportunities are still very difficult to come by.

"Things have gotten better when it comes to disabled people finding employment, particularly when they can go on site," D'Agostino said. "The opportunities for homebound workers, though, is a frontier we still have to work on."

Crisa agreed. "I think this program is great, but I'd like to see it expanded to other companies. There are a lot of companies in and around the New York area that could give disabled people the opportunity to work at home."

One group, called Lift, Inc., in New York, works with individuals to train them in computer programming and then places them in area companies. For the first year, the individuals are officially employed by Lift; but if things work out, they then become full-time company employees with all of the standard employee benefits.

D'Agostino said handicapped individuals represent a "vast, untapped pool of workers." What's holding things back, she added, is the misconception of some individuals who "equate having a physical disability with having a mental disability."

That's a myth that D'Agostino, Crissa, and others are rapidly working to dispel.

32 *The Terrors of Technostress**

John P. McPartlin

Are computers, those ubiquitous and strategic machines we have come to rely on, turning us into robots? Are they changing the very way we interact with our environment and each other?

Some psychologists feel that the more we work with machines, the more our minds try to think and act like machines—in other words, we are adapting to computers, rather than having computers adapt to us. This unnatural adaptation creates stress, a sign that we are fighting to keep our emotional and creative selves intact. This condition, called "technostress," can afflict anyone who interfaces with computers on a regular basis, whether at the desk or the automatic teller machine. Experts say those who manage computers and manage people who work on computers have to learn to cope with technostress.

According to the National Council on Compensation Insurance in Boca Raton, Florida, stress accounts for about 10 percent of occupational disease claims, up from 5 percent 10 years ago. Those claims can cost companies an average of $15,000 apiece, almost double the average physical injury worker's claim. And the problem is not going away. A study just released by the California Workers' Compensation Institute says that, in the state of California alone, there was a 700 percent increase in mental disorder or stress claims betwen 1979 and 1988. Allowing for the corresponding growth in the work force during that period, this still means a 500 percent increase in such claims. At the same time, general disability claims rose only 8 percent. If it's true that technology is one of the major factors in the increase of stress claims, it may be causing many American businesses to literally throw money out the window.

---

* Source: John P. McPartlin, "The Terrors of Technostress," *Information Week*, July 30, 1990, pp. 30–33.

If you think you've never experienced technostress, ask yourself these questions: Do you get aggravated when, during a phone call, you are put on hold for what seems like ages, even though it could only be a matter of seconds? Have you ever become incensed when your computer takes a few seconds longer than usual to perform a command? Have you ever yelled at your bank's ATM because it took too long to provide you with a receipt? Have you ever stopped working after a day in front of the computer and felt emotionally drained?

We have set expectations for information technology that are not always realistic. We have become used to the nearly instant gratification computers can provide, and we become abnormally impatient when we do not get immediate responses. We have also projected the "relationship" we have with computer equipment out to our interpersonal contacts and are sometimes disappointed that our associates' ideas and actions are far more disorganized than our computers'.

MAN VS. MACHINE

Next Monday, Rick Jandrt, former senior staff systems programmer for IDS Financial Services Inc., a subsidiary of American Express based in Minneapolis, will start his new job as an auto mechanic. Jandrt, 40, had worked in the data processing field for 14 years before deciding that job stress was detrimental to his relationship with his 9-year-old daughter Rebecca. "As a business's needs grow, it requires more and more computer uptime, leaving those of us in maintenance less time to fix. That cuts into our weekends, our late nights," he says. "I am a single parent. I found I was having less and less time to spend with my daughter. At work I held all the stress in, and then at home she felt the brunt of my frustration."

Jandrt is not alone. In his book *Technostress: The Human Cost of the Computer Revolution* (Addison-Wesley Publishing Co., 1982), Dr. Craig Brod, a psychologist in Oakland, California, coined the term *technostress* to describe the type of stress unique to computer users. He first noticed the phenomenon in his patients who worked in computer-related fields, particularly programmers from California's Silicon Valley. "We are all being socialized to be more at ease with technology than with people," he says. "We are now more at home with things than with each other." According to Brod, for those who have become accustomed to technology, any interaction with other people can produce stress.

Many psychologists warn that computers are weakening our empathy, altering our concept of the erotic, and have generally steamrolled over our emotional selves. If it's true that we become what we observe, then those who work with computers run the risk of becoming automatons who identify more with machines than humans. Sociologists and psychologists are concerned about what computers are teaching us about the rest of the world. "The machine is a socialization agent that teaches you a style of interaction which then is generalized and carried over to other situations," says Dr. Tim Lynch, president of New Wave Consultants, a North Quincy, Massachusetts-based firm that advises companies on the psychological effects of computers. The danger arises, he says, when people start treating each other like they treat their machines.

According to both Lynch and Brod, certain traits begin to crop up in people who use computers intensively. The first symptom is a growing impatience with social amenities and a lack of tolerance for people who do not exhibit machine-like performance. "Because the computer gives you immediate feedback, people begin to expect immediate feedback from other people within the company," Lynch says. "They want things and they want them now."

This attitude can even flow into a worker's personal life, particularly in romantic situations where a great deal of emotion is involved. "A lot of people I talked with said they went through a cyclical effect. They started to look for people in their personal lives that they could relate to, that matched qualities they found in the machine," says Lynch. "When they failed to find them, they simply went back to the machine. They found they were getting more satisfaction emotionally and psychologically from the machine than from people."

Brod says this intense man-machine relationship is both draining and addictive at the same time. "By the end of a day working with computers, you feel exhausted. There is no time for reflection. You just want to be left alone to recuperate." He says many burned-out computer professionals turn to alcohol and drugs so they don't come down from their "computer high." "One of the reasons we see so much drug use in Silicon Valley has to do with the hyper-computer culture that exists rather than the moral culture," he says.

He also notes that like Jandrt many young computer professionals tell him they want to get out of their fields at an early age and get into something completely unrelated to technology. "Humans can't sustain such [technology-intensive jobs] for very long. I know a lot of my baby boomer colleagues are looking for a way to get out," he says. "I see them take jobs as gardeners or working in bookstores. Anything to get away from computers."

Jandrt says that since he appeared on NBC's *Real Life With Jane Pauley* two weeks ago, fellow employees have been telling him they feel exactly as he does and wish they, too, could get out. "I'm 40 and still young enough to make the change," says Jandrt. "I can make just as much working as a mechanic 40 hours a week as I did working as a programmer for 60 to 70. I don't want to suddenly have a heart attack when I'm 50 and not be able to do anything with the rest of my life."

Those who decide to stick it out may find themselves adapting to computers in order to minimize the tension. Psychologists say that, like a corporate version of *Star Trek's* Mr. Spock, those who work closely with computers often come to stress logic over emotions. They get upset when situations require dealing with gray areas and fuzzy arguments. They lose patience with people who have trouble getting to the point. They prefer contacting other humans through computers, rather than face-to-face or on the phone. Lynch tells of one programmer shop where workers would send messages all day to people in the very same room and then leave without ever acknowledging each other's presence.

CREATIVITY CRUNCH

Others worry that computers will take away our sense of creativity and wonder. Lynch says he sees many cases where working closely with a computer can narrow workers' focus and often stifle their creativity as they try to become more like the machines they use. "In order to get things to work, [computer professionals] have to think in the way the computer dictates, the way the software works," says Lynch. "If you're using WordPerfect, you have to think as WordPerfect does. You start to think one straight way instead of having a broad perspective."

So what happens when programmers who have trouble interacting with others are promoted into management where they must supervise others with the same problem? "People who have been with a company 10 or 15 years will naturally start to move up, and this includes programmers," says Lynch. "There is an art and psychology to managing. If you don't know the subtleties and nuances of interacting, you can upset people and grate on them. This is not the best way to create an *esprit de corps*."

But MIS chiefs and microcomputer managers say that those are incredibly outdated generalizations. "When we first started into the microcomputer game there were more [computer jocks] around, but now [the technology] is being taken more in stride. You don't see as much obsessive curiosity now about what new things you can do with it," says John Haner, a partner at accounting/consulting firm Arthur Andersen in Chicago who oversees the company's PCs.

Bill Monteith, corporate director for IRM at Armco, Inc., a steel company based in Middleton, Ohio, agrees. "I see that kind of stress in certain managers, but I'm not sure it's for that reason. I think it's just a general aggression in managers." He adds, "I get irritable when my blood pressure goes up, but that's just a reaction to the way some projects are going."

Management consulting firms say the existence of stress in IS people may be more of a chicken-and-egg question. The reason some IS people may be so stressed out is that they were born with a personality prone to be stressed—a trait that may have drawn them into a career in the computer field. "People who want yes/no answers wanted them even before we had this kind of technology," says Madeline Weiss, VP of communications for the Society for Information Management and president of Weiss Associates, Inc., a business consulting firm in Bethesda, Maryland. "It's probably not accidental that those types of people went into computers."

IS PRESS COVERAGE HAZARDOUS?

But even people who are the most skeptical about the existence of technostress acknowledge they sometimes feel its symptoms. Bob Bettendorf, ex-IBMer and founder and president of the Institute of Office Ergonomics in Stamford, Connecticut, thinks the biggest cause of technostress is press reports about the hazards technology can cause us. "Reporting of these health studies has been very sensational and very unbalanced. Press coverage has contributed considerably to health concerns," he says.

However, Bettendorf, who suffered a heart attack while driving to work at IBM four years ago, does admit that his impatience with the speed of his PC causes him slight stress. "Where you used to take three days to get an answer to a question, now a few extra seconds is too long," he says. "I notice it more now. I use WordPerfect and I've installed new print cartridges and the response time went from two seconds to four seconds and it feels like eight. Every time I hit the retrieve command I wonder what the hell went [wrong] with the system."

Researchers insist that many symptoms of technostress will decrease once younger generations raised on technology start taking over the workplace. They will enter their jobs already well adjusted to computers. Older workers sometimes strongly resist technology, and this can create unnecessary stress. "It's tough to face any change for someone near the end of their career," Haner says.

"There is a problem with some senior management, people who have grown up and never dealt with computers and are afraid of them," agrees Monteith. "They think it's a perfect device, and they are afraid to make mistakes on it. It can be a very unforgiving device."

Older office workers—those used to a traditional office setup with typewriters and constant human interaction—are especially susceptible to technostress when adapting to terminals or PCs. Here, their relationship with the computer usually becomes one of disdain, rather than love. Workers such as telephone operators and data entry clerks often come to view the computer as the enemy, enslaving them and forcing them to perform endless routine and repetitive tasks. Add to that the policy of some companies to monitor the amount of keystrokes per employee to judge productivity and you have a tense working environment where both machines and management can be viewed as allied adversaries.

Lynch says he often gets called in when companies are making the switch from typewriters to computers. "Sometimes people find themselves going from secretaries to data entry clerks, and they lose a lot of the human contact that was there. Such isolation can lead to a great deal of stress.''

The Cleveland, Ohio-based 9to5, the National Association of Working Women, is one group that has been concerned with how workers adjust to office computerization; the organization has been campaigning to abolish the practice of keyboard monitoring, which they consider an intimidating management technique. In June, the group set up a toll-free hotline for workers who are being monitored to provide support and help organize lobbying for bills that will restrict or abolish such practices. The group estimates that as many as 26 million workers may now be under electronic surveillance, including airline reservation agents, telemarketers, sales representatives, and journalists.

''One of the women reservationists I've talked with said she began to feel like a robot,'' says Cindia Cameron, national organizer for 9to5. ''She was depressed and demoralized and felt like part of the computer.'' After a reorganization was done in that woman's office, Cameron says, she began to feel like a human being again and no longer dreaded coming to work. If changes hadn't been made, that company may have lost a good worker. ''More than half the people who are being monitored eventually quit,'' says Cameron. ''They refuse to put up with it.''

Whether for good or bad, younger people entering the work force have been already socialized into accepting computers as part of their lives. Computers have become as commonplace as blackboards in many classrooms. And while home computer sales have not been as high as predicted 10 years ago, sales of computer-driven video games have gone through the roof.

Having so much interaction with a computer at a time when social skills should be developing is dangerous, say some psychologists. ''Most families become technologically literate and emotionally illiterate,'' says Brod. ''They spend six hours a day watching television and playing video games, and then spend a few hours working on the computer and then go to bed. There's nothing else there.''

THE SOCIAL SOLUTION

What does MIS do when the people it's supposed to be managing are either deathly afraid of computers or so obsessed with them that they are almost unable to interact with other employees? Many companies conduct training programs and seminars to help workers deal with the stress. Psychologists suggest setting up the office so there is more direct human interaction and setting schedules that allow workers to get up, move around, and talk to their fellow employees. They also suggest more social gatherings either during or after work so people can relax and get to know one another as individuals. Since many people in the 1990s get their whole sense of community from their jobs, it's important they not lose that when their work becomes more technology-intensive.

For the individual who experiences technostress, Brod suggests that the key is to spend some time recuperating from a day spent doing intense computer work. "Allow yourself to make the transition," he says. "Go pick weeds in the garden. Do anything that brings you back to that bodily sense that you have lost. When you feel the need for that kind of computer speed in your personal life, you should count to 10 and reflect a little."

SIM's Weiss agrees. She says one of the key things to do outside of your work life is to get away from the self-imposed pressure for "polyphasic" or "multiprocessing" behavior—the need to be doing several things at one time. "You have to recognize that things are changing at such a rapid rate that it's impossible to keep up with everything, and it's okay if you can't. You've got to define limits," she says.

But Brod says the companies that call him in for consulting often get indignant when he suggests that changes must be made in the work environment or work schedule. "They tell me they want me to talk about the stress but not about any changes that have to be made. That's why those cultures are the way they are. We have a habit of blaming the victim."

Some firms are now realizing that, if changes are not made, they run the risk of facing a high turnover of workers. Technostress costs money in unnecessary retraining or rehiring. Even if they don't burn out, stressed-out workers are less productive and often become difficult to work with or manage. And no company wants to get the image of being uncaring toward its workers.

But most managers are still not willing to blame the computer for these problems, particularly those signs of stress that could just as easily be caused by other aspects of work. The possible reality of technostress, however, is still something to consider. Computers were supposed to free us from drudgery and make our jobs easier, but often they just give us more time to do more work. Unlike the machines we use and manage, humans need some time to recuperate, sort out the day's events, and relax. Otherwise that fine line that exists between man and woman and machine may grow even finer.